The State and Society

The State and Society
PERU IN COMPARATIVE PERSPECTIVE

by Alfred Stepan

PRINCETON UNIVERSITY PRESS
PRINCETON, NEW JERSEY

Library of Congress Cataloging in Publication Data will
be found on the last printed page of this book

Publication of this book has been aided by a grant from the
Paul Mellon Fund of Princeton University Press

This book has been composed in Linotype Baskerville

Clothbound editions of Princeton University Press books
are printed on acid-free paper, and binding materials are
chosen for strength and durability

Printed in the United States of America
by Princeton University Press, Princeton, New Jersey

To My Parents

Contents

List of Tables and Figures

FIGURES

List of Tables and Figures

Preface

My first book was about the military in Brazil. By the time I had finished the book, I was aware that military rule was only a part of a larger question concerning the role of the state as a major, "autonomous," actor in society. While I became increasingly convinced that the role of the state was a politically and intellectually urgent matter to address, I was dismayed to find that many of the most important theoretical approaches to politics—pluralist and Marxist alike—assigned very little independent weight to the state and did not provide the conceptual guidance I needed to put into context many new (and old) political patterns I observed, not only in Latin America but in Europe and elsewhere. My research, reflections, and teaching in the last five years have further convinced me that we need to find new ways of approaching what should be one of the central concerns of the discipline of political science—the relationship between the state and society. This book is an immodest effort (but only a modest achievement) in that direction. It is also an attempt to use the concept of the state to orient empirical research on politics in Latin America.

Though the term "state" is not widely used in contemporary political theory, or is dismissed as a vague abstraction from the past having little empirical meaning or researchable features, the term can refer to concrete structures and observable relationships. Max Weber provides a clearly focused discussion of some of the central features of the state in modern societies:

> The primary formal characteristics of the modern state are as follows: It possesses an administrative and legal order subject to change by legislation, to which the organized corporate activity of the administrative staff, which is also regulated by legislation, is oriented. This system of order claims binding authority, not only over the members of the state, the citizens, most of whom have obtained membership by birth, but also to a very large extent, over all action taking place in the area of its jurisdiction. It is thus a compulsory association with a

territorial basis. Furthermore, today, the use of force is regarded as legitimate only so far as it is either permitted by the state or prescribed by it. . . . The claim of the modern state to monopolize the use of force is as essential to it as its character of compulsory jurisdiction and of continuous organization.[1]

Elsewhere Weber states that "the state is a relation of men dominating men," and that "organized domination, which calls for continuous administration, requires that human conduct be conditioned to obedience towards those masters who claim to be the bearers of legitimate power. On the other hand, by virtue of this obedience, organized domination requires the control of those material goods which in a given case are necessary for the use of physical violence."[2]

First, then, the state must be considered as something more than the "government." It is the continuous administrative, legal, bureaucratic and coercive systems that attempt not only to structure relations *between* civil society and public authority in a polity but also to structure many crucial relationships *within* civil society as well. Consolidated modern states should be compared not in terms of whether they structure such relationships, but in terms of the degree to which, and the means through which, they do so.

Second, the state should be viewed as a mechanism of domination and control. The laws and bureaucratic procedures of the state may reflect civil society, but they may also give power to the state to shape the demands made by civil society on the state. A principal task of research is to determine the extent to which any particular state (a) is procedurally neutral and allows an autonomous and competitive process of interest aggregation to present binding demands on the state, (b) is a class instrument in which the full range of its coercive, administrative, and legal powers is used to dominate some class fractions and protect

---

[1] Max Weber, "The Fundamental Concepts of Sociology" in *The Theory of Social and Economic Organizations*, ed. Talcott Parsons (New York: The Free Press, 1964), p. 156.

[2] "Politics as a Vocation" in *From Max Weber: Essays in Sociology*, eds. H. H. Gerth and C. Wright Mills (New York, Oxford University Press, 1958), pp. 78, 80.

others, or (c) achieves some degree of autonomy from civil society and thus contributes its own weight to policy outcomes.

Third, a state is not necessarily unitary or monolithic. Each state is composed of various parts, such as the executive, the permanent administration, the judiciary, and the coercive apparatus. The degree to which a strategic elite in charge of the state apparatus in fact controls all the component parts of the state varies. Even in those cases where in theory the component parts are fused in the executive, actual control of the state apparatus may vary depending on the unity or disunity of the strategic elite. Any analysis of an attempt by that elite to use the apparatus of the state to structure society must therefore take into account the composition of the state and the ideological and organizational unity of the strategic elite.

Fourth, Weber stresses that "organized domination, which calls for continuous administration, requires that human contact be conditioned to obedience." This raises the question not only of the nature of the state's claims to obedience but also of whether they are made successfully and what the cost of this success might be. When we are considering attempts by strategic elites to install a new pattern of relations between the state and civil society, we must be aware of at least three different possible state-society relationships that can result: (1) installation of new state structures that achieve what Antonio Gramsci would term "hegemonic" acceptance in civil society, (2) installation in which civil society is conditioned to obedience only because of the overwhelming coercive power of the state, and (3) failure of installation due to effective resistance within civil society to the strategic elite's effort to establish "compulsory jurisdiction" and a "monopoly of force." One of the special concerns of this book is to examine the conditions that are supportive of or resistant to the state's installation of structures, and patterns of participation and control, which obtain hegemonic acceptance.

Finally, Weber says of the modern state that "this system of order claims binding authority, not only over the members of the state . . . but also to a very large extent over all the actions taking place in the area of its jurisdiction." In many countries of the Third World, foreign business enterprises and occasionally foreign governments carry out actions that are largely beyond the control of the government. This raises the question of whether the state in such countries can be called a state in Weber's sense of the term. It also directs attention to the strategies available to a regime to increase its capacity to control foreign actors such as multinational corporations.

In this book, the analysis of the state and Latin American politics is divided into two parts. The first part (Chapters 1-3) presents a conceptual discussion of the role of the state in various models of political analysis, and a comparative analysis of selected neo-corporatist regimes in which the state has an important function. These chapters raise certain broad issues about changing patterns of state intervention in civil society and suggest certain hypotheses about these changes. In the second part of the book (Chapters 4-8) some of the concepts about the state derived from Part One are applied in an analysis of the post-1968 attempt to restructure state-society relations in Peru. Peru offers an excellent setting for the application of these concepts because it represented a major attempt by a strategic elite (the military) to expand the power of the state apparatus and to use this power to restructure class, property, and participation patterns along new lines. The analysis of the initial successes and subsequent reversals of this effort will help give empirical and theoretical rigor to key concepts concerning the capacities and limits of the modern state.

Chapter 1 opens with an examination of two of the main approaches to politics in contemporary political science and the role assigned in them to the state. I argue that, in some of the main lines of argumentation in both liberal-pluralism and in the classic Marxist model of the bourgeois state, little independent weight is given to the role of the state in politics. The limitations of these approaches when applied to regimes in which the state plays an important part in structuring relations in the polity are identified, and conceptual modifications suggested. These two main approaches are contrasted with an important but neglected approach—that may be called "organic-statist"—in which the state is given a central role in the polity. The historical sources, normative content, characteristic state structures, and administrative policies of this approach are examined, and I present arguments why the organic-statist tendency should be seriously considered when studying Latin America.[3] Last, organic statism is

[3] For a brief definition of "organic statism," consult pp. 26-27.

considered as an abstract model of governance and is contrasted with the "classic-liberal" and "command-socialist" models, so that the inherent characteristics and predicaments of each model can be compared.

Although Peru during the 1968 to 1975 period was the Latin American regime whose articulated goals came closest to the organic-statist model presented in Chapter 1, I argue in Chapter 2 that the characteristic policies and state structures found in regimes that, in some respects, approach the organic-statist model are those traditionally called "corporatist." For this reason, Chapter 2 reviews the new literature on corporatism in twentieth-century Latin America. On the whole I argue that, while this literature is extremely suggestive, most of it is deficient concerning the role of the state and even the best of it does not help us differentiate between various types of corporatist experiments in Latin America, nor allow us to deal with the dynamics of attempts to install corporatist systems.

In Chapter 3, therefore, I attempt to overcome an important shortcoming of the literature on corporatism by distinguishing between two varieties of corporatism—"inclusionary" corporatism and "exclusionary" corporatism. The justification for considering these two varieties as distinct subtypes is presented, and the characteristic crisis conditions that give rise to each subtype are explored. I next advance five hypotheses concerning the outcome of attempts to install regimes that rely on inclusionary or exclusionary corporatist policies. On the basis of these hypotheses, several corporatist systems in Latin America are compared: Mexico (a successfully installed inclusionary attempt that achieved hegemony in civil society), Brazil since 1964 (a successfully installed exclusionary attempt that remains dependent on high levels of coercion), Argentina under Onganía (an unsuccessful attempt to install a system based on exclusionary policies), and Chile since 1973 (a highly coercive, exclusionary attempt whose outcome is still uncertain).

Part Two of the book elaborates the concepts and arguments discussed in Part One, on the basis of data collected during four field trips to Peru between 1972 and 1976. For the reasons mentioned earlier, Peru afforded an excellent opportunity to explore a dominantly (but not exclusively) inclusionary attempt in detail and to see whether the characteristic predicaments predicted by the organic-statist model on analytical grounds actually appear in a concrete situation. Part Two thus retains the analytic framework developed in Part One, at the same time that the focus shifts from *between-nation* comparisons to *within-nation* comparisons.

In Chapter 4 I address the question of why and how a strategic elite, the Peruvian army, developed an institution-wide perception of impending crisis. I show that this elite had achieved a substantial degree of doctrinal consensus before 1968 concerning the necessity for assuming control of the state apparatus in order to carry out structural reforms and inclusionary policies so as to forge a new and, as they defined it, more stable socioeconomic order in Peru. Unlike the Brazilian, Argentine, and Chilean cases discussed in Chapter 3, the conditions in Peru were more conducive to an inclusionary than an exclusionary installation attempt. However, while the military elite inherited a situation that initially gave them a relatively large degree of autonomy to impose their design on Peru, they faced more domestic constraints and very different world conditions than did the Mexican elite at the time of the installation of the inclusionary system under Cárdenas.

The next three chapters analyze in detail the problems and opportunities a strategic elite faces as it attempts to reorganize different sectors within a nation along organic-statist lines. Because the dynamics of state-society interactions are best studied at first-hand and over time, I narrowed my choice of sectors to three. My criteria of selection included the sectors' potential for shedding light on the theoretical questions and explicit hypotheses advanced in Part One, as well as their inherent importance for the model the military was attempting to construct in Peru. By limiting myself to three sectors, I hoped to be able to carry out the conceptually focused, concrete investigation needed at this stage of our research on the state. Also, it afforded me the opportunity to re-study each sector a number of times over the five-year period of my research so as to evaluate the dynamics of the state's attempt to restructure civil society.

Thus, in Chapter 5 I look at the question of how a strategic state elite can use inclusionary policies to "organize the weakly organized," specifically the urban squatters who make up approximately one-third of the total urban population of the country.

Chapter 6 focuses on my second sector, a working-class group. In this chapter I explore the much more difficult set of problems that emerges when a strategic elite attempts to use inclusionary policies to "reorganize the strongly organized," i.e., to incorporate into state-chartered structures an institutionally developed and ideologically committed sector of the working class, in this case the sugar workers. An additional reason the sugar sector is singled out for special attention in this book is because the state expropriated all the old sugar haciendas and handed them over to the workers as cooperatives. The cooperatives thus represent a test case of the theory of decentralized, self-managing, functional groups that are, as I show in Chapter 1, central to the theory of a society structured in accordance with the organic-statist model. Notwithstanding the limitations and even contradictions found in the sugar cooperatives, they represented one of the most elaborate experiments in worker self-management in Latin America (and outside of Yugoslavia, probably in the world), and hence a novel test of functional group participation in a political system that claims to be neither liberal nor Marxist. The analysis of the sugar sector allows me to explore the difficulties of incorporating a well-organized sector of society as well as the tension within the organic-statist model (hypothesized on analytic grounds in Chapter 1) between the organic-participatory and the statist-control components of the model.

In Chapter 7 I shift attention from the relationships between the state elite and lower-class groups to the relations between the state elite and upper-class groups, particularly foreign capitalists. This sector is especially salient because, while foreign capital and capitalists undoubtedly play a major role within the state boundaries—and thus according to Weber's discussion should be subject to state control—to a great extent the assets and institutional networks of foreign capitalists lie beyond the organizational format of the characteristic organic-statist structures used to encapsulate and control lower-class sectors. Notwithstanding this inherent limitation on state power, the military in Peru emerged in the late 1960s as a major innovator in using the power of the state to create new mechanisms to increase the capacity of the state to control foreign capital and to respond to the challenge multinationals present to the sovereignty and integration of a dependent state. My analysis of foreign capital opens with a general discussion of the variables that affect the power of a state in relation to such capital. I develop an analytic framework for assessing the capacity of any newly industrializing state to control foreign capital, and then I apply this analytic framework to Peru. While acknowledging Peru's undoubted innovations in this sector, I show how in the reorganization of the economy, the regime's intermediate (organic-statist) position between market-capitalist and command-plan communist modes of savings and investment presented the state elite with serious and never resolved dilemmas concerning capital accumulation that played a central role in contributing to the large scale retrenchments starting in 1975.

In the conclusion (Chapter 8) the analytic focus shifts from the question of *installation* to that of *institutionalization*. I explore two questions concerning institutionalization. Specifically, why was the Peruvian military not able to institutionalize the regime? And, more generally, does the organic-statist model itself present generic predicaments for the task of institutionalization?

In the nearly five years it took to write this book, I have received generous institutional, collegial, and personal support which it is my pleasure to acknowledge. My initial field research in Peru in 1972 was supported by a grant from the Joint Committee on Latin American Studies of the Social Science Research Council and the American Council of Learned Societies. Support for additional field research and writing time was provided by a John Simon Guggenheim Memorial Foundation Fellowship in 1974-1975. I am also grateful for a faculty grant from the Stimson Fund administered by the Concilium on International and Area Studies of Yale University.

Extended conversations in the initial stages of this book with the distinguished Peruvian scholars Julio Cotler, José Matos Mar, and Víctor Villanueva helped introduce me to Peru. Given the scope of the book I am more than normally indebted to colleagues from different specialties for thoughtful comments on drafts of chapters. Charles Anderson and Thomas Pangle helped me with interpretations of political philosophy. Three economists, Carlos Díaz-Alejandro, Shane Hunt, and Constantine Vaitsos, aided me in my maiden voyage into the difficult waters of the literature on foreign capital regulation. A legal scholar who works with multinationals, Stanley Rose, gave me a valuable perspective on how state regulations do, or do not, actually control multinationals. Peter Knight and Martin Scurrah generously shared with me some of the preliminary results of their long-term studies on the state and self-management. Luigi Einaudi kindly made available his unpublished material on the Peruvian military. Fernando Henrique Cardoso from Brazil, Douglas Chalmers from the United States, Ricardo Cinta from Mexico, Julio Cotler from Peru, and Guillermo O'Donnell from Argentina formed part of my personal "invisible college" of scholars who exchanged thoughts on how to reassess the role of the state. An appointment as a Research Fellow at the Lehrman Institute in New York gave me the rare opportunity to present several chapters of the book in an extremely agreeable setting to critical but supportive colleagues such as David Apter, James Chace, David Collier, Louis Goodman, Abraham Lowenthal, Juan Linz, Eric Nordlinger, Louis Ratinoff, Kenneth Sharpe, Paul Sigmund, and members of the Institute's staff, Benjamin Rowland and Nicholas Rizopoulos. Special thanks are due to Peter Cleaves, Louis Goodman, and Juan Linz for their patience in rereading the entire manuscript. David Collier was an invaluable colleague throughout the entire endeavor. In particular his penetrating and detailed comments served the function of encouraging me to rethink and rewrite some crucial sections before the book went to press.

During my field trips to Peru I of course incurred heavy debts of gratitude to Peruvians—both those involved in and those militantly against the experiment that originated in 1968. Wherever possible, I have acknowledged interviews and conversations in the text. In many cases, however, we agreed that their remarks would remain anonymous.

Scott Mainwaring and Shelly Pine generously helped compile and interpret data. Marty Achilles, Ann Carter, and Lynn Panza showed remarkable skill in deciphering my handwriting and typing the manuscript. At Princeton University Press, Gail Filion did prompt and painstaking copyediting, and Sandy Thatcher, once again, was just the sort of social science editor an author hopes to have. As always, I feel immense personal and intellectual gratitude to my wife, Nancy, who discussed all aspects of the project with me and who, during a particularly difficult period of my writing, took many days away from checking the final proofs of her book so that mine could one day reach that same stage.

Yale University
June 1977

PART ONE

The Role of the State:
Concepts and Comparisons

ONE · *Liberal-Pluralist, Classic Marxist, and "Organic-Statist" Approaches to the State*

A MAJOR, nearly worldwide trend since the 1930s has been the steady growth of the role of the state in political life. In the industrialized world, the emergence of the managerial state to combat the crisis of capitalism during the depression, the widened scope of executive power in World War II, and growing state regulative and welfare functions since the war, have all contributed to the expansion of the state. In the Third World it is even clearer that most development plans call for the state to play a major role in structuring economic and social systems.

Despite this expansion of the declared and undeclared functions of the state, there had been a significant decline in theoretical analyses of the impact of state policies on society. Starting in the mid-1950s, when the field of comparative politics underwent a major period of innovation, it was widely believed by members of the profession that this subfield of political science contained the most important new contributions. When we examine this period of innovation, however, there is a striking preoccupation with the search for the underlying economic, social, and even psychological causes of political behavior. The new approaches in comparative politics in most cases assigned little independent weight to the impact of state policies and political structures on the social system. Without denying the gains to comparative politics made by the move away from a sterile emphasis on descriptive studies of a formal-legal nature, it is clear that a price has been paid, namely a retreat from what should be one of the central concerns of the discipline. While almost everywhere the role of the state grew, one of the few places it withered away was in political science.[1]

[1] Indicative of the tone of mainstream North American literature is the fact that when I culled *World Politics* and *The American Political Science Review* for articles on the state in the period 1958-1972, the period in which comparative politics underwent intensive reconceptualization, I uncovered

The first task of this chapter, therefore, is conceptual, namely to examine what role the state plays in some of the major models used in contemporary political analysis. Is the state analyzed as an independent variable that has an impact on society, or is it treated as a dependent variable? If the latter, what problems for empirical research are presented by such conceptual approaches and what reformulations are indicated?

My second task in this chapter is analytical and empirical. Are there models that emphasize the role of the state that have been neglected by contemporary political science? Can an awareness of these alternative models help overcome some of the major conceptual and empirical lacunae that characterize much work in contemporary political science? And, less generally, are there political systems that have been influenced by these alternative institutional, administrative, and normative models? If so, it might greatly aid the analysis of politics in such societies to incorporate explicitly elements of these models into our research strategies.

I argue that there exists a recognizable strand of political thought, which I call "organic-statist," that runs from Aristotle, through Roman law, natural law, absolutist and modern Catholic social thought. I suggest that organic statism represents powerful philosophical and structural tendencies found throughout Western Europe, and especially in the Iberian countries and their former colonies, where organic statism was never as fully challenged by alternative political models as in the rest of the European cultural area. In addition, I argue that a modern variant of the organic-statist model of society provides a useful analytic framework with which to begin investigating the interrelationship of state and society in one of the more important and original political experiments in modern Latin American history—Peru.

---

only one major article that explicitly attempted a general theoretical analysis of the state. That article was J. P. Nettl, "The State as a Conceptual Variable," *World Politics* (July 1968). A telling analysis of the reductionist problem in the political development literature is Joseph LaPalombara's review article, "Political Power and Political Development," *The Yale Law Journal* (June 1969). A very useful general discussion of three major perspectives on the relationship between state and society is Reinhard Bendix, "Social Stratification and the Political Community," *European Journal of Sociology* (1960). Fortunately in the last few years there has been a renewed attention to the question of the state in social science and this book hopes to contribute to this reassessment.

But first it is necessary to review the basic assumptions about the role of the state in some of the major models of political life.

I begin with an examination of liberal pluralism and the classical Marxist model of the role of the state in capitalist societies, because in their various guises these two models are the most influential competing methodological paradigms used in contemporary political analysis.[2] As such, I think it is useful to indicate to what extent some of the major lines of development of both of these theories treat the political sphere as a dependent variable, and to indicate some of the empirical and conceptual problems created by an excessive reliance on either approach.[3] A brief discussion of these two approaches is an indispensable prelude to a more extensive analysis of the organic-statist approach for two reasons. First, as a body of literature, from the mid-nineteenth century on, much of the corpus of organic-statist writing has been developed and modified in explicit normative opposition to both liberal pluralism and Marxism. It is therefore important to clarify how these three approaches differ on most of the central questions of political philosophy—on the role of the individual, the nature of the political community, the common good, and most importantly, the state. Second, at the empirical level of twentieth-century Latin American politics, the major political leaders who have attempted to impose corporatist variants of the organic-statist vision of politics on their countries have invariably acted as though liberal and Marxist ideologies and structures were the major obstacles in their path. It is therefore imperative from the point of view of the present analysis to consider the interaction of liberalism, Marxism, and organic statism.

A final preliminary note. By no means do I intend to advocate the normative or analytic superiority of the organic-statist model over that of either liberal pluralism or Marxism. I do, however,

[2] The Leninist model of the state during the dictatorship of the proletariat is of course quite different from the Marxist model of the bourgeois state. In the concluding section of this chapter I contrast organic-statist and Leninist (or more generically "command socialist") models.

[3] Numerous exceptions exist, even within Marxist and Pluralist writings, to this sweeping statement, and this chapter does not intend, or pretend, to be a comprehensive survey of all approaches. Rather I have deliberately focused on major theoretical strands that assign little independent weight to the state because I feel it is intellectually imperative to confront directly the research consequences of these schemes.

5

want to make explicit the analytic implications of the different models. Most models usually fuse normative, descriptive, and methodological components. However, for analytic purposes these components can be separated. That is, in part, models are *normative statements* about what societies should be like. In part they are *empirical descriptions* of how societies are. In part they are *methodological approaches* suggesting what aspects of political life are important to study.

Classical Marxism and liberalism pluralism, in very different ways, contain vivid descriptions of what societies are like empirically that tend to portray the state as a dependent variable. Analysts working with either a classical Marxist or liberal-pluralist vision of the real world tend to use methodological approaches to study political life that, as I will attempt to demonstrate, all too frequently systematically draw attention away from consideration of the state as a possible independent variable. Normatively, both models also contain (for different reasons) negative evaluations of the state. My point in reviewing the literature on Marxism and liberal pluralism is not to dismiss them but rather to underscore characteristic research problems presented by both models and to suggest subthemes within both models that, if recast, are useful for contemporary research into state-society relations.

Organic statism, in contrast to liberal pluralism and classical Marxism, is seen most importantly as a normative model of the relations between state and society and not primarily as a methodological approach.[4] However, elites in many different societies, and in different historical periods, have used variants of the organic-statist model as a legitimizing formula—or at times even as a guide—for designing institutions, systems, and administrative structures. Where such state-structured interactions have played a role in shaping societies empirically, then the methodological implications are clear, namely, that at a bare minimum we must design research (even where Marxist or pluralist assumptions figure prominently) so that we are able to assess the comparative weight of the state and/or society in determining

---

[4] However, at the end of the chapter I recast organic statism so that it can be studied as an abstract model of governance with its own characteristic requirements and predicaments, just as David Apter has performed a similar task for his "secular-libertarian" and "sacred-collectivity" models in *The Politics of Modernization*, pp. 28-36.

political outcomes. My own analytic position, which will emerge more clearly as the book unfolds, is that all three approaches are in some basic respects seriously deficient. Liberal pluralism and a major strand of classical Marxism are deficient largely because of their presuppositions of the near autonomy of society, and organic statism because of its presupposition of the near autonomy of the state. I hope that this book will indicate the necessity of greater theoretical integration of the two obviously non-autonomous spheres: state and society.

THE LIBERAL-PLURALIST APPROACH TO THE STATE

In the liberal-pluralist approach the main normative, empirical, and methodological concern is with individuals who, pursuing their individual economic and political interests, together make up society. In pluralist theory, individuals may form into groups, but because they all have a variety of interests they tend to associate themselves with numerous and different groups whose interests cross-cut. A methodological and normative assumption among both political and economic thinkers in the liberal-pluralist tradition is that it is undesirable to use the concept of the general good. Instead, individual utility for the constituent members of society is most nearly achieved when individuals are allowed to pursue freely their own economic and political interests.[5]

The normative and empirical distinction between the "collective interest in the common good" and the "sum of individual interests," which in organic statism or in welfare economics going back to Pareto necessitates a major role for the state in the economy, is obliterated in classical liberal economics because of the supposition that the pursuit of individual interests will in itself produce the best good for society.[6] The classic formulation of the

[5] The literature is far too extensive and too well known to summarize here. Two excellent critical reviews of the literature that develop some of the points only briefly touched on here are Sheldon Wolin's, "Liberalism and the Decline of Political Philosophy," and "The Age of Organization and the Sublimation of Politics," Chapters 9 and 10 of his *Politics and Vision: Continuity and Innovation in Western Political Thought*, pp. 286-435. See also Theodore J. Lowi, *The End of Liberalism: Ideology, Policy, and the Crisis of Public Authority*, esp. chapters 1-3. A useful analysis and anthology of English liberal thought is *The Liberal Tradition: From Fox to Keynes*, ed. Alan Bullock and Maurice Shock.

[6] See my discussion of the significance of the common good in organic

7

"hidden hand" mechanism that produces this harmony of interests is, of course, that of Adam Smith: "Every individual is continually exerting himself to find out the most advantageous employment for whatever capital he can command. It is his own advantage, indeed, and not that of the society, which he has in view. But the study of his own advantage naturally, or rather necessarily, leads him to prefer that employment which is most advantageous to the society."[7]

For the classical liberal theoretician, the hidden hand of the market mechanism itself would appear to perform—and perform better—almost all the functions that in other theories are seen as being performed by the state. The clear injunction was to let society regulate itself without interference. Society was a homeostatic system with only minimal need for a state. Thus Jeremy Bentham argued, "The general rule is, that nothing ought to be done or attempted by government. The motto, or watchword of government, on these occasions, ought to be—Be quiet. . . . With few exceptions, and these not very considerable ones, the attainment of the maximum of enjoyment will be most effectually secured by leaving each individual to pursue his own maximum enjoyment."[8]

Though the role of the state is apparently reduced to a minimum because of the self-regulating market mechanism, it is often lost sight of that Adam Smith, in a much less well-known passage, in fact assigned three distinct duties to the state:

> First, the duty of protecting the society from the violence and invasion of other independent societies; secondly, the duty of protecting, as far as possible, every member of the society from the injustice or oppression of every other member of it, or the duty of establishing an exact administration of justice; and, thirdly, the duty of erecting and maintaining certain public works and certain public institutions which it can never be for the interest of any individual, or small num-

statism in this chapter. Pareto's distinction between the "utility of the collectivity" and the "utility of the members," and his argument that "far from coinciding these utilities often stand in basic opposition," is found in Vilfredo Pareto, *The Mind and Society. A Treatise in General Sociology*, Numbers 2110-2128, esp. Number 2115.

[7] *The Wealth of Nations*, Vol. I, p. 398.

[8] *A Manual of Political Economy*, reproduced in *The Liberal Tradition*, Bullock and Shock, pp. xxiii-xxiv, 28-29.

ber of individuals, to erect and maintain; because the profit could never repay the expense to any individual or small number of individuals, though it may frequently do much more than repay it to a great society.[9]

The point then, is, not that society is actually self-regulating but that the market mechanism is assumed to be self-regulating *only if* the state provides the indispensable neutral and impartial administrative, institutional, and physical infrastructures for capitalism to function. This is, in fact, quite a large task for the state to perform in any society, and, far from being automatic, its performance requires great political skill and power. When we turn to the task of the late developing countries, the fact that they are follower economies makes many of the indispensable infrastructure expenditures "unprofitable for any individual," and the role of the state more crucial.[10] Since 1964 Brazil, for example, has been widely regarded as following a liberal, market mechanism model of development. Yet Roberto Campos, a chief economic architect of the regime, believed that, in order to make the market mechanism work, large-scale and systematic state investment and intervention was required in almost all facets of the country's economic, and especially social, structures. The last decade of market mechanism rule in Brazil thus not so paradoxically ushered in one of the most important epochs of expansion of the scope of state power in Brazil's history.[11]

[9] *The Wealth of Nations*, Vol. II, pp. 180-81.

[10] For a seminal discussion of the role of the state in relation to the "timing" of industrialization, see Alexander Gerschenkron, *Economic Backwardness in Historical Perspective*, esp. pp. 5-30.

[11] Interview with Roberto Campos, minister of planning in the Castello Branco government, in Rio de Janeiro on September 15, 1967. For a detailed analysis of the expansion of the not-so-hidden hand of the state in order to make the market mechanism work, see Thomas Skidmore, "Politics and Economic Policy Making in Authoritarian Brazil, 1937-71," in *Authoritarian Brazil: Origins, Policies, and Future*, ed. Alfred Stepan, pp. 3-46. For a fascinating discussion of how the state created an Adam Smithean "public institution," the stock market, to allow the market mechanism to operate, see David Trubek, "Law, Planning and the Development of the Brazilian Capital Market," *The Bulletin*, nos. 72-73 (April 1971). For a careful analysis of the many aspects of the growth of the role of the state in the Brazilian economy since 1930, see Werner Baer, Isaac Kerstenetzsky, and Aníbal V. Vitella, "The Changing Role of the State in the Brazilian Economy," *World Development* (November 1973). Also see Werner Baer, Richard Newfarmer, and Thomas Trebart, "On State Capitalism in Brazil: Some New

Twentieth-century pluralism, especially the group-theory variant whose most noted exponents are Arthur Bentley and David Truman, allows for a more positive role for the state. Nonetheless, it implicitly shares with classical liberalism the presupposition that society is basically self-regulating.[12] The functional equivalent of the market's hidden hand in group theory is competition among groups combined with cross-cutting membership among groups. This is the essential self-regulating principle of group theory. In group theory, as in liberal theory more generally, the analysis begins with a concern with how individuals act: "No individual is wholly absorbed in any group to which he belongs. Only a fraction of his attitudes is expressed through any one such affiliation. . . . An individual generally belongs to several groups—a family, a church, an economic institution, and frequently a very large number of associations, perhaps sixty or seventy for active 'joiners' in our society."[13] After establishing the fact of multiple memberships, the next step in the analysis is to establish their cross-cutting character: "The demands and standards of these various groups may and frequently do come in conflict with one another. . . . We must start from the fact that the equilibrium of an individual consists of his adjustment in the various institutionalized groups and associations to which he belongs."[14]

In group theory the empirical and methodological consequences of multiple overlapping memberships are many and significant. It is the central argument used to dismiss the class basis of Marxist theory, on the ground that unified class consciousness (whether upper or lower class) is an untenable concept in the face of the fragmenting impact of multiple cross-pressures.[15] Also

---

Issues and Questions," *Inter-American Economic Affairs*, 30 (Winter 1976): 63-93.

[12] Pluralist group theory is particularly relevant for our analysis because organic statism is also a form of group theory, but one which, as we shall see, has fundamentally different premises. Although I draw somewhat different conclusions, I profited much by reading John F. Witte, "Theories of American Pluralism: The Writings of Arthur F. Bentley, David Truman, and Robert A. Dahl" (unpublished manuscript, Yale University, May 17, 1973).

[13] David B. Truman, *The Governmental Process: Political Interests and Public Opinion*, p. 157.

[14] Ibid., pp. 157, 162.

[15] For their arguments rejecting the Marxist concept of class, see Tru-

the central normative role for the state as being functionally necessary for the regulation of conflict, a role found in numerous variants of organic statism, is rejected by group theorists because in group theory conflict regulation is basically an autonomous outcome of the interaction of different groups. Pluralistic group theory sees the multiple cross-pressures in society as performing the function of inducing a tendency toward bargaining and compromise both in the individual and in the individual's groups, which strive to maintain group unity in the midst of cross-pressures. "The heterogeneity of membership that causes internal difficulties in all such groups tempers the claims of an occupational interest through the process of internal compromise and adjustment."[16]

This approach, while plausible in high consensus situations, is less appropriate in societies where cleavages are compounded or in crisis situations where, despite cross-pressures, some pressures assume greater salience in terms of the stakes involved than others. In both the above cases the hypothesized self-regulating process has little behavioral impact and the role of the state apparatus and strategic political elites often becomes crucial in determining the outcome.[17]

Bentley does not really discuss the empirical possibility of the state elite's altering the effective power of potential groups either by using repression to dismantle the organizational capacity of some groups or by seeking to broaden the social base for the state elite's programs by organizing from above a group that otherwise would not be able to organize effectively. His assumption is that "when we have a group that participates in the political system we have always another group facing it in the same plane."[18] Truman does not assert that opposing groups are actually organized, but he does place great weight on the fact that all inter-

---

man, *The Governmental Process*, pp. 165-66, and Arthur Bentley, *The Process of Government: A Study of Social Pressures*, pp. 207-208.

[16] Truman, *The Governmental Process*, p. 166, also p. 514. Bentley speaks of the "limitless criss-cross of groups"; *The Process of Government*, p. 206.

[17] For an excellent discussion along these lines see Eric A. Nordlinger, *Conflict Regulation in Divided Societies*, esp. pp. 93-101.

[18] Bentley, *The Process of Government*, p. 220. He presents no convincing evidence for this and does not address the question of comparative power. For a useful corrective to Bentley's approach, see Mancur Olson, Jr., *The Logic of Collective Action: Public Goods and the Theory of Groups*, revised ed. (New York: Schocken Books, 1971).

ests are potential interest groups and that, as such, other actual powerful groups will take them into account. Thus the balancing (or repressive) function does not need to be performed by the government because it is the "multiple memberships in potential groups based on widely held and accepted interests that serve as the balance wheel in a going political system like that of the United States."[19] In the writings of Bentley this methodological emphasis on group forces relegates the concept of the "state" to the "intellectual amusements of the past."[20]

As to the government's adding significantly to the sum total of interest group pressures, or being an agent reshaping the balance of forces in society, Bentley rules this out: "the governing body has no value in itself, except as one aspect of the process, and cannot even be adequately described except in terms of the deeplying interests which function through it."[21] He accepts the idea that the government or the permanent bureaucracy could be considered an interest group, but insists that as such it would have no autonomous interests because its interests would reflect other more fundamental interest groups in society.[22]

Although other variants of contemporary North American political science are not as reductionist as the interest group theorists, there is a widespread tendency to look for the underlying nonpolitical forces in society and to reduce greatly the autonomy of the state or the government. Significantly, in the elaborate

[19] Truman, *The Governmental Process*, p. 514. Once again little hard evidence is given to support this proposition and no discussion of the theoretical or normative problem of "non-issues."

[20] "The 'State' itself is, to the best of my knowledge and belief, no factor in our investigation," and "The 'idea of the state' has been very prominent, no doubt, among the intellectual amusements of the past, and at particular places and times it has served to help give coherence and pretentious expression to some particular group's activity. But in either case it is too minute a factor to deserve space in a book covering so broad a range as this." Bentley, *The Process of Government*, pp. 263-64.

[21] Ibid., p. 300.

[22] Ibid., p. 290. While his theory is mainly concerned with modern societies, Bentley argues that group theory would hold for all societies, even in the extreme case of absolute despotism. For the despot himself is merely an expression of the underlying balance of forces in society: "When we take such an agency of government as a despotic ruler, we cannot possibly advance to an understanding of him except in terms of the group activities of his society which are most directly represented through him. Always and everywhere our study must be a study of the interests that work through government; otherwise we have not got down to the facts" (pp. 270-71).

12

Parsonian schema, society, culture, and personality are judged to be worthy of relatively autonomous levels of analysis, but politics is not.[23] Gabriel Almond, in his influential introduction to *The Politics of Developing Areas*, a book that ushered in a decade of new field research, notes that "It was the conviction of the collaborators in this study that . . . the input functions, rather than the output, would be most important in characterizing non-Western political systems, and in discriminating types and stages of political development among them."[24] Later in the same introduction, Almond acknowledges that "While there is justification for having underplayed the governmental structures in this study, their neglect in the development of the theory of the functions of the polity represents a serious shortcoming in the present analysis."[25]

It is safe to say that, despite empirical refinements, there never was a major methodological advance in this approach in regard to the role of public policy or the state, and that, by and large, the prestigious Social Science Research Council Committee on Comparative Politics contributed heavily to the reductionist tendency to look for nonpolitical explanations of political behavior.[26]

Yet another attempt to analyze a total political system is that of David Easton.[27] His systems analysis approach shares an important dimension with Almond's functional approach, namely an elaborate discussion of inputs but a very cursory analysis of the role that the government plays in shaping inputs and generating its own policies or outputs. Easton does not deny that government can play a role in generating inputs, but even here he characteristically redirects attention back to the need to examine the

---

[23] See Talcott Parsons, E. A. Shils et al., *Toward a General Theory of Action*, pp. 28-29.

[24] Gabriel Almond, "A Functional Approach to Comparative Politics," in *The Politics of the Developing Areas*, ed. Gabriel A. Almond and James S. Coleman, p. 17. The four input functions were (1) political socialization and recruitment, (2) interest articulation, (3) interest aggregation and (4) political communication. In fact, all four "input functions" may be strongly structured by government policy as I demonstrate in other chapters.

[25] Ibid., p. 55.

[26] For an interesting critique along these lines by a prominent member of the SSRC Committee on Comparative Politics, see LaPalombara, "Political Power and Political Development," p. 1259.

[27] He has developed this in various publications. The two most important are his *A Framework for Political Analysis* (New York: Prentice Hall, 1965), and *A Systems Analysis of Political Life*.

overall cultural, environmental, and social backgrounds of the
"gatekeepers" rather than to the black box of government itself.[28]

A research strategy that is limited to the pluralist, interest-
group perspective, while it is certainly useful for some problems,
all too often takes for granted what it should be demonstrating,
namely that a plurality of interests plays a determining role in
shaping policy. This implicit assumption often contributes to a
systematic neglect both of the state's role in taking independent
policy initiatives, and of the impact of state policy on the structure of society, especially on the types of inputs that social groups
can in fact make on the state.[29] To cite one obvious example, in
many countries trade unions are subject to prohibitions against
organization, or at least are restricted to operating within a legal
and administrative network of regulations that has a profound
impact on how the unions' interests are organized and articulated.[30] A closely related neglected question concerns the role of
state policy in creating groups from above and then establishing
guidelines on how they can act.

These examples suggest that the neglect of the institutional,
class, and ideological context within which interest groups operate is a serious problem. The dominant supposition of group
theorists is that interest groups operate in an *unchartered* context. Significantly, Truman quotes approvingly Bentley's summary statement: "The very nature of the group process (which
our government shows in a fairly well-developed form) is this,
that groups are freely combining, dissolving, and recombining in
accordance with their interest lines."[31]

As a description of the real world, this suffers from the obvious
limitation that, for most societies throughout most of history,

[28] Easton, *A Systems Analysis of Political Life*, pp. 97-99.

[29] My specific intention here is to indicate conceptual and empirical
lacunae in regard to state policy in pluralist—especially group—theory.
There is of course a voluminous literature devoted to general critiques of
pluralism. Some of the more prominent attacks are Lowi, *The End of
Liberalism*; Peter Bachrach and Morton S. Baratz, "Two Faces of Power,"
American Political Science Review (December 1962); Michael Parenti, "Power
and Pluralism: A View from the Bottom," *Journal of Politics* (August 1970);
and *The Bias of Pluralism*, ed. William E. Connolly.

[30] In the next two chapters I document in extensive detail the effective
array of corporatist mechanisms the Brazilian and Mexican state elites have
constructed to control unions.

[31] Truman, *The Governmental Process*, p. 167, and Bentley, *The Process
of Government*, p. 359.

14

interest groups have not been at liberty to "freely combine." Quite often, as our later discussion of the organic-statist tradition will make clear, they have been very strictly *chartered* by the state in accordance with the state's, and not the groups', "own interest lines." Reliance on a theoretical scheme that posits freely combining interest groups and a passive, neutral state seriously limits the range of cases that can be considered because only with great difficulty can such a perspective deal with such contemporary architectonic party-states as China and the Soviet Union, where the party-based controllers of the state apparatus have clearly been reasonably successful in imposing their ideological and organizational designs on the body politic.[32] It leads also to historical parochialism, because even though it is clear that a promising area for political development theory lies in longitudinal historical analysis, many of the dominant theoretical schemes, with their view of the state as a dependent variable and their emphasis on relatively free and powerful interest groups,

[32] Schurmann's book on China, for example, begins with a clear acknowledgment of the power of the party-state to redesign and rebuild Chinese society: "Chinese communism came to power and created the present People's Republic of China. . . . They have rebuilt a great country, disciplined its people, improved the conditions of life, and laid the foundations for growth. . . . We are concerned with the systematic structures created by these men. Communist China is like a vast building made of different kinds of brick and stone. However it was put together, it stands. What holds it together is ideology and organization." See Franz Schurmann's *Ideology and Organization in Communist China*, p. 1. For a telling critique of the lack of usefulness of Almond's analytical framework for dealing with contemporary communist regimes, see Robert A. Dowse, "A Functionalist's Logic," *World Politics* (June 1966). This is not to imply, as the literature on totalitarianism had earlier, that attention to groups in strong party states is irrelevant. For an attempt at utilizing "interest group" analysis for the Soviet Union, see *Interest Groups in Soviet Politics*, ed. H. Gordon Skilling and Franklyn Griffiths. The Skilling approach, however, has a serious conceptual weakness: the confusion of "group politics" with "pluralist interest group politics." In fact a strong case could probably be made that the role of groups in Eastern Europe has more in common at the structural level with the organic-statist or corporatist traditions of chartered group politics than it does with the pluralist interest group tradition. One of the few scholars to begin to develop this potentially fruitful line of inquiry into the relationship of groups to the state in communist societies is Andrew C. Janos, "Group Politics in Communist Society: A Second Look at the Pluralist Model," in *Authoritarian Politics in Modern Society: The Dynamics of Established One-Party Systems*, ed. Samuel P. Huntington and Clement H. Moore.

have great difficulty in dealing adequately with major spans of Western political life. For example, in many Greek, Italian Renaissance, and Swiss city-states, the private sphere of interests was relatively small compared to the political sphere in which the government structured activities. The unchartered interest-group focus has even greater limitations as an analytic approach when the task is the study of power in such formative phases of European political history as the Roman Empire, seventeenth-century absolutism, or the two Napoleonic regimes, in all of which there was a major accumulation of power by the state at the expense of interest groups. As we shall see when we analyze the political philosophy and practice of organic statism in Europe, the state placed strict and effective controls on associations. Despite the rejection of some aspects of the organic-statist approach in the absolutist period, it is clear that state control of interest groups was, if anything, intensified.

Another problem for group theory relates to the question of selective access. Even in societies that were once assumed to approximate closely the pluralist political model, such as England or Sweden, the semi-planned nature of the political economy has given rise to a policy consultation stage that has significantly altered the nature of the input process by interest groups. Before new measures (which are increasingly drawn up by government initiative) are formally considered by the legislature, they are systematically vetted by a consultative committee consisting of the ministerial or public agency representatives delegated by the state, the representatives of employee organizations, the representatives of employer organizations, and occasionally a representative of a public interest group.[33] The crucial point is that the

---

[33] In Sweden such committees play a central role in the political process. In the 1961-67 period, 60% of the commissioners were civil servants (up from 41% in 1945-54) and the nonconflictual behavior of the other members is indicated by the fact that three-fourths of all commissions presented unanimous proposals; see Hans Meijer, "Bureaucracy and Policy Formulation in Sweden," *Scandinavian Political Studies*, pp. 103-116. For an interesting comparative study that makes a strong case that bureaucracies were the "most consistently important" group in shaping welfare policies in Britain and Sweden and that the earlier emergence of certain welfare policies in Sweden than in Britain was due more to variance in state administrative structures than to the power of organized political pressures see, Hugh Heclo, *Modern Social Politics in Britain and Sweden: From Relief to Income Maintenance*, esp. pp. 42-60, 301-321, quote from p. 301.

16

state plays a central role in determining which groups are represented in this policy process.[34] *Access capability* also has an impact on the strength or weakness of groups. Groups that can demonstrate reasonably good access capability are often in a superior position to maintain or even accrue support from constituents than those that are perceived to be outside this process of consultation. In addition, since group leaders want to maintain their own power and prestige, which often is derived from their membership on such a consultative committee, they often will be tempted to tailor their groups' demands to stay within the general policy framework being pursued by the government.[35] Because the state plays such a pivotal role in agenda setting, access granting, constituency support capability, and interest-group demand formulation, it obviously plays a central part in shaping the input process even in "pluralistic" politics.[36]

CLASSICAL MARXIST THEORY OF THE STATE IN CAPITALIST SOCIETIES

As in much of liberal-pluralist thought, a main line of argumentation in the classical Marxist theory of bourgeois society treats the state largely as a dependent variable.[37] Since this aspect

[34] Joseph LaPalombara discusses the question of "structured access" in his *Interest Groups in Italian Politics*, esp. pp. 258-70.

[35] This process has not received the attention it deserves. Two seminal works that begin to address the subject are by Samuel H. Beer, *British Politics in the Collectivist Age*, and Stein Rokkan, "Norway: Numerical Democracy and Corporate Pluralism," in *Political Opposition in Western Democracies*, ed. Robert A. Dahl, pp. 70-116, esp. pp. 105-10. Significantly, Rokkan cites no English language work that discusses this aspect of Norwegian politics.

[36] Philippe C. Schmitter's stimulating "Still the Century of Corporatism?" in *The New Corporatism: Social-Political Structures in the Iberian World*, ed. Fredrick B. Pike and Thomas Stritch, pp. 85-131, argues—correctly I think—that corporatist structures are becoming more prominent in countries such as Sweden, Switzerland, the Netherlands, Norway, and Denmark. However he argues that such structures have largely emerged from the interest groups themselves—thus his term "societal corporatism"—whereas I attach significant independent weight to the role the state has played in forging such structured interactions.

[37] By classical Marxist theory, I mean the theory found in Karl Marx and Frederick Engels. A number of good studies are devoted to this difficult subject. An analysis that places Marx's view of the state within the context of his general philosophy is Shlomo Avineri, *The Social and Political Thought of Karl Marx*, esp. pp. 17-64. A book that focuses specifically on

of Marxist thought has played a preponderant role in shaping subsequent "economistic" Marxist analyses of the state, I shall treat it first. Later I shall analyze subthemes in Marx's writings concerning hegemonic crises and Bonapartism that, if properly understood, offer rich, nondeterministic, theoretical insights about such crucial questions as the relative autonomy of the state. Unfortunately, Marx died before he was able to begin a full-scale systematic treatment of the state.[38] Nonetheless, he had already written enough about the relation of the state to society for us to discuss certain broad themes. For in fact Marx had always been interested in the question of the state. Significantly, his first major work, the critique of Hegel's *Philosophy of Right*, was largely devoted to a criticism of Hegel's view of the state.

In traditional liberal-pluralist thought, the analytical starting point is with the individual, who is seen as acting alone or with other groups of individuals to advance his private interests. Marx rejects the atomistic starting-point of liberal pluralism on the methodological grounds that it is impossible to discuss any individual without at the same time discussing the sum total of the relationships within which individuals are intermeshed.[39] For Marx, the most fundamental of these relationships involves the mode of production, and thus both individualist psychology and individualist politics are rejected. Marx's basic statement of the relationship of politics to economics is found in his famous preface to the *Contribution to the Critique of Political Economy*:

> . . . legal relations as well as forms of state are to be grasped neither from themselves nor from the so-called general develop-

---

the political theory of Marx and Engels is Robert Tucker, *The Marxian Revolutionary Idea*, esp. pp. 54-81. See also Ralph Miliband, "Marx and the State," *Socialist Register* (1965), 278-96; John Sanderson, "Marx and Engels on the State," *Western Political Quarterly* (December 1963); John Plamenatz, *German Marxism and Russian Communism*, pp. 135-64; and the important interpretations by Nicos Poulantzas, *Political Power and Social Classes*, and Jean-Claude Girardin, "Sur la théorie marxiste de l'Etat," *Les Temps Modernes* (September-October 1972).

[38] For Marx's intention to write such a work, see Karl Marx, "Preface to a Critique of Political Economy," in Karl Marx and Frederick Engels, *Selected Works*, Vol. I, p. 361.

[39] See Karl Marx, *The Poverty of Philosophy*, pp. 33-46. For an analysis of Marx's critique of "atomistic individualism" see Avineri, *The Social and Political Thought of Karl Marx*, pp. 17-18, 33.

ment of the human mind, but rather have their roots in the material conditions of life. . . . The anatomy of civil society is to be sought in political economy. . . . The sum total of these relations of production constitutes the economic structure of society, the real foundation, on which rises a legal and political super-structure and to which correspond definite forms of social consciousness. The mode of production of material life conditions the social, political and intellectual life process in general.[40]

The hidden hand of classical liberalism and the group competition and cross-cutting cleavages of pluralism imply there is fruitful competition and a minimum of systematic conflict or coercion. Though there is no sense of the collective community as such, as there is in organic statism, classical liberal pluralism in theory can result in a contribution to the greatest good of the greatest number. These assumptions are flatly rejected by classical Marxism. Once division of labor occurs, "every form of society has been based . . . on the antagonism of oppressing and oppressed classes."[41] Between classes the economic conflict is basically a zero-sum relationship: "Every advance in production is at the same time a retrogression in the condition of the oppressed class, that is, of the great majority. What is a boon for the one is necessarily a bane for the other; each new emancipation of one class always means a new oppression of another class."[42]

[40] Marx and Engels, *Selected Works*, Vol. I, pp. 362-63. Engels often formulated the relationship of the political superstructure to the economic structure in much less subtle and more deterministic language. See, for example, his prefaces to the German edition (1883) and the English edition (1888) of the *Communist Manifesto*, in *Selected Works*, Vol. I, pp. 24, 28.

[41] The *Communist Manifesto*, in Marx and Engels, *Selected Works*, Vol. I, p. 45.

[42] Frederick Engels, *The Origin of the Family, Private Property, and the State*, in Marx and Engels, *Selected Works*, Vol. II, p. 295. This essay is one of the most detailed treatments of the state to be found in the writings of Marx and Engels. All further references to this work refer to the *Selected Works* edition. For Marxist social science, the fact that Engels, not Marx, wrote most extensively on the state was unfortunate because, as noted, Engels's analysis of the relationship of the superstructure to the structure was often presented in much more mechanistic terms than that found in Marx. To this extent my strictures about "classical Marxism" apply more directly to Engels. Nonetheless, since Engels's works had a great influence

19

Given the fact that the economic structure is the basis for the political superstructure, the liberal assumption that the state will provide neutral procedural guarantees for free political and economic competition is rejected. The state, at least in Engels's formulation, is exclusively the coercive instrument of the dominant class: "The State, . . . in all typical periods is exclusively the state of the ruling class, and in all cases remains essentially a machine for keeping down the oppressed, exploited class."[43] The famous passage in the Communist Manifesto that "The Executive of the modern state is but a committee for managing the common affairs of the whole bourgeoisie" thus posits a relationship in which the state is the dependent variable and the economic system is the independent variable.[44]

Since for classical Marxism the state originally arose as a necessary means of coercion once division of labor occurred, the state remains as an instrument of oppression until the proletarian revolution eliminates all class distinctions by eliminating capitalism. This can only be accomplished when the proletariat in turn uses the state as a means of repression during the transitional stage of the "dictatorship of the proletariat."[45] Once private ownership is abolished, and class distinctions eventually eliminated, the need for the state as an instrument of class oppression no longer exists. At this stage classical Marxism shares with classical liberalism the assumption that society can essentially be internally self-managed. Emancipated society has the autonomous, noncoercive managerial capacity to regulate itself. In contrast to the basic assumptions of organic statism, the state in pure communism is seen as both functionally unnecessary, and normatively undesirable for society. As Engels said, "The society that will organize production on the basis of a free and equal association

---

on Marxist social science, it would be sociologically unacceptable to exclude his works when we are evaluating the legacy of classical Marxism in regard to the analysis of the state.

[43] Ibid., p. 294.

[44] Marx and Engels, *Selected Works*, Vol. I, p. 36.

[45] On the need for the revolutionary dictatorship of the proletariat, see Karl Marx, *Critique of the Gotha Program*, in *Selected Works*, Vol. II, p. 30. For Engels's attack on anarchic socialists who would not use authoritarian means to maintain the victorious revolution, see his "On Authority," in *Selected Works*, Vol. I, pp. 636-637. Also see V. I. Lenin, "The Immediate Tasks of the Soviet Government," in V. I. Lenin, *Selected Works* (New York: International Publishers, 1971), pp. 420-427.

of the producers will put the whole machinery of state where it will then belong: into the Museum of Antiquities, by the side of the spinning wheel and the bronze axe."[46]

The above summarizes a main line of argument of the classical Marxist theory of the state under normal conditions. As in classical liberalism, the state apparently does not play a relatively independent role in the political process. Until the classless society comes into being, the state is envisaged as the instrument of coercion of the dominant economic class, and as such, much research that confines itself to the above aspects of the classical Marxist tradition is directed almost exclusively to the underlying economic forces in society. As Nicos Poulantzas, himself a Marxist, laments, "a long Marxist tradition has considered that the State is only a simple tool or instrument manipulated at will by the ruling class."[47] As he acknowledges, this has often led to "economism" which "considers that other levels of social reality, including the State, are simple epiphenomena reducible to the economic 'base'. Thereby a specific study of the State becomes superfluous. Parallel with this, economism considers that every change in the social system happens first of all in the economy and that political action should have the economy as its principal objective. Once again, a specific study of the State is redundant."[48]

Such a methodological orientation leaves so little scope for overall dynamic analysis of situations that a number of neo-Marxists have argued that the treatment of the state is one of the weakest areas in much Marxist social science. As Ralph Miliband notes: "Marxists have made little notable attempt to confront the question of the state in the light of the concrete socio-economic *and* political *and* cultural reality of actual capitalist societies."[49]

[46] Engels, *The Origin of the Family*, p. 292. The even more famous passage describing the withering away of the state is found in the second chapter of the third part of Engels's *Anti-Dühring*.

[47] Nicos Poulantzas, "The Problem of the Capitalist State," *New Left Review*, no. 58 (November-December 1969), 74.

[48] Ibid., p. 68.

[49] See his *The State in Capitalist Society*, p. 6, emphasis in the original. He cites a similar judgment made by Paul Sweezy. A major exception that should be made is the work of the Italian Communist party leader and theoretician Antonio Gramsci. His concepts of hegemony and class fractions will be discussed and used in later chapters. Miliband's book and especially Poulantzas's *Political Power and Social Classes* are important attempts to invigorate the Marxist analysis of the state.

21

However, there are neglected subthemes in Marx and Engels that, if read properly and applied to the special conditions of late developing, dependent-capitalist societies such as those in Latin America, in fact provide much less theoretical foundation for the neglect of the state than do many conventional Marxist interpretations.

Classical Marxist writings give two major qualifications to the description of the state as a dependent variable: the nonhegemonic qualification and the qualification concerning the permanent tendency toward parasitic bureaucratic autonomy. Taken together, these should constitute an impressive a priori theoretical justification for considering the state as a major source of relatively independent political action even within the Marxist model.

Consider first the implications of the hegemony hypothesis. Engels asserts that the state "in all typical periods is exclusively the state of the ruling class." But how typical are "typical" periods? Apparently, for a period to be typical, a hegemonic class must exist. But how often does even Engels consider that there is a situation of class hegemony? His discussion of periods that are not typical merits quotation at length:

> By way of exception, however, periods occur in which the warring classes balance each other so nearly that the state power, as ostensible mediator, acquires, for the moment, a certain degree of independence of both. Such was the absolute monarchy of the seventeenth and eighteenth centuries, which held the balance between the nobility and the class of the burghers; such was the Bonapartism of the First, and still more of the Second French Empire, which played off the proletariat against the bourgeoisie and the bourgeoisie against the proletariat. The latest performance of this kind, in which ruler and ruled appear equally ridiculous, is the new German Empire of the Bismarck nation: here capitalists and workers are balanced against each other and equally cheated for the benefit of the impoverished Prussian cabbage junkers.[50]

[50] Engels, *The Origin of the Family*, pp. 290-291. In *The Civil War in France*, Marx gives a similar explanation of the rise of Bonapartism: "In reality, it was the only form of government possible at a time when the bourgeoisie had already lost, and the working class had not yet acquired, the faculty or ruling the nation," in *Selected Works*, Vol. 1, p. 518.

Writing toward the end of the nineteenth century, Engels saw, therefore, much of the seventeenth and eighteenth centuries as nonhegemonic, and extensive periods in the nineteenth-century history of the two major European powers as characterized by nonhegemonic class relations.

Whether or not there is a hegemonic class or fraction of a class capable of ruling politically in any given situation is thus not to be assumed. Rather it is to be determined by empirical investigation of the relationship between the economic structure and the class structure and by a detailed analysis of the relationship between class fractions and the control of the state apparatus.[51]

With reference to Latin America, numerous studies indicate that, within the context of late-industrializing, dependent economies, the national bourgeoisie has not been able to attain a hegemonic situation comparable to that achieved by the bourgeoisie in England, the United States, and some countries in Europe, *nor* has a hegemonic industrial proletariat emerged.

The reasons for the nonhegemonic class situation are complex but interrelated. The high degree of foreign ownership of industry reduces the relative size and power of the national bourgeoisie, while the national bourgeoisie itself often has a variety of credit, ownership, technological, and marketing dependency relationships with international capital. This, plus their frequent status as relatively recent immigrants, puts members of the national bourgeoisie in a weak political position to compete—in a nationalist environment—as an electoral force aiming at hegemonic acceptance for their position. The character of late dependent

[51] The lack of hegemony is not only due to economic equilibrium. In fact Poulantzas argues that, due to the *normal* difficulties preventing the bourgeoisie from achieving sufficient unity to create their own hegemonic political organization, the "relative autonomy of the state" is a constituent feature of capitalism and in this sense Bonapartism is the "religion of the bourgeoisie"; *Political Power and Social Classes*, pp. 281-85. Ralph Miliband, in his "The Capitalist State: Reply to Nicos Poulantzas," *New Left Review*, no. 59 (January-February 1970), p. 58, argues (correctly I think) that by labeling all capitalist states "Bonapartist" it is difficult to make the significant distinction between the meaning of "relative autonomy of the state" under fascism and under a social-democratic regime. At the very least, the debate highlights the fact that the creation of political domination via the state apparatus is the result of shifting coalitions of class fractions and that the forging (or nonforging) of a "hegemonic block" is a fit subject for independent analysis, whether by the political scientist, or—as in the case of Gramsci—by the Marxist party theoretician and tactician.

industrialization that has followed, not preceded, modernization means that, in comparison to Anglo-Saxon patterns, fewer workers are employed in industry at similar stages of development due to capital intensive methods, and the number of urban workers in the tertiary and marginal sectors is much higher. This pattern of industrialization has not been supportive of the consolidation of large, class-conscious, autonomous worker organizations.[52]

If something like this is in fact the case for much of Latin America and other parts of the Third World, then even from a Marxist perspective we should expect the state to play a large role in mediating conflict between nonhegemonic classes, and the question of the relative autonomy of the state apparatus should be central in any research strategy about politics in such systems.

The second major qualification about the state as a dependent variable in classical Marxism comes in the discussion by Marx and Engels of the tendency toward the parasitic autonomy of the bureaucratic apparatus of the state. Throughout their work they argue that, as class conflict intensifies, the repressive apparatus must become larger; this sets into motion a bureaucratic momentum whereby the state apparatus tends to play roles more self-determining than that envisaged in any mechanistic model of the state as a passive and maleable instrument of class coercion. Indeed, Engels goes so far as to say that this "transformation of the state and the organs of the state from servants of society into masters of society" is "an inevitable transformation in all previous states."[53] The tendency toward relative state autonomy is thus not restricted to nonhegemonic situations. Indeed, Marx and Engels see it as an actual, not latent, tendency in any society where there is a division of labor and therefore the need for a repressive

[52] For an excellent discussion of the structure and ideology of the bourgeoisie under such conditions, see Fernando Henrique Cardoso, *Ideologías de la burguesía industrial en sociedades dependientes (Argentina y Brasil)*. For a comparison with the pattern in the United States and Europe see his "The Industrial Elite" in *Elites in Latin America*, ed. Seymour Martin Lipset and Aldo Solari, pp. 94-114. For a brief comparative study of labor in Europe and Latin America see Kenneth Paul Erickson and Patrick V. Peppe, "The Dynamics of Dependency: Industrial Modernization and Tightening Controls Over the Working Class in Brazil and Chile" (paper prepared for the Latin American Studies Association, November 1974), and Brian H. Smith and José Luis Rodríguez, "Comparative Working-Class Political Behavior: Chile, France, and Italy," *American Behavioral Scientist* (September 1974).

[53] Introduction to Marx's *Civil War in France, Selected Works*, Vol. I, p. 484.

state. The numerous references by Marx and Engels to this phenomenon indicate that they took it seriously. Marx, for example, describes the state apparatus in nineteenth-century France as one in which the state "constantly maintains an immense mass of interests and livelihoods in the most absolute dependence; where the state enmeshes, controls, regulates, superintends and tutors civil society."[54]

If this is such a permanent tendency even under European conditions in a relatively well-developed civil society, one should expect that under twentieth-century Latin American conditions, where the state apparatus is often larger in comparison to civil society than it was in nineteenth-century Europe or North America, and where the state often "enmeshes, controls, regulates, superintends and tutors civil society," the problem would be even more acute.

Even in socialist societies a tendency toward bureaucratic aggrandizement rather than the hoped for withering away of the state is sufficiently prominent that it should be a central question for Marxist scholars.[55] Indeed, a major concern among some Marxists—especially Yugoslav Marxists—is, how to prevent the party-state apparatus from generating a new bureaucratic elite with special privileges that inhibit the evolution toward a more participatory, state-less communist society.[56]

[54] Karl Marx, *The Eighteenth Brumaire of Louis Bonaparte*, in Marx and Engels, *Selected Works*, Vol. I, p. 284.

[55] The League of Communists in Yugoslavia asserted, for example, that "bureaucratism is a great danger to socialism in the transition period," and warned against the tendency "of transforming the state into an all-embracing social force, a force above society which would in fact liquidate the direct social influence of the working masses on the policies of the state leadership —that is, the tendency of state idolatry." See *Yugoslavia's Way: The Program of the League of Communists of Yugoslavia*, translated by Stoyan Pribechevich (New York: All Nations Press, 1958), pp. 117-118. Svetozar Stojanović deals with similar issues in "The Statist Myth of Socialism," in his *Between Ideals and Reality: A Critique of Socialism and its Future*, translated by Gerson S. Sher, pp. 37-75.

[56] See, for example, Edvard Kardelj, "The Principal Dilemma: Self-Management or Statism," *Socialist Thought and Practice* (Belgrade) (October-December 1966), and Najdan Pašić, "Dictatorship by the Proletariat or over the Proletariat," *Socialist Thought and Practice* (October-December 1968). Other works by Marxist scholars which stress that the transition from socialism to communism cannot be assumed to be automatic and that it is particularly important for Marxists to analyze the state apparatus in socialist systems are Paul M. Sweezy, "Toward a Program of Studies of the Transition

A correct interpretation of what Marx and Engels say of the role of the state in nonhegemonic situations and of the permanent tendency toward parasitic bureaucratic autonomy means that any Marxist analysis of politics should devote extensive attention to the conditions in which the state acts with a significant degree of autonomy.

In the case of Latin America a number of central research questions flow from this discussion. For example, given a general context of late, dependent modernization that is relatively unsupportive for establishing class hegemony, how was a hegemonic block of class fractions nonetheless constructed in Mexico? The Marxist literature also often speaks of the role the state plays in the "reproduction of the means of production."[57] Analysis of this role as an independent variable becomes even more crucial when the question is that of the initial *production* by the state, rather than the mere *reproduction*, of the social and economic bases of capitalism. In such a case, as in Mexico, the state apparatus plays a central role in creating the political, ideological, and economic infrastructure necessary for the emergence of the national bourgeoisie. This raises extremely complex questions about the lines of domination in the relations between the state elite and the newly created economic elite.

Finally, what are the *limits* of the relative autonomy of the state? How far can a "revolution from above" by a fraction of the state apparatus (for example the military fraction in Peru) go in transforming economic and political structures?

THE ORGANIC-STATIST APPROACH TO THE STATE[58]

All too often post-World War II political science references to the theory of the organic state are restricted to Hegel or to twen-

---

to Socialism" in *On the Transition to Socialism*, ed. Paul M. Sweezy and Charles Bettelheim (New York: Monthly Review Press, 1971), pp. 123-135; Herbert Marcuse, "The Dialectic of the Soviet State," in his *Soviet Marxism: A Critical Analysis* (New York: Vintage Books, 1961), pp. 85-103, and the major study by Charles Bettelheim, *Class Struggles in the USSR: First Period; 1917-1923.*

[57] See for example the importance Louis Althusser attaches to this point in "Ideology and Ideological State Apparatuses" in his *Lenin and Philosophy and Other Essays*, pp. 128-136.

[58] The term *organic statism* needs some clarification. "Organic" here refers to a normative vision of the political community in which the component

tieth-century fascist or totalitarian regimes that proclaimed the supremacy of the state. This association contributes to the tendency to dismiss theoretical discussions of the state as belonging to a normatively aberrant and historically brief and closed epoch of political thought. Added to this negative moral and historical perception is a methodological critique. The concept of the state was often dismissed as a reification, as a nonquantifiable, Hegelian or medieval abstraction. Or, if it was acknowledged that the concept could refer to concrete governmental and bureaucratic agencies, the reductionist school of comparative politics tended to relegate the study of the state to the "legal-institutional-descriptive" school of traditional political science. Thus history, ethics, methodology, and scholarly fashion combined virtually to eliminate the state from the central concerns of modern political science.

Fashion and misguided methodology aside, this has been unfortunate. For of course there exists an important non-German approach to the state that greatly predates Hegel, and that, far from being philosophically aberrant, and despite its tendency toward authoritarian political formulas, has been a dominant strand of political thought since the time of Aristotle. Far from being historically closed, moreover, this approach is very much alive as a philosophical and structural influence, especially in southern Europe and the countries of Latin America. This corpus of political thought is not as textually and historically specific as classical Marxism or liberal pluralism. Nonetheless, there is a body of ideas running through Aristotle, Roman law, medieval natural law and into contemporary Catholic social philosophy that together make up what I call the organic-statist tradition of political thought.[59] As in the liberal-pluralist approach, the or-

---

parts of society harmoniously combine to enable the full development of man's potential. "Statist" is used because of the assumption in this tradition that such harmony does not occur spontaneously in the process of historical evolution but rather requires power, rational choices, and decisions, and occasional restructuring of civil society by political elites. "Organic" in this context thus is quite different from either the historical organicism of Burke or the monist organicism of Leninism. Even though the word *state* is a relatively modern term, I have used it to capture the sense that the organic unity of civil society is brought about by the architectonic action of public authorities—hence "organic-statism."

[59] Most contemporary political theory textbooks are interested in developing the body of ideas that have contributed to what is seen as the main line

ganic-statist approach has many, sometimes contradictory, variants. But just as a contemporary pluralist can select from Locke, Madison, de Tocqueville, Truman, and common law a reasonably coherent body of ideas stressing individualism, checks and balances, autonomous interest groups, and the central role of social forces, so a twentieth-century political theorist in Latin America can just as easily select out of Aristotle, Roman law, natural law, and the papal encyclicals a cumulative body of ideas stressing the political community, the concession theory of association, and the central role of the state in achieving the common good.[60] Both bodies of ideas have intellectual coherence and, as Charles W. Anderson has argued, a distinct "basic logic" as "paradigms of social choice."[61]

---

of historical evolution of the Anglo-Saxon (and to a lesser extent, French) political culture. There is a tendency to neglect the organic-statist tradition or to select out of it those aspects most relevant for the development of the liberal-pluralist tradition or that of its major contemporary opponent, the Marxist tradition. In many undergraduate courses, this means an ungainly leap from Aristotle to Machiavelli, in the process virtually leaving out a major component of the European cultural heritage.

[60] Two important caveats: First, just as liberal pluralism has variants that are not in the main line of development, so does organic statism. Twentieth-century fascist and totalitarian movements are extreme variations of the approach. I argue in Chapter 2, however, that in some fundamental ways these deviated from some of the basic ideas of organic statism and should not be considered essential to the model. Second, liberal pluralism and organic statism at times draw upon the same corpus of writing, such as Aristotle, but they select out of the corpus different elements. In the case of Roman law, to take an example, liberal pluralism has drawn upon the rational individualistic aspects of the doctrine of contract, while the organic-statist tradition has drawn upon the concession theory and sovereignty doctrines that grant the state authority to define and promote the common good and charter associational groups. In the economic sphere, the liberal-pluralist selection of ideas is supportive of a market based economy, while the organic-statist selection of ideas is supportive of mercantilist economies.

[61] He argues that: "A paradigm of public choice specifies the grounds that are appropriate for making claims within a given political order. It tells us about the kinds of arguments that are most likely to appear acceptable to political actors in arriving at policy conclusions. In this sense, it defines . . . the range of reasons that will be accepted as legitimate in political argument and debate." See his "Public Policy, Pluralism and the Future Evolution of Advanced Industrial Society" (paper prepared for the 1973 Annual Meeting of the American Political Science Association, New Orleans, September 4-8).

For liberal pluralism, the starting point is descriptive—the rational self-interest of the individual. For classic Marxism, the starting point is also descriptive—the dominant mode of production and its characteristic form of class struggle. For organic statism, the starting point is normative—the preferred form of political life of man as a member of a community.

From Aristotle to St. Thomas Aquinas to modern papal encyclicals, a central normative theme is that man's nature can only be fulfilled within a community. Thus Aristotle says: "The man who is isolated—who is unable to share in the benefits of political association, or has no need to share because he is already self-sufficient—is no part of the polis, and must therefore be either a beast or a god. . . . There is therefore an imminent impulse in all men towards an association of this order."[62] For Aristotle a corollary of man's political nature is the naturalness of political institutions. "It is evident that the polis belongs to the class of things that exist by nature, and that man is by nature an animal intended to live in a polis."[63]

A further corollary is that political institutions require order and power. Political authority as a concept is thus perceived as necessary and legitimate in the organic-statist tradition. Aquinas, for example, states that . . . "law must needs concern itself properly with the order directed to universal happiness,"[64] and, "order principally denotes power."[65]

It is from this perspective of man's nature, as requiring for its happiness and fulfillment participation in a well-ordered political community, that Aristotle argued: "The polis is prior in the order of nature to the family and the individual. The reason for this is that the whole is necessarily prior [in nature] to the part. If the whole body be destroyed, there will not be a foot or a hand. . . ."[66]

---

[62] Aristotle, *Politics*, Book I, Chapter II, Sections 14, 15, pp. 6-7 (all references to Aristotle's *Politics* refer to the Barker translation). One of the key Vatican II documents, *Gaudium et Spes* reiterated this theme: "by his innermost nature man is a social being, and unless he relates himself to others he can neither live nor develop his potential." (Article 12). Note however the stress is on man as a social being, not a political being.

[63] Aristotle, *Politics*, Book I, Chapter II, Section 9, p. 5.

[64] Aquinas, *Summa Theologica*, I-II, Question 90, Article 2, p. 612 (Pegis translation).

[65] *Summa Theologica*, III (Suppl.), Question 34, Article I.

[66] *Politics*, Book I, Chapter II, Section 12 and 13, p. 6.

Taken together, these arguments about the political nature of man, the necessity and legitimacy of power, and the ontological status of the political community, make the role of the state much more functionally central and normatively legitimate in the organic-statist tradition than in either liberal pluralism or the Marxist tradition. However, the differences go even deeper. The Aristotelian, Thomistic, and natural law concept that is central to the organic-statist tradition is that the state has a moral end, it has a moral *telos*. This is a significant difference between organic statism and liberal pluralism. Liberal-pluralist writings stress the neutral procedures of government within which social groups compete to define goals and policies. Organic-statist writings emphasize the ends of government and are less concerned with procedural guarantees. While Aristotle does not deny the utilitarian or instrumental advantages of political life, he always emphasizes that the higher goal is moral. Thus the polis is not merely

> an association for residence on a common site, or for the sake of preventing mutual injustices and easing exchange. . . . But it is the cardinal issue of goodness or badness in the life of the polis which always engages the attention of any state that concerns itself to secure a system of good law well obeyed. . . . Otherwise, a political association sinks into mere alliance . . . law becomes a mere covenant . . . 'a guarantor of men's rights against one another'—instead of being, as it should be, a rule of life such as will make the members of a polis good and just.[67]

The moral center of the organic-statist vision is thus not the individual taken by himself but rather the political community whose perfection allows the individual members to fulfill themselves: "The end of the individual is the same as that of the political community . . . but, even so, the end of the political community is a greater thing to attain and maintain, and a thing more ultimate, than the end of the individual."[68]

The concern for the pursuit of the common good leads to a de-emphasis or rejection of procedural forms and to a rejection of the legitimacy of "private interests" even if these private interests represent the majority: "The true forms of government, therefore, are those in which the one, or the few, or the many, govern

[67] *Politics*, Book III, Chapter IX, Sections 12 and 8, pp. 118-119.
[68] *Ethics*, Book I, Chapter II, Section 8 (Barker translation), p. 355.

with a view to the common interest; but governments which rule with a view to the private interest, whether of the one, or of the few, or of the many, are perversions."[69]

A standard contemporary treatise of Catholic social philosophy characteristically assigns a central role to the common good: "The common good is the prevailing principle that controls any other interest in its order. It is the creative principle, the conserving power of the body politic; it is the final cause of the state, its intimate end, it and nothing else gives the political, sovereign power its moral authority and legitimacy."[70] It should be noted that this "common good," while by no means intrinsically anti-democratic, lends itself to nonliberal legitimacy formulas in organic statism for two basic reasons. First, it opens the possibility that, since the common good can be known by "right reason," there is no need for a process whereby interest groups express their opinions and preferences in order for the leaders of the state to "know" what the common good is. Second, as the quotation above indicates, the pursuit of the common good (rather than elections or representation by group interests) is the measure by which the legitimacy of the state is evaluated.

This vision of the common good and the organic political community has led in the nineteenth and twentieth centuries to a moral rejection by all variants of organic statism of both liberalism and Marxism. Marxism is rejected in part because its view of class conflict violates the organic-statist ideal of the harmonious community, which is to be constructed by political action. For example, Leo XIII, in *Rerum Novarum*, presents the following argument:

> The great mistake made in regard to the matter now under consideration is to take up with the notion that class is natu-

[69] *Politics*, Book III, Chapter VII, p. 139 (Jowett translation).

[70] Heinrich A. Rommen, *The State in Catholic Social Thought: A Treatise in Political Philosophy*, p. 310. For a more extensive discussion, see the chapters "Organic View of the State," and "The State as a Moral Organism." Aquinas, in *Summa Theologica*, I-II, Question 94, discusses the content of the common good when he analyzes the three ends of Natural Law, which right reason dictates governments should follow. Like Aristotle—but less strongly—he emphasizes that man's nature requires some political participation for fulfillment. However, of course, neither is democratic in a "one-man one-vote" sense, because there is a tension between the claims of political participation and the claims of the more basic principle of the common good.

rally hostile to class, and that the wealthy and the workingmen are intended by nature to live in mutual conflict. So irrational and so false is this view, that the direct contrary is the truth. Just as the symmetry of the human frame is the resultant of the disposition of the bodily members, so in a State it is ordained by nature that these two classes should dwell in harmony and agreement, and should, as it were, groove into one another, so as to maintain the balance of the body politic.[71]

The liberal state and classical capitalism are likewise rejected because they lead to abuses and antagonism between classes, and because the state does not play its morally proper role of actively furthering the balance in the body politic by pursuing the common good. Thus, in the same encyclical, Leo XIII writes: "Some remedy must be found, and found quickly, for the misery and wretchedness pressing so heavily and unjustly at this moment on the vast majority of the working classes. . . . Workingmen have been surrendered, all isolated and helpless, to the hardheartedness of employers and the greed of unchecked competition."[72]

Forty years later, Pius XI, in his *Quadragesimo Anno* (On Reconstructing the Social Order), commented that Leo XIII, faced with what he perceived as growing class conflict and disintegration of the social order, had

> sought no help from either Liberalism or Socialism, for the one had proved that it was utterly unable to solve the social problem aright, and the other, proposing a remedy far worse than

---

[71] Leo XIII, *Rerum Novarum* (1881) in *The Papal Encyclicals in Their Historical Context*, ed. Anne Freemantle (New York: New American Library, 1963), p. 174. After Vatican II, the Catholic Church softened substantially its doctrinal criticism of Marxism. Nonetheless, a close reading of recent church documents shows that the preferred social solution still is normally one that eschews both Marxist ideas of class conflict and liberal ideas of unchecked competition in favor of more "communitarian" formulas. Thus in Peru, for example, the current military regime's initial program of imposed structural change in order to bring about a solidarist society with full communal participation was explicitly endorsed by leading church figures as being consistent with "the major new social teaching of the church." (Interview with Bishop Bambarén in Lima, November 12, 1972.) The complex relationship of the post-Vatican II church to the organic-statist tradition will be developed further in later chapters. Also see Luigi Einaudi, Richard Maullin, Alfred Stepan, and Michael Fleet, *Latin American Institutional Development: The Changing Catholic Church.*

[72] Ibid., p. 167.

the evil itself, would have plunged human society into greater dangers. . . . With regard to civil authority, Leo XIII, boldly breaking through the confines imposed by Liberalism, fearlessly taught that government must not be thought a mere guardian of law and of good order, but rather must put forth every effort so that through the entire scheme of laws and institutions . . . both public and individual well-being may develop spontaneously out of the very structure and administration of the State.[73]

The state in the organic-statist tradition is thus clearly interventionist and strong. However, it is important to understand that a just and stable organic order is not necessarily to be equated with the established order. The concept of the common good, with the moral obligation it imposes on the state to achieve the general welfare, leaves open the possibility that the state can formulate and impose on its own initiative major changes in the established order so as to create a more just society. From Aristotle to Aquinas to modern popes, there is therefore a strong normative tradition in organic-statist political thought in which the state is conceived of as playing a relatively autonomous, architectural role in the polity. A standard contemporary text of Catholic social theory, bearing the papal imprimatur, illustrates how the idea of imposed change and the need to create an organic order are closely interrelated:

A distortion in the social organism may disturb the balanced functioning and welfare of the whole. If this should occur, the supreme protector of the order, whatever its form, the state in that significant sense, has the right and duty to intervene. . . . Catholic political philosophy is aware . . . that the actual *ordo*, through the shielding of vested interests, can become unjust, that the changing circumstances in social and economic life demand the abolition of unintended privileges protected

[73] Pius XI, *Quadragesimo Anno* in Freemantle, *The Papal Encyclicals*, pp. 229-30. Further evidence of the strong directing role the state should exercise in order to contribute to the organic, harmonious society is found in Pius XII, *Summi Pontificatus* (*On the Function of the State in the Modern World*, 1939), where he argues "it is the noble prerogative and function of the State to control, aid, and direct the private and individual activities of national life that they converge harmoniously towards the common good." See *The Papal Encyclicals*, Freemantle, p. 266.

by the existing order; it knows, in other words, that the positive order may contradict the ideal order of peace and justice.

The order of laissez-faire capitalism thus has become unjust, creating unwarranted privileges of vested property rights against unjustly suppressed personal rights of the working classes. Formal right can, under our mode of existence, become material wrong. In these conditions the state needs power and must apply force for the sake of its own end. . . . *It must forcefully change parts of the actual order which have grown unjust . . . it must use force against the selfish resistance of the privileged interests that range themselves above the new and juster order.*[74]

Some of the paradoxes of contemporary Latin American politics become understandable if one keeps in mind this organic-statist principle, namely that the goal of a stable, organically integrated society might entail radical change in basic structures. The Peruvian military's "radical" land reform was organic-statist in this sense. The military perceived one class, the oligarchical land owners, as contributing to a revolutionary disintegration of society. In an action consistent with the implications of the organic-statist model, the military attempted to use their power to create a new organic relationship among Peruvians. The apparent radicalism of parts of the Catholic Church in Latin America also has strong organic-statist overtones. In 1968, the Latin American Bishops Conference endorsed the view that Latin America found itself in "a situation of injustice which could be termed one of institutionalized violence, because current structures violate fundamental rights creating a situation which demands global, bold, urgent, and profoundly renovating transformation."[75]

Thus in the organic-statist tradition of political thought, despite the concern for stability, there is a justification for rapid structural change and for a strong state that can impose this change. It is necessary, however, to note that two normative principles, in theory at least, are meant to restrict legitimate state action within the limits imposed by the concept of organic unity.

[74] Rommen, *The State in Catholic Thought*, pp. 203, 292 (emphasis added).

[75] CELAM (Consejo Episcopal Latinoamericano), *Documento Final de la Comisión No. 1*, Subcommittee II, Section III (Bogota, Colombia: September 1968).

The first principle is that, whatever its form, the state must pursue as its end the common good. For Aristotle, a government that did not rule with a view to the common interest was a "perversion." For Aquinas, an unjust law "seems to be no law at all." Consistent with this interpretation is the fact that the most extensive arguments for "tyrannicide" are found in the works of natural law theorists who stress that the ruler must always rule within the limits imposed by natural law.[76]

The second, and historically more important, principle is that, although the state is the most perfect political community, all the component parts (individual, family, private association) have a proper function of their own within the organic whole. Thus each part has a sphere of natural action that the state should not eliminate. Since the 1930s this concept has been explicitly referred to as "the principle of subsidiarity." A recent restatement by John XXIII shows that it is still meant to be a limiting parameter to what he saw as the necessarily increasing role of the state in the furtherance of the common good:

> This intervention of public authorities that encourages, stimulates, regulates, supplements, and complements, is based on the *principle of subsidiarity* as set forth by Pius XI in his Encyclical *Quadragesimo Anno*: "It is a fundamental principle of social philosophy, fixed and unchangeable, that one should not withdraw from individuals and commit to the community what they can accomplish by their own enterprise and industry. So, too, it is an injustice and at the same time a grave evil and a disturbance of right order, to transfer to the larger and higher collectivity functions which can be performed and provided for by lesser and subordinate bodies. Inasmuch as every social activity should, by its very nature, prove a help to members of the body social, it should never destroy or absorb them."[77]

76 The most coherent and explicit development of this theme is found in the work of the 16th-century political theorist, Francisco Suárez; see Bernice Hamilton, *Political Thought in Sixteenth-Century Spain: A Study of the Political Ideas of Vitoria, De Soto, Suárez, and Molina*, esp. pp. 61-66.

77 John XXIII, *Mater et Magistra* (Christianity and Social Progress, 1961), in *The Social Teachings of the Church*, ed. Anne Freemantle (New York: The New American Library, 1963), pp. 228-29. In Aristotle and Aquinas there is less emphasis on the rights of the parts against the whole. This emphasis in the modern church is a response to the secular claims of the liberal state and the total penetration claims of Marxist-Leninism.

The subsidiarity principle is the central feature that distinguishes the concept of "organic" in the organic-statist model from the concept of "organic" in the Leninist model of "command socialism." In contrast to liberal pluralism, both the organic-statist and Leninist models give an important place to the concept of organic political unity and give the state a major role to perform in achieving such unity. In Lenin's command-socialist model, however, the organic unity can emerge only after the dictatorship of the proletariat has abolished all elements of subsidiarity. For Lenin, "harmonious organization" is the end result of the total penetration and transformation of all units of society.

> The resolution adopted by the recent Moscow Congress of the Soviets advanced as the primary task of the moment the establishment of a "harmonious organization," and the tightening of discipline. Everyone now readily "votes for" and "subscribes to" resolutions of this kind; but usually people do not think over the fact that the application of such resolutions calls for coercion—coercion precisely in the form of dictatorship. And yet it would be extremely stupid and absurdly utopian to assume that the transition from capitalism to socialism is possible without coercion and without dictatorship. . . .
>
> The foundation of socialism—calls for absolute and strict *unity of will*, which directs the joint labour of hundreds, thousands and tens of thousands of people. . . . Revolution demands —precisely in the interests of its development and consolidation, precisely in the interests of socialism—that the people *unquestioningly obey the single will* of the leaders of labour.[78]

Such a model of the unified political community is built upon a monist relationship between the party-state and the citizens in which intermediate groups are perceived as serving neither a necessary nor a legitimate function. Thus, in *The State and Revolution*, Lenin argues: "accounting and control—that is the *main* thing required for 'arranging' the smooth working, the correct functioning of the *first phase* of communist society. *All* citizens are transformed here into hired employees of the state, which consists of the armed workers. *All* citizens become employees and workers of a *single* nation-wide state 'syndicate'. . . . The whole

[78] V. I. Lenin, "The Immediate Tasks of Government" in V. I. Lenin, *Selected Works*, pp. 420, 424-25 (emphasis in original).

of society will have become a single office and a single factory, with equality of labor and equality of pay."[79]

This distinction between the view of the organic community in command socialism and organic statism is so fundamental that it is one of the distinguishing characteristics of each as an analytic model, as I show in the concluding section of this chapter.

In terms of organic-statist normative theory, we have stated the main concepts: the political nature of man, the goal of the organically related community in which the subsidiary parts play a legitimate and vital role, the state's proper role in interpreting and promoting the common good, and the radical changes the state may legitimately impose to create an organic society. Any political tendency, if it is more than just a body of ideas, is however an amalgam of articulated norms and empirically identifiable sets of structures and practices.

A particularly influential set of structures and practices that are normatively congruent—and, in the Iberic and Latin American countries, historically associated—with the organic-statist tendency is Roman law. For our purposes, the impact of Roman law on interest association is especially salient. The Greek idea that the public common interest should prevail, and that organized private interests should be allowed only the freedom consistent with the organic functioning of society, took on new significance when transferred from the city-state to the context of the bureaucratic-state of the Roman Empire. Here, in the name of organic relationships, the statist element became extremely strong. The core assumption of group pluralists such as Bentley that the polity is composed of groups that are "freely combining, dissolving and recombining in accordance with their interest lines," is normatively and empirically alien to the Roman law "concession theory" of association. In contrast to group-pluralist ideas that interest groups are unchartered, Roman law posited that groups had to be "chartered" by the state. As the German legal historian

79 (Moscow: Foreign Language Publishing House, no date), pp. 161-62 (emphasis in original). He immediately adds that "this 'factory' discipline . . . is by no means our ideal, or our ultimate goal. It is but a necessary step for the purpose of thoroughly purging society of all infamies and abominations of capitalist exploitation, and for further progress." After the dictatorship of the proletariat has completed its tasks "then the door will be open for the transition from the first phase of communist society to its higher phase, and with it to the complete withering away of the state."

Rudolph Sohm observed, "With but few exceptions all societies were, on principle, prohibited. The law recognized no freedom of association. Only those societies were lawful which owed their existence to lex specialis, or 'privilege.' A lawful society—such was the view taken—cannot be the creation of a private individual; it can only be the creation of the State operating through the medium of a statute."[80]

In exchange for the privilege of official recognition, the association accepted obligations that in essence made it "part of the organization of the State."[81] Emile Durkheim, often mistakenly seen as an advocate of authoritarian corporatism, decried the impact of such controls on the workers' groups in Roman society because, he argued, "they ended by becoming part of the administrative machine. They fulfilled official functions; each occupation was looked upon as a public service whose corresponding corporation had obligations and responsibilities towards the State."[82]

In the late Roman Empire, and later in the Iberian and Latin American countries, this concession theory of interest groups, utilized in the name of organic unity, has given the state an important lever by which to shape the scope and content of demands articulated by interest groups.[83] Indeed, the concession theory also has provided the normative rationale for the complex mechanisms by which the state itself creates and charters interest groups from above, often leaving a structural legacy of high responsiveness on the part of interest groups to demands originating from the state.[84]

[80] Rudolph Sohm, *The Institutes: A Textbook of the History and System of Roman Private Law*, trans. J. C. Ledlie, pp. 198-199.

[81] Ibid., p. 199.

[82] Preface to the Second Edition, "Some Notes on Occupational Groups," in Emile Durkheim, *The Division of Labor in Society*, trans. G. Simpson, p. 8.

[83] This will be a major theme that is developed later in the book. For the argument that the establishment of state control of associations in the Roman Empire was motivated by "fears for public order" see W. W. Buckland, *Roman Law and Common Law: A Comparison in Outline*, p. 53. For a discussion and documentation of the influence of Roman Law concession theory in Spanish America, see Ronald C. Newton, "On 'Functional Groups,' 'Fragmentation,' and 'Pluralism' in Spanish American Political Society," *Hispanic American Historical Review* (February 1970), esp. pp. 16-17.

[84] Note that it is the restrictive chartering by the state rather than its role in association creation that is most analytically relevant for the question

One last historical-empirical note concerning the organic-statist tradition must be added. In the liberal-pluralist tradition, the absolutist period is seen as one of attack on the medieval church and feudal structures, laying the groundwork for the modern liberal constitutional state, which in turn put checks on absolutist power. In Iberian countries and their ex-colonies, however, absolutism, though it existed, was different in two key respects. First, because the Iberian peninsula did not experience the Reformation in full force, in the period of centralizing monarchy an effort was made to reconcile the principles of absolutist statescraft with natural law traditions. Second, because these countries did not fully experience the socioeconomic processes that accompanied the inauguration of the liberal constitutional state, the absolutist legacy in government and bureaucracy further strengthened the statist components of the organic-statist tradition.[85]

Intellectual awareness of organic statism furthers several analytical causes. Roman law and natural law were the predominant ingredients of the intellectual and political heritage of European philosophy since shortly after Christ until at least the sixteenth century. Many of the basic institutions of Western society—legal systems, bureaucracies, interest groups—were for much of modern history decisively shaped by organic statism and to this day, even in the non-Catholic countries of Western Europe, there are still

---

of the degree of subsequent autonomy. For example, the state may play a crucial role in the growth of associations, as in the case of the U.S. government's support for union organization given by the Wagner act. But, because the state did not at the same time build in extensive control mechanisms the unions subsequently became relatively autonomous sources of countervailing power. See, for example, J. K. Galbraith, *American Capitalism: The Concept of Countervailing Power*, pp. 128, 135-53. Contrast Galbraith's account with that by Kenneth Paul Erickson, "Corporative Controls of Labor in Brazil" (paper delivered at 1971 annual meeting of the American Political Science Association, Chicago). The construction of control mechanisms—and the subsequent system-level consequences of these mechanisms—is discussed later in this book in relation to the Vargas and Cárdenas governments.

[85] Sohm comments on the absolutist attitude toward association: "from the sixteenth century onwards the system of absolutist government, with its rigorous control of private life, struck root in Germany as elsewhere. Such a system was obviously quite as hostile to private societies as the Roman monarchy. It refused altogether to recognize the principle of free association, and required the sanction of the State for the formation of any society whatsoever." Sohm, *The Institutes*, p. 200.

understudied structural legacies. In addition, as one of the classic Western formulations of the relationship between the state and society, this body of ideas remains "available" for use and adaptation everywhere in the western European cultural area. It provides an intellectual framework for understanding movements, legitimacy formulas, administrative devices, and regimes that have been influenced by this tradition of political thought.

The organic-statist model seems to me to be particularly suitable for partial incorporation into analyses of political development when studying the Latin American pattern of development, where, as I have indicated, the strong normative and empirical tradition of government-chartered interest groups contrasts with some of the basic assumptions of pluralist associational patterns, and where the pattern of delayed dependent development has, from a Marxist perspective, contributed to nonhegemonic class relations that often give the state apparatus some autonomy.

My working hypothesis is that many of the political elites in Latin America have in fact responded to their perceptions of impending crises of modernization and control by invoking, in a variety of modern forms, many of the central ideas of the organic-statist, non-liberal, non-Marxist model of state-society relations described here, and have attempted to use the power of the state to forge regimes with marked corporatist characteristics.

Organic Statism as a Model of Governance

Organic statism as presented thus far in this chapter has coherence as a normative and historical tendency in political theory, as an ideology, and as a description of one possible mode of articulation between society and the state. In this concluding section, I wish to shift from normative, historical and concrete questions of organic statism to consider organic statism more abstractly as a model of governance. We will be particularly interested in two questions: first, how does it compare with other models, such as classic liberalism or "command socialism"?[86] Sec-

[86] I originally considered classic Marxism as an analytic approach to the state in capitalist societies. However, here I am concerned with the Leninist model of the state as an instrument to forge socialism. To use a more generic term than Leninism, I call such a model "command socialism." I have already considered some of the features of such a model in the extensive quotations from Lenin.

ond, what predicaments, tensions, or inherent contradictions exist within organic statism as a model?

As models of governance, command socialism and classic liberalism seem to arrive at "optimal" solutions by maximizing different principles of coordination. Classic liberalism, in theory, maximizes information, self interest, freedom, and competition to arrive at maximum economic efficiency and political equilibrium. Command socialism, in theory, maximizes control of the economy by state planning and achieves a perfectly integrated, monist political community by eliminating the autonomy of all groups and by building new collectivist values and structures. Organic statism in contrast, as a model of governance, does not maximize any of the polar principles of coordination of the two other modes of articulation between state and society. Such crucial features of organic-statism as the "concession theory" of private associations involve a far more interventionist role for the state in politics than posited in classical liberalism. However the "principle of subsidiarity" posits less penetration of society by the state in organic statism than that posited by command socialism. Organic statism, in theory, accords an important role for the decentralized political participation of semi-autonomous functional groups. This role is absent in the Leninist version of the harmonious organization of the political community in command socialism. The model of organic statism implies "limited pluralism" in the community, while the model of command socialism implies a "monist" community.

In classic liberalism the economic principle of coordination that is maximized is individual competition in the market; in command socialism it is centralized state planning. Organic-statist concepts of the priority of the political community and of the state's responsibility for the common good imply strong constraints on laissez-faire market individualism. However, the principle of subsidiarity implies equally strong limitations on the legitimacy of the state to act as the chief owner of the means of production and chief planner of the economy.

An economic formula congruent with organic statism is thus one in which the state plays a decisive role in constructing the parameters, rules, and infrastructure of a market economy. In addition, the limits to "egoistic individualism" and "state centralism" posited in the model leads to a key role for intermediate self-managing "labor-capital" functional groups that are assumed

41

to be a modern organic-statist industrial formula for arriving at the harmonious integration of the component parts of the economy.

To present graphically the differences between organic statism, command socialism, and classical liberalism as models of governance, we can place each model on a grid, illustrating the means through which political and economic goals are determined. (See Figure 1.1.)

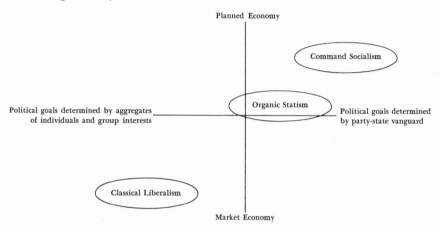

FIGURE 1.1. Location of three models in terms of means through which political and economic goals are determined.

Although no concrete regimes fit these abstract models completely, Apter has shown that, on analytic grounds alone, each of his somewhat similar polar models predictably faces characteristic tensions and predicaments. The predicament of classic liberalism is that some groups in society (including the government "group") may obtain greater political and economic power than others, upsetting the "perfect competition" assumed by the model. The predicament of command socialism is that coercion may become so high, and the flow of information so low, that distortions and irrationality affect both the economic and political system.[87]

Although in theory organic statism may represent a desirable balance between the two poles of classic liberalism and command

[87] Apter calls his polar models "the secular-liberatarian model" and the "sacred-collectivity model." For his presentation of these models with their characteristic predicaments, see *The Politics of Modernization*, esp. pp. 28-36.

socialism, in actuality it too contains inherent predicaments as a model. On the one hand, the statist component of the model implies a strong role for the state in structuring society so that it conforms with the model's assumption of functional parts that are perfectly integrated into a solidaristic whole. The role of the state is to ensure this integration between the parts and the whole. On the other hand, each of the parts is theoretically self-managing, so that there is a high degree of participation within state-chartered, organic structures. The predictable distorting tension in the model is that in the initial construction of the system from above, the state, in order to ensure integration and control, builds such strong control mechanisms into the new state-chartered functional groups that the meaningful participation posited by the model never becomes a reality. In later chapters I discuss numerous examples of concrete corporatist structures imposed from above by the state in which actual autonomy and participation is severely restricted. This, then, is the almost inherent distorting tension in organic statism stemming from the statist component of the model.

The other tension stems from the organic-participatory component of the model. If self-managing groups are in fact allowed to exercise a degree of decentralized autonomy, some groups may acquire political or economic control over others, and this violates the model's presupposition of organic harmony between the different functional groups within society. Thus either self-management and autonomy is allowed and the goal of intergroup balance and harmony is violated, or the state imposes restrictions on self-management and violates the supposition of decentralized group autonomy.[88]

[88] The organic-statist model, purely as a model, faces other logical and empirical problems. First, there are no obvious criteria for assigning exact representational weight to functional groups. Whatever criteria are selected there is the danger of over-enfranchising some functional groups while disenfranchising important nonfunctional groups based on ethnic, religious, linguistic, or regional identities. Second, the model assumes that vertical functional groups are the "natural" organic representational vehicles of modern society. However, in a complex modern society this is probably a more "artificial" representational vehicle than are broader, horizontal parties and movements. Third, multinational corporations challenge the very idea of an organic-statist society, but some of their major structures lie beyond the organizational formulas of organic statism. For a discussion of the first two problems along these lines, see Max Weber's section on "Representation by the Agents of Interest Groups" in *The Theory of Social*

Political elites who attempt to create systems that approximate the organic-statist model commonly come to power, as we shall see, in the context of elite perceptions of crises in pluralist systems and the failure of self-regulating mechanisms. In response to this perceived crisis, the role of the state is broadened and the perceived "responsibility" for the direction of the national economy is shifted from pluralist mechanisms of self-regulation to statist mechanisms. Yet, while the state comes to be considered responsible for the success or failure of the new order, the inherent limitations to state power that are implied in the organic-statist model may seriously impede its ability to achieve success. The new, controlled, functional group process posited by the model may never be brought into being because of the power and autonomy of major groups in society that emerged during the phase of pluralist politics. Short of totalitarian or revolutionary mobilization and penetration, it may be impossible for a state elite to restructure such existing interest groups. But such mobilization and penetration would not only be a violation of the model on theoretical grounds but would also risk alienating the original coalition that supported the state elite on the supposition that limited pluralism would be respected and mass mobilization avoided. The new organic-statist regime may thus be caught in the contradictions that flow from its intermediate position within the full range of alternative models of articulation between state and society.

Apart from this contradiction in the political sphere, organic-statist regimes face a parallel contradiction in the economic sphere. They commonly commit themselves to an intermediate statist model that is "neither capitalist nor communist," by replacing private initiative with overall public regulation in economic life, at the same time retaining the marketplace as the basic mechanism for distributing goods and services. They retain a system that is heavily dependent on entrepreneurial initiative and market flows, while to some extent undermining both. In the economic sphere, as in the political sphere, they may thus

---

and Economic Organizations, ed. Talcott Parsons (New York: The Free Press of Glencoe, 1964), pp. 421-23, and Juan Linz's "Totalitarian and Authoritarian Regimes" in *Handbook of Political Science*, 9 vols. (Reading, Massachusetts: Addison Publishing Co., 1975), ed. Fred Greenstein and Nelson Polsby, Vol. 3, pp. 175-441. I discuss the problems presented for the model by multinational corporations in Chapter 7.

face the problems of both of the principal alternative models, while benefiting from the advantages of neither.

Partly because of these inherent tensions in the abstract model of organic statism, in most concrete cases of regimes that initially announce organic-statist principles, there is a political tendency to move toward greater control over groups via manipulative corporatist politics (especially with regard to working class groups) than is theoretically posited in the model, and there is a tendency in economic policy to allow greater entrepreneurial freedom for capitalism than is posited in the model. Such regimes thus become authoritarian-corporatist capitalist regimes.[89]

Yugoslavia acquired added theoretical and political importance because it was an attempt to introduce greater degrees of self-management into the command socialist model. Tanzania became particularly important because of its endeavor to find a formula to reconcile revolutionary power in a one-party state with a significant degree of binding accountability of the rulers to the ruled.[90] Similarly, the Peruvian experiment gained special significance because it represented an attempt to develop new possibilities, and to resolve some of the central predicaments within a major model of governance—organic statism.

[89] Such concrete regimes are a subtype of Linz's general category of "authoritarian" as opposed to "democratic" or "totalitarian" regimes, in that they possess *limited*, but not *responsible*, pluralism. For his typological contrast between "democratic," "authoritarian" and "totalitarian" regimes see his initial statement "An Authoritarian Regime: Spain" in *Mass Politics: Studies in Political Sociology*, ed. Erik Allardt and Stein Rokkan (New York: Free Press, 1970), pp. 251-83, 374-81.

[90] For a perceptive analysis of the achievements and limits of Tanzania's 1965 election campaign for posts within the one-party system in which 22 out of 31 party officeholders were unsuccessful and 16 out of 31 MPs lost, see Henry Bienen, *Tanzania: Party Transformation and Economic Development*, expanded edition (Princeton: Princeton University Press, 1970), pp. 382-405. I discuss self-management in Yugoslavia in Chapter 6.

TWO · *"Corporatism" and the State*

As USED in this book *organic statism* and *corporatism* refer to two different things. Organic statism is a normative approach to politics that can also be formulated as an abstract model of governance. No modern state in its actual state/society relations has approximated pure organic statism, just as none has approximated pure communism. Yet like pure communism, organic statism is based on a strong philosophical tradition, and has been used and abused by modern elites in control of the state apparatus.

Corporatism refers to a particular set of policies and institutional arrangements for structuring interest representation. Where such arrangements predominate, the state often charters or even creates interest groups, attempts to regulate their number, and gives them the appearance of a quasi-representational monopoly along with special prerogatives. In return for such prerogatives and monopolies the state claims the right to monitor representational groups by a variety of mechanisms so as to discourage the expression of "narrow" class-based, conflictual demands. Many state elites past and present have used such corporatist policies for structuring interest representation.[1]

While organic statism and corporatism refer to different things, organic statism is sometimes connected as a guide to corporatist

[1] For more extended discussions of the distinction between pluralist and corporatist patterns of interest representation, see Philippe C. Schmitter, "Still the Century of Corporatism?" in *The New Corporatism: Social-Political Structures in the Iberian World*, ed. Fredrick P. Pike and Thomas Stritch (Notre Dame and London: University of Notre Dame Press, 1974), esp. pp. 93-105; and David Collier and Ruth Berins Collier, "Who Does What, To Whom, and How: Toward a Comparative Analysis of Latin American Corporatism" in *Authoritarianism and Corporatism in Latin America*, ed. James M. Malloy.

In Chapter 3, I distinguish between "inclusionary" and "exclusionary" forms of corporatism. Both forms are subtypes of what Linz would call authoritarian regimes. Inclusionary corporatist policies can, at least at the level of stated ideological intent, approximate the normative goals of organic statism, while exclusionary corporatist policies represent a fundamental violation of such norms.

46

policies, more often as a rationale, and frequently as a combination of guide and rationale. As a guide, state elites in the contemporary world attempting to use the state apparatus to forge the solidaristic, functionally interrelated society posited in the organic-statist tradition, will tend to establish institutional arrangements for interest representation that are more corporatist than pluralist in character. As a rationale, state elites who fear a crisis in the old pact of domination may seek to encapsulate the working classes in a new, state-chartered corporatist pattern of interest groups. If the new state elite has any aspiration to rule by hegemony rather than by coercion, they will need to provide the new institutional arrangements with ample normative justification. The strongest philosophical tradition that can be mined to provide a rationale is organic statism.

Given the obvious importance of the role of the state in contemporary politics, as well as the importance of state systems forged by political elites who reject pluralist and Marxist assumptions about state-society relations, it is useful to incorporate elements of the literature on corporatism into the present discussion. However, in order to build upon, or contribute to, this literature, it is essential to clarify four important problems or issues in recent discussions of corporatism. The first concerns the assumed association between corporatism and fascism. I argue that, although corporatism has overlapped empirically with fascism in some contexts, some fundamental institutional and ideological differences between the fascist and the corporatist vision of the state should be underscored. Second, I view corporatism primarily as an elite response to crisis, a response that involves the attempt by elites who control the state apparatus to restructure the relationship between sectors of civil society and the state. This "crisis response" explanation of the existence of corporatism competes with one in which corporatism is viewed as a function of historical continuity. In this chapter I compare the explanatory power of the two approaches. Third, some writers argue that the corporatist pattern of interest representation is a *reflection* of the way some civil societies (such as Mexico) are naturally organized. My own view is that corporatist patterns of interest representation are not so much a social input as a policy output, i.e., they are frequently the consequence of political structures consciously imposed by political elites on civil society. I assess the value of the two views on corporatism for the concrete case of Mexico. Fourth, while agreeing with those writers who focus on "corporatism as structure," I argue that the next essential step that must be taken if the literature on corporatism is not to stagnate into a new formalism involves the analysis of the great variation in the outcome and performance of virtually identical elite-forged corporatist structures.

CORPORATISM VERSUS FASCISM

If corporatism is to be a meaningful concept in comparative politics, a distinction must be made between corporatism and fascism. Unfortunately this distinction is often not made. The entry for "Corporatism" in the seventeen-volume *International Encyclopedia of the Social Sciences* contains exactly two words, "See Fascism."[2] While it is true that corporatism and fascism empirically overlapped in regimes such as Mussolini's Italy and Hitler's Germany, corporatism and fascism differ importantly in some aspects of policy and associated ideology. Concerning policy scope, the state in fascism (or the party that dominates the state apparatus) is presented as being without checks. Mussolini's formulation of the role of the state is not untypical of fascist thought: "The foundation of Fascism is the conception of the State, its character, its duty, and its aim. Fascism conceives of the State as an absolute, in comparison with which all individuals or groups are relative, only to be conceived of in their relation to the state."[3]

[2] See (New York: The Macmillan Company and The Free Press, 1968), Vol. 3, p. 404.

[3] From an article signed by Mussolini, written with the collaboration of Giovanni Gentile, and first published in *Enciclopedia Italiana* XIV (Rome, 1932) and reprinted as Benito Mussolini, *The Political and Social Doctrine of Fascism*, p. 13.

The Italian case is particularly complex because at the formal ideological level there were corporatist institutions in fascist Italy. In fact, almost none of these corporatist institutions became fully functioning. As the minister of corporations from September 1929 to July 1932, Giuseppe Bottai, acknowledged, "the operation of the state bureaucracy and the ideological conceptions of the government have killed corporatist institutions." Cited in Alberto Aquarone, *L'organizzazione dello Stato totalitario*, p. 220. Also see Aquarone's comments on pp. 3-5 and p. 189. Useful discussions of labor and corporatist institutions under the fascist state are found in Roland Sarti, "Italian Workers Under Fascism" (paper prepared for delivery at the annual meeting of the American Historical Association, 1973), and his "Fascist Modernization in Italy: Traditional or Revolutionary?," *American Historical Review* (April 1970).

48

In corporatist writing the state is of course given a major role in bringing about an integrated society, but this society is one in which the component parts are accorded their own spheres of action that should not be eliminated. Explicitly or implicitly, a form of the "subsidiary principle" discussed in Chapter 1 is normally found in formulations of corporatism, especially those from Ibero-America. When we analyze the speeches of Perón, who advocated a stronger state than either Cárdenas or Vargas, the contrast between his position and that of Mussolini's is striking: "To the Peronist doctrine, all economic goods were created and are created and exist for man. Therefore we condemn the principles of individualism and collectivism which put man at the service of the economy or the state and we maintain that the economy and the state must secure human happiness by promoting social well-being."[4] Elsewhere he writes, "The final objective of collectivism is the enrichment of the state, which will be realized with the pretext of enriching the community and which sacrifices all liberties on its altars demanding of the workers the tribute of opprobrious exploitation by the state."[5]

With regard to the vision of state-society relations found in fascist and corporatist ideology, the distinction made in Linz's well-known typology of totalitarian, authoritarian, and democratic regimes is useful.[6] Fascism characteristically tends toward totalitarianism. However, because of the lack of penetration and the de facto continued existence of limited pluralism, some fascist regimes, such as Italy during much of its fascist period, could be classified as authoritarian.[7] Corporatist regimes have charac-

[4] Juan Perón, *Expone su doctrina*, pp. 53-54.

[5] Juan Perón, *Mensajes de Perón*, p. 432. Though the labor codes constructed under Brazil's *Estado Nôvo* were undoubtedly influenced by the fascist Labor Charter of 1927, key *Estado Nôvo* publicists contrasted the mediatory role of the state in labor relations in Brazil with the totalitarian role of state-sindicato relations in Italy. Azevedo Amaral, for example, wrote that the Italian sindicato was "merely a bureaucratic tentacle through which the state exercises its arbitrary power upon the many sectors of the nation, which are oppressed and suffocated in the web of the totalitarian organization." See his *O Estado autoritário*, p. 183.

[6] See his "An Authoritarian Regime: Spain," in *Mass Politics: Studies in Political Sociology*, ed. Erik Allardt and Stein Rokkan (New York: Free Press, 1970), pp. 251-83, 374-81. Also to the point is David Apter's distinction between "bureaucratic" and "mobilizing" political systems in his *Choice and the Politics of Allocation*, esp. pp. 30-35.

[7] Much evidence for this is found, for example, in Roland Sarti, *Fascism*

teristically tended toward authoritarian and bureaucratic formulas and practices, but despite great difficulties, there may also be attempts within corporatist systems to expand the democratic components of the system.

Another major characteristic distinguishing corporatism from fascism concerns "mobilization." Politically, most major interwar movements that are commonly called fascist had a strong paramilitary component—such as the squadrists in Italy, the Heimwehr in Austria, and similar movements in the Baltic and Finland.[8] These paramilitary units had their origins in the very specific conditions of Europe in the period after the Treaty of Versailles. The limitations on the national armies of Austria, Italy, Germany, and Finland combined with post-treaty irredentist sentiments and fear of communist expansion after the Russian Revolution, contributed to the tacit tolerance of paramilitary units, which became an intrinsic part of fascist mobilization politics.[9] A key feature of most fascist movements was that they combined legal tactics with extra-legal ones as a way of achieving power.[10]

In regimes usually called corporatist, however, such as the *Estado Nôvo* of Brazil, Mexico since the late 1930s, or the current Peruvian military regime, the special conditions of post-Versailles Europe were absent, and corporatism has been the creation of a regime already in power. What mobilization there has been has characteristically taken the form of channeled, in-

---

and the Industrial Leadership in Italy, 1919-1940: A Study in the Expansion of Private Power Under Fascism. This is also the argument Aquarone develops in the final chapter of *L'organizzazione dello Stato totalitario*, pp. 290-311.

[8] Exceptions to this are the Rex movement in Belgium, where Degrelle wanted to come to power by legal means, and the Third Republic in France, which effectively controlled paramilitary organizations. Significantly, neither country had lost territory or had had restrictions imposed on the national army by the Treaty of Versailles.

[9] This point is amply documented in *Breakdowns of Democratic Regimes: The European and Latin American Experience*, ed. Juan J. Linz and Alfred Stepan (Baltimore: The Johns Hopkins University Press, forthcoming, title tentative). See especially the chapters by Linz, Farneti, and Lepsius, and the chapter on Finland by Alapuro and Allardt.

[10] The point is developed in Juan J. Linz, "Some Notes Toward a Comparative Study of Fascism in Sociological Historical Perspective," in *Fascism: A Reader's Guide; Analyses, Interpretations, Bibliography*, ed. Walter Laqueur.

stitutionalized participation, and normally the national military have jealously guarded their monopoly of armed force.[11]

Other distinguishing features between corporatism and fascism are more abstract but no less real. Almost all fascist movements have romanticized violence, most have had a "leader principle" and have frequently supported an expansionist nation-state.[12] Corporatist and neo-corporatist regimes, with their emphasis on order as a principle of legitimacy, on bureaucracy, and on reciprocal functional relations have (despite the frequent use of repression by the state) normally had both a normative and institutional bias against "non-legal" violence and have accepted existing state boundaries.[13]

Finally, and more generally, I would argue that for reasons that have to do with policies, political history and contemporary symbolism the term "corporatism" should not be tied too closely to the historically specific (and by now largely discredited) experience of the "fascist corporatist" policies attempted in Europe in the 1920s and 1930s. There were undeniable corporatist elements in the governments of Vargas, Cárdenas, and Perón. Nonetheless, it is essential to understand that, judged by their mass followings, these were (and remain) the most popular governments in the history of their countries. The policies these governments imple-

---

[11] Mobilization was briefly important in Mexico from 1934-38, but this was led by the president, Lázaro Cárdenas. Middle-class mobilization for a rightist coup played a role in Chile in 1973 and to a lesser extent in Brazil in 1964, but in both cases the military quickly confined this after taking power. The closest case to European mobilization was worker support for the then minister of labor, Juan Perón, in Argentina in 1944. However this never reached the level of uniformed, armed paramilitary units.

That authoritarian or bureaucratic regimes, corporatist or not, have important points of tension with mobilizational fascist movements, is underscored by the butchery of the Iron Guard Legionaires by the conservative monarchy in Rumania, the repression of the "integralistas" during the *Estado Nôvo* in Brazil, the demobilization and marginalization of the Falange by Franco and the military in Spain, and of the National Sindicalists by Salazar in Portugal.

[12] It could be argued that, although the leader principle was not prominent in early fascist formulations, it became a "standard accretion" as the movement developed. Hitler, for example, in 1930 rewrote two passages in *Mein Kampf* to greatly strengthen the leader principle; see the interesting discussion in Weiner Maser, *Hitler's Mein Kampf: An Analysis*, p. 56.

[13] For a discussion of order as a principle of legitimacy in such regimes see Apter, *Choice and the Politics of Modernization*, passim.

mented, and the legitimacy formulas they appealed to, are better approached by a more neutral label than "fascist corporatism." Terminology aside, at the very least one must be prepared to recognize and explain not only cases of what I would call "exclusionary corporatism," as in contemporary Chile, that rely heavily on coercion but also cases of what I would term "inclusionary corporatism" which in the most successful of cases, as in Mexico, have some possibility of winning a mass base of support and ruling with what Gramsci called "hegemony" in civil society.[14] These caveats stated, let us now evaluate competing explanations of the origins of corporatism.

CORPORATISM: HISTORICAL CONTINUITY OR CRISIS RESPONSE?

One important group of writers has argued that Latin American corporatist political patterns have their roots in medieval institutional conceptions of harmony, the common good, and the state.[15] As I argued in Chapter 1, this approach has the utility of drawing attention to a significant strand of Latin American culture that is distinct from the liberal strand of Anglo-Saxon cultures.[16] This strand of Latin American political culture can be useful to those elites attempting to legitimate the selection and installation of non-liberal political arrangements. Specifically, a body of ideas exists that can be drawn upon in the attempt to forge legitimacy formulas for a variety of regimes with marked corporatist components. For those writers who view corporatism as continuity, the fact that this tradition is drawn upon is one of the mechanisms through which this historical tradition operates. In addition, they frequently contend that many legal struc-

[14] The development of the distinction between "exclusionary corporatism" and "inclusionary corporatism" is a major theme of Chapter 3.

[15] Some recent but varied formulations of this argument are: Howard Wiarda, "Toward a Framework for the Study of Political Change in the Iberic-Latin Tradition: The Corporative Model," *World Politics* (January 1973); Glen Caudill Dealy, "The Tradition of Monistic Democracy in Latin America," *Journal of the History of Ideas* (October-December 1974); and Ronald C. Newton, "On 'Functional Groups,' 'Fragmentation,' and 'Pluralism' in Spanish American Society," *Hispanic American Historical Review* (February 1970).

[16] For the argument that there are almost no such corporatist strands in Arab political culture see Clement H. Moore, "Authoritarian Politics in Unincorporated Society: The Case of Nasser's Egypt," *Comparative Politics* (January 1974).

tures and political patterns linked to this past continue to exist. This continuity is most marked in the administrative law tradition of "chartered" associational groups and in patrimonial leadership patterns—both institutional characteristics that are congruent with modern corporatist patterns.[17]

Given this circumstance, it should not be surprising that in the continuing search for political models in Latin America there is frequent experimentation with a variety of corporatist approaches to state-society relations.[18] This said—and I think it an important contribution—a number of serious limitations to the "corporatism as continuity" argument remain.[19]

[17] Time and again historians studying contemporary political patterns comment on the marked institutional continuities. This is especially so for countries such as Mexico, which, unlike Argentina or Chile, never had a prolonged period of liberal politics. Two articles that develop such themes are Woodrow Borah, "Colonial Institutions and Contemporary Latin America: A) Political and Economic Life," *Hispanic American Historical Review*, 43 (August 1963): pp. 371-79; and Richard M. Morse, "The Heritage of Latin America," in *The Founding of New Societies*, ed. Louis Hartz, pp. 123-77.

[18] The point, however, should not be interpreted as implying that such corporatist traditions are either dominant or uncontested in Latin cultures. For example, one presumed traditional component of corporatist structures —the guilds—had virtually disappeared in 19th-century Spain while they were still significant in Germany and Switzerland. Also, from the ideological perspective, it is extremely important to note that the combination of the international disrepute of corporatist experiments in the interwar years plus the genuine elements of a liberal political tradition in countries such as Chile, Argentina, and even Brazil has meant that, after the epoch of the *Estado Nôvo* and Cárdenas, most Latin American political leaders have adamantly rejected the corporatist label. The current Peruvian leaders, for example, have explicitly contested any labeling of their regime as corporatist, and though Onganía privately felt that the only way to organize Argentina was along corporatist lines, some of his advisers urged him to avoid overly explicit references to his corporatist design.

In lieu of the above, any attempt to reformulate Harry Eckstein's concepts along the lines that corporatist stability in Latin America is due to cultural congruence would be excessively simplistic. Also, as I note later, there are new economic and political factors that have contributed to the emergence of contemporary corporatist experiments.

[19] Although in the next section I criticize those such as Wiarda who have placed excessive emphasis on the explanatory value of cultural characteristics, Schmitter's counterposition in "Still the Century of Corporatism?" seems an overreaction, which closes off some potentially important research areas. For example, Schmitter explicitly rejects the utility of a political culture approach to the emergence and consolidation of corporatist regimes. He tends to label any such endeavor as an indefensible form of *Weltan-*

Explanations based on continuity are relatively weak where the phenomenon to be explained is not so much continuity but the emergence of stronger and novel forms of corporatism after a period of relative abeyance. The simple fact is that neo-corporatist institutions are more prominent in the Latin America of the 1970s than they were in the 1950s, or indeed than in the "liberal" period in parts of Latin America from the late nineteenth century until the depression.

Another limitation of any broad cultural explanation for a large geographical area is that the presumed causal impact of the common cultural heritage cannot explain divergent political patterns within the geographical area. In the case of Latin America not only are corporatist political patterns unevenly distributed but corporatist politics are relatively weak in some countries such as Colombia and Ecuador, where the "Iberian Catholic" ethos is generally considered to be relatively strong.[20]

In contrast to the thesis of "corporatism as cultural continuity,"

---

schauung analysis. This seems to me to miss the point that a sophisticated analysis of political cultures includes such non-*Weltanschauung* concrete characteristics as different legal, institutional, and administrative historical traditions, as well as the important factor of the various paths by which capitalism developed in different cultures—all of which can contribute to contemporary attitudes towards corporatist experiments. Even within the terms of his own work, his rejection of any historically based explanation leads him to what are somewhat strained positions. For example, after having rejected as a "pseudoexplanation," any endeavor to identify some distinctive characteristics of the Iberian political tradition, he nonetheless acknowledges that, "it is, of course, quite conceivable at this early stage in research into these matters that what I have found to be a set of inter-related institutional practices coalescing into a distinctive, highly covariant and resistant modern system of interest representation may be quite limited in its scope of applicability, for example, only to Iberian authoritarian regimes." The question we are left with is, why? See his "Still the Century of Corporatism?" p. 95. Likewise, in his *Interest Conflict and Political Change in Brazil* (Stanford: Stanford University Press, 1971), while he correctly places an emphasis on the role of corporatist practices in structuring patterns of interest representation, he also documents that by and large a wide variety of elites accept this pattern as concurrent with the political culture into which they were initially socialized and which they operationally acquire. Given the importance of these attitudes it is rather surprising he offers so little in the way of pre-1930 material to explain their roots in Brazil.

[20] Schmitter develops a similar point in his "Still the Century of Corporatism?," in *The New Corporatism*, Pike and Stritch, p. 90.

it is my contention that corporatist institutional experiments have emerged out of *crises*, where elements of *discontinuity* are salient. For example, we see strong discontinuity in cases of "inclusionary corporatism," which aimed at recreating a new hegemonic base of support for the state by integrating new social groups, such as in the *Estado Nôvo* in Brazil, the revolutionary party in Mexico, and the current military experiment in Peru. Discontinuity is also seen in cases of "exclusionary corporatism," such as Chile, in which we see a sharp break with the pluralist pattern of politics and an attempt to create a more channelized system of state-society relations through reliance on coercion.[21]

Some of the problems of corporatism as "cultural continuity," as opposed to the "elite response to crisis," explanation are illustrated in Wiarda's influential article, "Towards a Framework for the Study of Political Change in the Iberic-Latin Tradition: The Corporative Model." Wiarda sees the basis of corporatism in traditional institutions such as the hacienda, the village community, the church, all of which he argues are in decline. New groups such as the development-oriented military, the "new" church, educated "técnicos," and various external actors are seen as ascendant and challenging traditional institutions. His conclusion is that the corporatist framework is experiencing a "crisis of major proportions" and may well be swept away.[22] Wiarda's emphasis on cultural continuity leaves him at odds with a substantial body of empirical evidence. He argues that corporatist culture resists change in traditional structures and states that "only in Mexico, Cuba, and perhaps Bolivia and Peru have there been sharp breaks with the past which destroyed the power of the traditionally privileged elites."[23] But if we are focusing on corporatist political institutions, a very strong case can be made that it was precisely the modern political elites' control of the state apparatus (the PRI in Mexico, the MNR in Bolivia, the *Estado Nôvo* in Brazil, and the military in Peru) that led to the installation of systems with marked corporatist characteristics. This is so precisely because many of the new elites Wiarda sees as challenging cultural corporatism, such as the "técnicos," the develop-

[21] See Chapter 3 for a discussion of the terms "inclusionary corporatism" and "exclusionary corporatism" and their relationship to crises.

[22] Wiarda, "Towards a Framework for the Study of Political Change in the Iberic-Latin Tradition: The Corporative Model," pp. 229-32.

[23] Ibid., p. 225.

ment-oriented military, even the multinational corporations and
the new church, have found state-directed, nonconflictual corporatist modes of participation a useful political device for their
crisis response projects of guided development. All these elites
have at least significant sectors that, for programmatic reasons
rather than for traditional cultural reasons, want to use the power
of the state to reconstruct civil society along new lines. What are
the programmatic goals of these elites?

The military elites in Brazil and Peru, in part because of their
"new professional" schooling systems, have come to perceive a
connection between internal security and national development
and to want to use the state apparatus to create a new pattern
of "integral security."[24] The most important component of Wiarda's new external actors are the multinational corporations,
and what they most frequently look for are consistent rules of
the game and a predictable labor environment. Although not
"cultural corporatists," they often find a strong state is the most
likely guarantee of these two requirements.[25] Many of the new
técnicos of economic planning share with the new military a

[24] I develop this argument in greater detail in "The New Professionalism
of Internal Warfare and Military Role Expansion," in *Authoritarian Brazil:
Origins, Policies, and Future*, pp. 47-65. See also General Edgardo Mercado
Jarrín, "La securidad integral en el proceso revolucionario Peruano," *Participación* (December 1972).

[25] The evidence for this is strongest in Brazil. A recent sample of 269
strategic elites selected from among high civil servants, congressmen, industrialists, financiers, bishops, and presidents of labor syndicates shows
that, on such criteria as similarity of view and regime support, these elites
feel one of the groups closest to the regime are the multinationals. The
survey was carried out by Philip Converse, Amaury De Souza, and Peter
McDonough, "Foreign Investment and Political Control in Brazil" (unpublished manuscript, Ann Arbor, 1974). The study concludes that "the
cumulative evidence is strong that elites make a positive connection between
foreign investment and political control. . . . One does not mechanistically
cause the other. But that they support and thrive off each other the elites
do not doubt . . . the (MNCs) benefit from and support the system; they
require and help sustain political control," pp. 84-85, 71. For a more
general development of this theme, see Luciano Martins, "The Politics of
U.S. Multinational Corporations in Latin America," in *Latin America and
the United States: The Changing Political Realities*, ed. Julio Cotler and
Richard R. Fagen, pp. 368-402. The support of the multinationals for a
strong state is not without tensions and contradictions, however, because
the state could attempt to use its strength to control the multinationals. We
will examine the complexities of such an attempt by Peru in Chapter 7.

penchant for social engineering, and share with the multinational corporations and the new military a desire for social peace that will allow state-designed projects (in which multinationals often benefit from the infrastructure investments or participate as partners) to go forward.[26] In most cases they see working arrangements with international sources of capital as crucial for the financing of their projects.[27] The low mobilization-high control alliance between new military, new multinationals, and new técnicos is most apparent in cases of "exclusionary corporatism."

The question of the "new" church is more difficult, and "exclusionary corporatist" regimes such as Brazil and Chile have had difficulty obtaining positive endorsement from post-Vatican II bishops. Nonetheless, despite new currents in the church, a large part of the church hierarchy, while rejecting the excesses of individualistic, egoistic capitalism, and while looking for methods

[26] On structural and normative grounds, we could predict that the incumbents of the new técnico "career-roles" would want more autonomy from the party-elite than that found in a mobilization regime, and more autonomy from the conflicting demands of interest groups than that found in unrestricted pluralism. This predicament, rather than traditional corporatist cultural values as such, is what frequently makes the técnicos receptive to modern corporatist formulas in Latin America. This argument draws heavily from David E. Apter, *The Politics of Modernization*, pp. 152-78, esp. p. 176.

[27] For example, in the previously cited sample by Converse et al., the three groups whom the elites viewed as the closest together on policy matters were the técnicos, the military, and the multinationals. In Mexico the regime has had a very close relationship with técnicos. A study of the appointments to the initial cabinets of the five presidents inaugurated between 1946 and 1970 classified 72% as "bureaucratic técnicos." See Roderic Ai Camp, "The Cabinet and the Técnico in Mexico and the United States," *Journal of Comparative Administration* 2 (May 1971), 208-12. A forthcoming study of top administrative officials in Peru by Peter Cleaves and Martin Scurrah argues that under the current military regime técnicos have filled more intermediate jobs and have been better renumerated than under previous regimes.

More generally, the whole question of top-level técnicos necessarily having any distinctive value orientations needs to be treated with caution. If the pool of available técnicos is large enough, different governments can usually recruit those closest to its own political beliefs. Thus Allende's government tended to recruit técnicos with "dependencia" orientations, while the current military regime has given many key positions to University of Chicago-trained classical economists. In addition there is the "chameleon" effect by which técnicos assume the political coloration of the government of the day.

to achieve greater participation, remain estranged from the idea of class conflict and thus are often open to the new forms of communitarian political and economic arrangements that an "inclusionary corporatist" regime might attempt to install.[28]

A final difficulty with the "corporatism as continuity" argument is that it ignores the question of conscious political and economic engineering in a crisis context. As a general theoretical point, I would argue that corporatist ideas of unity are not a function of unity or continuity but appeal to elites around the world precisely because there is a perceived threat of fragmentation. Frequently, there is widespread elite fear that the old modes of domination are breaking down, and they search for new mechanisms to link the lower classes to the state and new formulas to legitimize such mechanisms. In this context, both liberal ideas of individualism and competitive checks and balances, and Marxist ideas of class conflict, are rejected because they are seen as legitimizing conflict. From this viewpoint, organic-statist or corporatist arguments about the need for unity, the legitimacy of the common good over individual or class interest, and the key role of the state in social engineering are as natural a political response for Africans as for Latin Americans.[29] However, the fact that class-structured conflict is more widespread, and that organic statism has more "cultural carriers"—such as the legal system, or the Catholic church—in Latin America than in Africa or Asia, gives these ideas somewhat more resonance in Latin America than in other parts of the Third World.

In twentieth-century Latin America, the argument that corporatism is an elite response to the perception of the threat of fragmentation is strongly supported by the historical evidence. Brazil's corporatist *Estado Nôvo* became the ideology of a new, modernizing political and military elite who controlled the federal state apparatus that attempted to impose greater unity on a system in which the state of São Paulo's militia could challenge the federal army, where heavy interstate tariffs impeded the

---

[28] For example, one of the leading progressive bishops in Peru told me that "the revolutionary military regime is realizing many of the changes in social and economic structures that the church has been asking for." Interview in Lima, October 1972.

[29] See for example the very strong statements by African leaders along these lines cited in Aristide Zolberg, *Creating Political Order: The Party States of West Africa* (Chicago: University of Chicago Press, 1966), pp. 361 and 265.

growth of a national economic community, and where traditional modes of political control were beginning to be challenged
by the rise of a class conscious urban-labor union movement.[30]
The PRI in Mexico emerged from a period of revolutionary civil
war as a self-conscious attempt to impose unity and direction in
a highly conflictual political situation. The sectoral, neo-corporatist structure of the MNR in Bolivia after the revolution in 1952
was simultaneously a recognition of the different foci of power
in the movement and an attempt to bring them together in some
context.[31] The most recent stirrings of a corporatist experiment
are in Chile, where the military regime is considering constructing corporatist institutions to overcome the polarization of society, a polarization they feared so greatly that they waged
internal war to eliminate one pole.[32]

In almost all important cases of twentieth-century corporatist
experiments in Latin America, therefore, the hypothesis of corporatism as an outgrowth of continuity and/or unity has less
explanatory (and, I suggest, less predictive) power than corporatism as an elite response to crisis.

CORPORATISM: SOCIETAL REFLECTION OR POLICY OUTPUT?

A second interpretation of corporatism is "Corporatism as a
Reflection of Society." This interpretation of corporatism has
some similarity to the "corporatism as cultural continuity" explanation just discussed, yet it is sufficiently distinct and provocative to merit separate attention. From my perspective the most
unusual—the weakest—feature of this approach is the attempt

[30] The speeches of Getúlio Vargas are replete with these themes. See,
for example, *La Pensée Politique du Président Getúlio Vargas: Sélection,
classement systématique et traduction française*, ed. Hans Klinghoffer, pp.
103-136, 167-173. Also see the chapter "The Revolution of 1930 and the
Formation of the State Ideology," in Bolivar Lamounier, "Ideology and
Authoritarian Regimes: Theoretical Perspectives and a Study of the Brazilian Case" (Ph.D. dissertation, University of California, Los Angeles, 1974),
pp. 293-330. I discuss the general question of the integration of Brazil in "The
Continuing Problem of Brazilian Integration: The Monarchical and Republican Periods," in *Latin American History: Select Problems; Identity, Integration, and Nationhood*, ed. Fredrick B. Pike, pp. 259-296.

[31] See James M. Malloy, *Bolivia: The Uncompleted Revolution*, pp. 151-242.

[32] For a discussion of elite fears see Arturo Valenzuela, "The Breakdown of
Democracy in Chile," in *Breakdowns of Democratic Regimes*, Linz and Stepan
(forthcoming).

to explain the existence of corporatist politics without attaching any significant weight to the role of state-forged structures.

The most explicit example of the "corporatism as reflection of society" argument is found in the monograph by Ronald Rogowski and Lois Wasserspring, *Does Political Development Exist? Corporatism in Old and New Societies.*[33] The central thesis of this monograph is that it is societal characteristics (rather, by implication, than any state structured processes) that explain the existence of corporatist political patterns. They state that "We shall refer to any group linked by a common stigma as a segment. . . . We consider any society which consists of stigmatized groups (segments) to be *segmented*. . . . The existence of social segmentation in our view produces corporatism in politics."[34] The authors go on to say that, while their analysis is only a theoretical construction, they "believe that Mexican politics still approaches the polar type fairly closely."[35]

The formulation of corporatism by Rogowski and Wasserspring shares with some main lines of liberalism and Marxism the view that society is the independent variable and the political system the dependent variable. As a general approach, therefore, many of the criticisms I made of liberalism and Marxism in Chapter 1 apply here as well. More concretely, how does the Rogowski and Wasserspring approach actually help us understand Mexico—the only contemporary political system they specifically mention as approximating their "polar type" of corporatism? I will discuss the Mexican case at some length, not merely to criticize the "societal reflection" explanation of corporatism, but, more positively, to amplify and document my counterexplanation concerning the independent output impact that state-forged corporatist political

[33] Ronald Rogowski and Lois Wasserspring, *Does Political Development Exist? Corporatism in Old and New Societies* (Beverly Hills: Sage Publications; Comparative Politics Series, 1971). A work that shares some aspects of this approach but is more aware of its limitations is Ronald Newton, "Natural Corporatism and the Passing of Populism in Spanish America," in *The New Corporatism*, Pike and Stritch, pp. 34-51.

[34] Rogowski and Wasserspring, *Does Political Development Exist?*, pp. 19, 25. Concerning *stigma* they write, "any mark which has both low costs of information and high costs of conversion we shall call a *stigma*." "By this definition, race, sex, and accent are stigmata, with race and sex having the obviously higher cost of conversion," p. 19.

[35] Ibid., p. 45.

structures can have, given the right conditions, on presumed societal inputs such as the articulation and aggregation of interests.[36]

Significantly, the Rogowski-Wasserspring definition of corporatism excludes any mention of the state, except the notion that
groups themselves are like the nation-state: "We mean by 'corporatist' action the pursuit—consistently in norm and frequently
in practice—of group welfare over individual welfare . . . ," and
by 'corporatist' behavior . . . "we intend a kind of group sovereignty, very akin to the interaction of nation-states."[37]

The most important shortcoming of this approach is that it
accepts the groups as natural in their origins and relatively self-
directed in their political actions. In the Mexican case, however,
it is extremely difficult to analyze the political system without
studying how the political elite in control of the state apparatus,
and with it the PRI, has played a central role in shaping (and
in some cases creating) political groups. It has likewise continued
to play a crucial role in maintaining political boundaries between
groups, and plays a key role in monitoring the group leader selection process. The result is that many groups—especially working-
class and peasant groups—do not, and cannot, exercise group
sovereignty, but rather perform the role assigned to them in the
overall development model designed by the political elite of PRI.

The Mexican state has frequently played a decisive role in the
composition and conduct of groups. In the early years of the
Cárdenas era, the Mexican Federation of Workers (CTM) had
organized an impressive range of horizontally linked lower-class
groups. Cárdenas deliberately split the peasants from urban labor
by using the party and bureaucratic organization to organize peasant leagues in each state. These leagues were then united into
a National Confederation of Peasants (CNC), in which all beneficiaries of agrarian reform in the *ejidos* had compulsory membership. Cárdenas also removed the civil servants from the CTM
by a decree law in 1938, creating for them a separate union, and
later putting them in the popular sector of the party. The state,
against the desires of the private sector, also created compulsory

[36] The sustained attention to Mexico is especially useful because, although a
number of observers have labeled the system "corporatist," the Mexican system has, surprisingly, received much less systematic attention from contemporary analysts of corporatism than Brazil or Peru.
[37] *Does Political Development Exist?*, p. 7.

organizations for chambers of commerce (CONCANACO) and chambers for industrialists (CONCAMIN).[38]

Creation from above does not necessarily mean effective control. However, an analysis of the behavior and operation of these organizations does not bear out Rogowski and Wasserspring's idea of "group sovereignty, very akin to the interactions of nation-states." In his study of the political dynamics of the agrarian sector, Rodolfo Stavenhagen concludes that the CNC has been "an efficient vehicle for the control and manipulation of the rural population by the state."[39] When we examine the mechanisms available to the state, we can see why this is so. Elections for the executive committee of *ejidos* are presided over, and must be approved by, a member of the government's agrarian department, and at the state and local level, state governors frequently select the elected officials of the CNC.[40] In fact, one study asserts that "the elected head of the CNC has always been a member of the middle or upper class, usually lacking a rural background."[41] Indeed, in general the role of the state apparatus in rewarding, manipulating, and occasionally repressing groups has such a subtle and pervasive effect on the career patterns of interest group leaders that the autonomy of these leaders is questionable. As one authority notes, it is often "difficult to determine if they represent the state [poder público] or the members of their groups."[42] The

[38] Vicente Lombardo Toledano, a Mexican labor organizer, complains about fragmentation of the working class by Cárdenas in *México visto en el siglo XX: entrevistas de historia oral*, ed. James W. Wilkie and Edna Monzón de Wilkie, pp. 316-21. For a general outline of the state's creation of these organizations from above, see Frank R. Brandenburg, *The Making of Modern Mexico*, pp. 79-95, and Robert Scott, *Mexican Government in Transition*, pp. 125-139. Also see José Luis Reyna, "Movilización y participación políticas: discusión de algunas hipótesis para el caso Mexicano," in *El perfil de México en 1980*, pp. 503-35.

[39] See "Marginalidad y participación en la reforma agraria mexicana," in his *Sociología y subdesarrollo* (México: Editorial Nuestro Tiempo, 1972), p. 180.

[40] Patricia McIntire Richmond, "Mexico: A Case Study of One-Party Politics" (Ph.D. dissertation, University of California, Berkeley, 1965), pp. 189-91, 227-29.

[41] See Susan Kaufman Purcell, *The Mexican Profit-Sharing Decision: Politics in an Authoritarian Regime* (Berkeley and Los Angeles: University of California Press, 1975), p. 19. An excellent case study of a sugar cane ejidos' attempt to achieve greater autonomy is David Ronfeldt, *Atencingo: The Politics of Agrarian Struggle in a Mexican Ejido*.

[42] Rodolfo Stavenhagen, "Un modelo para el estudio de las organiziones políticas en México," *Revista Mexicano de Sociología* (April-June 1967). This

easy flow and rapid rotation of middle-level individuals from sectoral-spokesman positions to party, electoral, and government posts at municipal, state, and national levels, is one of the mechanisms by which the state apparatus renders the sectoral identifications of the leaders of Mexico's "segmented society" much less explicitly group referential than that postulated by Rogowski and Wasserspring.[43]

These mechanisms of state cooptation and control are not without consequences for the political behavior of peasant and working-class groups and for the resources these groups are, or are not, able to extract from the leaders of the state apparatus. Numerous studies of income distribution show that, despite the revolution, Mexican income distribution is "far below international standards," and indicate that the share of the bottom 5 deciles declined in the last period (1950-1963) for which good data are available.[44] The *ejido* sector, despite formally being one

---

theme is developed further, with interesting case studies that show the range of cooptation policies, in Bo Anderson and James D. Cockcroft, "Control and Cooptation in Mexican Politics," *International Journal of Comparative Sociology* (March 1966).

[43] Brandenburg, *The Making of Modern Mexico*, p. 157, estimates that "every six-year administration witnesses a turnover of approximately 18,000 elective offices and 25,000 appointive posts." The "no re-election rule" of Mexican politics is an important source of state leverage and further reduces links between societal groups and elected officials because it reduces incentives for elected officials to be responsive to their constituents in the hope of being reelected, and instead makes them dependent on subsequent bureaucratic posts after their term in office.

Studies of local PRI political structures show that though the PRI leaders are supposed to be recruited mainly from the functional base groups, many in fact regularly serve as bureaucrats. This once again tends to make the government rather than the functional organization the relevant reference group. For example, in Ensenado, from 1953-1967, of the 44 members of the PRI municipal committee, 31 had served in government bureaucratic posts, see Antonio Ugalde, *Power and Conflict in a Mexican Community: A Study of Political Integration*, p. 101. For a discussion of the effects of this type of career pattern, see Richard R. Fagen and William S. Tuohy, "Aspects of the Mexican Political System," *Studies in Comparative International Development* (Fall 1973).

[44] See Clark W. Reynolds's discussion of three income distribution studies in his *The Mexican Economy: Twentieth-Century Structure and Growth*, pp. 75-84. See also Ifigenia M. de Navarrete, "La distribución del ingreso en México: tendencias y perspectivas," in *El perfil de México en 1980*, Vol. 1 (México: Siglo Veintiuno Editores, 1970), pp. 15-71.

of the four corporate sectors of the official party,[45] has not been able to exercise much effective power in demanding state outputs in such vital areas as credit, transportation infrastructure, or new irrigation. Their period of greatest gains was when the government was organizing them into the official party in the mid-1930s. Once incorporated, their effective claim to scarce resources declined, as is shown graphically by their relative share of irrigated land in the 1930 to 1960 period (see Table 2.1).

TABLE 2.1

Net Yearly Change in Ejido and Non-Ejido Irrigated Land; 1930-1960
(in thousands of hectares)

	Organizational period of official peasant sector (1930-1940)	Post-Incorporation phase of peasants (1940-1960)
Ejidos	+ 77.5	+ 21.2
Non-Ejidos	− 72	+ 62.7

Source: Based on data in Stavenhagen, "Marginalidad y participación en la reforma agraria mexicana."

Urban labor has followed a similar pattern. From 1935 to 1938, Cárdenas championed their organizational mobilization and full integration into the national political party. When the party was reorganized in 1938, labor became one of the four official sectors. Once incorporated, however, labor became increasingly demobilized.[46] The combination of Cárdenas's undoubted charisma for much of labor and subtle classic corporatist "carrot and stick" mechanisms contributed to this demobilization.[47]

---

[45] Since the military sector was dissolved in 1940, there have been only three sectors. A guide to the formal organization of the PRI, written by the former press secretary of President Adolfo López Mateos, is Mario Ezcurdia, *Análisis teórico del Partido Revolucionario Institucional.*

[46] Much useful information about this general process of mobilization, incorporation, and demobilization is contained in Arnaldo Córdova, "La transformación del PNR en PRM: el triunfo del corporativismo en México" (paper presented to the IV International Congress of Mexican Studies in Santa Mexico, California, October 1973), and Wayne A. Cornelius, "Nation Building, Participation, and Distribution: The Politics of Social Reform Under Cárdenas," in *Crisis, Choice, and Change: Historical Studies of Political Development*, ed. Gabriel A. Almond, Scott C. Flanagan and Robert J. Mundt.

[47] For example, in order for a union to represent its members it has to

The full extent of labor's inability to press its demands effectively is seen in the wage and price figures for the decade following labor's incorporation. These indicate that, under Presidents Avila Camacho and Alemán, "real wages fell as much as one-third between 1940 and 1950."[48] Despite this decline in real wages, strikes in the decade after incorporation were almost half what they had been during the incorporation phase (see Table 2.2).

TABLE 2.2

AVERAGE NUMBER OF YEARLY STRIKES DURING AND AFTER URBAN LABOR'S
INCORPORATION IN CORPORATIST STRUCTURES IN MEXICO

Organizational period of labor sector (1935-1940)	Post-Incorporation phase (1941-1951)
480	250

SOURCES: México, *Anuario Estadístico*, 1940, 1943-45, 1953.

This pattern of low strike activity has endured. The comparison with the much higher mobilizational activity of labor in Chile and Argentina is noteworthy. In Mexico, with a population in 1965 of approximately 45 million, an annual average of 42,000 workers participated in strikes in the period between 1959 and

register with the minister of labor and meet strict legal requirements. If a union does not have formal registration or if it loses such registration, it loses protection under labor law. The state, in addition, has the right to declare strikes legal or illegal. Workers who participate in illegal strikes can be immediately discharged and lose the protection of the otherwise generous worker stability law. In addition, the range of cooptive devices is quite large. Most labor organizations are dependent upon financial subsidies that the regime can withdraw from an uncooperative union. The state-party apparatus also has the ability to coopt national trade union leaders to posts as senators or deputies. The ability of the top trade union leaders to control and reward regional unions is strengthened by the fact that they have the authority to deny official recognition to lower level unions. These mechanisms are amply documented in Richard Ulric Miller, "The Role of Labor Organizations in a Developing Country: The Case of Mexico" (Ph.D. dissertation, Cornell University, 1966), pp. 50-52; Michael David Everett, "The Role of the Mexican Trade Unions 1950-1963" (Ph.D. dissertation, Washington University, Missouri, 1967), pp. 21-25, 70-73; Richmond, "Mexico: A Case Study of One-Party Politics," pp. 201-24; and Purcell. *The Mexican Profit-Sharing Decision*, Chapter 2.

48 Roger D. Hansen, *The Politics of Mexican Development*, p. 73.

1965. This was a higher strike participation ratio than any previous period since 1935-1937. Chile, with a population of less than 8 million in 1965 (i.e., one fifth that of Mexico), had an annual average of 124,700 strikers in the same 1959-1965 period. On a per capita basis, therefore, Chile had a strike ratio that was over *14 times* that of Mexico. (See Figure 2.1 for longitudinal comparative strike data.)

My point is that government policy has had a major impact on the character of mobilization and demobilization of Mexican interest groups, especially the two organizational sectors of the peasants and urban labor. Once organized by the state, these "corporate groups" have been notable for their ineffectiveness in demanding corporate payoffs and for their secular passivity even in the face of their own poor results. The society-oriented theoretical perspective of Rogowski and Wasserspring, with its assumption of autonomous group maximizing behavior, has little analytic, or predictive power in the Mexican case, precisely because it leaves out of the equation the active role of the state.

CORPORATISM AS STRUCTURE: FUTURE RESEARCH PROBLEMS

The last body of literature on corporatism with which I deal views corporatism as a construction of the state, and is closest to my own view in its identification of the state as a major actor. The starting point in this approach is to treat corporatism from the viewpoint of the institutional characteristics of interest group representation. For example, Philippe Schmitter advances the following definition:

> Corporatism can be defined as a system of interest representation in which the constituent units are organized into a limited number of singular, compulsory, noncompetitive, hierarchically ordered and functionally differentiated categories, recognized or licensed (if not created) by the state and granted a deliberate representational monopoly within their respective categories in exchange for observing certain controls on their selection of leaders and articulation of demands and supports.[49]

Much of the burgeoning new literature on corporatism in Latin America shares this focus on formal institutional arrange-

[49] Philippe C. Schmitter, "Still the Century of Corporatism?," in *The New Corporatism*, Pike and Stritch, pp. 93-94.

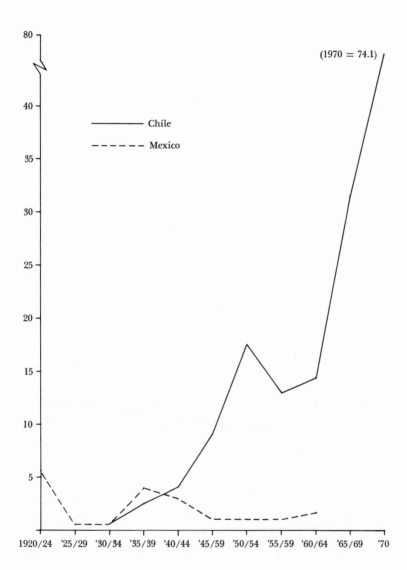

FIGURE 2.1. Strikers per 1,000 inhabitants in Mexico (1920-1964) and Chile (1930-1970). Sources: Chilean data based on International Labor Office, *Yearbook of Labor Statistics*, various years. Mexican data from Mexico, *Anuario Estadístico*, various years.

ments, especially as they are used to control the working class.[50]
As my analysis of Rogowski and Wasserspring's work indicates,
I perceive this as a crucial dimension to any analysis of how corporatism works as a political system. Nonetheless, some analytic
caveats and suggestions of important research that remains to be
done are called for.

As Schmitter recognizes, his definition presents an ideal type,
and no regime necessarily fulfills all his criteria. For example,
most writers would probably consider Mexico one of the most
fully structured corporatist regimes in Latin America. However,
even when we look at urban labor, which we would expect to
be the most fully institutionalized sector of the corporatist state,
we find a situation that differs in four out of nine of Schmitter's
criteria. The "singular" criterion does not apply, since Mexican
labor, even at the peak level, has been represented by two or three
organizations since the 1940s.[51] The criterion of "compulsory"
membership occasionally does not apply, because the "singu-
larity" criterion does not apply. The "noncompetitive" criterion
does not fully apply because, due to their somewhat greater autonomy and militancy, the "nonofficial" unions have presented
greater threats to the regime, and, as Brandenburg indicates, have
been able to extract somewhat more resources from the political

[50] The most detailed studies have been on Brazil. See, for example, Ken-
neth P. Erickson, "Labor in the Political Process in Brazil: Corporatism in
a Modernizing Nation" (Ph.D. dissertation, Columbia University, 1970);
Kenneth S. Mericle, "Conflict Regulation in the Brazilian Industrial Relations System" (Ph.D. dissertation, University of Wisconsin, 1974); and
Philippe C. Schmitter, *Interest Conflict and Political Change in Brazil*. For
Peru, see Julio Cotler, "Bases del corporativismo en el Perú," *Sociedad y
Política* (October 1972). Mexico, oddly enough, has been less well documented, though the theme runs through the literature. The most empirically specific treatment of the formal institutional characteristics of interest
representation is the second chapter of Purcell, *The Mexican Profit-Sharing
Decision*. The corporatist institutional mechanisms under Perón's first government are the principal theme of Robert J. Alexander's, *Labor Relations
in Argentina, Brazil and Chile*, pp. 139-222.

[51] For example, in Purcell's study of the politics of the National Profit-
Sharing Commission in the early 1960s, the following peak labor organizations made formal inputs: the Office of the Confederation of Mexican Workers (CTM), the mild oppositional General Labor Confederation (CGT), and
the somewhat more radical Revolutionary Confederation of Workers and
Peasants (CROC). See *The Mexican Profit-Sharing Decision*, Chapters 4
and 5.

elite than their official competitors.[52] The criterion of representational monopoly granted to organizations is also not applicable. Normally, the government, in its continuous attempt to coopt or contain the rival unions, grants them seats on major commissions and in congress.[53]

The implication of the above observation is that we must, as Ruth and David Collier have argued cogently, conceive of corporatism not as a "phenomenon that is either present or absent," but rather as a "series of traits that may be present or absent to varying degrees."[54] They have used such an approach to make a pioneering, systematic comparative study of the degree to which 36 different corporatist structural characteristics were present or absent in ten Latin American countries in the period 1905-1974.[55]

My discussion of the corporatist and noncorporatist structural features of the Mexican political system points to another set of considerations that must be borne in mind by the analyst of the structural dimensions of corporatism. Despite the claims of the regime's spokesmen (e.g. Salazar in Portugal) or the analyst's perspectives (e.g. on Mexico), *no* political system to date has approximated exclusive reliance on corporatist mechanisms to perform all the key political functions such as elite recruitment, articulation and aggregation of demands, and policy making. For example, in Mexico, no leader has ever emerged out of the two supposedly key sectors of the party—the labor or the peasant sector—to become the president of the country. Representative organizations do not figure prominently in the career patterns of the top decision makers in the country.[56] Since Cárdenas, all presi-

---

[52] *The Making of Modern Mexico*, passim.

[53] For example, in the early stages of the profit-sharing decision, the official CTM claimed that, as the largest union, it should receive all the labor seats on the study commission. However, the government, in order to get broad labor support for the decision, only gave the CTM 2 of the 10 seats, its other allies were given 5, and its opposition labor forces in the CROC and the FOR given 3. See Purcell, *The Mexican Profit-Sharing Decision*, p. 99.

[54] David Collier and Ruth Berins Collier, "Who Does What, To Whom, and How: Toward a Comparative Analysis of Latin American Corporatism," p. 493.

[55] Ibid. The project is also described in David Collier, Leslie Spencer, and Cherri Waters, "Varieties of Latin American 'Corporatism' " (paper prepared for the 1975 annual meeting of the American Political Science Association, San Francisco, September 2-5).

[56] As Brandenburg notes, "The politically ambitious enter any place

69

dents of Mexico have been former cabinet ministers, but the cabinet has been increasingly recruited by lateral transfers from the state bureaucracy and the recruitment process has bypassed not only interest-group representatives but even party activists.[57] Indeed, even the leaders of the representative associations at times have not worked their way up the representative group ladder, as we saw in the case of the peasant organization, where no peasant has ever been its president.

In the governmental apparatus of Peru, which was often seen as building a corporatist system, the three key decision-making structures during the Velasco presidency were the Council of Presidential Advisers (COAP), which initiated, examined, and coordinated almost all innovative proposals; the Council of Ministers, which normally met every Tuesday to formally resolve major decisions; and the presidency. In the first six years of experimentation with new forms of representation, the president, all the members of COAP, all of COAP's official advisers, and every cabinet-rank minister were recruited from institutions—the armed forces and the police—that were *outside* the supposedly new system of interest representation.[58] The analysis of the installation phase of such a regime must therefore concentrate on the internal tensions and requirements of the military as a strategic elite, and not just on the new political and social structures they claim to be forging.

The theoretical and political implications of this is that there are no fully corporate systems, but rather there are political systems, in some sectors of which (usually the working class) corporatist rather than pluralist patterns of interest representation

---

along the line—as private secretaries of ministers, as technicians in a state industry, as normal school teachers, or in one of hundreds of ways. The general tendency is for the educated, technically prepared young men, including the usual host of young lawyers, to enter the political system through the civil service. . . . Captive leaders of communal agriculture, civil service, trade, and other unions enter politics through the official party; their future rarely holds the promise of anything beyond a senatorship." *The Making of Modern Mexico*, p. 158.

[57] See Ai Camp, "The Cabinet and the Técnico in Mexico and the United States."

[58] The first civilian cabinet minister was not appointed until August 1975, and he was a técnico who had been an assistant to the new president in the Ministry of Economy and Finance.

predominate.[59] The research implications of my argument are that "corporatism as structure" is always only a *partial* sectoral phenomenon of the overall political system, and that supplementary analytical frameworks must be used to study other aspects of the system. For example, methodological and theoretical approaches used in non-corporatist systems to study machine or bureaucratic politics, clientelistic networks, or the military as a special form of a complex organization can—with appropriate contextual caution and modification—be applied to those political systems that display prominent corporatist features in some sectors.[60]

I now turn to an important topic that should be added to the research agenda on corporatism. The emphasis in the literature to date has been on the identification and discussion of corporatist structures. If we do not want to fall into formalism, however, we must take the next step and attempt to explain the great variation that exists in the performance of regimes with very similar corporatist structures. The formal identification of the existence of corporatist structures does not in itself help us analyze many of the crucial questions about the comparative, longitudinal dynamics of regime outcomes. For example, Regime A is able to install and consolidate a stable system with "xyz" formal, corporatist characteristics; Regime B, on the other hand, attempts

[59] It is dangerous to imply, however, as some studies have done, that it is *only* the working classes that are affected by corporatist institutions. For regimes that have had aspirations to rule by hegemonic acceptance in civil society (the PRI, the *Estado Nôvo*, the current Peruvian regime), this is misleading. The leaders of such regimes have endeavored to legitimate their organization of labor in these systems by their parallel claim that the new regime has eliminated some of the most offensive institutions of the former elites, and has the capacity to impose new negotiating frameworks on the propertied sector. Any analysis of how Perón, Vargas, and Cárdenas won such great labor support for their "inclusionary corporatist" experiments must also explore the new state mechanisms for the organization of non-working-class participants in the political system. This is not to claim that such mechanisms have been as effective as those constructed for labor, but rather to argue for their consideration in any systematic analysis.

[60] For example, John F. H. Purcell and Susan Kaufman Purcell have illuminated some important aspects of the Mexican system by drawing on the literature of machine politics. See their "Machine Politics and Socio-Economic Change in Mexico," in *Contemporary Mexico: Papers of the IV International Congress of Mexican History*, eds. James W. Wilkie, Michael C. Meyer and Edna Monzón de Wilkie.

to install a regime with similar "xyz" characteristics, but is unable to install a stable regime and the experiment disintegrates.

Another situation we want to be able to deal with is one where there are two relatively stable regimes operating with more or less identical formal structures but which are strikingly different in regard to their legitimacy. Regime A, for example, could be hegemonic, in the Gramscian sense in that there is a "consent given by the great masses of the population to the general direction imposed on social life by the dominant social group."[61] Regime B, on the other hand, may have little hegemonic acceptance of its policies in civil society, and has therefore to rely heavily on the "domination" imposed by the "apparatus of state coercive power."[62]

In the above cases— (1) successful installation vs. unsuccessful installation and (2) consolidation with hegemony and low coercion of civil society vs. consolidation with low hegemony and high coercion—we are forced to analyze not merely structures created by the state but also the relationship between the different types of corporatist state policies and different types of civil societies.

The attempt to construct concepts and indicators that will enable us to deal with such comparative questions about regime dynamics is the task of the next chapter.

[61] For this concept of hegemony, see Antonio Gramsci, *Selections from the Prison Notebooks*, p. 12, also pp. 57-59, 260-61, and Gramsci's *The Modern Prince and Other Writings*, pp. 164-88. For an analysis of Gramsci's use of "hegemony," see Gwyn A. Williams, "The Concept of 'Egemonia' in the Thought of Antonio Gramsci: Some Notes on Interpretation," *Journal of the History of Ideas* (October-December 1960), and Joseph Femia, "Hegemony and Consciousness in the Thought of Antonio Gramsci," *Political Studies*, 23 (March 1975): 29-48.

[62] Gramsci, *Selections from the Prison Notebooks*, p. 12.

THREE · *The Installation of Corporatist Regimes: Analytic Framework and Comparative Analysis*

THE most influential new work on corporatism is Philippe Schmitter's stimulating "Still the Century of Corporatism?"[1] However, this work leaves two questions unanswered. First, Schmitter's approach to corporatism does not address the question of the wide variation of the success or failure of political elites using the state apparatus to install regimes with strong corporatist characteristics.[2] Since this is a characteristic limitation of the available literature, my primary purpose in this chapter is to construct conceptually derived hypotheses with empirical indicators that enable us to analyze (and to increase our capacity to predict) variance in the outcome of corporatist installation attempts.

This task cannot be started, however, without briefly addressing the second question Schmitter's discussion leaves unanswered. His category "state corporatism" groups together political systems as different from each other as those inaugurated in Brazil in 1964 and Chile in 1973 on the one hand, and those installed by Cárdenas in Mexico in the 1930s, Vargas in Brazil between 1930 and 1945, and Perón in Argentina in the 1940s, on the other.[3] Since the political elites in all these political systems used the state apparatus to attempt to penetrate and restructure associational patterns along corporatist lines, it is useful at one level of analysis to group them together as examples of "state corporatism."[4] However, the question that arises is whether we can ade-

---

[1] In *The New Corporatism: Social-Political Structures in the Iberian World*, ed. Pike and Stritch, pp. 85-131.

[2] See his acknowledgment to this effect in ibid., p. 106.

[3] For Schmitter, a chief characteristic of "state corporatism" is that associational groups are dependent upon, and penetrated by, the state. He contrasts this with "societal corporatism" in which the associational groups are independent of the state and indeed penetrate the state. See ibid., pp. 103-105.

[4] David Collier and his colleagues have made a valuable contribution by empirically demonstrating the different policy mixes and coalitional patterns

quately analyze the dynamics of "state corporatism" without taking into account the extremely different policies followed by regimes within this category. On analytic grounds alone we can distinguish two policy poles within state corporatism. Near the "inclusionary pole" the state elite can attempt to forge a new state-society equilibrium by policies aimed at incorporating salient working-class groups into the new economic and political model. Near the "exclusionary pole" the attempt to forge a new state-society equilibrium can rely heavily on coercive policies to deactivate and then restructure salient working-class groups. The characteristic policies, coalitional partners, and hegemonic possibilities of each pole are so distinct that I suggest that an analysis of the dynamics of state corporatism requires that we distinguish between inclusionary corporatism and exclusionary corporatism (see Table 3.1).[5]

As analytic constructs, the two poles seem more than sufficiently different to warrant treatment as two subtypes. However, while new typologies are relatively easy to construct, they are of little

---

found along the state-societal corporatist dimension. One of their suggestions is that, given the salient and semi-autonomous role played by lower-class groups under Perón (especially from 1944-45) and Cárdenas, these be considered "intermediate cases" between state and societal corporatism. However, since the initiative for structuring lower-class associational groups along corporatist lines came from the state in these cases, I find it useful for my purposes to treat them as examples of "state corporatism." Nonetheless, there is clearly a need to distinguish between the "poles" of state corporatism. See David Collier and Ruth Berins Collier, "Who Does What, To Whom, and How: Toward a Comparative Analysis of Latin American Corporatism," and David Collier, Leslie Spencer and Cherri Waters, "Varieties of Latin American 'Corporatism'" (paper prepared for 1975 annual meeting of the American Political Science Association, San Francisco, California, September 2 to 5).

[5] With some modifications and qualifications, I am building upon the distinction between "incorporating populist-authoritarian" systems and "excluding bureaucratic-authoritarian" systems made by Guillermo A. O'Donnell in his excellent study, *Modernization and Bureaucratic-Authoritarianism: Studies in South American Politics*, pp. 53-114.

Both inclusionary corporatism and exclusionary corporatism employ policies that, if successfully implemented, restrict the autonomy of the groups they encapsulate. In no sense is the word "inclusionary" meant to imply liberal, democratic, or socialist policies. As already indicated, both inclusionary and exclusionary corporatism are classifiable as authoritarian subtypes in Juan Linz's well known typological distinction between "democratic," "authoritarian," and "totalitarian" regimes.

use unless they help point out significant and distinct patterns in phenomena that previously had been treated as a unit. Inclusionary and exclusionary corporatist subtypes in fact do correspond in broad outline to observable phenomena, even though of course no concrete regime perfectly fits all the defining characteristics of either pole.[6] Near one pole, we find that Brazil since 1964, the Onganía government in Argentina from 1966 to 1970, and the current military regime in Chile, are all identifiable as attempts to install new regimes by heavy reliance upon exclusionary corporatist policies. Near the other pole, the government of Cárdenas and, to a somewhat lesser extent, the first govern-

[6] Though Schmitter and most of the writers on corporatism do not explicitly make the distinctions between the characteristic policies, coalitional enemies and partners, and hegemonic prospects of the two subtypes as shown in Table 3.1, the distinction between the two subtypes is well grounded in the literature on "populism" and "post-populism," on which I have built and somewhat recast to fit my discussion of varieties of corporatism. For populism, see Torcuato di Tella, "Populism and Reform Latin America," in *Obstacles to Change in Latin America*, ed. Claudio Veliz, pp. 47-74. Also see Hélio Jaguaribe's discussion of "neo-Bismarckian" national capitalism in his *Desenvolvimento econômico e desenvolvimento político*. For an article that argues that the nature of Brazilian industrialization eroded the populist coalition and called for exclusionary policies to revive capitalist growth see Fernando Henrique Cardoso, "Associated-Dependent Development: Theoretical and Practical Implications," in *Authoritarian Brazil*, ed. Alfred Stepan. For an excellent discussion of the demise of "incorporating populist-authoritarian" systems and the rise of "excluding bureaucratic-authoritarian" systems in the industrially developed countries of Latin America, see O'Donnell, *Modernization and Bureaucratic-Authoritarianism*, pp. 53-144. Also see his "Corporatism and the Question of the State," in *Authoritarianism and Corporatism in Latin America*, Malloy, pp. 47-88.

As is obvious from the terminology I have used, there is much in common between my approach and O'Donnell's. There are also some differences. O'Donnell tends to restrict, and to link casually, the emergence of "excluding" systems to the economic requirements of highly modernized, dependent-capitalist systems. While I, too, accept this as frequently important, my use of "exclusionary" also embraces elite exclusionary motivations that are largely political and emerge in a context not as explicitly tied to the crisis of import-substitution in highly modernized dependent economies. I have in mind, for example, Franco's Spain and Salazar's Portugal. A less important difference is that, because of O'Donnell's focus on Argentina and Brazil, the role of peasants does not figure prominently. In systems where peasants are already mobilized, however (as they have been at times in Mexico, Peru and Bolivia), they become an important part of the "incorporating" or "excluding" process.

TABLE 3.1
The Two "Poles" of State Corporatism

	Inclusionary Corporatism	Exclusionary Corporatism
State elite's initial reaction to already activated, or potentially salient worker and/or peasant groups	Attempts to *incorporate* into support coalition for new political and economic system sought by state elites and to *encapsulate cooptatively* into state corporatist associational organizations	Attempts to *exclude* those autonomous organizations and demand making practices from the political arena that might obstruct the new political and economic system sought by state elite and to *coercively encapsulate* into state corporatist associational structures
Dominant state policies used to encapsulate salient worker and peasant groups in state corporatist associational structures	Primarily, distributive, symbolic and group-specific welfare policies; secondarily, coercive measures	Primarily, coercive measures; secondarily, group specific welfare policies and virtually no distributive policies in initial stages
State elite's policy toward functions of state apparatus	Attempts to expand distributive, regulative, arbitrative, control and planning capacities	Attempts to significantly expand scope and depth of coercive, control, and planning capacities
State elite's characteristic coalitional partners	National bourgeoisie and newly encapsulated workers and peasants	International bourgeoisie and technocrats

Characteristic enemies of state elite's coalition	Oligarchy, and traditional (non-industrial) foreign capital	Populist and radical political leaders and autonomously organized working class
State elite's characteristic stance toward structural reforms	Normally some nationalist and domestic reforms are made as part of the "constituent acts" of the regime	Few or no nationalist or domestic reforms. Emphasis on "post-populist," or "post-polarization" consolidation
State elite's orientation toward mobilization of worker and peasant groups	Attempts to sponsor limited controlled mobilization against coalitional enemies and *into* state chartered associational structures	Attempts to dismantle the organizational capacity of workers or peasants to mobilize against the policies of the coalitional partners and to demobilize into state chartered associational structures
Characteristic legitimacy principles of state elite vis-à-vis its coalitional partners	Political populism and economic nationalism	Political order and economic efficiency
Maximum hegemonic possibilities vis-à-vis salient working class	Diffuse support that contributes to hegemony of new political structures and facilitates effective control at relatively low coercion levels	Hegemony virtually impossible, passive acquiescence heavily dependent on coercive mechanisms

ments of Perón and Vargas were attempts to forge new regimes by the extensive use of inclusionary corporatist policies.[7]

Before going further with the analysis, an important distinction should be underscored. I have talked of inclusionary and exclusionary tendencies or *policies*, not *regimes*. This distinction is necessary for two reasons. One, any given attempt to install a regime using corporatist mechanisms could, and often does, combine inclusionary and exclusionary policies. Perón's policies, for instance, were predominantly inclusionary, but for the labor organizations opposed to him his policies were exclusionary. The military government in Brazil since 1964 is predominantly exclusionary, but in some rural areas where it has the resources and its economic model is not threatened, it is using some inclusionary policies, such as the extension of minimum wage and social security laws to the countryside, in order to help organize rural workers into state chartered syndicates. The label "inclusionary" or "exclusionary" when attached to corporatist systems thus refers to the *dominant* policy orientation of the state elite.

A second reason why it is imperative to emphasize policies and not regimes is that the same regime can shift from a pattern of inclusionary policies to one of exclusionary policies over a period of time. In Mexico under Cárdenas strong inclusionary policies dominated. But in the years following Cárdenas new demands have increasingly strained the inclusionary formula and hence some later presidents have turned more and more to exclusionary policies. In the case of Perón his government was much more inclusionary from 1944-1952 than from 1952 until his overthrow in 1955.

Having established that state corporatist installation attempts can follow very different paths, and that we are referring to dominant policy patterns, not regimes, let me briefly suggest the conditions that give rise to state corporatist experiments.[8] Inclusionary and exclusionary corporatism are elite responses to perceptions

[7] The self-styled "state-socialist" governments in Bolivia in 1936-1939 also approximated this pole. Peru, especially between 1968 to 1975, had several original features but nonetheless can also be included in the subtype.

[8] I say *briefly* both because my major task in this chapter is to discuss the neglected question of variance in the success or failure of corporatist installation attempts and because the analysis of the origins of corporatist experiments has been the major focus of the works of Cardoso, O'Donnell, and Schmitter with whom, with the exception of some differences I have already discussed, I am in substantial agreement.

78

of crises of participation and control, and both endeavor to use the power of the state apparatus to forge a new state-society equilibrium. However, different types of systemic tensions tend to be associated with attempts by elites to install regimes based primarily on inclusionary rather than exclusionary policies.

Inclusionary attempts are most likely when oligarchical domination is beginning to erode under the pressures of early modernization, where political mobilization, although increasing, is still relatively limited and uninstitutionalized, and where the industrialization process is still at an early stage. Under such circumstances public and private industrial managers, under the leadership of a new state elite, can forge alliances with the working classes against the old order of the rural and "comprador" oligarchy. Under some conditions, this multiclass alliance of the emerging industrial sector can also take the form of a nationalist attack against the presence of foreign capital in such traditional investment areas as extractive industries or utilities. Such inclusionary attempts have a hegemonic aspiration in the Gramscian sense in that the new state elites hope that, by integrating more fully (both economically and politically) the most strategically located of the lower class groups, a widely accepted pattern of carefully structured participation and political control can be constructed.

An exclusionary attempt, however, is most likely under either one of the two following conditions and frequently a combination of the two:

1. Political mobilization is more intense and ideologically differentiated than that which precedes inclusionary attempts. The elite that assumes control of the state apparatus, fearing a crisis of intense internal conflict, attempts to expand the scope, penetration and coercive capacity of the state apparatus so as to impose a new order on the political system. The state elite attempts to exclude from the political arena a variety of relatively autonomous, largely working-class based, institutional structures capable of resisting their political design, and then seeks to reintegrate the excluded groups into associational organizations designed and controlled by the state.

2. In a context of intense political mobilization the "crisis" of further development is perceived by the elites who assume control of the state coercive and planning apparatus (and nor-

79

mally by their private sector allies) as one in which further
national development—especially public and private investment
planning—requires the expansion of the scope and penetration
of the state apparatus and the initial exclusion and subsequent
controlled reintegration of the workers referred to above so as
to lower their capacity to make demands and to impede the implementation of the state's politico-economic development design.

Under the conditions of more advanced industrialization the
high investment requirements of the state planners often entails
a coalitional shift by the state elite toward an alliance with the
modern multinational industrial sector, which serves as a source
of scarce financial, technological and organizational resources.[9]

In the specific context of Latin America inclusionary corporatism thus is more likely in the earlier stages of import-substitution industrialization, where modern elites and urban working
classes perceive significant room for populist multiclass coalitions.
Exclusionary corporatism, on the other hand, is more likely to
be attempted if, after the import-substitution phase, the pattern
of industrial development begins to stagnate, the political and
economic struggle intensifies, and politics is increasingly perceived in zero-sum terms.

A final word about the relation of inclusionary and exclusionary corporatism to organic statism. Although I stated in Chapter
1 that organic statism can be seen as an abstract model of governance that no concrete regime approximates very closely, we can
nonetheless see that inclusionary corporatism, with its attempt
to create a state-constructed order based on the incorporation of
many of the major social groups into the political community, is
much closer to the organic-statist model than exclusionary corporatism. To some extent we can view exclusionary corporatism
as representing a profound distortion of the ideal of the social

---

[9] As I alluded before, O'Donnell's analysis of the origin of exclusionary
systems rests heavily on economic explanations found in number 2 above to
the neglect of number 1. This limits the utility of the concept because both
1 and 2 are often involved. Brazil since 1964 is a clear case where both numbers 1 and 2 played a role in the exclusionary attempt. In post-civil war Spain
number 1 was dominant; in Argentina from 1966-69 number 2 was dominant,
but the near absence of number 1 was, as I argue later, one of the reasons why
the installation attempt failed. In Chile since 1973 number 1 and 2 are
relevant, with number 1 being the immediate cause of the exclusionary
attempt and the major reason for the extremely high level of coercion the
new state elite has applied.

order posited in the abstract model of organic statism, in that the attempt to construct the political order by exclusionary policies results in the coercive deactivation of many groups, particularly labor. It represents a decrease, rather than an increase, of participation in the political community. However, *no* concrete inclusionary attempt satisfies entirely the pure organic-statist model either. The ideal posited in the model of participation through self-managing groups, for instance, has not been realized in any concrete regime based on inclusionary policies.

COMPARING INSTALLATION ATTEMPTS: A FRAMEWORK OF ANALYSIS

After distinguishing between inclusionary and exclusionary corporatism, the next step is to formulate hypotheses that permit comparative inquiry into attempts to install regimes with marked corporatist features. To take this step, we must attempt to specify the conditions that facilitate (or hinder) the installation of such regimes.[10]

The identification of these conditions will contribute to the task of the comparative analysis of such attempts not only among countries but also within countries because it will aid intracountry longitudinal and/or sectoral analysis. That is, we could use the conditions we have specified as facilitating or inhibiting the installation of inclusionary and/or exclusionary corporatism to evaluate the likelihood of successful installation at different times and also across different sectors within a given society, which may vary greatly in the degree to which they are amenable to attempts at corporatist restructuring by the state.

Before we can formulate hypotheses about supportive or resistant conditions we need to indicate which variables, on conceptual grounds, seem important to research for inclusionary corporatism and which for exclusionary corporatism. Obviously an historical analysis of any one case could identify an almost infinite variety of factors. The search here is for a parsimonious list of systemic variables that are of the greatest explanatory power in the comparative analysis of corporatist installation attempts.[11]

---

[10] In a less systematic way, I shall also attempt to indicate the conditions that facilitate (or hinder) the creation of hegemony for those regimes. The question of the consolidation of regimes will be analyzed in greater detail when I discuss Peru.

[11] By *systemic* I mean factors that are inherent in the structure of the economic, social and political aspects of civil society and the basic coercive,

The first variable that seems crucial to consider is the organizational strength and ideological unity of the state elite. The concern with this variable derives naturally from the analysis of corporatist experiments as elite responses to crisis. They are attempts by elites to *install* a new pattern of state-societal relations. As such, the elites' organizational strength and ideological unity is a critical variable affecting the success of both inclusionary or exclusionary attempts.

The second independent variable is the degree of development of autonomous political parties and interest groups. Because we are examining attempts to restructure society, it seems logical to assume that the relative autonomy, strength, and number of organizations already structured along noncorporatist lines in civil society affects the potential resistance to, or support for, both inclusionary and exclusionary installation attempts.

The third independent variable is the degree of societal polarization. The intensity of polarization is relevant for both inclusionary and exclusionary corporatism because it affects the coalitional possibilities available to the state elites. It also affects exclusionary corporatism because it can have an independent impact on both the will of the state elite to exclude and the degree

---

economic, regulatory, and legitimacy resources of the state. External resource flows of multinationals to Brazil since 1964 are in this case considered systemic because they are an inherent part of the structure of the development model being pursued by the state.

However, some international trends are nonsystemic and in individual cases can be decisive. Notwithstanding the longevity of the Franco regime and the effectiveness of its exclusionary policies, if Spain had participated in World War II on the side of the Axis the regime would have been overthrown by external forces. Likewise the defeat and discrediting of fascism in World War II contributed to a climate of opinion in Brazil (especially among the army who fought in Europe against Italy and Germany) and the world hostile to the explicit corporatism of the *Estado Nôvo*.

The quality of individual leadership is often also a nonsystemic variable. Cárdenas inherited favorable conditions for the creation of a regime by inclusionary policies but his masterful political leadership and his charisma for much of labor and the peasantry greatly strengthened the installation effort. A weak leader might have failed to capitalize on these favorable conditions.

Despite this inherent limitation to comparative analysis, a major advance can still be made toward the further identification of systemic conditions that support or resist the installation and consolidation of inclusionary and exclusionary corporatism.

to which a "constituency" for exclusionary repression by the state exists among some groups in civil society.

The final variable that appears relevant for both variants is the "ratio" of the state's coercive, economic, and symbolic resource capacity in relation to the effective demands made on the state by civil society. For inclusionary corporatism economic and symbolic resources would seem particularly important because they affect the capacity of the state to execute the distributive policies that help incorporate working-class and peasant groups into new corporatist structures. For exclusionary corporatism the coercive capacity of the state elite in relation to working-class demand-making capacity would seem to be the most salient relationship to explore.

One variable that may be central to inclusionary corporatism but less critical for exclusionary corporatism is the degree to which social welfare and other social reform programs have been elaborated prior to the installation attempt. This appears critical for inclusionary corporatism because it affects the extent to which standard reforms are still "available" to be used as vehicles for incorporating new groups into state-constructed corporatist institutions.

The following is a preliminary attempt to use these variables in hypotheses about the conditions that facilitate or hinder the installation and consolidation of regimes based on inclusionary or exclusionary policies. In all cases we are assuming that the elite in control of the state apparatus is attempting to install some form of corporatist regime.

Hypothesis One

[VARIABLE ONE: State Elites' Organizational Strength and Ideological Unity]

INCLUSIONARY CORPORATISM: *The greater the state elites' combination of organizational strength and ideological unity, the greater the possibility of installing the new regime.*

EXCLUSIONARY CORPORATISM: *Same hypothesis.*

The degree of ideological cohesion in support of the choice for inclusion (or exclusion) and of the institutional strength of the coercive elite is an independent variable of considerable importance. For example, if the elite that assumes control of some key sectors of the governmental coercive apparatus is itself weakly organized and/or internally divided, it may not be able to dominate the entire state apparatus, much less agree on an inclusionary or exclusionary design to impose on society. If the state elite attempting to forge corporatist structures is a military bureaucracy, their relative unity could be measured by answers to such questions as:

a. Has the organization, before assuming power, developed some general ideological-bureaucratic rationale for the assumption of this new role? Is this perceived as consistent with its military role?

b. Have they developed a minimal programmatic consensus?

c. As the "military as government" attempts to win new constituents, does this program solidify or threaten the cohesion of the "military as institution"?

There are, of course, other factors that affect the unity of civilian or military elites beside consensually evolved doctrine. For example, an elite's sudden perception of an intense threat may forge a "crisis unity" even in the absence of prior doctrinal or programmatic evolution. As Hypothesis Three will indicate, under some conditions, fear of polarization may strengthen the elites' will to use much higher levels of coercion than they would be willing to employ had polarization been less threatening. This source of elite cohesion becomes an especially important factor in analyzing the different orientations toward the use of coercion in exclusionary corporatist attempts.

Hypothesis Two

[VARIABLE Two: Degree of Development of Autonomous Political Parties and Interest Groups]

INCLUSIONARY CORPORATISM: *The lower the degree of development of autonomous political parties and interest groups, the greater the possibility of installing the regime.*

EXCLUSIONARY CORPORATISM: *Same hypothesis.*

Though lower levels of autonomous development help the installation chances of both inclusionary and exclusionary attempts, a medium (as opposed to high) level is relatively favorable to an inclusionary attempt, whereas a medium (as opposed to low) level is relatively unfavorable to an inclusionary attempt.

For exclusionary corporatism, if much of the political space is densely filled with ideologically based, relatively autonomous, noncorporatist political parties, trade unions, and other interest groups, the sources of opposition to the new regime will be more numerous and it will be more important (and difficult) to dismantle existing structures. At very high levels of development of autonomous political parties and interest groups, there will be greater "requirements" for the application of high levels of coercion by the state elite, and this in turn may place greater pressure on their ideological and institutional unity than would be the case if exclusionary policies were attempted in a context where there was a somewhat lower degree of development of autonomous political organization.

For inclusionary corporatism, a low, as opposed to medium, degree of development of autonomous political parties and interest groups means there is less institutionally based resistance to the integration of groups into new state structures of association, and there are more groups "available" to the state for such integration.

Hypothesis Three

[VARIABLE THREE: Degree of Polarization]

INCLUSIONARY CORPORATISM: *Conditions of polarized political mobilization are not supportive of the installation of the regime.*

EXCLUSIONARY CORPORATISM: *Opposite relationship expected.*

The logic here is that the broad multiclass coalitional possibilities and the non-zero-sum socioeconomic climate that aid inclusionary attempts tend not to be present in situations of high political polarization.

However, high prior political polarization favorably affects a number of crucial components of the exclusionary effort. In a situation of extremely high polarization, the state elite will feel the need, and the polarization will contribute to its will, to impose what may be unprecedented levels of coercion in the attempt to alter the old pattern of class or interest conflict, and by imposing exclusionary corporatist policies. The application of extremely high coercion by the state elite in turn further strengthens their will to maintain their exclusionary policies even in the face of resistance because the costs and obstacles to extrication are raised. Just as importantly, within exclusionary attempts, the greater the prior degree of polarization, the larger the subsequent "constituency" in civil society that, out of fear, will accept and even support policies of coercion against the enemies of the new regime. Extreme polarization helps to bind this initial constituency to the new regime in two ways. First, the more this constituency fears the consequences of societal polarization, the more likely they will be to endure passively the elimination of their former political institutions and even some economic hardships in return for the security and stability they hope the exclusionary policies will deliver. Second, the more intense the fear, animosity, and conflict generated by the polarization, the more difficult it will be for any eventual disaffected elements of the initial coercive constituency to form anti-regime alliances with the excluded sectors.

While my primary concern in this chapter is with predicting the success or failure of attempts to install regimes by inclusionary and/or exclusionary policies, I should note that, though polarization is functional for installation by exclusionary policies, there are costs for the regime. Precisely because of the societal polarization and the selective targeting of coercion, there is almost no chance, no matter how successful the regime might be in some of its subsequent economic policies, that it could achieve an ideologically hegemonic situation in the Gramscian sense. Given this "birth defect" of the regime, even economic growth and increased economic distribution will not greatly diminish the regime's dependence on visible and credible coercive mechanisms.

Hypothesis Four

[VARIABLE FOUR: Degree of Prior Social Welfare and Structural Reforms]

INCLUSIONARY CORPORATISM: *The lower the level of social welfare legislation and structural and sectoral reform the coun-*

try has attained before the installation attempt the greater the chance of installing the regime.

EXCLUSIONARY CORPORATISM: *Variable not utilized because less salient for exclusionary policies, and also unpredictable.*

The reasoning here is that, if great social welfare and structural and sectoral "reform space" is available for inclusionary policies (in the sense that there are logical and feasible reforms or measures that have not been carried out by previous regimes), the political elite has the opportunity to mobilize commitment to the regime by a series of major, often once-only, social reforms.

By social welfare reform, I am alluding to the broad range of citizen privileges and worker safeguards such as social security, minimum wage laws, and paid vacations. By structural and sectoral reform, I mean acts such as the first significant agrarian reform and the first major nationalizations. Other typical reforms include the first strong institutional and symbolic support for the role of labor in the economy, with the state playing a major role in ensuring the recognition and subsidy of labor unions, the establishment of state mediated bargaining procedures, and the creation of worker hospitals, funds, and vacation hotels.

All these reforms would be helpful for inaugurating any regime, but they are especially important for inclusionary installation attempts with hegemonic aspirations because they make possible the *simultaneous* creation of the new corporatist institutions *and* substantive and symbolic acts of distribution. Because the new corporatist institutions are thus often perceived by the newly incorporated groups as being intimately related to the new distributive policies of the state, these institutions are more likely to be perceived by the incorporated groups as legitimate. This is so notwithstanding the fact that the characteristic corporatist practices of such institutions (e.g. the legal right of the state to grant or deny official union recognition and the tying of union subsidies to official recognition) increase the capacity of the state to control groups in society.

This variable has not been included in the case of exclusionary corporatist installation attempts because it is less salient in the sense that major new groups are not being incorporated. Also, the direction of its impact is not sufficiently predictable to build into a hypothesis. In some contexts a preexisting high level of social welfare legislation (which is maintained) can provide a cushion for individual workers at the same time that their class organizations, such as unions, are under attack by the regime. This might make it easier to sustain the repressions. On the other hand, a low level of social welfare legislation could allow some room for the regime to take steps aimed at improving the well-being of individuals, which might lessen their resistance to the imposition of exclusionary corporatist policies on their class organizations.

Hypothesis Five

[VARIABLE FIVE: Resource/Effective Demand Ratio]

INCLUSIONARY CORPORATISM: *The greater the ratio of the state's resource capability—primarily economic and symbolic, and secondarily coercive—to effective demand, the greater the chances to install the regime.*

EXCLUSIONARY CORPORATISM: *The greater the ratio of the state's resource capability—primarily coercive, and secondarily economic and symbolic—to effective demand, the greater the chances to install the regime.*

This is a crucial variable for both inclusionary and exclusionary attempts. In pluralist regimes, much of the claim to legitimacy rests in the procedural adherence to formal representational institutions. In monist regimes, the revolutionary ideology and mobilization policies can keep effective demand low by the full penetration of all intermediate organizations of society. In corporatist regimes that do not emerge out of profound polarization, the claim to rule has a more instrumental basis—for instance, the argument that this is the only system by which to make the country prosperous, unified, or powerful. Because of these instrumental claims to legitimacy and the heavy reliance on high levels of unity within the state elite, corporatist regimes are less ideologically and institutionally protected than either pluralist or monist regimes against the problem of coping with a situation where effective demand significantly exceeds output capacity. Effective demand here is defined as a combination of the degree of social mobilization (in Karl Deutsch's specific sense of the term) and the institutional capacity of the organizations in civil society to press claims on the state.[12]

Economic and symbolic resources are particularly useful for the installation phase of inclusionary corporatism because the characteristic corporatist system of patron-client relations needs, as Hypothesis Four suggests, initial distributional outputs, both in order to coopt key power brokers and to incorporate groups into the emerging system. Once these mechanisms of incorporation are established, however, they themselves—as the analyses of Mexico in Chapter 2 showed—are important vehicles for containing future demand-making.

Coercive resources are more critical to exclusionary corporatism because in the initial stages of the installation attempt, the major policy instrument used by the state elite to restructure the demand patterns in civil society is coercion.

CORPORATIST INSTALLATION ATTEMPTS: FOUR CONCRETE CASES

At one level of analysis, varieties of state corporatism share common features. However, to analyze the dynamics of installation attempts, we have to be aware that a great range of concrete policies can be used to install a regime. Moreover, as I have just argued, conditions supportive for policies near the inclusionary pole can be very unsupportive for policies near the exclusionary pole. Thus, systematic analysis of the probabilities of success of any state corporatist attempt necessarily entails the use of the conceptual distinction between inclusionary and exclusionary corporatism. The analyst must also be sensitive to the extreme variation in the outcome of attempts to install state corporatism. Despite the initial appearance of great state strength and unity, the elite attempting installation may encounter such difficulties that it completely fails. At the other extreme our analysis must contain conceptual awareness that state corporatist installation attempts cannot only be successfully installed but can also achieve a Gramscian hegemony in civil society. I begin with an "opposite pair" analysis that explores such maximum variation in policies and outcomes. These are the inclusionary corporatist attempt in Mexico under Cárdenas, which ended in a successfully installed

[12] See Deutsch's "Social Mobilization and Political Development," *The American Political Science* (September 1961).

regime with hegemony in civil society, and the unsuccessful attempt by General Onganía to pursue exclusionary corporatist
policies to help install a regime in Argentina between 1966-1971.

I will then follow the more standard procedure in comparative
studies of a "matched-pair" analysis by examining two exclusionary attempts that followed similar socioeconomic policies, but had
different outcomes. The Brazilian military between 1964-1970
was able to use exclusionary policies to install a regime whereas
the Argentine military failed in a similar attempt. How much
of this variance is explainable in terms of the hypothesis we have
advanced?

Finally I will very briefly consider the newest exclusionary attempt, Chile, not so much to make a full-blown comparison but
rather to address the specific question of why the Chilean military regime that came to power in 1973 is applying a much higher
degree of coercion than did either the Brazilian or Argentine military, and to determine, from the perspective of our hypotheses,
what difference this might make for the outcome of the installation attempt.

While analyzing these concrete cases I will also explore the
question of the longitudinal relationship of different corporatist
regimes in the same country. For example, under what conditions
does a previous experience with inclusionary corporatism help
or hinder the later installation of a regime with exclusionary
policies? What special problems arise when a regime that has
relied extensively on exclusionary policies attempts to reduce the
degree of coercion? Finally, I will explore the question of hegemony in both inclusionary and exclusionary corporatism.

As cursory as this examination will be, it will provide a preliminary opportunity to test our hypotheses about corporatist
installation attempts.[13] It should be emphasized that the focus
of the present analysis is on predicting the success of installation
attempts once the basic choice between the inclusionary and exclusionary approach has been adopted. The broad conditions that
lead to the adoption of one or the other approach have been

[13] The apparent neglect of inclusionary cases is more than compensated
for in the next chapter in which, using the same hypotheses, extensive treatment is given to Peru where inclusionary policies were used to install a
regime successfully between 1968-72 but where—in contrast to Mexico after
installation—institutional consolidation and ideological hegemony were never
attained.

spelled out above, and will not be considered in this phase of the analysis.

Mexico vs. Argentina

In Mexico, for every variable the conditions were at least relatively favorable for the creation of a regime by inclusionary policies. In Argentina, on the other hand, conditions were extremely unfavorable for the installation of inclusionary corporatism and even unfavorable for the installation of a regime by the exclusionary policies they chose.

With regard to the state elite's organizational strength and ideological unity, the Mexican revolutionary military elite had already founded in 1929 the dominant party that has not lost a gubernatorial or presidential election to date. There is, of course, leadership competition within the party. However, by the 1930s no major social groups could effectively challenge the organizational strength and political resources of the revolutionary coalition, and by 1936 Cárdenas had established presidential dominance over the state and party apparatus by exiling former President Calles. The inclusionary policies of Cárdenas played a major role in the establishment of his dominance within the party, as well as in building crucial new controlled constituencies for the regime he consolidated. These constituencies contributed in turn to the support within the state elite for the inclusionary policies. The two revolutionary decades before 1930 had eliminated most prerevolutionary forms of sociopolitical organization. Thus Cárdenas was not faced with a densely organized or hostile associational network (variable two). The organizational development of Mexico at the advent of Cárdenas presented favorable conditions for the success of inclusionary policies. In terms of our third variable, Mexico was largely "post-polarized" by 1930. There was substantial room under the national revolutionary roof for the state elite to forge and sponsor an inclusionary coalition that sheltered the peasantry, urban workers, and the incipient industrial bourgeoisie.

Cárdenas inherited major opportunities for reform (variable four). He responded to these opportunities with consumate political skill by making major distributive and symbolic reforms while simultaneously mobilizing key worker and peasant groups against his remaining domestic and external opponents and incorporating these groups into the new corporatist institutions of

91

the party structure and state apparatus.[14] These organizations, in turn, were used by his successors to keep effective demand low from 1940 on. The Mexican state elite's task was facilitated by the fact that, in comparison to Onganía's Argentina, Mexico had far lower levels of social mobilization.[15] The low level of effective demand, combined with (and contributing to) the highest sustained growth rate in Latin America in the 1940-1970 period, has, in terms of variable five, kept government resources ahead of effective demand and allowed the regime to build and maintain the extensive patron-client machine which helps keep the regime intact, even though it has responded to the increasingly complex societal demands generated by the development process by selective—but very systematic—exclusionary policies.[16]

[14] For this crucial period, see Jorge Basurto, "Populismo y movilización de masas en México durante el régimen cardenista," *Revista Mexicana de Sociología* (October-December 1969); Joe C. Ashby, *Organized Labor and the Mexican Revolution Under Lázaro Cárdenas*; Lyle C. Brown, "General Lázaro Cárdenas and Mexican Presidential Politics, 1933-1940; A Study in the Acquisition and Manipulation of Political Power" (Ph.D. dissertation, University of Texas, 1964); the many interesting oral histories in James W. Wilkie and Edna Monzón de Wilke, *México visto en el siglo XX: entrevistas de historia oral* and Wayne A. Cornelius, "Nation Building, Participation, and Distribution: The Politics of Social Reform Under Cárdenas," in *Crisis, Choice, and Change: Historical Studies of Political Development*, ed. Gabriel A. Almond et al.

[15] One study has used Deutsch's indicators to create a composite index of social mobilization for the 20 countries of Latin America using mid-1960s data. The highest index score was Argentina's at 217, and Mexico's was sixth at 115. Obviously the Mexico of the 1930s, when the installation attempt began, would have had even a much lower index score whereas the Argentine index reflects the level of social mobilization the Onganía installation attempt encountered; see David Scott Palmer, " 'Revolution from Above': Military Government and Popular Participation in Peru, 1968-1972" (Ithaca: Cornell University, Latin American Studies Program, Dissertation Series, Number 47, January, 1973), pp. 6-9, 35.

[16] The special circumstances of post-revolutionary Mexico, while very favorable to inclusionary corporatism, would also have been moderately favorable to exclusionary corporatism. Variable two was moderately favorable to exclusion because of the organizational weakness in civil society. Variable five was moderately favorable in that in the post-revolutionary situation, even with exclusionary policies, the state could have had sufficient coercive, economic, and symbolic resources to keep effective demand low. The polarization variable was more favorable to inclusionary than exclusionary corporatism but in the revolutionary aftermath a victorious state elite could have at least neutralized the effect of this variable by "creating" enemies to support exclusionary politics. Likewise the relative organizational strength

In contrast to Mexico, the military elite that assumed state power in Argentina in 1966, while having temporarily resolved some of their past divisions,[17] were basically divided over the central question of whether to attempt to install any variant of corporatism or not. From the beginning, key civilian allies as well as some major military factions, such as that led by General Lanusse, had serious reservations about General Onganía's corporatist designs for Argentina.[18] As the design became more explicit, and as civilian opposition grew, the divisions within the military grew apace. The internal division was especially significant in the Argentine case because, unlike Mexico, the coercive elite could not draw upon any broader revolutionary or institutional mystique to bolster its new regime.[19] In terms of these factors, Argentina under

---

of the state elite was increased by inclusionary politics but even if they had decided on exclusionary policies, the state elite would not have been weak enough to merit a negative score on the variable of organizational strength.

This exercise helps clarify how the Mexican regime that won diffuse support and created powerful institutions by its inclusionary policies did not lose control in the decades after Cárdenas as its policies shifted in the exclusionary direction.

[17] O'Donnell in *Modernization and Bureaucratic-Authoritarianism*, pp. 158-65, shows how, due to professional organizational evolution, they had achieved a new degree of internal cohesion. He also discusses the initial unity and later fragmentation of the military in "Modernización y golpes militares: teoría, comparaciones y el caso Argentino" (Buenos Aires: Instituto Torcuato Di Tella, Documento de Trabajo, September 1972).

[18] O'Donnell's forthcoming study of the Onganía period convincingly documents the corporatist design of Onganía. He also analyzes the latent ideological and structural conflicts between Onganía's goals and the goals of the liberal-international and nationalist wings of the military as well as the goals of some of the new regimes' most weighty allies from the technocracy and internationalized big business.

[19] A survey taken a few months before this attempt at installation shows widespread skepticism about the military. In response to the question as to which group had "so much influence over the way the government is run that the interests of the people are ignored," the military was the most frequently cited group. See Jeane Kirkpatrick, *Leader and Vanguard in Mass Society: A Study of Peronist Argentina*, pp. 128, 242. The author concluded, "all categories of the population shared a generally antimilitary orientation" (p. 133), and "more than three-fourths (78.2 percent) of Argentines opposed military intervention in principle, approximately two-thirds (63.9 percent) denied that military interventions had saved the country from chaos, and 57.2 percent said they would oppose a party supported by the military" (p. 132).

Onganía ranks somewhat lower on variable one than did Mexico under Cárdenas.

Moreover, unlike the Mexico of Cárdenas, Argentina in 1966 was already a densely organized society in which extensive social reform had already been carried out (variables two and four). During the inclusionary corporatist phase of Perón from 1943-1955, much of the available institutional space had been filled and the previously "available" masses committed. For example, the crucial indicator of social security coverage reveals that from 1919 to 1943 the number of workers covered had increased only from around 200,000 to less than 500,000. Under Perón, this figure soared to about 5,000,000 by 1955.[20]

In addition, Perón created the complex system of working-class resort hotels and vacation plans, greatly extended hospitalization and medical coverage programs for workers, established paid vacations and the Christmas bonus of a month's pay, as well as improved legal provisions for job security and work conditions.[21] These benefits, coupled with worker gains in real pay and the workers' strong symbolic identification with Perón, meant that after 1955, with Perón alive and possibly capable of making a political comeback, the Peronista movement remained important. The overwhelming electoral victory of the Peronistas in 1973 and 1974 show how loyal this constituency remained. Of central importance was the fact that the movement retained an organized core in the massive, relatively autonomous trade union movement, which had well-developed institutional capabilities both at the national and, perhaps even more crucially, the local levels.

The Onganía installation attempt thus occurred in a context where much of the social welfare and ideological space had been filled. The government, which began with questionable claims to legitimacy, was faced with a political system that offered few opportunities for inclusionary policies and where the exclusionary policies were directed at political groups with a capability for powerful, autonomous demand making. Widespread polarization might have created a middle-class constituency for very high levels of coercion; but, as we shall see when we contrast the Brazilian

[20] Argentina, Ministerio de Trabajo y Seguridad Social, *Análisis económico financiero de las cajas nacionales de seguridad social* (Buenos Aires, 1963), p. 41.

[21] A well-indexed compilation that brings together much of this legislation is Alejandro Unsain, *Ordenamiento de las leyes obreras Argentinas.*

and Argentine cases, there was little political polarization prior to the installation attempt in Argentina. The installation attempt thus began without a wide constituency for coercion and with few polarization-generated obstacles to the middle class using their considerable demand-making capability in cross-class coalitions against the exclusionary regime.

Despite an initial period of relative passivity and acceptance, Onganía, with his fledgling corporatist policies, faced—in strong contrast to Cárdenas—an ideologically and institutionally defined society with great capacity for resistance, extremely high levels of intergroup information, and strong demand-making powers. It is not surprising, then, that Onganía's March 1969 speech introducing a new series of neo-corporatist measures elicited open discussion of a possible coup by the liberal wing of the military and negative reactions from a broad range of organized interests in civil society.[22]

With resistance to the attempted installation of exclusionary corporatist measures and increasing division within the military itself, the ratio of regime resource capability to effective demand (variable five), which was always lower than that in Mexico, deteriorated sharply. Demonstrations, frequently involving students and middle-class elements as well as workers, occurred in Rosario, Corrientes, Mendoza, and almost every large Argentine city. It was in this context that the major uprising in Córdoba—the "Cordobazo"—occurred, severely testing the regime. Following a period of social conflict and policy indecision, the Onganía government fell in June 1971. Onganía was succeeded by General Levingston, who attempted to add some inclusionary policies to the installation attempt. However, the political and economic conditions (high organizational development and commitments, extensive prior social welfare legislation, unfavorable economic and symbolic resource/effective demand ratio) were, in terms of our hypotheses, overwhelmingly unsupportive to successful use of inclusionary policies, and the modified installation effort was a total failure.

[22] For a skeptical discussion of these measures by a major newsweekly see "Onganía: hacia el Nuevo Estado" *Primera Plana* (April 1, 1969), pp. 76-79. Key passages from the government document outlining some of these measures are contained in the May 13, 1969, issue of *Primera Plana*. The April 29, 1969, issue discusses opposition to Onganía by the liberal wing of the military.

Faced with the option of either greatly increasing the level of coercion or beginning to extricate itself from its installation attempt, the military chose the latter and backed away from massive confrontation. The military leaders thus began the search for an understanding with the Peronista forces that would allow for their inclusion in the political formula and allow the extrication of the military from direct rule as a way of preserving their severely threatened institutional unity.[23]

The foregoing discussion has shown how the conditions in Mexico were much more supportive of the installation of a regime with marked corporatist characteristics than they were in Argentina. But what of the question of ideological hegemony in Mexico? What is the relation between value patterns in civil society and the regime? We have already argued that the Argentine installation attempt failed partly because the society was one where high demand capabilities were coupled with low regime acceptance.

Mexico by the 1960s, in contrast, could be characterized as a society where low demand capabilities co-existed with attitudes of high regime acceptance. Table 3.2 shows how sharply different the orientations toward politics are in Mexico and Argentina. Coupled with the citizens' perception that the Mexican government has little impact on their lives is a strikingly high degree of acceptance of the proposition (an extremely supportive normative orientation for corporatist regimes) that state goals should be accorded greater legitimacy than individual goals (see Table 3.3).

The Mexican attitudinal patterns revealed in these tables must, of course, be seen as having a reciprocal cause and effect relationship with the elaborate mechanisms of "incorporation" created during the period of Cárdenas and discussed in Chapter 2. The result was effective control coupled with broad societal acceptance of the political system. Mexico thus merits classification

[23] For this period, with special attention to the Cordobazo, see Beba Balvé et al., *Lucha de calles, lucha de clases*, pp. 169-89, Francisco Delich, *Crises y protesta social: Córdoba, mayo de 1969*, pp. 7-67; and Juan Carlos Agulla, *Diagnóstico social de una crisis: Córdoba, mayo de 1969*, pp. 15-62. For indicators of increased generalized resistance to the Onganía government and for the erosion of elite unity and will to impose their corporate design, see a forthcoming study by Guillermo O'Donnell. This study also has invaluable material on the contradictions of the Levingston policies and an interesting analysis of the post-Levingston extrication formula.

TABLE 3.2

PERCENTAGES EXPRESSING "HIGH INFLUENCE OF NATIONAL GOVERNMENT
ON SELF": RESPONSES FROM SIX COUNTRIES

Argentina	U.S.	Germany	U.K.	Italy	Mexico
41	41	38	33	23	7

SOURCES: The data for all countries but Argentina are from Gabriel Almond
and Sidney Verba, *The Civic Culture: Political Attitudes and Democracy
in Five Nations* (Princeton: Princeton University Press, 1963), p. 80. The
question was repeated in Argentina in 1965, see Kirkpatrick, *Leader and
Vanguard in Mass Society*, p. 159. The implications of such an opinion pattern for Argentina are discussed by O'Donnell in his *Modernization and
Bureaucratic Authoritarianism*, pp. 148-154.

TABLE 3.3

"THE INDIVIDUAL OWES FIRST LOYALTY TO THE STATE AND ONLY
SECONDARILY TO HIS PERSONAL WELFARE":
RESPONSES FROM FIVE COUNTRIES

	Agree	Disagree	Don't know	No Answer
Mexico	91.9%	4.8%	3.3%	—
Italy	48.1	32.7	19.2	—
Germany	40.6	44.7	14.7	—
U.K.	37.8	54.8	7.4	—
United States	25.0	68.3	6.6	0.1%

SOURCES: Inter-University Consortium for Political Research, *Codebook for
the five-nations study*, cited in Kenneth S. Sherrill, "The Attitudes of
Modernity," *Comparative Politics*, 1 (January 1969): 190.

as a regime that achieved hegemony in civil society. Following
Gramsci, we stress that an important requirement for hegemony
is a rough congruence between the dominant values of civil society and those of political society. However, while concurring
with Gramsci's emphasis on the importance of ideology for maintaining a regime, Louis Althusser's point that the state apparatus
plays an active role in shaping the values in civil society seems
particularly relevant in the analysis of corporatism in Mexico.[24]
Ideological hegemony in Mexico was not achieved spontaneously,

[24] See "Ideology and Ideological State Apparatuses (Notes Towards an
Investigation)," in his *Lenin and Philosophy and Other Essays* (New York
and London: Monthly Review Press, 1971), pp. 127-86, esp. pp. 141-48.

but has been maintained through the continued action by the state in order to protect itself from being challenged effectively. The leaders of the state, in the few instances where they have felt threatened, have used their coercive powers to repress the organized expression of antiregime sentiment.[25] More routinely, they have used the full resources of the state apparatus to marginalize ideological opponents and to coopt and promote middle-rank activists who are willing to collaborate ideologically. Hegemony exists in Mexico. Rule is not primarily a function of the domination of civil society by the state. Nonetheless, this hegemony itself is partially achieved by the selective use of the coercive apparatus of the state.

Brazil vs. Argentina

I now want to consider a somewhat more difficult case: post-1964 Brazil. Why, unlike Argentina, were the military strategic elite in Brazil able to use the state apparatus to install a regime that relied heavily on corporatist mechanisms? This regime does not have the hegemony of Mexico; nonetheless it possesses some stability, though it is not fully institutionalized.[26] The answer is not to be found in the types of economic models selected, for both were exclusionary corporatist attempts to use the power of the state apparatus to redirect the economy and the political system along new, "efficient" directions after the populist and the import-substitution period of industrial growth had encountered severe difficulties. Since our comparison is between two exclusionary installation attempts we will only analyze the four variables relevant for exclusionary corporatism.

The difference can be explained in part by the polarization variable. The 1964 coup in Brazil had been preceded by increasing political mobilization on the left and had been countered by

[25] For a discussion of two major challenges—the railroad workers' strike of 1959 and the students' demonstration before the Olympic Games in 1968—that resulted in large-scale imprisonments and deaths, see Jorge Carrión, "La represión también es militante," in Fernando Carmona et al., *El milagro Mexicano*.

[26] I discuss important conflicts between the "military as government" and the "military as institution" in the period 1964 to 1970 in *The Military in Politics: Changing Patterns in Brazil*, pp. 213-71. For the regime's problems with institutionalization, see Juan Linz, "The Future of an Authoritarian Situation or the Institutionalization of an Authoritarian Regime: The Case of Brazil," in *Authoritarian Brazil*, ed. Stepan, pp. 232-54.

mobilization on the right.[27] The 1966 Argentine coup was not preceded by major mobilized polarization. Under the circumstances, neither the military elite nor their potential civilian allies believed it possible or necessary to impose their policies through high levels of coercion. Significantly, the extensive national sample taken less than eight months before the coup does not show a pattern of cleavage or polarization more pronounced than that found in many European democracies.[28] The fears of the middle class, the industrialists, and the military officers were greater in Brazil in 1964 than they were in Argentina in 1966. In this sense the polarization variable was more favorable to exclusionary policies in Brazil than in Argentina because a larger group in civil society was willing to "abandon" their political power to the military in exchange for the protection offered by the new regime which would repress labor and the left.

Another independent variable for explaining variance in this paired comparison is the degree of development of autonomous political groups (variable two). The key target for control in both regimes was the industrial workers. The task was substantially greater in Argentina. Data for 1960 show that 25.1 percent of the economically active population in Argentina was employed in industry, whereas in Brazil the comparable figure was only 8.9 percent.[29] Even more important was the question of the relative autonomy of labor in each country. Much of the Brazilian urban labor force was unionized or "reunionized" under the inclusionary corporatist policies of Vargas from 1930-1945. As with Cárdenas and Perón, these incorporation measures were accompanied by a series of basic welfare reforms and symbolically gratifying acts toward labor that made Vargas the most popular figure among labor in Brazil's history.[30] Despite the fact that the struc-

---

[27] The process of growing polarization is discussed in Part Three of Stepan, *The Military in Politics.*

[28] See for example the date in Kirkpatrick, *Leader and Vanguard in Mass Society.*

[29] See *Statistical Abstract of Latin America: 1971* (Los Angeles: Latin American Center, December 1972), p. 102.

Over-all, Argentina scores much higher than Brazil on Deutsch's indicators of social mobilization. In the study previously cited, Brazil had a composite index of social mobilization of 73 compared to Argentina's 217, see Palmer, " 'Revolution from Above,' " p. 9.

[30] One recent study summarizes the period in the following way: "Among other things legislation brought the first effective regulations of working con-

tures into which unions were organized in this period later constrained labor's freedom of action, Vargas is still affectionately known as "O pai do povo" (the father of the people) and won the presidency in a freely competitive election with strong labor support in 1950. Like Cárdenas, he inherited a major opportunity for creating new working-class organizations.[31]

Subsequent governments found these mechanisms so useful that they were never dismantled. Even under a populist government such as that of Goulart, labor in Brazil never achieved a significant degree of autonomy.[32] Thus when the military assumed power in 1964, by and large they did not have to struggle to impose an alien corporatist system on labor, but merely had to utilize fully the existing mechanisms that had been in operation for a quarter of a century. The post-1964 regime was therefore able to eliminate important strike activity almost completely during the installation period.[33]

---

ditions via the creation of a Ministry of Labor. It also granted important new fringe benefits, extended the coverage and scope of social security programs, and established a minimum wage system. This legislation represented a real and immediate social and economic advance for the working class. . . . Labor leaders were attracted by Vargas' program also. They gained access to legislative and administrative bodies through the system of corporatist representation." . . . This quotation is from a basically critical study of corporatism in Brazil by Kenneth S. Mericle, "Conflict Regulation in the Brazilian Industrial Relations System" (Ph.D. dissertation, University of Wisconsin, 1974, pp. 65-66. See also Azis Simão, *Sindicato e Estado*, where he lists major social welfare and labor legislation passed in the period 1900 to 1940. Of the 85 measures taken in this period affecting urban labor, 72 were taken under Vargas; see pp. 90-98.

[31] For a general review of the corporatist mechanisms created by Vargas, see Thomas E. Skidmore, "Politics and Economic Policy Making in Authoritarian Brazil, 1937-71," in *Authoritarian Brazil*, ed. Stepan, pp. 3-46. For a detailed discussion of the compulsory syndical tax, the labor court system, and the social security system, which enmeshed labor in a subtle network of corporatist control mechanisms, see Kenneth P. Erickson, *Brazilian Corporative State and Working Class Politics* (Berkeley: University of California Press, 1977).

[32] For the unsuccessful struggle of labor under Goulart to achieve greater autonomy, see Erickson, *Brazilian Corporative State and Working Class Politics*.

[33] This point is amply documented in Mericle, "Conflict Regulation in the Brazilian Industrial Relations System," esp. pp. 219-25. To be sure, in those cases where the control mechanisms did not work, the military and police units have used naked force. Nevertheless, most of the time much of the

The situation in Argentina was quite different. Under Perón, much of labor had been incorporated initially into inclusionary corporatist structures, but the subsequent fate of these structures was different from those in Brazil in two crucial ways. In the formative years of the corporatist system under Vargas, Vargas' coalition with the military was strong, and labor remained a useful, but dependent, and except for brief periods unmobilized, adjunct to the core coalition. The role of labor was very different in Argentina. Perón, in his initial rise to power, was almost blocked by the military. He was saved by his mobilization of labor, and, despite the existence at a formal level of many of the control mechanisms of corporatism, labor remained in fact a dynamic part of Perón's core coalition.[34] Because in the post-Perón, liberal restoration movement, some corporatist mechanisms were viewed as part of the Peronist-labor power base, some of them were dismantled.[35] In the years leading up to the attempt by Onganía to impose an anti-Peronist corporatist system, labor retained its institutional strength and autonomy. At medium levels of coercion the task of controlling labor was too great, as we have seen, and the Onganía government was eventually faced with extremely high levels of resistance, which reached a crisis point during the Cordobazo.

---

containment comes from the mechanisms themselves. Mericle, writing in 1974, concludes that "the Contagem and Osasco strikes are the only important strike movements which have occurred since the military takeover of 1964," p. 225. Both of these occurred in 1968.

[34] This highlights an important point. While the classic formula is that of Cárdenas's "mobilize-incorporate-demobilize," the Perón sequence of mobilization, which turns into autonomous power, is of course possible. I will explore this possibility in the case of Peru in Part Two of this book.

[35] The most important of these was the reform of Perón's Law of Professional Associations by decree 9270 (May 1956), which eliminated the process by which unions needed official recognition by the state—a process that is a classic corporatist control device to selectively reward or punish unions. Compare Perón's Law of Professional Associations found in Unsain, *Ordenamiento de las leyes obreras Argentinas*, pp. 383-94, with Decree 9270 found in Deveali, *Derecho sindical y de previsión sindical*, pp. 403-407. Under Frondizi a new law of association was introduced, but the point remains that Argentina did not maintain consistent mechanisms for the control and co-option of labor. Another important change was the Law on Collective Bargaining, which was altered to reduce the role of the state in settling wage agreements. For a number of interesting documents about labor after Perón see, Santiago Senén González, *El sindicalismo después de Perón* (Buenos Aires: Editorial Galerna, 1971).

The foregoing discussion clarifies the relation of the two exclusionary attempts to the first part of variable five. The Brazilian state had a comparatively greater ratio of coercive resources to effective demand than the Argentine state. The second part of variable five refers to the state's economic resources. The relative weakness of the Argentine state's coercive resources, demonstrated during and after the Cordobazo, adversely affected its ability to attract international economic resources. Conversely, the relative strength of the Brazilian state's coercive resources favorably affected foreign capital inflows. Figure 3.1 graphically shows how the Cordobazo correlates with a decline in direct investment from the U.S. multinationals to Argentina and how, after five years of solidly established control in Brazil, the multinational investment flows to Brazil dramatically increased and gave the regime important new resources in its installation attempt. In 1969 Brazil only received $57 million more in direct U.S. investment than did Argentina. In 1973 Brazil received $696 million more.

The final variable that is relevant to exclusionary corporatism is the state elite's organizational strength and ideological unity in favor of exclusionary policies. In both cases there were important divisions within the central state elite—the army. However in Argentina the critical split was between the military government and those members of the military elite such as Lanusse, who did *not* favor the imposition of new corporatist policies. In Brazil, by contrast, the critical tensions were between the military government and those hard-line members of the military institution who wanted the regime to go *even further* in the exclusionary direction. In addition, there was no divisive debate in Brazil over the formulation and imposition of corporatist control mechanisms for labor, for as we have seen these already existed.

Thus, on every single variable, the systemic conditions in Brazil were more supportive of the installation of a regime with marked exclusionary policies than they were in Argentina.

Let us shift now to the question of hegemony. Does the military elite in Brazil rule only by force? Or were there attitude patterns in civil society that lent strength to the exclusionary installation attempt? First, the fact that the basic control mechanisms were created by Vargas to some extent cloaks the appearance of naked force, because by now labor is so powerless it cannot

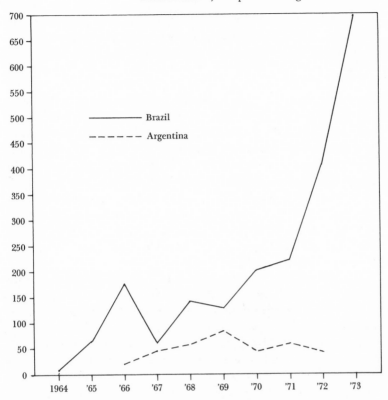

FIGURE 3.1. Total annual net new U.S. direct investment in Brazil (1964-1973) and Argentina (1966-1973) (in millions of U.S. dollars). SOURCES: U.S., Dept. of Commerce, *Survey of Current Business*, vols. 42-54. 1973 figures are preliminary estimates. The Inter-American Development Bank, *Economic and Social Progress in Latin America: Annual Report 1974* (Washington, 1975), p. 471, aggregates net private direct foreign investment from all countries and estimates that in no year between 1970 and 1973 did such investment exceed $11 million in Argentina, whereas Brazil's lowest year was 1970 ($131 million) and its highest year was 1973 ($941 million).

function without some of the rewards his system supplied. For example, in Mericle's study of trade union presidents in São Paulo, over 54 percent of them wanted to retain compulsory membership and automatic collection of fees by the minister of labor,[36]

[36] Mericle, "Conflict Regulation in the Brazilian Industrial Relations System," p. 134.

even though most studies have demonstrated that these are crucial instruments of the overall corporatist system of control.

Accurate data about mass attitudes are of course difficult to obtain and evaluate under authoritarian conditions such as exist in Brazil. Nonetheless a few polls have been taken that yield interesting insights. A survey in the northeastern city of Salvador in 1971 asked people, "What should be the government's main concerns?" Of the six possible choices, only one percent listed as the first choice, "to create a climate of greater liberty and democracy."[37] In answer to a question probing whether they would prefer an "elected government even if it were less efficient," only 32.5 percent said they would prefer it.[38] Another study, based on a national sample, showed that, while over 50 percent of the respondents agreed that they "were interested in knowing what the government does," only about 16 percent said they considered themselves interested in political questions.[39]

It is difficult to interpret these studies. At most they indicate that, under the conditions of high economic growth from 1968 to 1974, adroit manipulation of ideological appeals to the emerging "big power status" of Brazil, and systematic government repression of effective political criticism or competition, much of the citizenry will be oriented toward the output side of government and relatively passive about the input side of politics. In this context the regime won some modest degree of acquiescence to its exclusionary style of corporatist rule.

However there is no evidence in Brazil of ideological hegemony as in Mexico. In March 1974 the "fourth government of the revolution" was inaugurated and began a cautious policy of "distensão," or decompression. The Geisel cabinet decided to hold relatively open elections for the federal congress and the state legislature.[40] Roughly an hour of free television time each day

[37] Bolivar Lamounier, "Ideology and Authoritarian Regimes: Theoretical Perspectives and a Study of the Brazilian Case" (Ph.D. dissertation, University of California, Los Angeles, 1974), p. 268.

[38] Ibid., p. 264. The least educated, contrary to the lower-class authoritarian personality hypothesis, were the group most opposed (38%) to this statement.

[39] Survey by Philip Converse, Amaury DeSouza, and Peter McDonough and reported in Peter McDonough, "Foreign Investment and Political Control in Brazil," (manuscript, 1974), p. 88.

[40] While a step toward distensão this was less risky for the regime than it sounded because the president, governors, and mayors of capital cities are in-

was given to the official opposition party, MDB, and to the government party, ARENA.[41] Despite 10 years of rule and six years of one of the highest GNP growth rates in the world, the government party had overwhelming losses in precisely those developed regions that at the aggregate level benefited most from the regime's economic policies.[42] The government's response was to argue that its original intention had been to create a strong party *system* and not merely a strong government party. The chief spokesmen of the government defined as a healthy party system one in which an opposition party has at least the prospect of winning significant power.[43] While the experiment was important, the obstacles to distensão are so serious that they underscore the difficulties of relaxing exclusionary policies once a regime has been built upon them, and of transforming acquiescence into hegemonic support sufficient to allow reintroduction of any significant pluralistic competition.

In this context, three assumptions held by the architects of distensão are open to question. First is the assumption that ARENA's losses will reinvigorate the party. So long as all the key policy decisions are made by the military and their high-level civilian technocratic allies, the party will be hard-pressed to recruit strong, politically attractive candidates. Second, the government assumes that, in return for containing its own "ultras," the MDB will contain theirs. Nothing in the recent history of electorally based parties indicates that this is a reasonable expectation. The third questionable assumption is that the political system can be restored to a measure of competition without disrupting elements in the regime's preferred economic model.

---

directly elected. The Congress, though then directly elected, remained sharply curtailed in that it could not, even before the additional restrictions of April 1977, originate money bills or override major presidential bills or measures.

[41] The campaign is discussed in "Eleições: a redescoberta da política," *Visão* (November 18, 1974), pp. 20-27; "Eleições: e agora?" *Opinião*, No. 108 (November 29, 1974), pp. 4-5.

[42] For example in the state assemblies the opposition won 45 of the 70 seats in the state of São Paulo, 65 of the 94 seats in the state of Rio de Janeiro, and won control of the state assemblies in the dynamic agricultural states of Paraná and Rio Grande do Sul. For a breakdown of the election results at the state level see the table in *Veja*, No. 325 (November 27, 1974), p. 45.

[43] Interviews with some of the key cabinet officers involved in the distensão policy in Brasília, December 1974, provided valuable insights into the government's political and economic strategies at this critical juncture in the regime's development.

The opposition won ground largely by calling attention to such issues as the denationalization of Brazilian industry, poor income distribution, and systematic violations of civil liberties. To be politically competitive in a more open electoral arena, the government will have to take positive action on these explosive issues. However, while the development plan for 1975-1979 identifies these as important policy areas, the structural constraints imposed by massive reliance on foreign loans and investment—estimated by the financial community as approximately 10 billion in 1978 alone—means that significant improvements in these areas along the lines suggested by the opposition (greater controls on incoming foreign investments, greater restriction on profit expatriation, and fewer controls on trade unions) would most likely create difficulties for the economic model that is at the heart of the regime.[44]

If the government policy of distensão is perceived by its military constituency as endangering either political stability or the economic model there could be a crisis of the kind that occurred in 1965-1969, where the military as government was strongly checked by the military as institution. Thus distensão to date has met with severe internal and external constraints. After fourteen years of rule, the regime in Brazil, despite the fact that it has a significant external and internal constituency among those elites who have profited most from the political and economic model, would still be confronted with great difficulties if the political elite significantly relaxed the exclusionary policies used to install the regime.

Chile: The Centrality of the Polarization Variable

Finally, the question in Chile is where the post-Allende military government fits into our analysis. The combination of mobilized polarization, high levels of ideological and institutional commitments, relatively filled reform and first-step social welfare space, and the high demand/low economic and symbolic resource position of the government, means that the military in Chile would

---

[44] For the development plan see, República Federativa do Brasil, *Projeto do II Plano Nacional de Desenvolvimento (1975-1979)* (Brasília; September 10, 1974). The government is indeed taking some bureaucratic measures to protect Brazilian industry and to provide greater welfare services, but the question remains whether these will have enough political impact to counter the more sweeping demands of the opposition.

have virtually no chance of creating a hegemonic inclusionary corporatist system as in Mexico, even if this were its intention. However, the situation is more complicated if the question is simply: can the military use exclusionary policies to install a new regime? Here the index value of polarization is different. The extremely high polarization before and after the overthrow of Allende has a "favorable" effect on a number of our variables. It unified the coercive state elite—the military.[45] The polarization and fear also created a large constituency in civil society that supports this coercion as the price for protection. This combination of circumstances contributed to a level of coercion that was much higher than in the immediate aftermath of the coup in 1964 in Brazil and the 1966 coup in Argentina. This, in turn, has "favorably" affected the effective demand/resource ratio in that, despite the economic crisis, the massive repression used by the military has contained effective worker demand.

The violence imposed by the military on working-class leaders becomes in itself a "will hardening" factor. It makes an "extrication formula" like that of the Argentine military after the collapse of the Onganía corporatist experiment more institutionally threatening to the military-state elite because of the military's fear of reprisals. Thus, though the outcome of the Chilean corporatist attempt remains in doubt, we can say that a number of elements conducive to "successful" installation are present in Chile that were absent in Argentina: there is a stronger constituency for a highly coercive corporatist state, the military are meeting dissent with much more systematic and unrelenting repression, and the costs for failure are much higher.

Coercive capabilities will remain central to the Chilean case, even though the leaders of the military government speak of emulating the Brazilian economic formula that has won their Brazilian peers some support. A Chilean "economic miracle" along Brazilian lines seems very unlikely. The Brazilian model has depended heavily on high foreign investment, which in turn has

45 Fears of "communism," polarized class conflict, and their own institutional disintegration unified the bulk of the military in favor of the coup. This majority in turn enforced further ideological "purity" within their ranks by court martials and formal and informal purges before and after the coup. See for example, *Las fuerzas armadas y el golpe de estado en Chile*, ed. Pío García, pp. 263-84, and Joan Garcés, *El estado y los problemas tácticos en el gobierno de Allende*, pp. 20-54.

been postulated on (1) selling manufactured consumer goods to the large domestic market, (2) using Brazil as the low-cost export platform for the rest of South America, (3) investments in a wide range of extractive and refining industries, and (4) the multinationals' assumption that Brazilian labor will remain effectively controlled by the state. All these factors are more problematic in Chile: (1) Chile's population is only one-tenth that of Brazil, (2) many multinationals have already located their major export oriented plants in Brazil, (3) with the exception of copper, Brazil is much more richly endowed with scarce raw materials than Chile, and (4) the "scare of multinationals" in 1970-1973 was greater in Chile than the comparable scare of 1962-1964 in Brazil, and labor has a history of much greater autonomy in Chile than in Brazil.

The extremely high coercion levels may prove instrumental in the installation of the regime. However the costs in terms of any eventual ideological hegemony have already been prohibitive. Indeed, the international campaign against the violation of human rights has not only severely eroded the symbolic resources of the regime but is having some success in impeding the flow to the regime of vital economic resources such as governmental loans and even some private investments.[46]

SOME COMPARATIVE CONCLUSIONS

I do not claim to have arrived at hard quantitative indicators for the five variables introduced in this chapter. Nonetheless, the variables are useful for assessing the systemic conditions that facilitate or hinder the installation of regimes using inclusionary or exclusionary corporatist policies. If they appear useful to other scholars, it is hoped they can be refined, variables added and/or deleted, and more rigorous steps taken toward their quantification.

Even at this stage of analysis, however, we may conveniently summarize our foregoing discussion by the use of a table in which an attempt is made to classify for each variable the conditions

---

[46] In the United States, for example, the human rights pressure groups succeeded in getting Congress to put such restrictions on aid, and loans and military sales to Chile that Chile even briefly alluded to refusing any further assistance, see "Chile Moves to Rebuff U.S. Economic Assistance in Anger over Curbs," *New York Times*, 21 October 1976, p. 8.

in each country as to whether they were "very favorable," "moderately favorable," "neutral," "moderately unfavorable," or "very unfavorable" to the installation of the particular type of corporatism (inclusionary or exclusionary) that was selected.[47] Since the argument rests or falls on our verbal discussion, this table is presented for its heuristic, rather than independent analytic, value. Table 3.4 presents this five-category summary of the values on each variable.[48]

Although only four cases have been discussed in detail, these hypotheses should be useful in analyzing any corporatist installation attempt. More cases would, of course, help refine the hypotheses and also help determine under what conditions which of the five variables carries more explanatory or predictive weight in analyzing outcomes.

Although they need to be researched in greater detail by specialists, a number of cases spring to mind that could be profitably explored using this framework.[49]

[47] My original intention was to have a binary classification system of "favorable" / "unfavorable." However, this system could not depict some important aspects of the range of variation I repeatedly encountered as I tried to complete the classification. On some variables, for example, Brazil and Mexico had more favorable conditions than Argentina and both could get a "favorable" while Argentina received "unfavorable." However if the conditions in Mexico were much more favorable than in Brazil it seemed useful to have the category "very favorable" and by extension, if conditions in Chile were more unfavorable than in Argentina, the category "very unfavorable" seemed useful. Finally the category "neutral" seemed necessary for those cases where, due to cross-pressures or other factors, the conditions could not clearly be labeled favorable or unfavorable. Thus my reluctant shift from a two point to a five point classification system.

[48] Although I do not think each variable should be given equal weight, if, purely for heuristic purposes, we wanted to give numerical values ranging from +2 for "very favorable" to −2 for "very unfavorable," we could get an average value for all applicable variables presented in Table 3.4. On a scale where +2 is the top and −2 the bottom, Mexico would receive +1.6, Brazil +1, Chile 0 and Argentina −1.25.

[49] Our detailed examination of the cases graphically underscores our methodological argument that we cannot make predictions about the conditions that are supportive or resistant to the installation of "state corporatism" as such but only about "inclusionary corporatism" or "exclusionary corporatism." This is so because the conditions that may be supportive of one can be resistant to the other. For example, if we omit consideration about the strength of the commitment to inclusion or exclusion (variable one), we note that Brazil received a "moderately favorable" for all remaining variables relevant to exclusionary corporatism. Using the procedure set forth in foot-

TABLE 3.4

SUMMARY OF CONDITIONS AFFECTING THE SUCCESS OF CORPORATIST INSTALLATION ATTEMPTS

Variable	Mexico (1935-1940) Inclusionary	Brazil (post-1964) Exclusionary	Argentina (1966-1971) Exclusionary	Chile (post-1973) Exclusionary
Organizational strength and ideological unity of the state elite	Moderately favorable	Moderately favorable	Neutral	Moderately favorable
Development of autonomous political parties and interest groups	Very favorable	Moderately favorable	Very unfavorable	Very unfavorable
Polarization	Moderately favorable	Moderately favorable	Moderately unfavorable	Very favorable
Prior social welfare and other reform space	Very favorable	Variable not applicable	Variable not applicable	Variable not applicable
Resource/effective demand ratio	Very favorable	Moderately favorable	Very unfavorable	Moderately unfavorable

The Torres government that came to power in Bolivia in 1970 made overtures that implied it was considering inclusionary corporatism. By all indications the Torres faction of the Bolivian military had been influenced by the Peruvian experiment. However, because—the Bolivian military—unlike the Peruvian military had not undergone any extensive period of prior ideological and institutional preparation for the installation attempt, it soon divided sharply. In this case the organizational unity of the coercive elite was probably so low that it alone would have proved decisive even if the other variables were favorable—and some were not.

In the 1950s General Rojas Pinilla of Colombia was obviously interested in a Perón-style inclusionary corporatist attempt. However in this case variable two was decisive. That is, even though political party conflict had been so intense that it precipitated military rule, the breadth and intensity of party identification—even among much of labor—meant that very little political space was available, and it was hard to mobilize new followers. Even more importantly, the party elites, in the face of this challenge, closed ranks and constructed a consociational formula that brought about the fall of Rojas Pinilla and the advent of the consociational democratic regime.[50]

The Colombian case raises the question of whether the consociational formula would be a viable response to the exclusionary corporatist challenge in Chile. While one cannot rule out a Christian Democratic-Communist party consociational attempt if

---

note 48, the average value for these variables would be +1. However, if we had assessed the conditions for inclusionary corporatism, the relatively high polarization would then receive a "moderately unfavorable" value for variable three. The high degree of prior social welfare legislation by Vargas would result in a "moderately unfavorable" value for variable four. The resource/effective demand ratio—which for inclusionary corporatism weighs symbolic and economic resources more heavily than coercive resources— would result in at best a "neutral" value and quite possibly a "moderately unfavorable" value for variable five. Variable two would suffer a similar shift in value. Thus whereas Brazil had an average value of +1 for variables two-five for exclusionary corporatism its average value for these variables for inclusionary corporatism could be as low as −1. Chile of course would have an average value for inclusionary corporatism even lower.

[50] For "consociational democracy," see the seminal article with that title by Arend Lijphart in *World Politics* (January 1969). For a review of the literature see Hans Daalder "The Consociational Democracy Theme," *World Politics* (July 1974).

the military becomes severely fragmented, it appears much more difficult because of the extreme political polarization in Chile. In Colombia, polarization was between two multiclass parties. In Chile polarization was along class lines. More Chilean center-right politicians have been willing to abandon the party system than in Colombia because of the higher value they attached to security, which they see as being achieved *only* by the coercive apparatus of the exclusionary military state. In Colombia consociational agreement among upper-middle-class party elites itself brought about reduction in societal conflict. Under Colombian conditions the elite saw the military as expendable.[51] In Chile they do not.

When we examine the case of post-civil-war Spain, we see a situation in which the state had few economic resources, political identifications were strong, and polarization intense. According to our hypotheses such conditions were unfavorable to the successful installation of inclusionary corporatism. Nonetheless, the unity of the coercive elite in the aftermath of the war was high, and the repressive apparatus of the state was aided to some extent by the diffuse societal fear of the renewal of intense conflict. These conditions contributed to the consolidation of a regime with exclusionary characteristics.

The situation in Portugal was quite different from that in Spain. In the first years of Salazar, the structural conditions would have probably allowed either an exclusionary or inclusionary outcome. However the ideological commitment to stability without mobilization, the strength of the bureaucratic structure, and the lack of developmental commitment of the state elite contributed to the exclusionary outcome.

The Italian case is extremely complex. Mussolini clearly had inclusionary aspirations, and he did carry out some inclusionary policies. However, unlike Vargas, Perón, and Cárdenas, he encountered unfavorable conditions in Variable 2 and Variable 4. Much of the political space in Italy was already filled with party loyalties. Preexisting, noncorporatist party identifications were so strong among many syndical institutions that corporatist institu-

[51] For an analysis of Colombia within the context of the consociational democracy literature see Alexander Wilde, "Conversations among Gentlemen: Oligarchic Democracy in Colombia" in *Breakdowns of Democratic Regimes: The European and Latin American Experience*, ed. Juan Linz and Alfred Stepan (Baltimore: The John Hopkins University Press, forthcoming).

tions never became as effective as they did in Mexico or Brazil.[52] Not only were party identifications high, they were mobilized and polarized. Despite some inclusionary policies, the regime increasingly relied on exclusionary policies, for which the conditions were somewhat more favorable. The fall of the regime, of course, flowed directly from the "nonsystemic" variable of defeat in war.

These further examples suggest that our hypotheses can usefully be extended to a variety of different cases. Our analysis has obviously not had the goal of "verifying" these hypotheses in any formal sense. It is evident, however, that they are a valuable tool in the analysis of patterns of success or failure of corporatist installation attempts.

[52] See for example Alberto Aquarone in *L'organizzazione dello Stato totalitario*, pp. 151, 188-89, 220.

PART TWO

Peru: An Organic-Statist Experiment

FOUR · *Evolution of the Peruvian Army*
as the Strategic State Elite:
Context and Content

THE organic-statist experiment that began in Peru in 1968 is one of the most interesting cases of this type of political system to appear in Latin American history. The impressive success with which the regime was initially installed, the rapidity with which it carried out major structural reforms, and the shift away from the initial goals of fundamental reform beginning in 1975 have all attracted widespread attention, both among political leaders in the Third World and in the scholarly community. How does one explain the initial success of this regime? What factors facilitated its initial installation and the bold execution of its initial reforms? What accounts for its subsequent transformation?

Part Two of this book addresses these questions. The present chapter analyzes the conditions that led to the success of the initial installation of the regime by placing the Peruvian case within the framework of comparison developed in Chapter 3. Chapters 5 through 7 then attempt to explain the differing degrees of success of this government in three crucial areas of public policy by applying this same explanatory framework to each of these policy areas. A final chapter discusses the factors that make the *institutionalization* of this regime, as opposed to its initial *installation*, virtually impossible.

In this chapter I argue that the initial phase of the Peruvian military government under General Velasco (1968-1975), was inclusionary in its policies, and that its design for restructuring Peruvian society approximated the organic-statist model. This period in Peruvian history is now called "Phase I of the Peruvian Revolution" and has been followed by Phase II, which has been dominated by more consolidationist policies and philosophy. The policy differences between Phase I and Phase II in Peru have some similarity to the policy differences between the Cárdenas and post-Cárdenas periods in Mexico. Velasco, like Cárdenas, installed a new regime by the use of inclusionary policies. How-

117

ever, unlike Mexico in the post-Cárdenas period, Peru in Phase II does not have a regime that is solidly institutionalized, nor does it have a regime that has ideological hegemony in civil society. Indeed, as I show in the concluding chapter, the problems were severe enough that by 1977 a search for some formula for extricating the military from direct power by 1980 had begun. In itself, Phase I is nonetheless extremely important for two reasons. First, it represents one of the longest and most interesting reform periods in Latin American history. Second, in Phase I the first Latin American regime to be forged by inclusionary policies in the last twenty-five years was—notwithstanding the later retrenchment and crises of Phase II—installed.

To explore the origins and some of the constraints of Phase I, I first examine whether the system-level conditions that precipitated—and facilitated—the attempt to install an inclusionary (as opposed to an exclusionary) system conformed in broad outlines to the argument developed in Chapter 3. More extensively, I analyze the ideological, educational and institutional evolution of the military as a strategic elite, and examine the factors that led them to seize and transform the state apparatus in order to restructure Peruvian society.[1]

[1] In my effort to analyze in depth some special problems in state-society relations, I have not tried to provide a comprehensive account of contemporary Peruvian politics. An extensive literature exists that both enables, and excuses, my more restricted focus. The best overview of pre-1968 Peru is probably François Bourricaud's *Power and Society in Contemporary Peru*, trans. Paul Stevenson. Julio Cotler's "Peru: A Structural-Historical Approach to the Breakdown of Democratic Institutions," in *Breakdowns of Democratic Regimes*, ed. Linz and Stepan, is a perceptive study of the growing pressures on representative institutions and their inability to respond that is indispensable for understanding the context in which the military regime emerged. For a detailed institutional analysis of the Peruvian military, consult Víctor Villanueva, *Ejército Peruano: del caudillaje anárquico al militarismo reformista*, and Luigi Einaudi and Alfred Stepan, *Latin American Institutional Development: Changing Military Perspectives in Peru and Brazil*. For a provocative, well-documented collection of essays on such questions as income distribution, agrarian reform, education, social property, and other policy matters see *The Peruvian Experiment: Continuity and Change Under Military Rule*, ed. Abraham F. Lowenthal. Lowenthal's opening essay in that volume provides an excellent overview of the performance and predicaments of Peru's "Revolutionary Government of the Armed Forces." The policies of the regime have stimulated considerable controversy as to their character. The most influential, early indictments of the regime's economic and political models were Aníbal Quijano's *Nationalism and Capitalism in Peru: A Study*

Phase I Peru: An Inclusionary, Organic-Statist Experiment

In a very schematic fashion, let me indicate some of the major policy measures and ideological positions of Phase I that, despite its original features, warrant labeling the regime's dominant policy orientation "inclusionary" and its dominant ideological orientation "organic-statist."

The government carried out a number of distributive policies and structural reforms. Agrarian reform was sweeping. A study concluded just before the military seized power asserted that "the oligarchy today consists of a central nucleus made up of the sugar and cotton growers of the coast."[2] In a 1974 revision of his well-known neo-Marxist study of the elites of Peru, Carlos Malpica, one of the most stringent critics of the military government, acknowledged:

> As a consequence of the Agrarian Reform Law . . . all the agricultural enterprises with any economic significance have been expropriated or are in the process of expropriation. The most important, that is to say, the sugar producers, were the first to be transformed into agro-industrial cooperatives. Practically speaking, the agrarian elite has disappeared as a power group.[3]

For the urban migrants living in squatter settlements, who constitute almost a third of Peru's urban population, the military government implemented a program of title-granting and infrastructure improvements that was unprecedented in South America.[4] For industrial workers, the government initiated an "industrial community" law that was supposed to allow the workers gradually to acquire shares of ownership in their own enterprises

---

in Neo-Imperialism, and Julio Cotler's "Bases del corporativismo en el Perú," *Sociedad y Política* (October 1972). Despite the government's "anti-Communist," "anti-Capitalist," self-definition, some of the most forceful defenses of Phase I came from orthodox Marxists. See Jorge del Prado, "Is there a Revolution in Peru?," *World Marxist Review* (January 1971), pp. 17-27. Eric Hobsbawm rebuts Quijano's charges along similar lines in "Peru: The Peculiar 'Revolution'," *New York Review of Books* (December 16, 1971).

[2] Magali Sarfatti Larson and Arlene Eisen Bergman, *Social Stratification in Peru,* p. 262.

[3] Carlos Malpica, *Los dueños del Perú,* p. 4. The achievements and limitations of the new worker-run sugar cooperatives will be studied in Chapter 6.

[4] This program is analyzed in Chapter 5.

until they owned as a "community" 50 percent of the enterprises in which they worked, and in theory to exercise managerial control commensurate with their equity.[5] There were also significant changes in education, health care, and communications, and the state nationalized many foreign firms in sectors such as mining, communications, fish-meal plants, and banking.

Although each of the reforms carried out by the military had its share of problems and critics, among recent Latin American change-oriented regimes, only Cuba has managed actually to carry out as many bold structural changes as were accomplished in Phase I Peru. Phase I Peru however, was quite different from Cuba in its philosophy and structure. One of the central concerns of the military elite in charge of the Peruvian state was not so much to eliminate the principle of private ownership of the means of production as to lessen class conflict and to increase the integration of the masses into the national society. In the agricultural area this goal was sought by removing the owners of larger estates and giving ownership, normally in the form of cooperatives, to the laborers who worked the property. Because the old oligarchy no longer owned the land, the regime also transformed the National Agrarian Society, which was one of the major symbols of oligarchical power and one of the more important interest groups representing the oligarchy.

In the industrial sector the state elite attempted to forge a more "organic unity" by reducing the ownership powers of capital and by giving both equity and managerial patricipation to labor.[6] The hope was that in time this would transform both the capitalist outlook of owners and the class-consciousness of labor. The state elite in particular hoped that trade unions, which they saw as a logical response of labor to situations where capital owned all the means of production, would wither away in response to the structural changes introduced by the state to make workers both owners and participating managers.[7] To underscore that old

[5] Chapter 7 examines Phase I ownership and participation policies in industry and shows how Phase II policy makers have watered down key aspects of the "industrial community" law.

[6] Two types of industrial arrangements, the social property sector and the state-owned sector, are discussed in Chapter 7.

[7] As the then director-general of the Labor Communities of the Ministry of Industry, José Segovia, expressed it: "We want to create structures that do not produce confrontation. We want to reach a point where labor understands that to have a strike will be to strike against themselves. In the not

associational forms based on "capitalist interest" were not preferred under the new regime, the government first made the National Industrial Society include workers in its directorate, later took away the right of the society to call itself "national," and finally prevented the society's president from returning to the country following his outspoken opposition to the regime's policies.[8]

To summarize, the peak organizations of class interest (whether representatives of labor or capital) were under a series of ideological and institutional attacks in Phase I.

As is characteristic of inclusionary attempts, the government used distributive policies to embark upon a program to incorporate the population—especially those lower-class groups such as peasants, squatters, and industrial workers whom the regime saw as the major beneficiaries of the structural reforms—into new state-chartered associational groups. The major state agency initially charged with this task was the National System to Support Social Mobilization (SINAMOS). The basic law creating SINAMOS said it should

> promote the organization of the population into dynamic functional and territorial units of communal and cooperative nature

and

> foment and stimulate the dialogue between the government and the national population in order to orient the conscious participation of the people in the basic decisions that effect their environment, their interests and their communal objectives

as well as

---

too distant future I think the labor union tradition will decline but this can only happen if the managerial tradition of conflict with the workers also disappears." Interview in Lima, June 22, 1972.

The chief of the Presidential Advisory Office (COAP), General Graham Hurtado made similar points. He stressed: "The goals of the Industrial Community are various. We want to create a sense of solidarity, to relieve tension. This will in turn create a stronger industrial base because development needs industrialization. We need both solidarity and development." Meeting with the author and other social scientists, June 14, 1972, in Lima.

[8] The Industrial Society complained bitterly that "in its 77 years of institutional life it never had faced so serious a problem," *Industria Peruana: Una publicación de la Sociedad de Industrias*, no. 492-93 (1974), pp. 10-11, and that there was no "possibility of dialogue at high levels with the government," ibid., no. 499 (1974), p. 25.

foment the systematic linkage between the coordinated actions and services of the government and those of the organized population.[9]

The state apparatus, working through SINAMOS and relevant ministries, had by 1974 organized the agricultural sector into a local, provincial, and finally a peak National Agrarian Confederation. The industrial counterpart was the National Confederation of Industrial Communities. The emerging organizational model emphasized the vertical integration of functional groups.[10]

The dominant policies of Phase I thus approximated the inclusionary pole presented in Table 3.1 in that (1) there were significant distributive and symbolic acts in favor of lower-class groups aimed at integrating these groups into the emerging economic and political systems being constructed by the state elite, and (2) the state elite linked these distributive acts with a major effort to encapsulate the beneficiaries into new state-chartered associational structures.

The dominant normative orientation of Phase I was what I have called "organic-statist." The regime explicitly rejected both the liberal emphasis on the "individual" and the Marxist emphasis on "class" as organizational principles of society. The vision was "organic" in that the goal was the nonconflictual, functional unity of civil society in which decentralized, participatory, self-managing groups were to play a key role. The regime was "statist" in that the elite perceived that this functional unity would not occur spontaneously but rather required power, ra-

[9] Decreto Ley No. 18896 *Ley de Movilización Social* June 22, 1971, articles 1, 5. SINAMOS is the acronym for: Sistema Nacional de Apoyo a la Movilización Social. Also in Spanish the words "sin amos" mean "without masters." By 1975 SINAMOS had become so controversial that the government announced a plan to reorganize it and change its name.

[10] While the Phase I government received official support from the Communist party and from such revolutionary figures as Fidel Castro, a major attack from the intellectual sector of the left was that the "verticalization" the state was introducing had the goal of destroying "class consciousness" and class organization among the workers by preventing horizontal linkages between the working class, which was being fractionalized into separate, vertically organized, categories. The most important formulation of this critique was by Cotler in "Bases del corporativismo en el Perú." A discussion of SINAMOS from the perspective of corporatism is James Malloy, "Authoritarianism, Corporatism and Mobilization in Peru," in *The New Corporatism: Social-Political Structures in the Iberian World*, ed. Pike and Stritch.

tional choices and decisions, and, where necessary, fundamental restructuring of civil society by the state elite. Organic unity of civil society was thus to be brought about by the architectonic action of public authorities—hence the regime's model of governance was "organic-statist."[11]

PRECIPITATING CONDITIONS FOR AN INCLUSIONARY VS. EXCLUSIONARY ATTEMPT: AN ASSESSMENT

I argued in Chapter 2 that corporatism does not arise from cultural continuity but rather is the result of an elite's response to the perception of impending crisis. I further specified in Chapter 3 that whether the elite's response is dominantly one of inclusionary or exclusionary policies depends on the nature of the systemic tensions. Specifically, it was suggested that, in Latin America, inclusionary attempts are most likely when oligarchical domination is beginning to erode under the pressures of early modernization and that exclusionary attempts are most likely if, after the import-substitution phase is quite advanced, industrial development begins to stagnate, the political and economic struggle intensifies, and politics is increasingly perceived in zero-sum terms.

The evidence from Peru supports this argument. There were indeed many signs of increasing systemic tension in Peru, but these tensions were very different from those that led to exclusionary attempts in Brazil, Chile, and Argentina. In the early 1960s, Peru was experiencing rural unrest and mobilization that one observer called "unquestionably one of the largest peasant movements in Latin American history."[12] In terms of numbers of peasants and land seizures involved, it was probably larger than any peasant movement then being experienced in the Third World. One source argued that "no less than 300,000" peasants were involved in the process.[13] Another study reported approximately 140 land invasions in Cuzco alone from August 1963 to

[11] The specific characteristics—and predicaments—of Peru's organic-statist design are analyzed much more extensively in Chapters 5-8.

[12] Howard Handelman, *Struggle in the Andes: Peasant Political Mobilization in Peru* (Austin: University of Texas Press, 1975), p. 12.

[13] Comité Interamericano de Desarrollo Agrícola, *Tenencia de la tierra y desarrollo socio-económico del sector agrícola: Perú* (Washington, D.C.: Pan American Union, 1966), p. 396.

March 1964 and estimated that the "total number of invasions may well have been between 350 and 400" in Pasco, Junín, and Cuzco in this period.[14] These invasions affected a wide variety of properties, from foreign-owned grazing land to traditional haciendas. Land seizures occurred throughout much of Peru, involving almost all the departments of the highlands.

For many elites these rural invasions began to have an urban analogue as land was seized and traditional property laws challenged by urban squatters who asserted their rights to claim land around the cities. In 1955 Lima had a squatter population of only 120,000. By 1970 this population had grown to over 750,000.[15]

A second area of tension was the economy. Having long prided themselves on their relatively stable currency, Peruvians were shocked by the 44 percent devaluation of the sol in 1967. The devaluation was widely interpreted as a sign of the political bankruptcy of the Belaúnde government and of the intrinsic limitations of the model of economic development then being pursued.[16]

The sense of crisis that arose from the peasant mobilization and economic difficulties was further enhanced in the later 1960s by a dramatic failure of political reform in the Belaúnde period in the 1960s, a serious crisis of the party system, and the occurrence in Peru in 1965-1966 of a small but nonetheless politically important rural guerrilla movement.

Clearly, then, Peru had been undergoing a process of growing societal crisis in the period before the military seized power. But how should we characterize this crisis? The main locus of tension was in the traditional sectors, and its most volatile expression occurred in peasant-landlord conflicts. This contrasts with the conflicts preceding the exclusionary attempts in Chile, Brazil and Argentina. In these countries, with their advanced import substitution economies, conflict centered in the modern industrial sector and the structural tensions manifested themselves through such

[14] Handelman, *Struggle in the Andes*, p. 121.

[15] I analyze and document this trend in Chapter 5.

[16] The impact of the devaluation in military circles is discussed in Augusto Zimmermann Zavala, *El Plan Inca, objetivo: revolución peruana* (Lima: Empresa Editora del Diario Oficial "El Peruano," 1974), p. 33. For an informed account of economic problems during the Belaúnde period see, Pedro-Pablo Kuczynski, *Peruvian Democracy under Economic Stress: An Account of the Belaúnde Administration, 1963-1968* (Princeton: Princeton University Press, 1977).

124

"stress indicators" as high strike and inflation levels and growing external indebtedness.

If we compare Peru with Brazil, Argentina and Chile in terms of these indicators, Peru scores relatively low. Taking inflation, for example, as a partial measure of the intensity of demands on the government made by classes and groups competing for shrinking resources, we see that the average rates of inflation for the five-year period prior to the exclusionary attempts in Brazil, Chile, and Argentina were far higher than in the five-year period preceding the inclusionary attempt in Peru. Argentina experienced an average inflation rate of 29.1 percent, Brazil 60.5 percent, and Chile 102.5 percent. The comparable figure for Peru is only 13.1.[17]

In the case of strikes, labor mobilization had been growing in Peru and from 1957-1962 the average number of strikes per year was 269. For the next six-year period the figure rose to 398 per year.[18] If we look at strikers per thousand inhabitants, Peru in 1965-1967 averaged 11.4.[19] This is a noticeably greater percentage than Mexico, which even during the Cárdenas period never experienced more than 5 strikers per thousand inhabitants, but it is dramatically lower than Chile, which, even before the figure soared in the years immediately preceding the exclusionary attempt in 1973, had 74.1 strikers per thousand inhabitants in 1970.[20]

---

[17] These inflation rates are calculated from data in *International Financial Statistics*, a publication of the International Monetary Fund. The Chilean and Peruvian data are from Volume 28, no. 1 (January 1975), p. 35. The Brazilian data from Volume 19, no. 1 (January 1966), p. 33. The Argentine data from Volume 21, no. 1 (January 1968), p. 33. Arturo Valenzuela cites data that show that from July 1972 to July 1973 the percentage increase in prices in Chile was 323.6. See "The Breakdown of Democracy in Chile," in *Breakdowns of Democratic Regimes: The European and Latin American Experience*, ed. Juan J. Linz and Alfred Stepan (Baltimore: The Johns Hopkins University Press, forthcoming), table 3.9.

[18] Perú, Ministerio de Trabajo, *Las huelgas en el Perú: 1967-1972* (Lima: 1973), p. II-2.

[19] Absolute number of strikers given in ibid., p. III-2.

[20] For the Chilean and Mexican data, see the sources cited in Figure 2.1. Total strikes in Chile went from 1819 in 1970 to 3325 in 1972, the year before the military assumed power. The contrast with Peru is dramatic; with a somewhat larger total population Peru had only 364 strikes in the year before the military assumed power. For these and other comparative data see Evelyne Huber Stephens, "The Politics of Workers' Participation: The Pe-

The external financial dimensions of Peru's crisis were much less severe than those that preceded exclusionary attempts in Latin America. As the devaluation indicated, Peru had been undergoing stress in its trading and balance-of-payments situation. An important indicator of this stress was that, despite generally favorable export prices, its ratio of external public debt service to value of exports had climbed from an annual average of 7.4 percent in the period 1960-1964 to 11.1 percent in the period 1965-1969. However, this was significantly lower than the ratios found in the countries immediately before the three exclusionary attempts we have considered. Brazil's average annual ratio for the period 1960-1964 was 31.5 percent, Argentina's was 20.5 percent for the period 1961-1965, and Chile had reached a ratio of 20.5 percent by 1971.[21]

Brazil, Chile, and Argentina were experiencing crisis and stagnation at advanced levels of modernization before the exclusionary attempts, whereas Peru was just beginning its industrialization process. Its average annual gross domestic product growth rate for 1961-1967 was a healthy 6 percent, which placed it sixth among the 20 Latin American countries in this period.[22] This contrasted with Argentina, which had the third lowest in Latin America in this period; with Brazil, which had a negative per capital growth rate the year before the exclusionary attempt; and with the severe economic problems of Chile.

We conclude therefore that the crisis in Peru was not so much about how to exclude and contain the modern industrial labor force, but rather about how to include and integrate the marginal rural and urban masses so as to lay the groundwork for incipient modernization and industrialization. However the crisis was no less real. Should the state elite be unable to clear away the obstacles to such modernization, explosive disintegration of the oligarchical order seemed a possibility, as the peasant land invasions indicated. Thus the crisis in civil society in Peru was more consistent with an inclusionary policy response than an exclusionary policy response.

---

ruvian Approach in Comparative Perspective" (Unpublished Ph.D. dissertation, Yale University, 1977), table 6.6.

[21] For Peru and Brazil see, Inter-American Development Bank, *BID Annual Report: 1972*, p. 57. For Chile and Argentina, *BID Annual Report: 1973*, p. 77.

[22] Inter-American Development Bank, *Economic and Social Progress in Latin-America: Annual Report 1972*, p. 4.

General systemic conditions, however, are not sufficient causes of inclusionary installation attempts. Such attempts are conscious endeavors by a strategic elite to create a new pattern of state-society relations. Thus it is important to examine why a particular strategic elite actually arrives at the ideological and organizational position that enables it to seize the state apparatus and begin to impose new policies on society. In the Peruvian case, the strategic elite that must be examined is the military, particularly the army.

THE MILITARY AS A STRATEGIC ELITE: ITS CHANGING PROFESSIONAL ROLE AND THREAT PERCEPTION

From the moment the military seized power in Peru, they saw themselves not as caretakers of liberal democracy, but as a radicalizing group that would restructure both state and society. The question that needs to be explored is how the Peruvian army perceived the tensions just described. Why did these tensions heighten their sense of institutional insecurity? What process of ideological evolution and professional role-transformation led this strategic elite to seize power? Had the army developed a "core programmatic consensus" before assuming power? If so, what were the limits to this program? Also, how wide was the institutional base of the military government's reform program? Had the military prepared themselves institutionally for a new mission consistent with their military organization?

One way to explore these questions is to examine the publications of the military in the years preceding the coup. I carried out a content analysis of the articles published in Peruvian military journals in the fifteen-year period before the military assumed power.[23] This investigation built upon my earlier study of organizational and educational changes in the Peruvian army, and was supplemented by extensive interviews with former faculty members and students of the military schooling system and

[23] The only major military archive accessible to scholars is the *Centro de Estudios Histórico-Militares del Perú*, Lima. The two most important army journals are *Revista Militar del Perú* and *Revista de la Escuela Superior de Guerra*. I read all the available articles in the latter since its foundation in 1954 and all in the former since World War II. Unfortunately approximately 10 percent of the issues were missing. More randomly, I also consulted other military publications such as *Actualidad Militar*. In all, slightly over a thousand articles were read.

127

with visits to the Center of Higher Military Studies (CAEM) in 1972 and 1974.[24]

I looked, first, to see whether, even at the level of the most public and widely disseminated military publications, there had been an emergence of a "new professional" concern about the nexus between internal security and national development. Second, if there was such an emergence, I wanted to ascertain the programmatic content of the new professional articles. This second point was crucial because in Brazil the policy content of new professionalism was dominantly exclusionary. Was the policy content in Peru dominantly inclusionary? And if it was—why?

In Samuel Huntington's important discussion of military professionalism he argues that modern warfare demands a highly specialized military; the military cannot master the new skills required to carry out their tasks while at the same time "remaining competent in many other fields."[25] The scope of the military function "is presumed to be a highly specialized one. . . . A clear distinction in role and function exists between military and ci-

---

[24] CAEM (Centro de Altos Estudios Militares) was founded in the early 1950s. Its organization, curriculum and institutional impact on military role-redefinition are discussed in "The New Professionalism of Internal Warfare and Military Role Expansion," *Authoritarian Brazil: Origins, Policies, and Future*, ed. Stepan. There, I hypothesized that "new professionalism" played an important role in Peru. Here I examine that hypothesis. Also see Einaudi and Stepan, *Latin American Institutional Development: Changing Military Perspectives in Peru and Brazil*.

[25] Samuel Huntington, *The Soldier and the State: The Theory and Politics of Civil-Military Relations*, p. 32. As Huntington correctly insists, his model of professionalism holds only in conditions where the military develop their professional skills for conventional warfare against foreign enemies. In his later writings he notes that, if the focus shifts from interstate conflict to domestic war, it will encourage a different pattern of civil-military relations than that expounded in the following quotations. Since many later writers have failed to note this qualification, the concept of military professionalism is still widely misunderstood, and it is useful to formulate explicitly the difference between the old professionalism of external warfare and what I call the new professionalism of internal security and national development. Two excellent articles by Huntington that discuss the role of the military in political situations where the old professionalism does not hold are "Patterns of Violence in World Politics" in *Changing Patterns of Military Politics*, ed. Samuel P. Huntington (New York: Free Press, 1962), esp. pp. 19-22, and "Praetorianism and Political Decay" in his *Political Order in Changing Societies*, pp. 192-263.

128

vilian leaders."[26] Huntington asserted that the content of this professionalism contributes to apolitical attitudes within the officer corps because "the vocation of officership absorbs all their energies and furnishes them with all their occupational satisfaction. Officership, in short, is an exclusive role, incompatible with any other significant social or political roles."[27] The impact of this professionalism on military attitudes toward politics is that "civilian control is thus achieved not because the military groups share in the social values and political ideologies of society, but because they are indifferent to such values and ideologies."[28] Politicians can contribute to civilian control by "professionalizing the military" and by thus "confining it to a restricted sphere and rendering it politically sterile and neutral on all issues outside that sphere."[29]

I call the professionalism Huntington alludes to, the "old professionalism of external defense" and concur that the nature of military professionalism is of cardinal importance. However, it is my contention that the "new professionalism of internal security and national development" that is dominant in such countries as Peru, Brazil, and Indonesia (and by no means absent even in developed countries such as France and the United States during times of internal stress) is very different from "old professionalism" in its content and consequences.[30] By the early 1960s the military in these countries assumed that the major focus of professionalism should be the nexus between internal security and development. This focus led to an expansion of military professional education to include subjects such as economic planning and the identification of obstacles to development and internal security. In a political context where the military conclude that civilian leaders cannot carry out the development policies they deem necessary for internal security, the new professionalism

[26] Samuel Huntington, "Civilian Control of the Military: A Theoretical Statement," in *Political Behavior: A Reader in Theory and Research*, ed. H. Eulau, S. Eldersveld, and M. Janowitz, pp. 380-81.

[27] Ibid., p. 381.   [28] Ibid.

[29] *The Soldier and the State*, p. 84; "Civilian Control of the Military . . . ," p. 381.

[30] For the limitations of "old professionalism" in the context of the United States in the late 1960s see Bruce M. Russett and Alfred Stepan, "The Military in America: New Parameters, New Problems, New Approaches" in *Military Force and American Society*, ed. Russett and Stepan, pp. 3-14.

129

contributes to a military role expansion that, in some circumstances, lead to seizure of power and the use of the state apparatus to impose a policy of internal security and national development.[31] The contrast between these two "paradigms" of military professionalism is shown in Table 4.1:

TABLE 4.1[a]

CONTRASTING PARADIGMS: THE OLD PROFESSIONALISM OF EXTERNAL DEFENSE
THE NEW PROFESSIONALISM OF INTERNAL SECURITY AND NATIONAL DEVELOPMENT

	Old Professionalism	*New Professionalism*
Dominant function of military	External security	Primarily internal security
Military skills required	Highly specialized skills incompatible with political skills	Highly interrelated political and military skills
Scope of military professional action	Restricted	Unrestricted
Impact of professional socialization	Renders the military politically neutral	Politicizes the military
Impact on civil-military relations	Contributes to an apolitical military and civilian control	Contributes to military political managerialism and role-expansion

[a] Reproduced with permission of Yale University Press from Stepan, "The New Professionalism of Internal Warfare and Military Role Expansion," p. 52.

To what extent did "new professionalism" exist in Peru before the military assumed power in 1968? In 1954 the General Staff School founded a new journal, *Revista de la Escuela Superior de Guerra*. I decided to code all the articles appearing in this journal from its founding up through 1967, the year before the formation of the new military regime. I was fortunate to be able to interest an independent scholar in the classification effort.[32] To a degree

[31] The above argument on old and new professionalism is developed in greater detail in my "The New Professionalism of Internal Warfare and Military Role Expansion," pp. 47-65.

[32] My colleague in this content analysis was Jorge Rodríguez, who at the time was engaged in research on the Peruvian military for his doctoral dissertation at the University of York, England. He will also discuss the results of our content analysis in his dissertation. The general methodology we used is discussed in greater detail in Clarence L. Abercrombie III and Major Raoul

130

this provided an "intercoder reliability check." After a discussion of possible categories and a pretest on some issues of the *Revista Militar del Perú* we agreed on six all-inclusive categories (see Table 4.2).[33]

Upon completion of our independent classification, we had both classified 363 of the 405 articles in identical categories. In the language of content analysis the "co-efficient of intercoder reliability" was 89.6 percent, which allows a reasonably high confidence level in the results.

If we eliminate categories V and VI, which refer to general culture articles and which were much smaller than we expected, we eliminate 9 articles, or only 2 percent of the total. The universe of articles then becomes 396. By combining categories III and IV ("Internal War and Engineering Social Change" and "Sociopolitical Analysis"), we obtain the composite category of "New Professionalism of Internal Security and National Development."

Figure 4.1 shows how "new professional" articles increased from only 1.7 percent in 1954-1957 (before the Algerian war, Cuban revolution, U.S. export of counterinsurgency programs, and major peasant land invasions in Peru) to over 50 percent in 1963-1967, immediately before the military seized power and began using the state apparatus to restructure Peruvian society. The questions of internal war and sociopolitical analysis had clearly become a major concern of the Peruvian military well before it seized power in 1968.[34]

Let us turn now to the specific content of the articles and related material. What does it say about the hypothesis that inclusionary attempts follow the perception by a strategic elite that

---

H. Alcalá, U.S. Army, "The New Military Professionalism" in *Military Force and American Society*, Russett and Stepan, pp. 34-58.

[33] We decided to include all content articles, national and foreign, and exclude editorials, news sections, and short notes.

[34] A significant interest remained in classic professional topics as would be anticipated in a military institution that sees a lightning conventional war with Chile, and to a lesser extent with Ecuador, as a persistent possibility. This comment represents a change in emphasis from my original "new professional" article. In that article I neglected to stress that a military organization always retains its external concerns and that the internal security emphasis itself has important implications for the military's ability to carry out its external defense missions.

TABLE 4.2

I. *Classic Military Professionalism*
   Use of weapons, military technology, military organization. Discussion of traditional military values (discipline, leadership, patriotism). Traditional geopolitics not related with internal problems. External war and essentially military aspects of strategy and tactics. Note: When the tactics of guerrilla warfare are discussed without reference to wider social issues they are classified in this category as is psychological warfare when the target is an external enemy.

II. *History of Classical Military Professionalism*
   Biographies of military heroes. Discussions of non-contemporary, non-national military conflicts or other aspects of foreign military history. Discussions of Peruvian military conflicts or other aspects of Peruvian military history (pre-Colonial, Colonial and Republican). Note: The articles in this category must respond to a "classic" viewpoint as defined in Category I. If an article on the Algerian war written in the late fifties emphasizes the social aspects of internal war it should be classified in category III.

III. *Internal War and Engineering Social Change*
   Guerrillas, civil disorders and other forms of violent political action and their linkage with ideologies, parties, and the social structure of the country. Military and social tactics for preventing or opposing such violence, such as agrarian reform, national integration, civil-action, psychological warfare, etc. Also included are articles that stress that the content of classic military professionalism should be transformed due to new forms of warfare (irregular), and their nexus with social structure, and those which argue for an important role for the military (as managers or instruments) in social change.

IV. *Sociopolitico Analysis*
   Articles concerned with different aspects of national and international development (political, social or economic) from a social science perspective in which the central concern does not appear to be military. Articles on planning techniques, the protection and development of national resources and discussions. Articles on social psychology and the management of public opinion that are not explicitly concerned with internal war. Articles that relate the armed forces to society from a wide perspective without having as a central concern internal war.

V. *Non-Military Scientific or Technical Subjects*
   Discussions of scientific or technical matters which make no clear attempt to relate these matters directly to military affairs.

VI. *General Knowledge*
   Articles aimed at providing information on general topics which are neither of a scientific/technical nor socio-political nature. For example, an article on horseback riding is placed here.

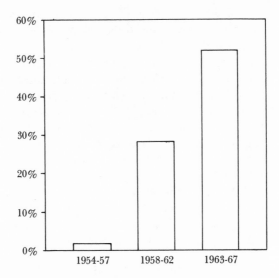

FIGURE 4.1. Growth of "new professional" articles as percentage of coded articles in *Revista de la Escuela Superior de Guerra* 1954-1957, 1958-1962, 1963-1967.

the old system is entering a stage of dangerous disequilibrium and that stability requires both structural and symbolic changes and an effort to integrate the most salient lower-class groups into new economic and political structures?

The evidence is strong that the army elite perceived the country to be in a severe crisis.[35] The first article, published in 1960, to raise the theme of growing crisis was written by a young lieutenant-colonel recently returned from military schooling in France.[36] He argued that the communist revolutionary strategy represented a new form of warfare; that such revolutionary warfare had already started in Peru; and that the old military tactics were irrelevant for the new challenge. He also stressed that the open-

[35] I discuss the growing army perception of crisis in "The New Professionalism of Internal Warfare and Military Role Expansion," pp. 47-68, and in Einaudi and Stepan, *Latin American Institutional Development: Changing Military Perspectives in Peru and Brazil,* see esp. pp. 21-31. This theme is also discussed in Victor Villanueva. *¿Nueva mentalidad militar en el Perú?* Julio Cotler, "Crises política y populismo militar" in *Perú: hoy,* José Matos Mar et al., pp. 86-104; and François Bourricaud, "Los militares: por qué y para qué?" in *Fuerzas Armadas, poder y cambio,* Luis Mercier Vega et al., pp. 101-171.

[36] He had attended the General Staff School of the French army.

133

ness of workers and campesinos to communist appeals was directly related to their living standards.[37] By 1964 the General Staff School, after a study of strikes, land invasions, and the proliferation of revolutionary parties, concluded in a lesson plan that "we now are in the stage of revolutionary war." Even after a guerrilla campaign was defeated by the army in 1965 the official army report emphasized that Peru remained in a state of "latent insurgency."[38] In an important article published in 1967, General Edgardo Mercado Jarrín listed a series of structural problems in Peru (such as great income inequality and explosive land tenure problems), that he believed contributed to the dangerous disequilibrium of the country. He argued that the guerrillas would reappear unless reforms and structural charges were accelerated.[39]

In numerous interviews—and during informal conversations with Peruvian officers in my four field trips since 1972—a theme

[37] Lt. Colonel Enrique Gallegos Venero, "¿Debe preocuparnos la guerra subversiva?" *Revista de la Escuela Superior de Guerra* 7 (January-March 1960): 18-20. In 1957 General Romero Pardo, the Director of CAEM, went to Algeria to observe the counter-guerrilla campaign. Upon his return he gave a number of lectures at CAEM, "Charlas sobre Argelia" (January 2nd and 3rd, 1958) that stressed the importance of the social and political aspects of revolutionary warfare and the necessity for fusion of civil and military powers in the army struggle against subversion.

[38] Perú, Ministerio da Guerra, *Las guerrillas en el Perú y su repressión* (Lima: 1966), p. 80.

[39] General Edgardo Mercado Jarrín, "La política y la estrategia militar en la guerra contrasubversiva en la América Latina," *Revista Militar del Perú,* no. 701 (1967), pp. 4-33, esp. p. 17. Until his retirement in 1975 General Jarrín held central positions within the military government including foreign minister, minister of war, and prime minister. Mercado's theme—that the political and structural issues are more important in revolutionary warfare than purely military issues—was frequently sounded in the journals. For example, a lieutenant colonel recently back from attendance at the French General Staff School criticized the first phase of French strategy in Algeria for paying attention only to repression and neglecting socioeconomic action. See Lt. Col. Miguel de la Flor Valle, "La guerra en Argelia," *Revista de la Escuela Superior de Guerra* 9 (October-December 1962): 19-44. Like Mercado Jarrín, he became a ranking general and important cabinet minister under the military government. The Peruvian military's emphasis on structural change contributed to their skepticism about U.S. strategy in Vietnam. In this context it is significant that as early as 1967 the *Revista Militar del Perú* devoted space to translating three long articles by Moshé Dayán in which he concluded that the United States would never be able to win in Vietnam because they offered no alternative plan of fundamental socioeconomic change.

emerged explicitly that is only implicit in the articles. The army supported the candidacy of Belaúnde in 1963 because it saw him as the last hope to bring about changes democratically. By the mid 1960s, however, the army felt that party conflicts and the internal and external influences stemming from Peru's economic dependency had eroded the possibility of parliamentary-induced structural change. The military's own studies at CAEM, and in its intelligence schools, indicated that more peasant and guerrilla insurrections would inevitably (and a number of officers stressed "justifiably" and "necessarily") develop. From my interviews it is clear that the military's newly expanded intelligence services had penetrated what they analyzed as complex networks between external capital and domestic elites that produced a dependent political system unable and unwilling to carry out structural changes and more nationalist policies.[40] The intelligence services evidently assumed a more radical position than that expressed in the official journals. A faculty member who taught at CAEM before and after the guerrilla campaign observed:

> the effect of the guerrillas on the military was great but more on the intelligence services than on CAEM. The intelligence services argued intensely for the need for quick structural change. . . . The intelligence services are better organized than CAEM and their studies more continuous and better researched. The greatest part of the officers who made the Revolution were from the intelligence services, not CAEM.[41]

The intelligence services' concrete studies of the guerrilla groups on the one hand and the "dependencia networks" on the other made them especially sensitive to the need for change, and to the structures impeding such change. The specific institutional dilemma this presented for the army was that, should no structural reforms be undertaken, the military would have to continue acting as the "watchdog" of the oligarchy by repressing demands for change because there would inevitably be other revo-

---

[40] The process by which the Peruvian military linked their "internal security" studies with the "dependencia" critique of conventional development strategies is crucial to understanding why, in Phase I, they attempted to construct more nationalist policies than any previous inclusionary experiment. This theme receives special attention in Chapter 7.

[41] Interview, Fall 1972, Lima.

lutionary movements it would have to put down.[42] Some officers also implied that, should a revolution be successful, the military, as the coercive force of the oligarchy, could suffer institutional dissolution and even the firing squad. Such had been the fate of the Cuban regular army. What was the way out of the dilemma? To seize power and to use the power of the state to impose change and eliminate the structural disequilibrium impeding Peru's internal stability and national power.

Thus, in a context of growing systemic pressures in Peru, the "new professionalism" helped contribute to the emergence of a strategic elite that (1) perceived that its corporate survival required fundamental changes to be made in Peru's social, economic and political structures, (2) concluded that the traditional political system could not make these fundamental changes, (3) had developed within its own schooling and intelligence systems an alternative program of structural change and societal development, (4) was confident that these same schooling and intelligence systems had formed the necessary military cadres to implement their program, and (5) believed that it, and only it had the power to impose the program.

By 1968, therefore, the stage was set for a major effort by a strategic elite to install a new regime. The specific programs of this strategic elite, namely the new professional army, however, needs further examination.

PROGRAMMATIC CONSENSUS: CONTENT AND LIMITS

In Chapter 3 I argued that the greater the strategic state elite's prior doctrinal consensus about the general need for, and the specific content of, inclusionary policies, the greater its internal unity and therefore capacity to impose its design. Note; I am not assuming that the state elite is ever a "unitary actor." However, the newly ascendent "bureaucratic politics" approach so emphasizes the lack of ideological or programmatic unity within bureaucracies that it is extremely important to make empirically

[42] In numerous speeches after taking power, the military admitted that they had played the role of sustaining the oligarchy in the past. See for example a revealing interview with General Graham Hurtado in *Granma* (Havana) (September 17, 1972), p. 2. Also see the first authorized account of the origins of the "revolution" which says that the officer corps was "fed up with playing this role," Zimmerman, *El Plan Inca*, p. 57.

grounded assessments of the degree to which programmatic unity exists within any given state elite and to identify the limits of this consensus.[43]

There is considerable evidence that, in the case of the Peruvian army, a core programmatic consensus indeed existed before the army assumed power, and that this consensus provided a source of policy direction and internal cohesion in the first years of the military government. At the same time, several key political issues were omitted from the consensus, and a study of these issues provides important insights into the sources of the policy conflicts that emerged toward the end of Phase I, and into the policy reversals of Phase II.

The structural issue on which the most solid consensus existed was the need for agrarian reform. This was closely linked to attacks on the oligarchy. One of the strongest and clearest formulations of military thinking on the issue was contained in a report on peasant mobilization. In 1962 in response to a massive peasant movement in La Convención Valley, the military government of 1962-1963 made Lieutenant-Colonel Gallegos the "Coordinator-General of the Socio-Economic Activities of La Convención and Lares." A later article written by Gallegos neatly captured the military's perceptions of the dangers presented by the old system and the prospects for successful restructuring by the military.[44] Because La Convención became a powerful symbol for the military, and the young colonel became one of the leaders of Phase I six years later, I will discuss the report at some length.[45]

The report presents the traditional order in La Convención as one in which the peasants live in "subhuman conditions on numerous haciendas." Gallegos deplores the "exploitation suffered by the campesinos due to the medieval conditions of work" and

[43] Some leading examples of the bureaucratic politics approach are Graham Allison, *Essence of Decision: Exploring the Cuban Missile Crisis* (Boston: Little, Brown, 1971), Morton Halperin, *Bureaucratic Politics and Foreign Policy* (Washington: The Brookings Institution, 1974), and Abraham F. Lowenthal, "United States Policy Toward Latin America: 'Liberal,' 'Radical,' and 'Bureaucratic' Perspectives," *Latin American Research Review* 8 (Fall 1973); pp. 3-25.

[44] Without belaboring the point, it is obvious that the picture he presents is much more conducive to an inclusionary than an exclusionary policy response.

[45] Lieutenant Colonel Enrique Gallegos Venero, "Un combate victorioso en guerra contrarevolucionaria," *Revista de la Escuela Superior de Guerra* 10 (July-September 1963): 7-26.

the fact that the campesinos receive almost no aid from the state authorities, who "in many cases are in the service of the large hacendados." He then focuses on the opportunity such conditions give communist organizers. The conditions are "ideal for exploitation . . . a hate accumulating for centuries is agitated by specialists." When he arrived at La Convención, police posts were being attacked, haciendas invaded, and the campesinos had been grouped into powerful organizations by "red lawyers" and were demanding land and other reforms. The military's response was twofold: a wave of repression against the leaders and the inauguration of an active program to convince the campesinos the military would introduce systematic reforms. A special agrarian reform measure for the area was passed despite "pressure from the hacienda owners of all the country." Gallegos affirms that, once the campesinos saw the military were sincere about introducing structural changes, their allegiance shifted dramatically in favor of the military reformers. A campesino rally was held, and "the masses were delirious with happiness, their discipline perfect, and their faith great." Gallegos argues that as the agrarian reform went forward the military would "have the glory of having removed, in support of democracy, one of the oldest structures which, like walls, impeded the progress of the country." He ends his article by arguing that "the only way to attract the population is demonstrating that democracy is capable of giving them social justice, equality of rights, equality of treatment, equality of opportunities, the power to attain a human level of life and in addition to all this to be able to think freely, to argue and act independently."

Other articles in military journals joined in this advocacy of agrarian reform. The Peruvian officers were particularly interested in Bolivia, and they published an article by two Bolivian officers detailing the social gains brought about by that country's agrarian reform.[46] The year before the Peruvian military assumed power, General Mercado Jarrín asserted that the weakness of the guerrilla revolutionary attempt in Bolivia was largely due to the fact that

> Boliva was the only country in South America which by means of agrarian reform, in spite of its problems, has transformed

[46] "La reforma agraria en Bolivia," *Revista de la Escuela Superior de Guerra*, Vol. 11 (January-May 1964), pp. 99-116.

138

the land tenure pattern. A great part of the Bolivian peasantry owns the land they work. Communism has very little or almost nothing to offer them, consequently the guerrillas could not count, and will not be able to count in the future, on popular support.[47]

He argued that the same phenomena held true in the 1965 Peruvian guerrilla movement in La Convención. Significantly he underscored that accelerated agrarian reform was necessary but that the strong opposition of special economic and political interests was sabotaging the reform. The first popular authorized account of the organization of the revolutionary military movement stressed that the 1965 counter-guerrilla campaign had "wounded the rebellious heart" of Colonel Gallegos and that much of the army was "fed up" with playing the role of protecting the oligarchy against the legitimate demands of the masses.[48]

The evidence is very strong, then, that the army had arrived at a consensus to promote agrarian reform and to cease protecting the rural oligarchy.

The second area of programmatic consensus concerned nationalism and in particular the need to nationalize the International Petroleum Company (IPC). As far back as 1959 the commandant of CAEM had been the president of a civil-military group that urged the restoration of IPC to Peru[49] and in 1960 the Joint Staff, over the signature of the commanding general of the army, asserted that the existing agreements with IPC were "harmful to national sovereignty."[50] Articles on the protection of raw materials occurred less frequently, but as early as 1961-1962 three general articles about mineral deposits were printed. The last article concluded that: "The strategy of the large industrial states is thus to conserve their mineral resources while exploiting those

[47] "La política y la estrategia militar . . . ," p. 11. Earlier articles in this vein were by Capitan Lizandro Mejía Zagastizábal "Acción cívica en el campo laboral," *Revista Militar del Perú*, no. 680 (January-February 1964), pp. 100-115, and Coronel Oscar Cebreros Rueda, "Algunos aspectos del problema agropecuario en el Perú," *Revista Militar del Perú*, no. 681 (May-April 1964), pp. 80-86.

[48] Zimmerman, *El Plan Inca*, pp. 46, 57.

[49] Approved typescript of an interview with General Marcial Romero Pardo by Jorge Rodríguez (Lima; March 13, 1972).

[50] See Einaudi and Stepan, *Latin American Institutional Development: Changing Military Perspectives in Peru and Brazil*, p. 30.

of the underdeveloped countries . . . National companies extract 8.4%, and foreign companies . . . 91.6%. . . . In mining Peru has not yet gone beyond the stage of economic colonialism."[51] And in the year before the revolution an intelligence officer argued that "the mobilization of energy resources in our country has neither followed lines of adequate planning nor has it been carried out in accordance with the national defense strategy."[52]

Other policy themes that emerged were the need to strengthen the planning powers of the state and the role of the state in mediating conflicts between capital and labor. From the military perspective, numerous articles emphasized that the military must greatly increase its domestic intelligence capacity and domestic public opinion-shaping capacity because these are major arms in the struggle for internal security.[53]

A final area where one is tempted to say a consensus had emerged concerns the new role definition of the military. Over half the articles in the four-year period before the military assumed power were "new professional" in orientation. An underlying theme of these articles was that the military should play an expanded role in the reorganization of the state apparatus and that the state apparatus should play a more pervasive mana-

[51] "Derecho de mineria," *Revista Militar del Perú*, no. 667 (November-December 1961), pp. 95-104. A strong defense of the 200-mile claim as being necessary to protect sea resources was "Sobre nuestro mar territorial," *Revista Militar del Perú*, no. 669 (March-April 1962), pp. 17-31.

[52] Coronel de Inteligencia, Alejandro Rivas Gago, "Primer foro nacional de la energía," *Revista Militar del Perú*, no. 690 (January-February, 1966), pp. 53-54.

[53] There are too many articles to cite. However, for a detailed discussion of the need for intelligence officers of large military units to collect intelligence on any potential labor disputes, peasant movements and urban disorders see Colonel Enrique Gallegos Venero, "Inteligencia y guerra no convencional," *Revista de la Escuela Superior de Guerra* 13 (July-September 1966), pp. 7-18. For characteristic articles discussing the necessity for greater state planning see "La planificación del desarrollo," *Revista de la Escuela Superior de Guerra* 12 (July-September 1965), pp. 61-83, and "El Estado en la planificación," in volume 10 of the same journal. For the argument that the state must play a greater role in labor-management conflicts see the article written by a captain who is described as an "expert in industrial relations," "Conflictos laborales: causas y medidas de prevención," *Revista Militar del Perú*, no. 603 (July-August 1964), pp. 67-79. For the need for the military to create tools to affect public opinion see "La información pública: 'nueva herramienta del ejército,'" *Revista de la Escuela Superior de Guerra* 7 (July-September 1960), pp. 46-53.

gerial role in civil society in the attempt to restructure the development process so that it contributes to internal security and national strength.[54] The cautionary note that should be sounded is that nearly half the articles were not new professional. The two are not necessarily in tension. If the military as a corporate institution perceives the most severe threat to be internal (as it did in the 1965-1972 period), the new professional orientation can be institutionally compelling even to an old professional officer previously oriented toward external security missions. However, if external threats loom, and if some of the specific policies the new professionals are pursuing are perceived by the old professionals as exacerbating external threats, the internal military consensus over the correct mission will be subject to erosive pressures.[55]

What themes are relatively absent from this literature? On the basis of the published articles, what seem to be issues about which no consensus was established? Did Phase I policies conform to, or go beyond, the prior consensus?

Given the policies the regime later proclaimed, the most striking omission was any discussion of political participation. There were frequent expressions of worry about the fact that the mass of people was not integrated into the political system, and to military men this low identification with the nation-state was cause for alarm.[56] There was also a series of articles favorable to

---

[54] The clearest statements of this shift are contained in the writings of Edgardo Mercado Jarrín. See "El ejército de hoy y su proyección en nuestra sociedad en período de transición," *Revista Militar del Perú*, no. 685 (November-December 1964), pp. 1-20; "La política y la estrategia militar . . . ."; and his essays brought together in Perú, Ministerio de Guerra, Biblioteca Militar del Oficial No. 38, *Ensayos por Edgardo Mercado Jarrín: Primer Ministro, Ministro de Guerra y Commandate General del Ejército* (Lima: 1974). Other officers also participated in the role re-definition; see for example. Lt. Colonel Carlos Bobbio Centurión, "¿Que ejército necesita el Perú?" *Revista Militar del Perú*, no. 675 (March-April 1963), pp. 132-136.

[55] As we shall see in the concluding chapter, such pressures began to build after the fall of Allende contributed to a more threatening external geopolitical situation for the Peruvian military.

[56] A number of officers argued that, unless the social strata from which enlisted men were recruited received some benefits from the nation-state, the enlisted men would make unreliable soldiers against a guerrilla force promising structural changes. See for example Major Agustín León Zeña, "La infantería en la guerra revolucionaria," *Revista Militar del Perú* (March-April 1963). This is an extension of a more general Peruvian army

141

the general idea of cooperatives and even collective modes of agricultural production following agrarian reform.[57]

But while a major theme of the articles was the endorsement of state policies that could integrate the population, a theme consistent with the philosophy of organic statism and the characteristic structures of inclusionary policies, no article addressed systematically the question of active national political participation. From mid-1971 on, the articulation of new theories of participation and the creation of SINAMOS became a major concern of the core group of Phase I officers. Virtually none of this participation program is prefigured in the pre-1968 articles. The final two years of Phase I saw an increasing debate in the country and within the military about the role of SINAMOS, and in Phase II its role has been reduced significantly.

What of the question of capitalism and the preferred economic model? Here the record is more difficult to interpret. At the philosophical level, the goals of greater state direction and greater worker involvement in the enterprise were affirmed, but organizational recommendations about the shape of the economy were vague. There was always, of course, a sharp rejection of communism and Marxism. While capitalism was not attacked systematically, nowhere was it defended as an economic or moral system, and there were frequent attacks on liberalism, which was seen as the philosophy of capitalism. The defects of liberalism were often cited as being conducive to the emergence of Marxist revolution.[58] Philosophically, many of the articles fell almost per-

---

preoccupation that the state was militarily weakened by the fact that much of the population was not integrated. Indirectly this military concern for integration later became a source of support for both the structural reforms that gave the Peruvian masses "something to defend" and for the concept of organized participation in functional groups.

[57] Almost all the initial organizational principles of post-1968 policy for cooperatives are found for example in Lt. Colonel Víctor M. Escudero, "El movimiento cooperativista," *Revista Militar del Perú* (September-October 1964). Collective production for indigenous communities and much of sierra agriculture is endorsed in the previously cited "Augunos aspectos del problema agropecuario en el Perú," p. 80 and in "Las comunidades indígenas en el Perú: el ayllu o comunidad en la República," *Revista Militar del Perú*, no. 693 (July-August 1966), pp. 5-6.

[58] This is the main thesis for example of "La revolución: fin ultimo del Liberalismo y Marxismo," *Revista Militar del Perú*, no. 677 (July-August 1963) esp. p. 89. Another article argued that "the cupidity and social in-

fectly into a modern version of the normative tradition I called "organic-statist" in Chapter 1. For example, in 1963 three articles by a French economist, based on lectures he gave at the Escuela Superior de Guerra, were replete with classic organic-statist arguments. Liberalism and capitalism were attacked for engendering the "free manifestation of interests and the egoism of the individual without any discipline and without any restraint."[59] In the context of developing countries, this was seen as contributing to a "state of inconceivable misery of the masses." The "concepts of capitalism . . . are the principal cause of the expansion of communism." Finally there was the call for the state to act in the general interest because its "intervention has become more and more necessary."[60]

This fairly general military discontent with traditional liberal capitalism, linked with specific programmatic consensus over the expropriation of IPC, provided a broad institutional base for the new regime to use foreign policy as an instrument in its attempt to forge a more nationalist, less dependent and more statist economic model. However, the policy vagueness and the cold war anticommunism characteristic of the articles did not provide a very firm doctrinal consensus for the aggressive and innovative pro-Third World, anti-*dependencia*, economic foreign policy that became a hallmark of Phase I.

What can we conclude from this analysis of the published articles? First the two major and critical reforms of the Revolutionary Military Government, the expropriation of IPC, and the agrarian reform, had solid prior doctrinal endorsement within the army. Second, a reasonably strong doctrinal consensus had developed for a much more active role for the state in restructuring economic and social systems.[61] Since these were the major

---

sensitivity of capitalism created . . . communism," "Introducción al estudio de la guerra revolucionaria," *Revista Militar del Perú*, no. 663 (March-April 1961), p. 132.

[59] The attacks on "egoism" and "interests" were a major feature of post-1968 military rhetoric.

[60] These articles were written by Phillipe Guignabaudet, see in particular his "Concepción de una economia racional," *Revista de la Escuela Superior de Guerra* (October-December 1963). These articles are also quite consistent with the frequent utterances of the Revolutionary Government of the Armed Forces that it is "neither communist nor capitalist."

[61] However the state was never accorded the all-consuming role it is given

policy initiatives of the government in its first three years, we can say that the installation attempt began with an institutionally based "core programmatic consensus."

However, two of the major policy questions that dominated the 1972-1975 period—the nature of participation and the nature, structure, and foreign policy position of a political-economic system that was "neither communist nor capitalist"—were issues that went beyond the most widely disseminated doctrines in the army.[62]

AN EVALUATION OF THE CONDITIONS FOR AN INCLUSIONARY ATTEMPT

Since what transpired after October 1968 was clearly a major attempt to install a new pattern of state-society relations, let us examine the initial conditions in Peru in light of the five hypotheses advanced in Chapter 3. To what extent were conditions in Peru in 1968 supportive of, or resistant to, the installation of a regime based on inclusionary policies? How did conditions in Peru for installation—and less rigorously, for hegemonic consolidation—compare with those for Mexico, Argentina, Brazil and Chile?

---

in fascist ideology. I argued in Chapter 1 that in the modern version of organic statism the state is given a major role in shaping society but that this is limited by the "principle of subsidiarity." Interestingly, one article published just before the military assumed power argued for the state to play a greater role in society but cautioned that "this state intervention that foments, stimulates, organizes, protects and completes [society] rests upon the *Principle of Subsidiarity* that Pope Pius XI established in the encyclical Quadragesimo Anno," *Revista Militar del Perú*, no. 705 (July-August 1968), p. 88 (emphasis in the original).

[62] This judgment is reinforced by an interview with a civilian professor who had taught at CAEM since 1959. In answer to my questions about how much of the military's program had been formulated at CAEM before the revolution, he replied, "the period of programmed changes with a link to prior military ideology has now [1972] been reached." Interview with Jorge Bravo Bresani, Lima, June 22, 1972. Later in this chapter I discuss the very real possibility that the intelligence service had a more fully articulated program than that revealed in the military journals. The fact remains, however, that such programs were not fully aired within the officer corps as a whole and are thus beyond what I would call a "programmatic consensus" within the army as an institution. On this general point, see the balanced argument by Lowenthal, "Peru's Ambiguous Revolution," in *The Peruvian Experiment*, pp. 21-36, esp. p. 36.

State Elite's Organizational Strength and Ideological Unity

The discussion of the Peruvian army (the strategic state elite) showed that, for over a decade before they assumed power, they had evolved a core programmatic consensus on the necessity of structural reforms. This commitment to reform was further strengthened by being grounded in a strong institutional perception that (1) the reforms were necessary for the military's own self-preservation, and (2) that the military had to assume control of the state apparatus in order to ensure that these changes were made.

In terms of the variable of elite unity and organizational strength, the Peruvian inauguration attempt thus began in conditions that were at least moderately favorable to the use of inclusionary policies.

However, the tone, and by 1972 the substance, of the government's policies went beyond the programmatic consensus arrived at in CAEM and implicitly formulated in the articles in the military journals prior to 1968. Some of the new policies undoubtedly emerged partly as a response to new pressures and opportunities once in power and partly as a response to the suggestions of civilian allies. However, another possible source of ideas about how to reorganize much of the population into new units of representation and control, and new patterns of property ownership, was the military's intelligence services. In the first authorized account of the origins of the military revolution, four colonels— Leonidas Rodríguez Figueroa, Enrique Gallegos Venero, Jorge Fernández Maldonado, and Rafael Hoyos Rubio—are specifically listed as having been recruited by General Velasco both to help organize the military movement and to draft the long-term plan of the government. One thing is certain about the plan—it went well beyond the programmatic consensus contained in the journal articles.[63]

Although CAEM is frequently credited as having been the source of the ideas of the revolution, and undoubtedly did play an important role in creating the general philosophy and the institutional consensus about this philosophy, none of these four key colonels of Phase I was a graduate of CAEM.[64] All, however,

[63] Zimmermann, *El Plan Inca*, p. 41. The origins of the plan, "Plan Inca," are discussed in the book. However, the plan, though bearing the date October 3, 1968, was not published until July 1974.

[64] The full list of military and civilian graduates of CAEM from the

had strong connections with army intelligence, and all by 1975 had been promoted to the highest general rank, held key political or security posts, and were judged by close observers—together with General Graham Hurtado—to have constituted the core of the radical officers within the army in Phase I. At the time of the overthrow of Belaúnde, Gallegos was chief of the Army Intelligence Service and Rodríguez Figueroa was the sub-director.[65] Hoyos in 1974 was director of the National Intelligence Service and therefore undoubtedly had been formally trained in intelligence. Fernández Maldonado had been chief of the Army Intelligence Service and before that a professor at Army Intelligence School.[66]

In addition, one of the key generals in the group of nine organizers of the seizure of power in 1968, Mercado Jarrín, helped found the Army Intelligence School in the early 1960s.[67] It is likewise striking that in my content analysis of articles, I found that those articles signed by officers who identified themselves as members of the intelligence service tended to be much more specific in detail and sweeping in their recommendations for changes.[68]

My point is that much of the group that emerged as the most radical group within the army in Phase I had a career experience, the very nature of which kept them somewhat apart from the rest of the institution. Thus while the institutional unity of the military could be judged to have been reasonably high, there were from the beginning differences in orientation as to how far

first class of 1951 to 1971 is presented in Document 12 of Víctor Villanueva, *El CAEM y la revolución de la Fuerza Armada*, pp. 220-227.

[65] Zimmermann, *El Plan Inca*, p. 36. Many details of Gallegos's military career up to 1964 are contained as an editorial note to his previously cited article "Un combate victorioso en guerra contrarevolucionaria," p. 8.

[66] Details of the military careers of all ministers in 1973 including General Fernández Maldonado are contained in *5 años de revolución* (Lima: Propersa, 1973), no pagination. General Graham Hurtado had links both with CAEM, where he was a faculty member, and with intelligence, having served as the G-2 of the most powerful army division, the "División Blindado" headquartered near Lima. For most of Phase I Graham Hurtado headed the crucial Council of Presidential Advisors (COAP). For biographical details see *5 años de revolución*.

[67] Interview with Mercado Jarrín on October 10, 1974, Lima. At the time of the interview he was minister of war and prime minister.

[68] The best example of this is Gallegos's article.

and fast to push structural changes. Therefore, despite initial programmatic consensus, I score elite unity only "moderately favorable," not "very favorable." However, ideological differences
within the army were less important in the installation period
of the regime (1968-1972) than in the consolidation phase that
began around 1973. In this latter phase (especially in 1975-
1976), crucial debates about the exact nature of participation
and the structure of an economy that was "neither communist
nor capitalist," issues that had not been dealt with in the military journals before 1968, became the central policy questions
facing the regime.[69]

Degree of Development of Autonomous Political Parties and Interest Groups

Concerning this variable, a complex combination of "moderately unfavorable" and "moderately favorable" conditions for an
inclusionary attempt faced the military government when it assumed power. The net value of these conditions could be termed
at most "neutral" for installation, but, taken as a whole, the
conditions for hegemonic consolidation over the long run were
"moderately unfavorable."

The major mass party in Peru is APRA. In the late 1920s and
1930s, APRA had a strongly reformist, anti-imperialist platform
and highly disciplined mass cadres. Since World War II, the
leader of APRA, Haya de la Torre, steadily softened his anti-
imperialist international position, and between 1956 and 1968 the
party, in return for expected favors, entered into a series of coalitions with conservative political parties. This change in APRA's
position led it to lobby against an agrarian reform bill that would
affect the coastal sugar palntations, and not to take a militant
position on the expropriation of IPC. For these reasons, APRA
suffered a progressive erosion of its support, especially among
younger activists.[70] In the installation period, 1968-1972, the military implemented many of the original Aprista programs, and
active APRA opposition to the military was muted.

However, for the long-run task of hegemonic consolidation,
APRA presented problems of a sort not faced in Mexico, where

[69] The demise in Phase II of the core group of Phase I radical army
officers is discussed in the concluding chapter.

[70] For this phase of APRA see Carlos A. Astiz, *Pressure Groups and Power
Elites in Peruvian Politics*, pp. 94-111.

147

Cárdenas did not have to cope with the continued existence of a powerful, prerevolutionary, mass-based party. Although the military adopted much of APRA's program, they remain hostile to the idea of APRA as a party organization. The fact that APRA's cadres and organizations, though reduced, remain intact and ideologically committed to APRA, with a bitter historical memory of conflict with the army, means that APRA's members are, to a significant extent, "unavailable" for enthusiastic (as opposed to merely mechanical) incorporation into the new inclusionary structures created in Peru.[71] In this particular area, therefore, institutional space for inclusionary structures was reduced.[72] The Peruvian strategic elite faced a constraint that Cárdenas in Mexico did not. This constraint was not too important in the installation phase because the government was carrying out many historic APRA policies. However it remains a major obstacle to the consolidation of the regime because such consolidation would threaten the existence of APRA as a political party.[73]

In the crucial area of national labor organizations, the initial power of APRA's trade union confederation, CTP (Confederación de Trabajadores del Perú), complicated the task of organization for the new government. In order to create a countervailing power to APRA in the trade union sector, the military government granted official recognition and valuable support to a national Communist party trade union confederation CGTP (Confederación General de Trabajadores del Perú). The CGTP and the Communist party in return gave the new government much needed support in the installation period. But by the time the government was ready to launch its own labor confederation, the CGTP had consolidated its position. The official confederation thus found much of the organizational space filled. Here the Mexican state during the Cárdenas period encountered fewer obstacles to its reorganization of labor than did the Peruvian state.

The rest of the political arena, however, presented favorable conditions for the installation attempt in Peru. The other major

71 For a discussion of the historic conflict between the army and APRA see Liisa North, *Civil-Military Relations in Argentina, Chile, and Peru.*

72 The ambivalent participation of APRA-organized sugar workers in the new sugar cooperatives, despite the fact that they are the major beneficiaries, is discussed in Chapter 6.

73 Again and again the military has insisted that being a militant within the revolution is incompatible with membership in any political party.

electoral party was the personalist reform party, Acción Popular, centered on Fernando Belaúnde. Belaúnde had created the party in 1956 as a personal vehicle, and the party was never characterized either by strong organization or by the strong ideological commitment of its followers. In fact, before the military assumed power, the more progressive wing of the Acción Popular party had broken with Belaúnde.[74] A small but intellectually prestigious democratic-reform party, the Movimiento Social-Progresista, had been founded in 1955, but its leaders were demoralized by their failure to attract any mass following in the 1962 election.[75] The Christian Democratic party in Peru, unlike those in Chile or Venezuela, never was able to develop into a major electoral party. Among the non-electoral forces, the most significant political movements were the guerrilla movements of 1965-1966. However these movements were solidly defeated by early 1966.

Two factors, then, came together to create reasonably great "coalitional space" for an inclusionary attempt in Peru by 1968. First, a significant percentage of the change-oriented elites was available for collaboration with the military. These elites represented a wide variety of ideologies. The inside strategy for structural reform—electoral politics—seemed exhausted, either because of compromise with the oligarchy (APRA), the ineffectualness of those in power to bring about the promised reforms (Acción Popular), or the inability to attract a mass following for reform programs (Social Progressives and Christian Democrats). The outside strategy for structural change—guerrilla revolution —seemed unfeasible given the crushing defeat of guerrilla movements in the period 1965-1966.[76]

Second, unlike Chile or to a lesser extent Brazil and Argentina, Peru had an extremely weak liberal tradition of competitive politics. The only recent competitive periods were 1945 to 1948, 1956-1962, and 1963 to 1968. In the last of these periods, the strange congressional alliance of APRA with the oligarchical Unión Nacional Odriista (UNO), which blocked reform, weak-

74 Belaúnde's growing loss of support in his own party is discussed by a former secretary-general of the party, Edgardo Seoane, in his *Ni tiranos ni caudillos: cartas y hechos del proceso político 62-68.*

75 For a brief description of the ideas of the party see Augusto Salazar Bondy, *Historia de las ideas en el Perú contemporáneo.*

76 The significance of the collapse of both the "inside" and "outside" strategies was first brought to my attention by Luigi Einaudi. Later in my interviews with key civilian activists within the military government, a number of them made a similar point.

ened the legitimacy of liberal parliamentary politics. A case could be made that, in the core programs of APRA (in its original 1930s version); in Christian Democracy, with its emphasis on communalism and solidarity; and in the guerrillas' concern with agrarian reform, there was always a greater commitment to social change than a commitment to liberal parliamentary political procedures and guarantees as such. When the military came to power with a program that rejected liberal parliamentary norms, but began to carry out structural changes that had been previously advocated by the political groups, few, if any, of these political groups launched ideological attacks based on liberal principles against the installation attempt.

Degree of Polarization

The peak period of peasant mobilization was from the late 1950s to mid-1960s. With the defeat of the guerrilla campaign in 1965-1966, conflictual polarization lessened, but the hopes for change that had been raised in the election campaigns of 1962 and 1963 and the peasant movement still existed. Conditions in Peru were therefore moderately favorable to inclusionary policies because, when the military came to power in 1968, there was a relatively low level of polarized mobilization.

Coalitional space can be marginally expanded or diminished by "timing." The timing in Peru was favorable to the installation of a regime by the use of inclusionary policies and structural reforms. Given the fact that most of the revolutionary forces seemed spent or defeated, Peru at the advent of the regime was momentarily "post-polarized." The military's actions were thus not those of repression and exclusion as in Chile in 1973 and Brazil in 1964. In the earlier period of 1965-1966 the Peruvian military had responded to guerrilla threats with repression. But by the time the army came to power they faced no immediate threats and their first visible acts were associated with nationalism (the expropriation of IPC) and structural change (the agrarian reform). The regime was thus born, in national and international spheres, under a reform star.

Given these special circumstances, the military was able to recruit important activists from every major political group, one of the most prominent being Carlos Delgado, formerly a key member of APRA who had left the party because of its increasing conservatism. Delgado was given the second most powerful post in the regime's major instrument for organization, SINAMOS, and was one of the most important ideologues of Phase I.[77] Héctor Béjar, one of the few guerrilla leaders not killed in the 1965-1966 counter-guerrilla campaign, and a prominent figure within the international revolutionary left, joined SINAMOS in 1972 as director of youth activities.[78] SINAMOS, in particular, became the base for attracting prominent members from almost all change-oriented movements in modern Peru.[79] This situation contrasts sharply with those exclusionary cases growing out of high polarization that we examined in Chapter 3. In Brazil since 1964 and Chile since 1973, there has been virtually no active regime collaboration from left-of-center intellectuals and party leaders.

Degree of Prior Social Welfare and Structural and Sectoral Reforms

This variable was at least moderately favorable to an inclusionary installation attempt. A number of studies have documented that many of the reforms the regime carried out had been "in

[77] Two collections of his articles explaining Peru's revolutionary process are, *El proceso revolucionario peruano: testimonio de lucha* (México: Siglo Veintiuno editores, 1972), and *Revolución y participación* (Lima: Ediciones del Centro, 1974).

[78] His book on the guerrilla struggle was the 1969 non-fiction winner of Cuba's *Casa de las Americas* prize. It has been published in English as *Peru 1965: Notes on a Guerrilla Experience* (New York: Monthly Review Press, 1970). Along with Delgado he became a major spokesman for the Phase I government against important critics from the left in Peru. See, for example, his attack on Aníbal Quijano, "El neocapitalismo del Señor Quijano," *Participación* 1 (December 1972), pp. 17-22. Bejar discusses his years in SINAMOS in *La revolución en la trampa* (Lima: Ediciones Socialismo y Participación, 1976).

[79] *La Prensa* (April 20, 1972), p. 5, printed the list of the initial top officials of SINAMOS. The list included representatives of virtually every important left-of-center political faction in Peru. Two of the four deputy director generals of SINAMOS, Hélan Jaworski and Francisco Guerra came from the Catholic left; another, Jaime Llosa, had a long interest in Yugoslavian-style reforms in participation. The director general of Labor Organizations was José Luis Alvarado, a former Communist party trade union leader who organized Peru's first major bank strike in the early 1960s. The Social Progressive's presidential candidate in 1962, Ruiz Eldredge, was named director of the newspaper *Expreso* after it was expropriated, and Social Progressives such as Augusto Salazar Bondy played an important role in educational reform, while Virgílio Roel was involved in formulating the Industrial Community Law. This list could be greatly extended.

151

the air" for a long time, but never executed.[80] Agrarian reform is the obvious example. Numerous groups had advocated land reform in theory, and peasants were demanding it. Peru had one of the most unequal systems of land distribution in the world.[81] This was an obvious area for reform, and the military moved decisively. Another area was the question of nationalism. Shane Hunt, in his excellent study of the history of Peru's policies toward foreign capital, shows that Peru had been one of the most laissez-faire countries in Latin America and that public-sector investment was extremely low by the standards of other major countries in the region.[82] Indeed, the financial capacity of the state was so weak that, as Abraham Lowenthal observes, "taxes could be collected by a private banking firm which actually charged the government for the use of its own revenue," and "Peru's Central Bank was still directly responsive to the private sector."[83]

The high degree of regional inequality, and often isolation, gave the government considerable scope for carrying out important steps in the direction of national integration.[84] On a whole range of reforms, thus, Peru lagged behind almost all the other major countries in Latin America. Many opportunities for reform were available for the military regime to fill in its quest for constituents.

Resource/Effective Demand Ratio

In comparison to Chile or Argentina, the "politically relevant strata" in Peru are quite small. In terms of Deutsch's indicator

[80] This is a major theme that runs through the policy studies contained in *The Peruvian Experiment*, ed. Lowenthal. Especially see the introduction.

[81] On a Gini Index of land distribution for 57 countries, Peru received the highest index of inequality, see *World Handbook of Political and Social Indicators*, ed. C. L. Taylor and M. C. Hudson, second edition (New Haven: Yale University Press, 1972), pp. 267-68.

[82] "Direct Foreign Investment in Peru: New Rules for an Old Game" in *The Peruvian Experiment*, ed. Lowenthal, pp. 302-49.

[83] Lowenthal, "Peru's 'Revolutionary Government of the Armed Forces': Background and Context," in *Political-Military Systems: Comparative Perspectives*, ed. Catherine McArdle Kelleher.

[84] For example Irma Adelman and Cynthia Taft Morris classified seventy-four countries according to their national integration and sense of national unity on an A to D scale. Argentina and Chile were classified "A," Brazil "B," and Peru "C+." See their *Society, Politics, and Economic Development: A Quantitative Approach* (Baltimore: The Johns Hopkins Press, 1967), pp. 54-56.

of social mobilization, of the twenty countries of Latin America, only the Dominican Republic, Guatemala, Honduras, and Haiti had lower scores than Peru.[85]

Also, as we have shown, at the time the military assumed power, most of the organized political forces were in disarray. Numerous observers have noted that the military stepped into a power vacuum and that the military state had a relatively large degree of autonomy. The military's power vis-à-vis effective demand was, thus, relatively great at the start of the regime. Their coercive power gave them control over one of the major resources for which there was high demand at the start of the regime, namely land. The military were thus able to respond to many of the initial claimants—the sierra peasants, coastal plantation workers, and urban squatters—for regime outputs by introducing major rural and urban land-granting programs.

The regime therefore started the installation phase with a relatively high ratio of resources to effective demand. However, in the long run a major question was whether the regime could extract sufficient resources from the national and international environment to allow it to push forward its social and economic policies, and to consolidate its new institutions. Here the nationalist policies of the regime encountered serious constraints.[86]

Summarizing our analysis, Table 4.3 places Peru in the comparative context of the four cases analyzed in Chapter 3.

CONDITIONS FOR INCLUSIONARY POLICIES IN PERU: COMPARATIVE ANALYSIS

One of the perennial questions about military regimes in Latin America is why Chile, or Argentina, or Brazil did not attempt to take the path chosen by General Velasco and his followers in Peru, or by General Cárdenas in Mexico. All too often the questioners limit their inquiries to differences in the military establishments in each country. Our analysis of the conditions that are supportive of or resistant to installation by inclusionary policies puts the question of the policy direction of these military

[85] Peru's score was 63 compared to Argentina's 217 and Chile's 121, see David Scott Palmer, "'Revolution from Above': Military Government and Popular Participation in Peru, 1968-1972" (Ithaca: Cornell University, Latin American Studies Program, Dissertation Series, No. 47, January 1974), p. 9.

[86] Chapters 7 and 8 address this question.

TABLE 4.3

SUMMARY OF CONDITIONS AFFECTING THE SUCCESS OF CORPORATIST INSTALLATION ATTEMPTS IN FIVE COUNTRIES

Variable	Mexico (1935-1940) Inclusionary	Brazil (post-1964) Exclusionary	Argentina (1966-1971) Exclusionary	Chile (post-1973) Exclusionary	Peru (1968-1972) Inclusionary
Organizational strength and ideological unity of the state elite	Moderately favorable	Moderately favorable	Neutral	Moderately favorable	Moderately favorable
Development of autonomous political parties and interest groups	Very favorable	Moderately favorable	Very unfavorable	Very unfavorable	Neutral
Polarization	Moderately favorable	Moderately favorable	Moderately unfavorable	Very favorable	Moderately favorable
Prior social welfare and other reform space	Very favorable	Variable not applicable	Variable not applicable	Variable not applicable	Moderately favorable
Resource/effective demand ratio	Very favorable	Moderately favorable	Very unfavorable	Moderately unfavorable	Moderately favorable

governments into a larger, comparative perspective that more adequately treats societal, as well as purely military, variables. If we exclude the first variable, which involves a degree of subjective choice, the other variables largely concern initial objective socioeconomic and political conditions. We can thus, for heuristic purposes, assess the conditions for a hypothetical inclusionary installation attempt for variables 2, 3, 4, and 5 for each of the five countries we have analyzed. (See Table 4.4.)

The table shows that conditions in Peru were much more supportive to the installation of a regime by the use of inclusionary policies than in Chile, Argentina, or Brazil. Although Peru faced obstacles (such as a foreign exchange shortage, the existence of well-organized Aprista and Communist trade unions, and a New Professional Army which blocked the creation of a party of the revolution), obstacles that eventually constituted insurmountable impediments to the full institutionalization of the regime, Peru shared with Mexico (though to a lesser degree) generally favorable conditions for installing the regime.

The variables were constructed primarily to facilitate comparative analysis of the initial macrolevel conditions facing installation attempts. However, a study of the attempt to install a new regime necessarily must go beyond a consideration of the initial conditions to a consideration of the ongoing within-nation, microlevel, interactions between state policies and different sectors in civil society. That is our next analytic task.

TABLE 4.4

SUMMARY OF CONDITIONS AFFECTING THE SUCCESS OF HYPOTHETICAL INCLUSIONARY
INSTALLATION ATTEMPTS FOR VARIABLES 2, 3, 4 AND 5 IN MEXICO, PERU, BRAZIL, ARGENTINA AND CHILE[a]

Hypotheses for Inclusionary Corporatism	Mexico: 1934 (at advent of Cárdenas government)	Peru: 1968 (at advent of military government)	Brazil: 1964 (at advent of military government)	Argentina: 1966 (at advent of military government)	Chile: 1973 (at advent of military government)
Variable Two: "The lower the degree of autonomous development of political parties and interest groups, the greater the possibilities of installing the regime."	Very favorable	Neutral	Moderately unfavorable	Very unfavorable	Very unfavorable
Variable Three: "Conditions of polarized political mobilization are not supportive of the installation of the regime."	Moderately favorable	Moderately favorable	Moderately unfavorable	Neutral	Very unfavorable

Hypotheses for Inclusionary Corporatism	Mexico: 1934 (at advent of Cárdenas government)	Peru: 1968 (at advent of military government)	Brazil: 1964 (at advent of military government)	Argentina: 1966 (at advent of military government)	Chile: 1973 (at advent of military government)
Variable Four: "The lower the level of social welfare legislation and structural and sectoral reform the country has attained before the installation attempt, the greater the chance of installing the regime."	Very favorable	Moderately favorable	Moderately unfavorable	Very unfavorable	Very unfavorable
Variable Five: "The greater the ratio of the state's resource capability, primarily economic and symbolic, and secondarily coercive, to effective demand, the greater the chances of installing the regime."	Very favorable	Moderately favorable	Moderately unfavorable	Very unfavorable	Very unfavorable

ᵃ If we followed the procedure in footnotes 48 and 49 of Chapter 3 whereby we gave a numerical value of $+2$ to "very favorable" and a -2 to "very unfavorable," we could get an average value for the four variables presented in Table 4.4. On a scale where $+2$ is the top and -2 is the bottom, Mexico would receive $+1.6$, Peru $+0.75$, Brazil -1.0, Argentina -1.5 and Chile -2.0.

FIVE · *Organizing the Weakly Organized:*
The State and Urban Squatters

POLITICAL thinkers and political actors in the organic-statist tradition attach great value to the goal of a harmonious political community. Since such a community seldom comes into being spontaneously, the state is pictured in this tradition as having a legitimate role to perform in actively structuring society. As we have seen, the organization from above into state-chartered institutions is a central part of the organic-statist strategy to control and unify society and to forge nonpluralist modes of interest representation that are intended by the state elite to lessen society's vulnerability to organized class conflict. Whether the military regime in Peru could in fact restructure civil society into new functional organizations, and whether such state-chartered organizations would contribute to the regime's desired goal of solidarity, were central questions for the regime's overall political strategy.

In this and the next chapter I compare—within the broad context of the hypotheses advanced in Chapters 3 and 4—the ability of the Peruvian government to incorporate two different lower-class groups, the urban squatters and the sugar workers, into new state-chartered institutions. Analysis of these two sectors allows me to explore in much greater detail some of the arguments previously advanced.

In his excellent work on the squatter settlements in Lima, David Collier notes that the settlements were frequently referred to by such perjorative labels as *aberración social* and *cancer social* and that the settlements "had generally been viewed by the established classes of Lima as a 'belt of misery' and a breeding ground of political radicalism which threateningly surrounded the city and which, in some dimly imagined political upheaval, could dangerously cut off the capital from the rest of the country."[1] From the perspective of an organic-statist regime,

[1] See his *Squatters and Oligarchs: Authoritarian Rule and Policy Change in Peru* (Baltimore: The Johns Hopkins University Press, 1976), p. 3. Also

158

such an "unintegrated" sector, strategically located (either geographically or economically) in society, not only violates the normative value of solidarity posited by the organic-statist model but, more saliently, is often perceived by the state elite as threatening the stability of the regime because of the sector's potential for anomic violence or its openness to "agitational" appeals from anti-regime groups. The typical inclusionary solution to such a problem is to attempt to use distributive policies to reorganize the sector from above, to "preempt" the organizational space and link the group to the state and thereby reduce their availability to anti-regime forces. This approach has characterized the large-scale attempt in Peru to incorporate the squatter population into new political organizations.

The sugar workers constitute another lower-class sector that has been the object of large-scale reorganization by the state particularly through the introduction of worker participation in ownership and self-management. Prior to 1968, however, the two lower-class groups were organized differently. The sugar workers had a high degree of autonomous organizational resources, strong ideological, union and party commitments, and were linked with powerful national political movements. The squatters had an important, reasonably effective organizational tradition of elected neighborhood associations.[2] However, these associations tended to be clientelistic rather than autonomous, instrumental in their goals rather than ideological, and had ephemeral linkages with national political movements.[3] My working hypothesis, therefore, based on the arguments presented in Chapter 3, was that the sugar workers would offer greater challenges to state reorganization than the squatters. In fact, whereas the state elite has indeed been reasonably successful in implementing its inclusionary policies toward the squatters, the state's task in the sugar sector has been much more difficult. A comparison of the two sectors supplements the perspective provided by Chapter 3 con-

see his "Squatter Settlements and Policy Innovation in Peru" in *The Peruvian Experiment: Continuity and Change Under Military Rule,* ed. Abraham F. Lowenthal (Princeton: Princeton University Press, 1975), p. 137.

[2] See William Mangin, "Squatter Settlements," *Scientific American* 217 (October 1967), pp. 21-29 and Henry Dietz, "Political Participation by the Urban Poor in an Authoritarian Context: The Case of Lima, Peru," *Journal of Political and Military Sociology* 5 (Spring 1977): 63-77.

[3] A substantial body of evidence to support this characterization of squatter organizations will be offered later in the chapter.

cerning the conditions affecting the success and failure of inclusionary policies in concrete situations. This comparison permits the further exploration of such issues as the opportunities for and limitations of state organization from above to control lower-class groups and to construct new forms of political and economic participation for such groups.

THE SQUATTER "PROBLEM" AND THE STATE'S RESPONSE

When the military came to power, Peru's urban squatter population was experiencing extremely rapid growth. From 1956 to 1970 the squatter population of Lima increased from 120,000 to what was conservatively estimated as over 760,000, or from 9.9 percent of the total Lima population to 26 percent. The trend was not restricted to Lima. In fact in 1970, of the six most populous cities in Peru, Lima had the second lowest percentage of squatters.[4]

The radical potential of such urban migrants has been a subject of much study. The initial theoretical and policy assumption was that the massive waves of urban migrants who came to live in shanty towns represented a radical force. Subsequent research in Africa, Asia, and Latin America has qualified this hypothesis, and the evidence shows that the first generation of migrants, for a host of reasons, is not initially disposed to radical political behavior. Remaining in the balance is the question of what happens in the long run if aspirations are not satisfied.[5] For our

[4] The fishmeal boom city of Chimbote had the highest, with 70%. But Trujillo had 62%, Arequipa 37%, and Chiclayo, 35%. Only Cuzco, with 21% was lower than Lima. The 1970 figures are from Perú, SINAMOS, Dirección General de Pueblos Jóvenes y Áreas de Subdesarrollo Urbano Interno, *Diagnóstico nacional de la problematica de los pueblos jóvenes: documento de trabajo* (Lima: September 1973), pp. 146-149. The 1956 Lima data is from José Matos Mar, "Censo de las barriadas de Lima (1956)," in his *Urbanización y barriadas en América del Sur*, p. 65.

[5] An excellent review of the literature is Joan Nelson, *Migrants, Urban Poverty, and Instability in Developing Nations* (Cambridge: Harvard University, Center for International Affairs, Occasional Papers in International Affairs, No. 22, 1969). William Mangin, "Latin American Squatter Settlements: A Problem and a Solution," *Latin American Research Review* (Summer 1967), is a review and a critique of the anomic hypothesis for Latin America. An extensively documented article is Wayne Cornelius, Jr., "Urbanization as an Agent in Latin American Political Instability: The Case of Mexico," *American Political Science Review* (September 1969). Also see

purposes, however, the social science literature is less relevant than the perception of the situation by the military regime. It should be remembered that the regime in Peru came to power after the defeat of Ché Guevara in the Bolivian countryside had led to a shift among many revolutionaries in Latin America from a rural to an urban guerrilla strategy. Military journals in Peru in the period leading up to the coup of 1968 show a growing concern with the potential threat of urban violence originating in the mushrooming *barriadas*.[6]

In the first days of the military regime, despite the confusion of seizing power and the international furor caused by the new government's expropriation of IPC, the new government demonstrated a clear interest in formulating a policy toward squatter settlements.[7] After less than a week in power the head of the military government, General Juan Velasco, personally phoned one of the bishops of Lima, Bishop Bambarén, to ask him what the Church was doing in the squatter settlements and what sug-

---

the section on "The Hypothesis of Anomic Urban Agitation" in my article, "Political Development Theory: The Latin American Experience," in *Journal of International Affairs* (1966). The second-generation radicalization argument is most forcefully presented in Samuel P. Huntington, *Political Order in Changing Societies*, pp. 281-83.

[6] As early as 1965 the Peruvian army journal *Revista de la Escuela Superior de Guerra* featured two articles on urban revolutionary warfare. Interestingly, whereas in many countries "civic action" has been a largely rural program, in Peru since the early 1960s an important element of the civic-action program entailed military programs in urban squatter settlements. Also significant are the repeated references to the intelligence-gathering potential of military civic-action personnel, such as doctors. See Col. Alfonso Icochea de Vivanca, "La sanidad militar en la acción cívica," *Revista de la Escuela Superior de Guerra* 12 (1965), pp. 65-68. Collier also notes that in the early days of the military government "the concern with radicalization in settlements was apparently expressed frequently by the members of the armed forces" working on squatter programs. *Squatters and Oligarchs*, p. 108.

[7] Numerous studies deal with the social-economic and political situations of squatters in the period before the military assumed power. A bibliographical guide with 342, mostly annotated, entries is Eileen Welsh, *Bibliografía sobre el crecimiento dinámico de Lima, referente al proceso de urbanización en el Perú*. A very useful study based on a 1967 survey of Lima's urban population, which includes as one of its major categories the barriada population, is Jaime Gianella, *Marginalidad en Lima Metropolitana: una investigación exploratoria*. This study contains 84 tables with data on migration, employment, union membership, and housing patterns, as well as some data on political attitudes.

gestions the Church had for a government policy. Bambarén's initial response was that the new government needed to approach the question at the national level and to look for an "integrated program." During the five preceding years, the Bishop and a group of volunteers had been active in the barriadas. His main purpose had been to encourage the dwellers to self-help action instead of reliance on sporadic, paternalistic government programs. Bambarén, along with a growing number of scholars and urbanists, believed the barriadas should be viewed not as "shanty towns" but as positive responses by poor migrants to the crisis of rapid urbanization. With this in mind, he created for the first time in Peru the term *Pueblos Jóvenes* (Young Towns, or Towns in Formation), and in January 1968 renamed his organization Pueblos Jóvenes del Perú, or PUJOP.[8]

By October 1968, President Velasco had established a nine-man commission, five of whose members were drawn from PUJOP. The commission's report on the barriadas, after being vetted by key military groups, was approved on December 13, 1968, and a National Office for the Development of Pueblos Jóvenes was established reflecting many of Bishop Bambarén's ideas.[9]

[8] Interview with Bishop Bambarén, November 12, 1972, Lima.

[9] For the mission and guidelines of the new organization, the Oficina Nacional de Desarrollo de Pueblos Jóvenes (ONDEPJOV), see Decreto Supremo No. 105-68-FO. The Bishop's ideas were closely related to a growing school of thought in Peru that emphasized the hopeful and politically dynamic nature of the squatter settlements, especially as contrasted to the more densely populated and decaying slums, "callejones," of the inner city. A pioneer effort to create a typology of different types of lower class urban settlements in Peru was by John F. Turner. See for example his "Lima's Barriadas and Corralones: Suburbs vs. Slums," *Ekistics* (1965). See also Mangin, "Latin American Squatter Settlements: A Problem and a Solution." The most theoretically focused development of this approach is Carlos Delgado, "Tres planteamientos en torno a problemas de urbanización acelerada en áreas metropolitanas: el caso de Lima," originally published by the Oficina del Plan de Desarrollo Metropolitano in 1968 and reprinted in Carlos Delgado, *Problemas sociales en el Perú contemporáneo* (Lima: IEP-CAMPODÓNICO ediciones, 1971), pp. 119-58. Important work in this area in Peru has also been done by Diego Robles and Hélan Jaworski. Significantly, Delgado, Robles, and Jaworski were named to important posts in SINAMOS when that organization was created. This is but one of many examples where the Phase I military acquired an important degree of legitimacy and assistance from social thinkers or technocrats because they were perceived to have the will—and the power—to impose ideas that had been given intellectual expression but had been politically frustrated in

The role of Church organizations in the establishment of a major program highlights a characteristic aspect of decision making in an organic-statist regime. The government played the leading role in creating the commission and in nominating its members, and in the final formulation and approval of policy. Within these parameters, however, it encouraged and accepted the participation of a major institutional group with whom it shared a general policy perspective, and whose support, or at least non-opposition, it desired. The government's eventual program was indeed national and integral.[10] The program built upon a num-

---

the past. It should also be noted that the self-help and road building components of the program had been a part of the military's civic-action program. This civic-action experience made the policy less controversial within military circles and contributed to the quick movement from the decision, to the implementation stage of the government's squatter policy.

[10] My discussion and evaluation of the government's policy toward squatters is based on a variety of sources. The government (in 1972) considered the program a successful example of their new pattern of participation, and, as such, officials were willing to make available to me most of the government documents concerning how the system was run, and in particular the method of organizing elections. These documents are cited in the appropriate places. The assessment of any new program, however, requires extensive interviews and observations at all the major bureaucratic levels, especially at the level of the field workers charged with implementing the policy. Adequate evaluation also requires independent analysis of the program from the point of view of the people affected by it. Consequently, in carrying out research I pursued two parallel lines of inquiry.

My study of the government's attitudes and mode of operation entailed interviews with chief officials at all three major governmental levels. At SINAMOS national headquarters, which after June 1971 absorbed the original office in charge of the Pueblos Jóvenes, I interviewed the second in charge of the Dirección General de Pueblos Jóvenes y Áreas de Subdesarrollo Urbano Interno, on October 31 and November 7, 1972, about the installation period of the regime's squatter policy. At the regional office level for Lima and Callao, I interviewed the Director de Organización Vecinal, Décima Región, SINAMOS, November 9 and 19, 1972. His office had the task of installing and supervising the regime's new electoral system for all Pueblos Jóvenes in greater Lima. At the field level, I accompanied a number of "promotores" whose job it was to work nights and weekends with the squatters to create the new system of participation and distribution.

My study of the effect of the program on the squatters entailed visiting, on my own, between October and November 1972, a number of Pueblos Jóvenes to observe, more as a political anthropologist than as a political scientist, how the squatters were reacting to the new system. I had open-ended interviews with elected representatives from six different Pueblos Jóvenes in Lima and Chiclayo. I selected one large Pueblo Joven, which

163

ber of policies that had been advocated and even tried in the past, such as self-help, mutual savings associations, gradual legalization, and the attempt to use the settlements as easily mobilized bases of political support via demonstrations.[11] What was new and distinctive about the government's policy was its architectonic, organic-statist design of political and social engineering. This design called for a comprehensive, national organization that could penetrate every settlement block in Peru and link those blocks to hierarchal, state-chartered structures of control and distribution.[12]

A nationwide program for Pueblos Jóvenes was established to implement this design. Lima was divided into four sectors, each with its own central office, and the rest of the country was divided into twenty-one regional offices. To clarify the scope of the squatter problem, a special door-to-door national survey of Peru's entire squatter population was carried out in 1970. The survey identified 610 distinct squatter settlements with a combined population of 1,516,488. Lima alone had 273 settlements, with a population of over 760,000.[13] For electoral and organizational purposes, each of the distinct settlements, later called Pueblos Jóvenes, was to be broken down as much as possible into square blocks. Each square block was to be organized by state officials so as to elect its own neighborhood committee of representatives (Comité Vecinal). For the Pueblos Jóvenes of greater Lima alone, this amounted by mid-1972 to 4,875 neighborhood committees.[14]

---

must remain anonymous, for intensive observation, and was allowed to attend on a regular basis over a period of several weeks the meetings of the Pueblo Joven organization at all three levels. These meetings were held late at night in the homes of the residents of the Pueblo Joven.

By the end of 1972 the basic pattern of installation had been set. In 1974 and 1975 I returned to assess some of the problems and prospects of the "post-installation" period and repeated on a smaller scale my 1972 interviews and observations.

[11] See Collier's *Squatters and Oligarchs*, Chapter 7, for an excellent comparative analysis of different governments' policy approaches to the squatter settlements.

[12] Referring to the above design, Collier observes that it is "an attempt to establish an elaborate hierarchal structure of political control that has no precedent in earlier periods." Ibid., p. 130.

[13] Perú, Presidencia de la República, Oficina Nacional de Desarrollo de Pueblos Jóvenes, *Censo de población y vivienda de pueblos jóvenes: cifras preliminares* (Lima: February 1971), p. 10.

[14] As of September 31, 1972. The official figures for that date indicate that the complete cycle of neighborhood organizations, elections and leader-

The massive system of block-level elections was a forerunner of the regime's later approach to organized participation within state-chartered institutions. By 1971 the regime had created SINA-MOS and charged it with the task of organizing the population into "dynamic functional and territorial units" and establishing "the systematic linkage between the coordinated actions and services of the government and those of the organized population." The announced goal of this organizational effort was to foster "the conscious and active participation of the national population in the tasks that demand economic and social development."[15] The elections were an integral part of this policy of participation by the "organized population." A senior official in the Pueblos Jóvenes program argued in an interview that the government "wants the marginal masses of people to participate in the process . . . in the past there was no real identity between the leaders of the barriadas and their residents because the government intervened directly and gave services. In the past the settlers' associations were also often controlled by outside political forces who did not live there."[16]

The official in charge of organizing Lima and Callao into neighborhood committees stressed "We want participation but it should be organized participation. We want to make as many people as possible homeowners, then they will act responsibly towards their community and have a stake in it."[17] His allusion to ownership refers to the question of giving the squatters legal title to the land on which they built their homes following invasion.

DISTRIBUTIVE POLICIES AND BINDING STRUCTURES

The question of property title raises issues that are central, both theoretically and in terms of policy, for an analysis of the

ship seminars had been carried out in 64.2% of the Pueblos Jóvenes; data supplied by the office of the Organización Vecinal, Décima Región, SINA-MOS. In August 1974, the same office estimated that over 8,000 neighborhood committees had been formed and that 95% of the squatter population was incorporated.

[15] These quotes are from Decreto Ley No. 18896, *Ley de Movilización Social*, June 22, 1971, articles 1, 5.

[16] Interview, Dirección General de Pueblos Jóvenes y Áreas de Subdesarrollo Urbano Interno, SINAMOS, November 7, 1972, Lima.

[17] Interview with the Director de Organización Vecinal, Décima Región, SINAMOS, November 9, 1972.

regime's inclusionary policy toward squatters. Past presidents of Peru—particularly the populist General Odría—had often tolerated or even encouraged "invasions."[18] But though presidents extended services to squatters, they seldom granted them legal title to the land. Despite some important similarities between the patron-client model of linking the lower classes to the state and the organic-statist model, crucial differences are revealed when we analyze how the issuing of titles is dysfunctional for the control strategy of one model and functional for the other.

In the patron-client model the president (or a political leader) extends services and protection to the legally precarious squatters in exchange for their support in mass demonstrations and in elections. But the exchange in such a patron-client relationship is based on power asymmetry, and is thus unequal.[19] As long as the squatters do not have property titles, the president can legally use coercion to remove them from the land. The absence of title —the maintenance of squatters in a situation of institutionalized illegality—is therefore a key to the continued dependence of the squatter clients on their patrons. In this system, the granting of titles by the president would mean losing a major component of his patronal leverage.[20] The logic of this model of elite-mass politics requires the maintenance of legal and institutional marginality.

In the organic-statist model, however, control is sought by incorporating the lower-class groups in a complex web of binding legal relationships in which benefits flow from membership in state-chartered institutions. Membership thus gives the lower classes structural incentives for working within the institutions

[18] The first systematic discussion of this process is in Collier's *Squatters and Oligarchs*, Chapter 3. His conclusion is that "the government role was crucial in the formation of more than a quarter of the settlements in Lima at the very *least*," p. 46 (emphasis in the original). José Matos Mar is currently engaged in an analysis of the economic aspects of presidential involvement in settlement formation.

[19] For the concepts of "unequal exchange" and "power asymmetry" as they apply to the patron-client relationship, see John Duncan Powell, "Peasant Politics and Clientelist Politics," *American Political Science Review* (June 1970). For a discussion of the 1961 legislation that in theory (but seldom in practice) allowed squatters to acquire legal title, see Kenneth A. Manaster, "The Problem of Urban Settlement in Developing Countries: Peru," *Wisconsin Law Review* (1968).

[20] See Collier, *Squatters and Oligarchs*, pp. 60-63.

of the political community.[21] In the case of the squatter settlements, this would imply an attempt to incorporate the squatters into formal, legally sanctioned, property and political units.

If my argument is correct, that the political logic of the two models is distinct in this respect, and if the Peruvian military was in fact following a model of elite-mass relationships that was organic-statist, it should manifest itself in a different pattern of title granting from that of the previous patron-client period. To check my tentative working hypothesis I examined the records of squatter title-granting in the 1961-1968 and 1969-1974 periods.[22] The data show that in fact the military regime sharply increased title-granting (see Figure 5.1).

Clearly title granting by the military government could potentially be classified as significant distributive and symbolic acts that are often evaluated, in retrospect, as important "constituent acts of the regime." The most successful inclusionary institution-building examples in Latin America are found in the field of urban labor under Vargas, and in the area of the peasants under Cárdenas. As we have seen, all entailed material distribution and symbolic recognition with the *simultaneous* creation of new institutions. These institutions, because of their association with distributive and symbolic acts, were granted some legitimacy by the very groups they encapsulated. The result in all cases was

[21] Again and again the Phase I military leaders justified structural reforms on the grounds that it incorporated the masses and gave them something to defend. For example, one of the architects of the Industrial Community Law said, "The Industrial community gives some ownership to the workers, it seeks to motivate the Peruvian citizens. . . . When our workers realize they are owners of productive property they will have to defend this property, they will have to commit themselves to the ownership because it is the guarantee of the subsistence of their children, of their homes." See General José Graham Hurtado, Jefe del Comité de Asesoramiento de la Presidencia de la República, *Filosofía de la revolución peruana: la comunidad laboral, la comunidad pesquera* (Lima: Oficina Nacional de Información, 1971), p. 19.

As we saw in Chapter 3, a key part of the system Vargas created to tie labor to the state was to link most of the social welfare benefits to membership in officially recognized unions.

[22] The classic period of the patron-client model was during the Presidency of General Odría (1948-1956), during which almost no titles were granted. The movement toward legalization had, of course, begun well before the period under study here. The first steps to enable the legalization of settlements were in 1961 and in mid-1968, prior to Velasco's assumption of power, see Collier, "Squatter Settlements and Policy," pp. 141-43.

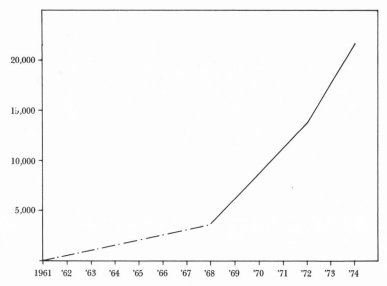

FIGURE 5.1. Comparative rates of squatter title distribution in Lima and Callao in "patron-client" policy period (1961-1968) versus "organic-statist" policy period (1968-1974). Source: Data points for October 1968, October 1, 1972, and August 31, 1974, obtained from Oficina de Promoción de Organización, Décima Región del SINAMOS.

that complex control mechanisms were built into the new institutions, making the newly incorporated population highly responsive to the state's demands.[23]

In the Peruvian case, during the populist-clientelist phase, most particularly during the Odría government (1948-1956), titles were withheld to maintain patronal leverage. In the organic-statist phase, however, titles are still a form of leverage, but are exchanged for the incorporation of workers into new structures that bind them in new and more systematic ways to the state. Thus while there has been a great increase in title granting in the organic-statist phase, its ordered pace is guided by the regime's desire to use the title-granting opportunity to eliminate or preempt existing—especially political—organizations and to create new state-chartered organizations. In visits to various Pueblos Jóvenes, and during attendance at block meetings of the squatters, I could see that a major incentive for cooperation in the state's massive new organizational structure was the oppor-

[23] See Chapters 2 and 3.

tunity to qualify for receipt of title. The regime normally grants a title only after the entire barriada has completed all phases of the organizational training and election processes of the Pueblo Joven program.[24]

This raises another crucial question. After the "once-only" period of title granting is finished, what continuing linkage in theory will maintain the newly incorporated groups within the bounds of the state-chartered institutions?

The design calls for local elections that will generate "authentic" leaders who will represent local communal economic demands, instead of national political goals. The elected leaders will then act as the only conduits through which all subsequent outputs to the Pueblos Jóvenes sector will flow. In order to systematize this linkage, all requests for state services, and all distribution of state services, are coordinated by the twenty-six regional offices of the Pueblos Jóvenes. The representative system and the distributive system do not, therefore, interact at numerous points, as they might in a pluralist system of interest articulation. Rather, by design, they meet only at one bureaucratic point, the regional office director.

Because of the key position the regional director occupies, it is useful to determine how regional directors are recruited and how they respond to the community. Almost all of the regional directors in fact wear two hats. One hat makes them a member of the regime's organization charged with creating a system of participation, SINAMOS. The other hat is often a military one. Of the twenty-five regional officer directors when the system was first established, twenty-three were military officers. This in itself would not clearly demonstrate the nature of their responsiveness to the military, as opposed to the participatory, organization. An officer on leave from operational command, for instance, might consider his primary duty to lie in his membership in the new organization in which he worked full-time. This is a common

[24] In an interview, the official in charge of Lima's Pueblos Jóvenes electoral organization made a rough estimate that 100,000 families needed titles in 1972. It might well have been higher. An extensive survey of residence patterns in Lima indicates that an average of 5.8 people lived in each housing unit in the barriadas. See Gianella, *Marginalidad en Lima Metropilitana*, p. 133. For the 750,000 estimated Pueblos Jóvenes population in 1972, this would come to almost 130,000 housing units. In any case the 13,452 titles distributed by October 1972 meant that at least 85% of the population did not have titles at that time.

organizational and psychological phenomenon. In Peru, however, this possibility was significantly diminished by the fact that twenty of the officers were attached to operational commands and most of them were, in fact, the commanding officers of these commands.[25] The primary chain of authority within which they are promoted and evaluated is thus not the system of participation, SINAMOS, but the military system. In essence, then, the structures of representation, distribution, and potential coercion are bound together at one key point, the regional office director.

THE PUEBLOS JÓVENES ELECTION AND DEMAND-ARTICULATION SYSTEM

Elections are central to Peru's version of organic-statist politics. In the case of the Pueblos Jóvenes, the regime organizers have gained a sense of self-legitimacy because they believe they have created a realistic system of electoral representation that is able to present accurately and authoritatively the priorities of each Pueblo Joven to the government.

In my interviews in 1972 with well over a dozen regime activists concerned with organizing Pueblos Jóvenes, every one argued strongly that the system was an example of grass-roots democracy, in which political authority and choices were correctly focused on the problems that most directly affected the peoples' lives and about which they were most informed. It should be noted that, despite any reservations outside observers may have, activists' belief in the legitimacy of the system was an impotant strength of the regime itself. This is especially so because there are important classic liberal strands in Latin American political culture. Liberal critiques have often been an important erosive force from within previous inclusionary experiments in Latin America. Loss of support from key regime collaborators because of their ambivalence over the regime's conflicts with liberal principles was a major reason for the fall of the Vargas regime to-

[25] For example, in 1971 the director for the Cuzco office of the Pueblos Jóvenes program was also commanding general of the 4th Military Region headquartered in Cuzco; the director of the Ayacucho Office was chief of the 51st Infantry Battalion garrisoned in Ayacucho; the Talara director was the chief of the 11th Fighter Group based in Talara, etc. For a list of the 21 office directors outside of Lima and their military or governmental affiliations, see *Censo de población y vivienda de pueblos jóvenes*, pp. 5-6. The affiliation of the four Lima office directors was confirmed by direct observation.

ward the end of the World War II, and to a lesser extent the first Peronist regime. In this respect, the permanence of the neo-corporatist system in Mexico is partly due to the regime's self-image (that it is in fact democratic) and to its ability to convince many national, and just as importantly, international, observers that its dominant party system is at least an embryonic democracy.

This said, what is the system of representation in the Pueblos Jóvenes? In what sense, if any, is there organic grass-roots participation? The government's plan of organization called for each of the more than 600 barriadas identified in the special 1970 census to be organized according to the following format.[26] The basic unit of organization is the Comité Vecinal (Neighborhood Committee) at the "block" level.[27] Each family on a block sends a "head of the household" to a general assembly, which in turn elects a three-person Comité Vecinal. The committee is composed of a secretary of coordination, a secretary of organization, and a financial secretary.[28] In a large Pueblo Joven of over 20,000 peo-

[26] The explanation that follows is based on direct observation, interviews, and on the official organizers' handbooks. The most detailed of the handbooks is the 132-page *Organización vecinal* prepared by the Oficina Nacional de Desarrollo de Pueblos Jóvenes, SINAMOS (n.d.). A more popular illustrated version with answers to standard questions that might be asked of the organizers, is *Guía para la organización de los pueblos jóvenes*, issued by the Oficina Nacional de Desarrollo de Pueblos Jóvenes (n.d.). This will be referred to as *Guía* hereafter. For a description and analysis of such structures see Sara Michl, "Urban Squatter Organization as a National Government Tool: The Case of Lima," in *Latin American Urban Research*, vol. 3, ed. Francine F. Rabinovitz and Felicity M. Trueblood (Beverly Hills, Calif.: Sage Publications, 1973), pp. 155-80.

[27] By "block" (manzana) is meant all the dwellings that are included in the four sides of a square block. If the terrain or dwelling layout is such that no recognizable block exists, the government will often try to create one with a bulldozer. Until this time, a Comité Vecinal is defined in the *Guía* (p. 5) as being composed normally of 30 neighboring families.

[28] The duties of the three elected officials are spelled out in the booklet, *Organización vecinal*, pp. 21-23. On the basis of this, interviews with officials holding these positions, and my direct observations at committee meetings, it is clear that the coordinator is the chief official and that one of his or her chief responsibilities is to ascertain the block's priorities in regard to self-help projects or to win support for projects recommended by SINAMOS or a higher Pueblo Joven committee. If the project is agreed upon, then the coordinator supervises the assignment of financial and work quotas. The organizational secretary keeps the official minutes and is charged by SINAMOS regulations with the task of keeping an accurate census of the block, noting the ages, marital status, employment, and in-

171

ple, there would normally be over 150 electoral units each with its own election of a three-person Comité Vecinal. Thus 450 dwellers in a large Pueblo Joven would serve as directly elected officials of the Pueblo Joven.

The next echelon brings together all the elected coordinators of all the blocks in one of the major zones in the Pueblo Joven.[29] These block coordinators constitute ex-officio the zone's Committee of Promotion and Development, which in turn acts as the selecting agency for the six top officials.[30] For small Pueblos Jóvenes, this is the highest echelon. For large Pueblos Jóvenes, the same procedure is followed, at an additional echelon, whereby all the chief elected officials of each zone constitute the Executive Committee for the entire Pueblo Joven, and they select the chief officer from among their own members. It is the chief officers of the Executive Committee who then receive the official recognition of the state to act as the legal representatives of the Pueblo Joven.

The key actors in the system are thus members of the Executive Committee of the Pueblos Jóvenes and the regional office director of SINAMOS. The Executive Committee makes its requests for government service to the office director, and the SINAMOS office director asks for the cooperation of the Executive Committee in carrying out general policies.

This is formal structure. How does it work in practice? What are the political implications of this type of organization? What types of representatives are selected? What types of demands are made? Does the structure make any difference?

First let us examine more closely the recruitment process for

---

come of all residents. The organizational secretary is also in charge of coordinating legal papers for application for titles to the residents' lots, and is the day-by-day coordinator of self-help projects. The financial secretary collects the financial quota from the residents for the self-help projects.

From this account of their duties, it should be clear that the elected members of the Comité Vecinal are not only interest representatives. One is reminded of Durkheim's observation about the effect of Roman Law regulations on corporations, that "they ended by becoming part of the administrative machine. They fulfilled official functions."

[29] An average zone could be composed of somewhere from 20 to 50 blocks, and a Pueblo Joven of approximately 20,000 people could have from 6 to 10 zones.

[30] Called the Junta Directiva Central.

representatives. The guidebook lists four prerequisites for election. These are:

(1) A candidate must be a resident in the Pueblo Joven that he or she will represent.

(2) A candidate must be older than 18 years and know how to read and write.

(3) A candidate must have a recognized occupation (*ocupación conocida*).

(4) A candidate must have a good police record (*tener buenos antecedentes*).

The official position is that these prerequisites are simple, logical requirements, given the system of representation. The residency requirement ensures that the residents' own demands are listened to. Literacy is required because elected officials must keep financial records (to account for the monies collected for self-help projects) and write requests for state services. Officials stress that the requirement of recognized employment is not meant to exclude people who are temporarily unemployed, but to assure that elected officials are serious, hard-working members of the community who do not live off crime or who would not be tempted to profit financially from their elected position. Finally, the "buenos antecedentes" requirement is depicted as a vehicle for ensuring that criminals do not have access to the financial and political power of the community.

Extensive interviews with both field election organizers and elected officials show, however, that the prerequisites, as actually interpreted, have a wider impact than indicated in the official explanations. As a top SINAMOS official acknowledged, the residency requirement "in effect cuts down greatly on the political party or trade union control of the Pueblo Joven organization. In the past all too often the residents' organizations were controlled from the outside."[31] The *buenos antecedentes* requirement is more ambiguous. Normally it is presented as a simple veto of candidates with criminal records. However, a number of field organizers admitted that it has been used to disqualify people with a "subversive" political background. One organizer said that a union activist who had a record of encouraging damaging strikes or pursuing narrowly based "class" action could

[31] In an interview not for direct citation.

also be disqualified. The "recognized occupation" prerequisite is also seen as a formula for barring a full-time political activist who might be sponsored by a political party or trade union organization to take up residence in the Pueblo Joven in order to become a full-time organizer.

Taken together, these prerequisites provide a powerful mechanism to ensure that the Pueblos Jóvenes are not horizontally linked with other lower class or radical political organizations. This is consistent with the regime's view that the preferred mode of participation is that of numerous functionally or geographically specific organizations vertically linked to the state.

The echelon system of representation also deserves comment. The regime organizers stress that the advantage of the system is that all leaders are selected by small groups of people personally familiar with the candidates. In practice this means that though over a million people live in Pueblos Jóvenes in Peru, no single election ever involves as many as fifty voters. This is so because the only direct election is at the block level, which by statute is restricted to approximately thirty heads of families, each with one vote. The chief zone officers are in turn individually selected by the twenty to thirty block coordinators in the zone. The final election of the chief representative of an entire Pueblo Joven of, say, 50,000 people, is made indirectly by an even smaller pool of approximately six to ten zone chiefs of the Pueblo Joven. The potential for explosive, direct, competitive election campaigns waged among the entire population of a Pueblo Joven is dampened because there is no one election focusing on the demands of the entire Pueblo Joven. Instead, in a Pueblo Joven of about 50,000 people, this potential explosiveness is diffused throughout the approximately 300 block elections, where the local and purely personal component is reasonably large.

THE SUPPORTIVE CONDITIONS FOR INCLUSIONARY POLICIES

By 1974 the majority of urban squatters had been reorganized from above into the state-chartered Pueblos Jóvenes. Titles and services were being distributed to the squatters at an accelerated rate, and government distribution policies were being carried out within the new system of the Pueblos Jóvenes. Judging from the fact that there were virtually no parallel institutions left in the squatter settlements to challenge or compete with the newly formed structures,[32] that there was only sporadic and scattered resistance to the creation of the new political institutions (in sharp contrast to the sugar sector, as we will see later), that there were no significant antiregime movements based on the support of the squatter settlements, and that, at regime-sponsored political rallies, one of the largest contingents was from the Pueblos Jóvenes, we can say that, from the regime's perspective, inclusionary policies in the squatter sector had been installed with relative success as of 1974.[33]

When we examine the squatter sector from the perspective of the variables described in Chapter 3, we see that all the variables were supportive of inclusionary policies. The most salient were the variable of the ratio of resources to effective demand (variable five), the variable concerning social welfare and reform space (variable four), and most importantly the variable concerning the degree of autonomous development of political organization and interest groups (variable two).[34]

Consider first the question of reform space and the relationship

[32] The absence of parallel institutions is discussed and documented later in the chapter.

[33] Not withstanding this overall judgment, two important caveats should be borne in mind. First there obviously was some resentment and resistance to the re-organization attempts, especially in those settlements with strong organizations that had to be dismantled as the price of eligibility for titles and services. Second, the institutional agent of incorporation—SINAMOS—was normally resented, and even before the end of Phase I the search had begun within the government to get some other agency to administer the system set up by SINAMOS. For resentment of SINAMOS, see Henry A. Dietz, "Bureaucratic Demand-Making and Clientelistic Participation in Peru," in *Authoritarianism and Corporatism in Latin America* ed. Malloy, pp. 450-53.

[34] Conditions were also supportive for the two other variables. Concerning variable three, despite the fact that the government feared potential anomic violence in the squatter sector, Collier's book clearly shows that there was still a relatively low level of polarization in the sector when the military came to power. Elite unity (variable one) has never been shaken gravely over squatter policy (as it has been over policies toward newspapers, for example) partly because in the installation period it did not appear to present any conflicts with other regime goals or to generate strong organized resistance and because prior military civic-action projects had built up a degree of policy consensus about squatter policy within the military. Most significantly there was a close fit between the military as institution's general concern with internal security and political control and the specific policies being implemented in the squatter sector by the military as government.

175

between demands and resources. Fortunately there exists a baseline study of settler attitudes and requirements carried out before the military began its new policy. This study is useful for assessing potential reform space and the "fit" between citizen wants and policy outputs. The survey, a carefully drawn, multistage probability sample that encompassed the entire squatter population in Lima, polled squatter attitudes toward twenty-six government service areas.[35] The survey attempted to estabilsh indicators for the "extent of dissatisfaction" and the "intensity of dissatisfaction."[36] The results are shown in Figure 5.2.

As we see, there is a very close fit between the regime's policy outputs in the Pueblo Joven sector since 1968 and the squatter demand pattern as determined by the 1967 poll. The major focus of the Pueblo Joven program in regard to services has been on street leveling (and later paving), water, sewage, street (and eventually house) lighting, and the delivery of property titles.[37] The extremely high intensity of concern over the lack of legal property titles confirms that this was a major area of potential reform space available to the government. The squatters' concern to legalize their position is understandable given the fact that some Latin American governments, especially Brazil, have used police and bulldozers to raze entire squatter settlements.

The government's capacity to respond to demands in the squatter sector is aided by a number of factors. Most squatters are on government-owned land. Satisfaction of title demands thus does

[35] The results are reported in Frank M. Andrews and George W. Phillips, "The Squatters of Lima: Who They Are and What They Want," *The Journal of Developing Areas* (January 1970). The survey was carried out in 1967. When the article was published, Andrews was senior study director at the University of Michigan's Survey Research Center. By focusing on government services the survey unfortunately neglected the important area of employment.

[36] "The Extension Index (simply the percentage of respondents who were less than satisfied with a given service) indicated how widespread was the problem. The Intensity Index indicated how important was the problem *to those who had it.* (This Index was computed by determining the percentage of dissatisfied people who were *very* dissatisfied.)" Ibid., p. 217. Emphasis in original.

[37] Based on my interviews with Pueblos Jóvenes and government officials and direct observation. Also the vast majority of notices concerning new services that the government puts in the official newspaper, *El Peruano*, fall into these categories. The only major demand that the regime has not specifically addressed is the location of medical services.

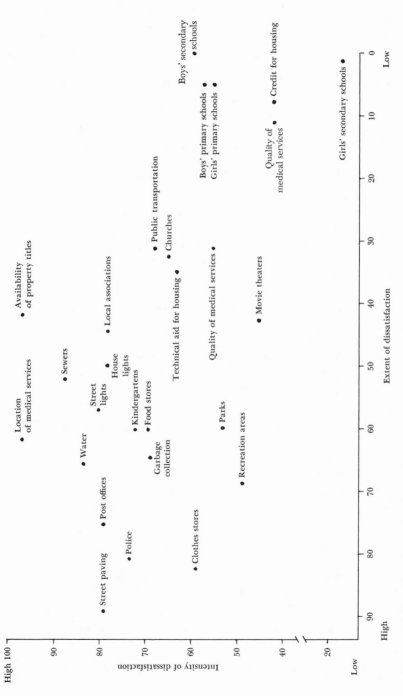

FIGURE 5.2. Squatter demand pattern for twenty-six urban services, Lima, 1967. Source: Frank M. Andrews and George Phillips, "The Squatters of Lima: Who They Are and What They Want," *The Journal of Developing Areas* 4 (January 1970): 211-24.

not entail the politically costly priority-resolving conflict that normally accompanies basic change.[38] For example, unlike sweeping agrarian reform, title granting does not require state expropriation policies. And unlike industrial reform, it does not need state-enforced policies of profit sharing or state insistence on worker participation in management decisions. In addition, since most of the squatters' land is in previously unused desert, title granting does not entail immediate revenue losses. Title granting is not, however, an unlimited free resource. Granting of property titles entails opportunity costs for future state use of the land. Also, the more the resource is exhausted close to the city, the more "costly" become future allocations to the recipient in terms of time and money spent in travel to work sites in the city.

The government's general policy toward other services is geared toward bringing demand into rough balance with supply. The basic principle is that no non-educational services are completely free. Electricity, paving, water, etc., only come to a Pueblo Joven *after* the settlers, via their representation system, have agreed on priorities and back their highest priority task with a cash down-payment. This down-payment is based on a quota system for each household and is collected by the secretary of finance of each block. The residents of the Pueblo Joven also agree to help with their labor. The state administration believes the system has the merit of avoiding the paternalism of the past, where the government, especially under General Odría, frequently gave services without payment. The present system is also congruent with their version of a participatory, self-help community.

As a response to the revolution of rising expectations, the system has the advantage for the state that dwellers normally have not asked for everything at once. The cash down-payment principle diminishes the levels of demand and endows the provision of services with an aura of governmental responsiveness, because in theory each Pueblo Joven has arrived at its own priority for services after collective discussions.[39]

[38] A number of other studies support the thesis that home ownership is the central politically oriented demand among squatters. See for example, Henry Dietz, "Urban Squatter Settlements in Peru: A Case History and Analysis," *Journal of Inter-American Development* 11 (July 1969): 353-370. Even among industrial workers in Lima, home ownership was the central objective. See Guillermo Briones and José Mejía Valera, *El obrero industrial*, p. 71.

[39] In a number of cases I observed, however, the government officials made

Thus because of the low cost of the resource being distributed, the demand-dampening effect of the self-financing principle, and the reasonably close fit between the government's program and the squatters' prior demands, the variable of demand/resource ratio and the variable of reform space were reasonably favorable to the government's inclusionary policies in the squatter sector.

The final and in this case the most important variable to consider concerns the squatters' history of organizational development, ideological and party identification, and goal-oriented political participation (variable two).

Analysis of voting records of the 36 districts constituting Lima Province in the Department of Lima for the presidential election of 1963 (the last before the military regime assumed power in 1968) and the municipal elections of 1963 and 1966, does not reveal any strong pattern differentiating districts with high barriada populations from those with low barriada populations.[40] The popular myth is that barriada populations supported disproportionately the authoritarian populist Odría. However, in 1963 Odría received exactly the same percentage of the vote (36.2 percent) as Belaúnde in the three districts in which over 70 percent of the population were barriada residents.[41] Moreover, the leader of Peru's best organized party, APRA, polled only 26.5 percent in the three barriada districts.[42] The inference is that when the military came to power they did not have to confront a population that, as a group, was strongly committed to an existing party or political figure. The barriadas did, however, have a tradition of organization, namely the neighborhood associations. As was noted earlier the associations had a tradition of local elections and were reasonably effective vehicles for the squatters' purposes. However this tradition of local organization

---

very strong recommendations as to which services were most needed. The estimate most often given the author by government officials was that the settlers would pay approximately 10% of the total cost of the project.

[40] See the study by Sandra Powell, "Political Participation in the Barriadas: A Case Study," *Comparative Political Studies* 2 (July 1969): 195-215.

[41] Ibid., p. 200. He did, however, exceed his Lima average in these three districts by 1.4%, while Belaúnde was 2.2 percentage points below his Lima average. This is not enough, however, to sustain the myth of strong barriada support for Odría. Odría did receive a greater share of the votes in the particular settlement area most closely associated with his populist policies, San Martín de Porras.

[42] Ibid., p. 200.

entailed low ideological commitments to national political organizations. As Dietz summarizes, settler "participation frequently revolves around local community associations and their activities, tending . . . to be instrumental, rather than ideological or partisan."[43] Part of the settler organizational heritage is that they are clientelistic in nature largely oriented toward getting government services in exchange for support. Collier notes, "In general, these settlement associations have not tended to make demands on the political system. They exist largely for the purpose of carrying out community projects and for cooperating with any state or private aid programs that are available, often changing their leadership at the beginning of the term of a new national president to maximize such cooperation."[44]

On analytic grounds one would predict that the squatters' organizational legacy would aid the government in its efforts to impose an inclusionary policy with low levels of coercion. This has in fact been so.

As clientelistic organizations the squatters had a tradition of exchanging their support for political patrons or brokers who could speak authoritatively on their behalf before the key distributive or coercive agencies of the state. Under the military regime, however, the old political parties and patrons do not have significant access to these distributive or coercive agencies of the state. Thus the legacy of barriada organization as clientelistic structures oriented toward state power meant that most of the dwellers were relatively well disposed toward the idea that their new dweller organizations tacitly support a group (i.e., the military government) that appeared for the time being to have a de facto monopoly of all the means of distribution and coercion that could affect them.[45]

43 Dietz, "Political Participation by the Urban Poor in an Authoritarian Context: The Case of Lima, Peru," p. 65.

44 David Collier, *Squatters and Oligarchs*, p. 62.

45 A number of studies of squatters' associations stress that, to the extent the state bureaucracies are seen as responsive to squatter goals, there is a shift away from interest in the squatter association as an instrumental vehicle toward the state bureaucracy, which is then viewed as the most relevant organization. See for example Dietz, "Urban Squatter Settlements in Peru: A Case History and Analysis," p. 365. Also see Daniel Goldrich, Raymond B. Pratt and C. R. Schuller, "The Political Integration of Lower-Class Urban Settlements in Chile and Peru," *Studies in Comparative International Development* 3 (1967-1968), pp. 8-9.

The regime's inclusionary policies were also facilitated by the fact that there were almost no ideologically committed organizations to dismantle coercively. More subtly, one could predict that because the squatters did not want to jeopardize the instrumental relationships between their organizations and the state apparatus, the squatters, not the state, would perform many of the tasks of containing or removing militant, antiregime activists who might emerge from the Pueblo Joven electoral structure. The pattern of candidate selection that I observed is consistent with this hypothesis. In most cases where radical or antiregime candidates for election were declared ineligible, the dwellers themselves played a major role in this evaluation. Normally the SINAMOS field promoters implied that the preliminary check to see if the prospective candidate fulfilled the "buenos antecedentes" prerequisite had raised some doubts about the suitability of the candidate. In most cases, however, the government representative did not declare the candidate ineligible. The block dwellers, nonetheless, after consultation among themselves, asked the candidate to step down because they believed he or she would be a less effective broker with the state than a more "acceptable" candidate. This is not to say that coercion was absent, but that unobtrusive anticipatory squatter self-censorship rather than confrontation and overt state coercion seems to have been the norm in the installation period.[46]

To conclude, the political identifications and structures the military regime encountered in the squatter sector were not strongly resistant to the imposition by the state of inclusionary policies. The squatters did have a history of local, service-oriented organizations. But the goals of these organizations were such that they could be preempted by, and finally almost completely subsumed within, the new structures of representation and distribution devised by the regime. Indeed we can conclude not only that the instrumental, clientelistic heritage of these organizations gave ample latitude for the construction by the state elite of new

[46] Dietz, on the basis of his observations of demand-making patterns of the squatter representatives in the governmental office for Pueblos Jóvenes, makes a similar judgment, "the most fundamental rule of behavior in approaching [the government office] is simply not to break any rules. . . . Any display of belligerence or hostility would normally be considered not only bad form, but also prejudicial and harmful to the undertaking." "Bureaucratic Demand-Making and Clientelistic Participation in Peru," p. 421.

inclusionary structures but that the local, self-help, nonpartisan orientation of the previous settler organizations were reasonably congruent with the organizational structures the military regime favored.[47]

POST-INSTALLATION POLITICS: CONSEQUENCES, TENSIONS AND PROSPECTS

From May to November of 1972, when I first began my study of the squatter sector in Peru, the regime had defined its policy toward the squatters, was reasonably content with the results, and bureaucratic extension of the program rather than heated ideological debate characterized the government's activity in the sector. In this section, I want to explore the consequences, tensions, and prospects of this kind of political organizational effort, as assessed by my follow-up studies of the squatter sector in Peru in 1974 and 1975.

Once inclusionary structures have been established in a sector, a key question concerns their impact on the future emergence of other patterns of interest articulation and aggregation. Do the structures really matter? In the discussion in Chapter 2, I indicated the ways in which the inclusionary organizational structures for labor established by Vargas in Brazil and by Cárdenas in Mexico impeded the formation of competitive and more autonomous or especially antiregime, organizations in the labor sector. How do the Peruvian government's policies in the Pueblos Jóvenes sector impede or facilitate the appearance of alternative structures of interest articulation?

The most obvious effect of these policies is that, in principle, every Pueblo Joven in Peru will eventually have an official organization down to the block level. By late 1972, for example, the office in charge of organizing block committees in the greater Lima area had already completed the full cycle of elections and leader training seminars for over 4,800 committees, or almost 65 percent of the total blocks.[48] Since all titles and service distribu-

---

[47] Dietz makes a similar observation when he notes that the settlers "are not forced into a pattern of authority relationships unfamiliar or even undesirable to them." Ibid., p. 442. For elements of congruence between the prior pattern of settler organization and the military government's design, also see Collier, *Squatters and Oligarchs*, p. 107.

[48] Figures supplied to the author by the Décima Región of SINAMOS.

tions are linked to this representative system, at least formally, the state has filled almost all the organizational space. This does not make entry by antiregime groups impossible, but clearly the squatters are not easily available to anti-regime organizations claiming to be in a powerful position to help deliver services to the Pueblos Jóvenes. The fact that most of the squatters are already paying their dues to official organizations will make it especially difficult for dissident squatter groups to build parallel organizations with voluntary contributions by the squatters. An even more serious obstacle is presented by the fact that the official Pueblos Jóvenes structures are variants of the "concession" theory of organization discussed in Chapter 1. The Pueblos Jóvenes are granted official status as the only legal representative of the squatters. Only these officially recognized organizations have the right to enter into contractual negotiations with the state bureaucracy in regard to output functions of the state. In fact neither in 1972 nor in 1974 did I encounter any significant overt parallel political organizations in the squatter settlements.[49] This is a concrete example of the general argument I outlined in Chapter 1, namely that state structures can have a powerful impact on the capacity of latent interest groups to actually aggregate their interests.

The analysis of organic-statist inclusionary policies necessarily involves close examination of the power relationships between the state and the specific sectors of society. However, it also requires the evaluation of the material, political, and ideological costs of organizing each sector from the perspective of other major regime goals. How does the government's policy toward the squatter sector affect its relations with other sectors, and does

[49] The question of parallel organizations is crucial. If research indicates that parallel organizations exist and that many of the citizens articulate and aggregate demands via parallel organizations, the state-chartered organizations obviously have not been able to take over effectively the function of interest representation and run the risk of being paper organizations. When I asked citizens how they got something done, they normally said they contacted their Pueblo Joven representative. A foreign scholar carried out a survey in Pueblos Jóvenes in Trujillo from January to August 1974. In a private communication he noted that the only real political network in the settlements was between the officially recognized Pueblo Joven committees and SINAMOS, and that no significant parallel organizations existed. He also asked people where they would go to have a problem solved, and a very high percentage said "go to Comité Vecinal."

it support or hinder the attainment of more fundamental regime goals?

One of the stated goals of the regime was to structure Peru into a new set of organic organizations which would decrease class conflict and violent breakdowns of the law. In particular, there was a strong desire to reduce the role of violence as the normal mode by which the poor achieve their goals. The widespread peasant land invasions in the Andes, and the quickening pace of urban squatter invasions in the coastal cities in the early and mid 1960s, had instilled in the military and the socioeconomic elites a fear that the rule of law was breaking down.

The regime's policy toward both agrarian reform and squatter reform was to supervise the creation of new property relationships that would incorporate both peasants and squatters into the legal arrangements of the new society. To the extent that the regime's policies can be considered radical, they closely approximate Apter's category of "radicalization for embourgeoisement."[50] In the case of the squatters, this has meant a desire to turn "invaders" into property holders and tax payers. The establishment of controlled *legal* settlement growth was meant to decrease the possibility of radical sponsorship of generalized attacks on the concept of property or the new socioeconomic order. To the extent that government policy only granted title to publicly owned land, and helped to check invasions on privately controlled land, the policy was widely interpreted by the middle and upper classes and the military as a low-cost, non-zero-sum reform. Thus both the economic and political costs, from the viewpoints of other sectors, were low, and the policy was generally supportive of the wider regime goal of creating new organic structures.

However the regime's desire to supervise a new controlled system of property distribution that would not jeopardize other goals has not been completely successful. In May 1971 there was a sudden, large-scale squatter occupation in the Pamplona area of Lima. The government used coercive measures against the invasion. The hostile reaction by the regime seemed motivated by three considerations. First, the unexpectedly large-scale invasion raised concern that nonregime forces were controlling the

---

[50] See David Apter, "Radicalization and Embourgeoisement: Some Hypotheses for a Comparative Study of History," *The Journal of Interdisciplinary History* 1 (Winter 1971), pp. 265-303, and his *Choice and the Politics of Allocation*, pp. 36-38.

new squatters.[51] Part of the land was privately owned and thus seemed to threaten the regime's long-range policy of making private property (within the context of the new organic community that was being constructed) respected.[52] Third, it appeared that the regime's policy of gradual location of squatters in approved areas had completely broken down.

Faced with the crisis, the government declared a spacious desert area south of Lima a new zone of legal settlement, and within two weeks had forceably trucked most of the squatters to this area. The president announced a major program of the installation of the basic infrastructure of a city—bulldozed roads, sewage, and some lighting, thus turning the gigantic new Pueblo Joven, El Salvador, into what government planners hoped would be a model of orderly urban growth.[53] The new settlement was created overnight in May 1971. The government believed it was designing far into the future with its plan to put in infrastructures to support the target population of 250,000 by 1980.[54] By 1975 El Salvador's population already approached 150,000, making it one of the largest cities in Peru.

The government's response to the Pamplona crisis highlights a number of system-level problems about the state's squatter policy. The agrarian reform has a secondary goal of slowing urban migration by making the peasants' life more just and the

[51] This fear even triggered off the rather panicky jailing by General Artola, minister of the interior, of Bishop Bambarén, who had worked closely with the military to establish the Pueblos Jóvenes program. The crisis was resolved only when the bishop was released, and the general soon thereafter retired. The Pamplona episode was widely reported in the Lima press from May 7 to May 14, 1971. See in particular, "Bambarén: Uds no son invasores sino fundadores de nuevo pueblo," *Correo*, May 10, 1971, p. 2, and "Ministro del Interior denuncia agitación en zona de Pamplona," *El Peruano*, May 11, 1971, p. 1.

[52] This point was brought home to me when I was shown the invasion site by one of the high officials of the government's Pueblos Jóvenes program. He waved to the land and told me it was privately held and said emphatically, "If we had allowed that, then nothing we are trying to build would be sacred."

[53] See the glowing two-page center spread about El Salvador in the pro-government newspaper, "Villa Salvador: el pueblo joven de la esperanza," *La Crónica*, May 14, 1971, pp. 14-15. See also the report of the president's personal visit, "Velasco en Villa Salvador: todo deve estar planificado," *Correo*, May 17, 1971, p. 1.

[54] Interview with the architect in charge of planning of El Salvador, November 12, 1972.

185

entire agricultural sector more dynamic. However, in the short run, the pressures toward urbanization and thus squatter invasions are continuing. Wanting neither to employ the high level of coercion needed to stop invasions nor to tolerate the invasion of private property that could run counter to the regime's "stable society" goals, the military has responded by attempting to channel the bulk of the new squatters into state designated zones. This policy, while solving the legal and property problems, may well contribute to other difficulties. The receptive policy toward squatters appears to have increased the rate of rural migration. In 1973 SINAMOS replicated the 1970 census of the Pueblos Jóvenes and found that the total number of settlements had increased from 610 to 976, and the total population had soared from 1,516,488 to 2,677,660—an increase of 77 percent in a three-year period.[55]

The SINAMOS report and my later interviews with officials indicate that in some areas the political and economic cost of the spreading settlements is increasing, because some of the new settlements have encroached upon land the Ministry of Agriculture had hoped to make productive by extending the irrigation systems. Another problem is that, by and large, the organic-statist response to the squatters has been political—the channeling of squatters into organizations that allow the state simultaneously to control the situation and respond to some of the squatters' demands relating to their squatter environment. However, this cooptive sectoral approach has not been directly linked to the basic question of creating jobs for new squatters, and the 1973 report shows unemployment in the Pueblos Jóvenes had increased.[56] The state has made some plans in the area, but to date there has been little in the way of concrete results.[57]

[55] Perú, SINAMOS, *Diagnóstico nacional de la problemática de los pueblos jóvenes*, pp. 146-47. There is some evidence that the government began to slow the rate of title-granting in 1975-76. This may have been a deliberate policy effort to reduce incentives for urban migration.

[56] Ibid., p. 142.

[57] For example, the state has set aside land for an industrial park that will run parallel to El Salvador. However, planners indicated to me that new investment plans in no way match the job needs of the new squatters. By mid-1976 the park was still empty. The director of the "Comité Vecinal" system for Lima and Callao estimated that in El Salvador 40% of the working-age male population were fully employed, 30% had partial employment, and 30% had no employment. Interview, August 1, 1974, Lima.

What is the political future of the state chartered Pueblos Jóvenes organizations? In 1972 the political organizers of SINA-MOS were reasonably satisfied with the self-contained system focused on titles, elections, and services in each of the Pueblos Jóvenes. By 1974-1975, they were less certain about the organizational design. There was both more apathy at the bottom of the system and more complex demands at the top of the system than that posited in any organic-statist formula.

The state organizers had hoped that by linking services to the representation system, the representation system would retain the degree of vitality it possessed in the initial drive to organize for titles. However, in those areas where the titles and the major "once-only" services, such as lighting and paving, have been installed, interest in competing as a candidate for electoral position within the Pueblos Jóvenes has dropped. The director of the Lima-Callao electoral system estimated that, for approximately 20 percent of the positions, there were no candidates, and the government field workers have had to search for applicants.[58] As the title granting and provision of infrastructure proceeds, the problem of growing apathy at the lowest levels may well force changes in the electoral system. At the top of the system of representation, the local service orientation has come under some attack. In those municipalities where the Pueblos Jóvenes population constitutes the bulk of the population, the contradiction between the government's position of urging participation within the Pueblo Joven structure, while still directly appointing from above the chief officials of the municipality, has led to growing demands that the Pueblos Jóvenes directly elect the municipal officials and that these officials be granted wide powers to handle problems that go beyond those originally defined as appropriate for consideration by Pueblo Joven committees.[59] Another pres-

[58] Ibid.

[59] See for example the report of the first convention of the Pueblos Jóvenes of the "Zona Norte" of Lima, "Líderes de PP.JJ. piden subrogación de 3 alcaldes: sugieren elegir a los reemplazantes," *La Prensa* (May 27, 1974), p. 1. One of the top SINAMOS officials for the national Pueblo Joven program estimated that pressures were building for wider powers for the Pueblo Joven representatives in Chimbote, Trujillo, and the Northern and Southern "Zones" of Lima. Interview, October 1, 1974. For a frank acknowledgment by a former high SINAMOS official about the failure to link base organizations either to local government or development planning, see Hélan Jaworski, "La planificación participante y la planificación de

sure, especially in El Salvador, is to give economic content to the Pueblos Jóvenes structures by channeling "social property" firms into the Pueblos Jóvenes.[60] Finally, the fact that the regime has filled virtually all the organizational space in the Pueblos Jóvenes may impede overt parallel organizations of a political nature in the Pueblos Jóvenes. If the economic pressures intensify, however, the inclusionary structures in themselves cannot prevent the participation by settlers as individuals in anomic demonstrations in the city, nor do they totally preclude the possibility that groups of settlers might make direct demands on the regime, or play an important supporting role in a general strike situation. There was ample and mounting evidence of all three types of squatter activity in 1975-77. In early 1975 squatters participated in the widespread looting and anomic disturbances during the police strike. In April 1976 "some 10,000 inhabitants of El Salvador began a march on Lima in support of a list of demands that has been ignored by authorities."[61] In the general strike of July 19, 1977, squatters played a particularly effective role in blocking bus traffic on the outskirts of Lima, a role they also performed in Cuzco during that city's general strike of November 1977.[62]

To date neither the political nor economic demands that have originated within the Pueblo Joven structures have constituted a sustained threat to the regime's programs, although these demands are causing the regime to reevaluate the structures it installed in 1969-1972.

Privately, those Phase I officials high in the Pueblos Jóvenes program and SINAMOS who were advocates of increased participation stated, as early as 1974 that, although they had been successful in installing the system, the system did not have a great enough political base because the settlement residents were not owners, or at least part-owners, of any of the means of production. These officials thus had shifted their hopes for more mean-

---

base en el Perú," *Revista Interamericana de Planificación*, 9 (June 1975), pp. 5-15.

[60] This is a major theme in *Comunidad*, the official newspaper of El Salvador. Significantly El Salvador has changed its name to *Comunidad Urbana Autogestionaria "Villa El Salvador."*

[61] See *Latin America* (May 21, 1976), p. 159.

[62] For details of squatter political activities see, *Marka* (November 25, 1977), p. 7; *Latin American Economic Report* (October 14, 1977), p. 176; and *Latin American Political Report* (August 19, 1977), p. 251.

ingful participation to economic areas. In the next chapter I examine the political and economic problems of worker-self management in an area of high worker organization—the sugar sector. Both because of the economic content of worker participation, and because of the previous history of political and trade union organization in the sugar sector, the regime's organic-statist organizational model met problems that were substantially more complex and difficult than those in the Pueblos Jóvenes sector.

SIX · *Reorganizing the Organized: Statism versus "Participatory" Self-Management in the Sugar Cooperatives*

DURING Phase I, the Peruvian government began one of the major modern experiments in developing new forms of ownership, worker self-management, and participation. Restructuring civil society into new functional units that would contribute to its announced goals of solidarity, equity, and meaningful participation was one of the most challenging—and ultimately intractable—problems the Peruvian military elite faced.

Since "participation" can mean such different things in different systems, let us briefly see how "participation" as defined in Phase I, contrasted with the role of participation in liberal democracy and in a communist mobilization regime such as China.

For many contemporary theorists of liberal democracy, the word has a restricted but vital meaning. For these theorists, the defining criteria of democracy revolve around the institutional arrangements that allow non-elites to participate in periodic, openly contested elections that select the government elite. In J. A. Schumpeter's influential discussion, "the democratic method is that institutional arrangement for arriving at political decisions in which individuals acquire the power to decide by means of a competitive struggle for the people's vote."[1]

For Robert Dahl, a "key characteristic of a democracy is the continuing responsiveness of the government to the preferences of its citizens, considered as political equals." To achieve this responsiveness, he argues, contested elections are central. The "three

[1] Schumpeter, *Capitalism, Socialism and Democracy* (New York: Harper Torchbook 1962), p. 269. Elaborating on Schumpeter Juan J. Linz argues for the analytic utility of restricting the word "democracy" to procedural arrangements and against building into the definition of democracy the quality of outputs; see his "Crisis, Breakdown and Reequilibration of Competitive Democracies," in *Breakdowns of Democratic Regimes: The European and Latin American Experience*, ed. Linz and Stepan.

190

necessary conditions" for the citizens' participation in this public contestation are that they have the right to formulate preferences, signify preferences, and have preferences weighed equally in the conduct of government. For these three conditions to be met, Dahl offers eight institutional guarantees.[2]

Whatever other meanings the term "participation" may have for these theorists, without the citizen's free participation in competitive elections a system would not meet their definition of electoral democracy.[3]

In a communist mobilization regime such as China, participation also plays a crucial role. Here the emphasis is on the maximum *involvement* of the people in the *execution* of the party's policies. This intensive and extensive mass participation in itself is one of the principal processes to ensure the responsiveness of party leaders to the masses. A study of the Chinese style of participation before the Cultural Revolution concluded that (1) "the major function of participation" is the "execution of Party policies," (2) it "emphasizes direct contact between cadres and masses as the surest means of eliciting popular participation and keeping political leaders in touch with popular demands," (3) it "insists that popular political action support a supreme, unified national interest as defined solely by the Communist Party," (4) it "emphasizes the quality and morality of political leaders, rather than legal and institutionalized popular controls, as the guarantee of good government," and (5) it "recognizes no theoretical limits to the extension of demands for political activity and no private obligations that can take precedence over public ones."[4] During the Cultural Revolution, workers' management

[2] Dahl, *Polyarchy: Participation and Opposition*, pp. 1-3.

[3] In keeping with this approach, a recent, extensive review of the literature on participation explicitly confined the analysis to "democratic societies that have well-established legal opportunities for political activity—in particular the right to vote in meaningful elections." See Norman H. Nie and Sidney Verba, "Political Participation" in *Handbook of Political Science*, ed. Fred I. Greenstein and Nelson W. Polsby (Reading, Mass.: Addison-Wesley Publishing Company, 1975), Vol. 4, pp. 1-74, quote from page 3. For the argument that participation within democratic theory should be defined more broadly see Carol Pateman, *Participation and Democratic Theory*, esp. pp. 1-44, 103-11.

[4] James R. Townsend, *Political Participation in Communist China*, pp. 3-4. In 1974 Cuba, with local elections in the province of Matanzas followed in 1976 by the election of a national assembly, began an interesting experiment to devise formulas for combining meaningful electoral participa-

teams and revolutionary committees were created in the factories to increase worker participation. The Marxist theorist Charles Bettelheim considered this a major advance in meaningful worker participation because it altered the relations of production.[5] Some later scholarship indicates, however, that the pattern of participation that existed before the Cultural Revolution is re-emerging, especially in the larger factories.[6]

The philosophy of the military elite in Phase I Peru was much closer to an organic-statist than to a liberal or Marxist view of society. The major doctrinal spokesmen of Phase I depicted the role of the state apparatus as that of restructuring civil society into functional units that would contribute to the formation of a "solidaristic, participatory, communitarian" harmony and would lessen class conflict and individual egoism. In such a society, participation would play a key role, but the emphasis was not on the institutional guarantees for the individual voter as in liberal democracy, nor on the intense involvement under party direction in the execution of party goals as in communist mobilization regimes. Instead the locus of participation in Peru, at least in the early stages of the regime, was to be within state-chartered functional organizations. The exercise of participation

---

tion and political and economic decentralization with vanguard party mobilization. Much valuable material on the Cuban experiment is contained in the special issues of *Center for Cuban Studies*, 2 (October-December 1975), and *Cuba Review*, 6 (September 1976). A first-hand account by sympathetic Chilean journalists is contained in Marta Harnecker, *¿Cuba: dictadura o democracia?* (México: Siglo Veintiuno, 1975).

[5] The fascinating changes he observed seem to me to represent a deepening, rather than an alteration, of the communist-mobilization model of participation. He argues (approvingly) that the Chinese workers' management teams "have nothing in common with the Yugoslav practice of self-management." I would agree. Yugoslavia, with its experiment in a labor-managed, decentralized, market economy is not a communist mobilization regime. The role of participation in Peruvian and Yugoslavian labor-managed enterprises will be compared later in the chapter. Bettelheim's book is *Cultural Revolution and Industrial Organization in China: Changes in Management and the Division of Labor*, translated by Alfred Ehrenfeld (New York and London: Monthly Review Press, 1974), p. 29.

[6] See for example, Christopher Howe, "Labor Organizations and Incentives in Industry, before and after the Cultural Revolution," in *Authority, Participation and Cultural Change in China*, ed. Stuart R. Schram (Cambridge: Cambridge University Press, 1973), pp. 233-56, and Mitch Meisner, "The Shenyang Transformer Factory—A Profile," *The China Quarterly*, 52 (October-December 1972), esp. p. 731.

in theory, was to consist in the management and control by occupational groups of those problems closest to their day-to-day
work life. Occupational groups played a key role in the doctrine
of participation. Such groups were supposed to help overcome the
egoism of the individual, which was seen as a major defect of
liberal capitalism, and to avoid total control by the state, which
violated the subsidiarity principle and which was seen as a major
defect of communism. In this respect the Phase I doctrinal emphasis on occupational groups echoed the classic formulation by
Emile Durkheim:

> A society composed of an infinite number of unorganized indi-
> viduals, that a hypertrophied State is forced to oppress and
> contain, constitutes a veritable sociological monstrosity. For
> collective activity is always too complex to be able to be ex-
> pressed through the single and unique organ of the State. . . .
> Where the State is the only environment in which men can
> live communal lives, they inevitably lose contact, become de-
> tached, and thus society disintegrates. A nation can be main-
> tained only if, between the State and the individual, there is
> intercalated a whole series of secondary groups near enough
> to the individuals to attract them strongly in their sphere of
> action and drag them, in this way, into the general torrent of
> social life. . . . Occupational groups are suited to fill this role,
> and that is their destiny. . . . since these occupations today
> absorb the major part of our collective forces. . . . What we
> especially see in the occupational group is a moral power ca-
> pable of containing individual egos, of maintaining a spirited
> sentiment of common solidarity in the consciousness of all the
> workers.[7]

For the core group of Phase I, the state's restructuring of ownership patterns so as to give the workers a significant share of
ownership in the enterprise was a necessary precondition for the
authentic participation of such occupational groups. This was so
because of their belief that for the participation of occupational
groups to be real, participation must have an economic base or
such groups would be manipulated by the owners, as in capitalism, or by the state, as in communism. As an important spokesman for SINAMOS expressed it: "In capitalist systems represent-

[7] Durkheim, "Preface to the Second Edition—Some Notes on Occupational
Groups" in his *The Division of Labor in Society*, pp. 28, 10.

ativeness is merely formal. In an authoritarian-socialist regime there is no real economic base for workers' participation. We want to give an economic base to groups so that they can really participate."[8]

The Peruvian regime in Phase I attempted to give functional groups this economic base by creating a series of agricultural cooperatives and industrial communities, and by beginning to generate a social property sector. These different economic sectors, together with the state sector (which includes much of mining, telecommunications, and the new metallurgy industries) and a private sector would, in the official doctrine of the regime, provide the economic pluralism that would preclude either statist or capitalistic domination.[9] The goal, in President Velasco's words, was to bring together the best of the "libertarian, socialist, and Christian traditions" by:

> constructing in our country a democracy of full participation, that is to say a system based on a moral order of solidarity, not of individualism; on an economy fundamentally self-managing (autogestora) in which the means of production are predominantly of social property, under the direct control of those who by their work generate the wealth; and a political order where the power of decision, far from being a monopoly of political or economic oligarchy, is diffused and rooted essentially in the social, economic, and political institutions and managed, without, or with a minimum of, intermediaries, by the men and women which form them.[10]

For the Peruvian state elite, then, the organic order of solidarity that they were attempting to construct was seen as flowing to a great degree from the participatory, self-managing, functional

[8] Interview with Jaime Llosa, the director-general of Rural Organizations, SINAMOS, Lima, October 30, 1972.

[9] For a review of the range of these new ownership and participation formulas see Peter T. Knight, "New Forms of Economic Organization in Peru: Toward Workers' Self-Management" in *The Peruvian Experiment*, ed. Lowenthal, pp. 350-401.

[10] Speech given before the Second Ministerial Reunion of the Group of 77, Lima, October 28, 1971, and reproduced in General Juan Velasco Alvarado, *Velasco: la voz de la revolución*, (Lima: Ediciones Participación, 1972), vol. 2; p. 285. Another official presentation of the ideology of the regime closely follows this statement; *Bases ideológicas de la Revolución Peruana* (Lima: Oficina Central de Información, February 25, 1975).

groups they were forging. But how realistic was this attempt to create an organic order?

I argued earlier that, as an abstract model of governance, the organic-statist model differed from the command-socialist model in that it contained greater political pluralism and, in theory at least, greater decentralized self-management within the organic structures. In any concrete organic-statist experiment that takes this theoretical commitment seriously, the predicament becomes one of how to reconcile the statist control implicit in the model with a high degree of participation in the new structures created by the state. In all regimes to date whose stated ideology would place them in the category of organic statism, or inclusionary corporatism, a degree of limited pluralism has existed within the authoritarian political structure, but the statist thrust has virtually eliminated significant participation in functional groups. The Phase I state elite never did fully spell out how the functional groups they were creating would feed into national decision making. In the conclusion of this book I analyze the profound generic predicaments entailed in such an endeavor. In this chapter I explore the dilemmas of state control and participation at the subnational level, in one of the most important occupational groups—the sugar workers.

THE SUGAR COOPERATIVES: THE BACKGROUND

While on normative grounds the organic-statist model has been attractive to a broad variety of political elites for a number of reasons, the logic of such a model implies tension and inevitable conflict between the participatory and statist components. The special importance of the Peruvian experiment, especially in Phase I, was that it was one of the most concerted efforts to resolve this conflict by allowing a significant element of participation while maintaining the state's power to carry out sweeping programs to restructure civil society.

The Peruvian regime devised various formulas and mechanisms for increasing participation and new forms of worker-ownership and management. These included the creation of new industrial communities and plans to create a "social property" sector, both of which are discussed in Chapter 7. In theory the social property sector was to eventually be more important than the cooperative sector, but given the retrenchments of Phase II

195

it was in the sugar cooperatives that worker ownership and self-management actually advanced furthest and where participation based on self-management was most fully put to the test. It was the sugar cooperatives that the government initially singled out as the area where "the revolution has begun to carry out its ideal of constructing in Peru a social democracy of full participation."[11] For these reasons the quality of participation within state-chartered organizations, and the types of conflicts between participatory organizations and state goals inherent in organic statism, are best examined through a study of the sugar sector in Peru.

The sugar haciendas represented the most advanced sector of agro-industry in Peru when they were expropriated by the military in June 1969. After a twelve to fifteen-month transitional period of direct state management, all twelve of the haciendas were legally transferred to the workers in the form of new sugar cooperatives, although the state maintained numerous electoral restrictions. By April 1972, however, direct elections were allowed whereby the workers in the cooperatives selected all the representatives to general assemblies and the presidents of the cooperatives. An official bulletin issued by the government claimed that these elections represented the largest step yet taken by the government to "arrive at a democracy of producers, authentically participatory, and responsible."[12]

From the perspective of the military, the sugar cooperatives were by no means a showcase of participation in a marginal area. On the contrary, the economic stakes were high. The sugar haciendas had been one of the chief economic bases of the old oligarchy in Peru. They continue to be important to the military because they are one of the largest earners of foreign exchange and also allow the government to subsidize a significant item of domestic food consumption.[13] The political stakes were also high

[11] Official SINAMOS bulletin printed in *El Peruano: Diario Oficial* (April 13, 1972), p. 1.

[12] SINAMOS bulletin printed in *La Crónica* (April 19, 1972), p. 2.

[13] In 1972 sugar exports represented 9.1% of the total value of Peru's exports. In 1975, an exceptionally good year, sugar exports represented 18.9% of the total value and were Peru's leading export item. See, Perú, Central Reserve Bank, *Aide Memoire on the Economic Situation of Peru* (Lima: 1976), Table 8. Over half the total sugar production is sold to the domestic market at prices normally well below the world level. For the role of sugar in Peru's economy see the excellent work by Santiago Roca, "The Peruvian

since the sugar workers had a long tradition of political organization and ideological commitment. The sugar workers in fact formed the backbone of the Aprista party and trade unions, the historic opponent and competitor of the military.[14] The sugar cooperatives therefore presented a test case of the regime's philosophy that self-managing, apolitical cooperative organizations could erode prior trade union support, and through increased worker participation, ownership, and management, contribute to an organic, solidaristic society.

In the analysis that follows, three broad problems are examined. The first is why the government's attempt to add some exclusionary features to its original inclusionary sugar policy failed. This failure will be analyzed within the context of the hypotheses developed in Chapter 3. The abandonment of the exclusionary features by 1972 led to the government's decision to experiment with much greater organic-statist participation.

The second problem is the nature of this participation. In particular, I probe the predicament of reconciling participation, as seen from the perspective of the occupational group that is in theory self-managing, with strong statist direction of society. Where, and how, was this participatory self-management most significant? Where, and how, was it limited by the state?

Sugar Cooperatives: Some Fundamental Economic Problems, 1968-1972" in *Selfmanagement in Peru*, Peter T. Knight, Santiago Roca, J. Vanek and F. Collazo (Ithaca: Cornell University, Program on Participation and Labor-Managed Systems, No. 10, 1975), pp. 5-7. A revised version is available in Spanish as *Las cooperativas azucareras del Perú* (Lima: ESAN/Campodónico ediciones, 1975). For between-the-lines complaints by the sugar industry about selling at a low price to the domestic market see, Central de Cooperativas Agrarias de Producción Azucarera del Perú, *Caña de azúcar: plan de cultivo en base al incremento de la demanda interna* (Lima: 1974).

14 The bitterest conflict between the Apristas, the sugar workers, and the army was the 1932 Trujillo revolt, where an Aprista group, largely composed of workers from the Laredo plantation, after taking the O'Donovan garrison, executed ten officers. One scholar estimates that after the revolt was put down "over fifteen hundred civilians were executed by order of the military." See Peter F. Klarén, *Modernization, Dislocation, and Aprismo: Origins of the Peruvian Aprista Party, 1870-1932*, p. 141. A useful study of the political history of the plantations, especially in the period immediately after they were expropriated is Julio Cotler and Giorgio Alberti, "La reforma agraria en las haciendas azucareras del Perú" (Lima: manuscript 1971). A revised version will be published by the Institute de Estudios Peruanos in a special book on the sugar cooperatives.

The third problem is to assess the participatory versus statist predicament from the perspective of the state's goals. The Peruvian regime's assumption was that participation within functional groups would contribute to its larger goal of creating a solidaristic, communitarian society. Yet on analytic grounds, as we have argued, there seems to be a range of inherent contradictions between the goals of participation and the larger goals of the state. How have the claims of each functional unit to be self-managing been reconciled with the goal of equity within the sector? What are the implications of the model of self-managing cooperatives for the state's effort to construct organic unity and equity in the rest of the political system? What resources are available to the cooperatives to resist integration with other sectors, and what resources are available to the state to deal with this resistance without violating its goal of autonomous participation within each sector?

To explore these problems I selected for research eight of the twelve sugar cooperatives in existence in Peru since 1969. These cooperatives were Casa Grande (the largest, with 4,552 workers and a residential population of 33,000), Tumán, Pucalá, Paramonga, Pomalca, Cayaltí, Cartavio, and Laredo (the smallest of the eight, with 1,472 workers). Together these cooperatives employ 91.6 percent of the almost 24,000 workers in the sugar sector, and produce 92.5 percent of the sugar.[15] The cooperatives were visited in 1972 and again in 1974. Since in some cases I was asked not to cite interviews or documents directly, let me briefly indicate how I proceeded and the range of material upon which my evaluations are based. Wherever possible I interviewed officeholders of the three most important internal organizations within each cooperative: elected officials of the cooperatives (delegates to the General Assembly, and members of the Administrative and Vigilance Councils);[16] the secretary-general and secretary of de-

[15] Basic data on all the cooperatives are contained in Perú, SINAMOS, *Problemas económicos fundamentales que afrontan las cooperativas azucareras* (Lima: 1972), p. 31.

[16] Each of the twelve sugar cooperatives also elects four delegates to their national organization, CECOAAP (Central de Cooperativas Agrarias de Producción Azucarera del Perú). The forty-eight delegates in turn select the members and officers of their Administrative and Vigilance Councils. Various delegates to CECOAAP, including a former president of the Administrative Council, were interviewed.

198

fense of the trade unions;[17] and the business manager *(gerente)* of the cooperative.[18]

I also interviewed key officials and collected policy working papers from the major organizations of the state apparatus concerned with the sugar sector. In fact, because of the economic and political importance of the experiment in the sugar sector, the government created a special state agency to monitor the finances, production, and participation of the cooperatives. This agency, *Sistema de Asesoramiento y Fiscalización de las Cooperativas Agrarias de Producción* (SAF-CAP) is headed by a uniformed colonel at each cooperative, is commanded by a general, and has a large civilian research staff.[19] In addition, the Ministry of Agriculture and the Office of Rural Organization of SINA-MOS (the first concerned largely with production and the second with problems of equity and participation) are actively involved in the sugar cooperatives.[20]

Throughout my research, I tried to determine power flows,

[17] Of the eight cooperatives only Tumán, the most patriarchically run of the old haciendas, does not have a union.

[18] Under the terms by which the government gave the workers ownership of the cooperatives, each cooperative is obligated to pay, over a twenty-year period, part of the assessed value of the land and equipment. This *adjudication debt* provides the rubric by which the government claims the right to oversee some financial and managerial aspects of the cooperatives. In the case of the *gerente* each cooperative draws up a list of three nominees for the post but the final designation is made by the minister of agriculture. CECOAAP also has a gerente, who in coordination with the Administrative and Vigilance Councils, carries out marketing, long-range financing, diversification, and research activities.

[19] Its national headquarters are in Chiclayo, where I interviewed the executive officer of SAF-CAP, as well as senior staff members of the sociopolitical section and the legal office. It is formally an agency of SINAMOS but some observers say it is also associated with military intelligence. The duties of SAF-CAP are detailed in Resolución Suprema No. 285-71-AG (May 11, 1971) and Decreto Supremo No. 003-72-PM (February 29, 1972).

[20] The broad range of institutional actors, and the importance of the issues being debated, contributed to a relatively open, adversary style of public sector research. In addition to the line agencies, the government has created a center to research the various experiments in agrarian reform. This center (CENCIRA) conducts original field research and trains new agrarian reform personnel. To aid in the latter they have on file in their Lima documentation center surprisingly frank working papers of the various agencies involved in agrarian reform. I gratefully acknowledge the permission given me to use this documentation center.

the parameters and consequences of participation, and the major areas of conflict and change.

WORKER RESISTANCE TO INCORPORATION AND THE STRUGGLE TO EXPAND CHARTERED PARTICIPATION

The military government's expropriation of the sugar haciendas in June 1969 had the immediate intention of removing the economic base of a major sector of the old ruling elite as well as to give the agrarian reform a good chance of success by including the most wealthy agricultural units in the reform. A longer-range intention was to erode the base of the APRA party by incorporating the sugar workers into new inclusionary structures and transforming the haciendas into apolitical worker cooperatives. Implicit in the government's orientation was that, once the trade union members were the actual owners, the trade union mentality, and its political party expression, would fade. Ideally, from the government's perspective, what had been a source of strength for APRA, namely the APRA trade unions, could, by inclusionary policies, be transformed into a base of support for the new regime.

During the initial period of direct state management, the state interventor teams encouraged attacks on the abuses of the old oligarchical system and gave lectures preparing the workers for the eventual assumption of power in worker-managed cooperatives. As the date for the workers to elect their own leaders approached, however, the government became worried about how to reconcile what it saw as its revolutionary social and economic program, which needed strong state direction (and thus control), with its commitment to participation. A few weeks before the scheduled election, two decrees were issued that introduced "exclusionary" features into the original inclusionary design by curtailing the participation of workers with recent trade union or political party experience, and giving the government substantial powers to appoint delegates to the General Assembly.[21]

[21] Decreto Supremo No. 019-70-PM, and Decreto Ley No. 18299, both issued May 29, 1970. The four provisions provoking the greatest worker opposition were: (1) Any cooperative member who in the past had received time off from normal work obligations to carry out trade union duties for which he had been elected (*licencia sindical*) was ineligible to be a candidate for any office for the total length of time he had ever held

When queried about the reasons for the decision, one official acknowledged that there had been a debate within the government about how to foster participation while "guaranteeing the production structure" in a foreign exchange-earning sector.[22] A civilian lawyer in SAF-CAP who helped draft the 1970 election law that strictly chartered participation was more specific:

> The fundamental reason for the restrictions was to prevent the cooperatives from falling into the hands of APRA, which was both a traditional enemy of the army and was seen by the army as a group in alliance with rightest forces who wanted agrarian reform to fail . . .
>
> If the cooperative movement was to work it had to have time to develop. The restrictions were not against participation as such, but against participation by anti-revolutionary forces. The purpose of government selection of delegates was not to control the delegates but to neutralize the opposition.[23]

There is no hard evidence about how long the government believed these restrictions would be in force, but since the restrictions were linked to the agrarian debt, which was scheduled to be paid over a twenty-year period, the implication is that they would last considerably longer than the twenty-one-month period they in fact endured.

Why did the state's attempt to charter participation by means of these exclusionary features collapse so quickly?

---

licencia sindical (Decreto Ley, art. 10). (2) Any member who had held any political party post in the last three years was ineligible for any office in the cooperative (Decreto Supremo, art. 9). (3) The government could appoint delegates to the General Assembly in direct proportion to the adjudication debt that had not yet been paid. Once the cooperative had completely paid the adjudication debt, it could elect all the delegates (Decreto Ley, art. 7). (4) The members of the cooperative were divided into four functional groups; Group A, manual field workers, Group B, manual industrial workers, Group C, administrative and service workers, Group D, high level technocrats and professionals. Each group would elect 25% of the delegates to the General Assembly. The General Assembly would then elect three members of Group D, and two each from Groups A, B, and C to the Administrative Council (Decreto Ley, art. 7; Decreto Supremo, art. 35, 98).

22 Interview with staff member, Dirección General de Organizaciones Económicas de Interés Social, SINAMOS, Lima, November 7, 1972.

23 Interview, SAF-CAP National Headquarters, Chiclayo, November 13, 1972.

Certainly it was not because of worker resentment based on absolute economic deprivation stemming from the restrictions. A careful study of wages in the sugar cooperatives concludes that between 1968 and 1972, after adjusting for inflation, the *obreros* increased their real per capita income by 78 percent, the *empleados* 27 percent, and the *eventuales* 20 percent.[24]

Despite these significant wage increases—especially among the *obreros*, the core of union strength—the sugar workers fought against incorporation into the government-chartered cooperatives as long as they contained "exclusionary" features. Signs were painted on walls proclaiming "The State is the New Patron." In the residential sections of the cooperatives, political hand-outs and occasional loudspeakers denounced the inconsistency between the government's initial pronouncements in favor of egalitarian participatory cooperatives, and the reality, in which technicians were over-represented in the decision-making councils of the cooperatives and where the workers with trade union and political party leadership backgrounds were excluded. The workers' organizations also managed to obtain and divulge data documenting the wide differential between the pay-scales of technicians and workers, and to call attention to cases where technician-dominated councils awarded themselves disproportionate pay increases. The constant accusation was that the original ideals of the cooperative were being systematically violated.[25]

What explains the motivation and strength of worker resist-

[24] Roca, "The Peruvian Sugar Cooperatives," p. 17 and Table 7. "Eventuales" are field workers who are not members of the cooperative because in theory—but often not in reality—they are part-time workers who return to work land they own in the sierra. The special problems of this group will be discussed later in the chapter. "Obreros" refers mainly to factory workers, and "empleados" to low- and intermediate-level administrative workers. I will also refer to "technicians," most of whom are engineers, agronomists, or university-trained administrators.

[25] Many examples of this protest material are reproduced in *Campesino*, 3 (Lima 1970), which is entirely devoted to the struggle in the sugar cooperatives. The technicians came under particularly intense emotional attack at Tumán, the ex-hacienda that had had the strongest patriarchal tradition and the only one where the owners had managed to forestall the creation of a union. In the absence of any prior history of worker-technician bargaining relationships that had tempered the technicians' personal autocratic power, neither the technicians nor the workers adapted easily to the cooperative, and the hacienda cadre of technicians, with only one exception, were driven away, or fled the cooperative.

ance to the state-chartered cooperative formula? In Chapter 3, I hypothesized that the presence or absence of a prior history of autonomous organizational development and ideological commitment may be a key variable for predicting levels of resistance or acceptance in civil society to exclusionary, state-organizing efforts.[26] Much of the reason for the intense resistance by the workers to the state's attempt to incorporate them into rigidly chartered institutions was the threat such incorporation posed to their own organization and ideology.

Intrinsic to the government's vision of cooperatives was that they were apolitical. Also, since in the cooperatives the workers would become owners, the government argued that there was no place for unions. The official position eventually became that, as the cooperative assumed all the vital functions of sugar production and management, the unions would "wither away."

However, before 1968 labor gains had been closely tied to labor unions, most of which in turn were linked to political parties or movements, especially the Apristas. Thus, in the midst of the state intervention period, when the government was making its argument for cooperatives without unions, a poll taken at one of the cooperatives showed that 78 percent of the workers wanted the unions to remain.[27]

Given this background, the government's prohibitions against the participation of the former trade union or political leaders in the cooperative elections naturally brought the resistance not only of the leaders but of many of their followers. In addition to the electoral prohibitions, trade unionists' anxiety and resistance were heightened by clear indications that members of the state apparatus were trying to hasten the "withering away" of the unions by removing some of the key institutional supports the unions had won in their collective bargaining pacts with the haciendas. The two most important institutional supports were the compulsory universal union dues checkoff, which provided the union with an autonomous source of financing to carry out its activities, and the *licencia sindical*. The latter provided

[26] Hypothesis two stated "the lower the degree of development of autonomous political parties and interest groups, the greater the possibility of installing the regime."

[27] Alphonse L. MacDonald, (Jefe de los equipos), *La reforma agraria en dos complejos agro-industriales Cayaltí y Tumán: informe preliminar*, p. 86. The poll was taken at Cayaltí.

the elected union leaders time off from normal work duties to carry out union tasks such as inquiring into members' job complaints, pension problems, and acting as general watchdogs to see that management honored all the clauses of the contracts the union had won in the collective bargaining pacts.

Thus, despite the major economic gains the obreros made in 1968-1972, the union leaders led the intense opposition to incorporation, whose terms precluded their authoritative participation in the formative years of the cooperative. Strikes and work-stoppages broke out, to which the government responded with increasing severity. In Cartavio in September 1971 the secretary-general and the secretary of defense of the union were expelled from the cooperative.[28] In Pucalá, five trade union leaders were accused of sabotaging agrarian reform and were imprisoned.[29] In Cayaltí some key leaders were dismissed in 1970, but a 1971 strike brought their reinstatement. By late January 1972 the situation had so deteriorated that the government intervened with armed troops at Tumán, and there were sudden arrests in the three surrounding cooperatives.[30]

However the workers' organizational strength and ideological commitment made repression by the state apparatus difficult and costly. The well-developed cell tradition of the Aprista unions meant that, even when key leaders were imprisoned, others were capable of assuming their role.[31]

In most cooperatives the government's attempt in 1970 to abolish union dues failed. A government report about Cartavio

[28] Interview with trade union officers, Cartavio, November 20, 1972.

[29] A letter by the Federation of Peruvian Sugar Workers to President Velasco protesting and documenting the arrest of union leaders is reprinted in *Perú Sindical*, no. 67 (July 1971), pp. 16-17.

[30] The secretary-general of the Union at Cayaltí, who was himself arrested, said 17 worker activists at Cayaltí were arrested. Interview, November 14, 1972.

[31] For example, after the arrest of 17 worker leaders at Cayaltí, the government began a major campaign to eliminate the automatic dues check-off and *licencia sindical* at Cayaltí. The resistance of the workers was nevertheless strong enough to retain elements of both these traditional privileges.

This situation, where the rank and file can operate even without their leaders, contrasts sharply with the situation among the peasant leagues in the northeast of Brazil. Because the leagues had not developed any organizational depth, once the military jailed the leaders of the leagues, most of these organizations rapidly diminished in size and significance.

observed that "pressure from the union leadership and the rank and file" led the government to a compromise. The government allowed check-off of dues on an individual basis, if workers personally signed a petition that dues be docked from their pay checks. The report went on to add that, by January 1972, "since the union has strengthened its ascendency with its rank and file the number of workers who had individually signed the trade union deduction has grown progressively. Presently, of a total of 1,470 workers, approximately 1,050 have signed."[32]

Another source of the sugar workers' strength vis-à-vis the state was their strategic location in a capital-intensive, export-oriented sector. In contrast to groups such as most peasants or the urban squatters, the sugar workers have the power to withhold their labor, and even to damage the multimillion-dollar sugar mills and stop production completely.[33]

By September 1971 various state agencies active in the sugar cooperatives began to reevaluate the consequences of restrictive chartering and to consider new options.[34] By early 1972 at least three agencies had published very candid internal reports. One study acknowledged that the principle of equal representation for each functional sector worked out in practice to massive over-representation of the technicians. Although technicians constituted only 1.8 percent of the membership of the cooperative studied (Casa Grande), they received 30 delegates, the same number as the field workers, who composed 48.2 percent of the cooperative members.[35] The combination of over-representation of technicians, government nomination of delegates in accordance with the unpaid adjudication debt, and restrictions against for-

[32] Perú, Presidencia de la República, Oficina Nacional de Desarrollo Cooperativa, *Apreciación sobre la situación económica, financiera, organizativa, sindical y social de las cooperativas agrarias de producción azucarera del Departamento de La Libertad* (January 1972), p. 62.

[33] As one engineer noted, the extremely centralized process of refining sugar means that one mill worker can (and he argued did) shut down the entire mill by deliberately damaging a key part of the refining process, such as the press.

[34] Interview with a senior officer of SAF-CAP, November 13, 1972, in Chiclayo.

[35] Perú, Centro Nacional de Capacitación e Investigación para la Reforma Agraria, *Participación, organización y poder en Casa-Grande* (April 1972), p. 3. For the smaller cooperatives with less than 30 technicians, this meant 100% representation, whereas the campesinos and plant workers might have less than 1 representative per 100 men.

205

mer trade union leaders, led to almost total domination of the cooperatives' Administrative Councils by nonlabor groups.

Another report noted that despite the government's assertion that unions would have no real function to perform in the cooperatives, they had in fact grown stronger because "while the formal structure of power was the General Assembly of Delegates, real power rested with the Administrative and Vigilance Councils which were dominated by technicians." In this situation "the lack of real channels of participation for the members of categories A and B [field workers and factory workers] has meant that they channel their demands through the union."[36]

When I queried government officials about the decision to drop the restrictions and allow direct elections for the governmental organs of the cooperative, they agreed that a major reason for the decision was a recognition that the restrictions were not strengthening the cooperative structure, but rather were contributing to turmoil.

A high-ranking army officer in charge of SAF-CAP admitted that, during the period of restrictions, the government faced serious problems in seven of the eight cooperatives that I was studying. He added that, because of the restrictions, the workers did not take any responsibility for any hard decisions about running the cooperatives and that "all the demands that were won by the workers were won by the unions."[37]

The military government became extremely concerned that one of their major structural reforms was turning sour. The head of SINAMOS personally visited some of the cooperatives and at mass meetings heard the workers' demands. Shortly after, the government issued new election rules that abolished all four of the contested restrictions. Thus, despite the significant distributive dimension of the government's policy toward the sugar workers, the workers strongly resisted the exclusionary features and were successful in their campaign to get the state to broaden the scope of their participation. The way was thus paved for the

---

36 Perú, *Apreciación sobre la situación económica, financiera*, . . . , p. 78. A separate study directed by Jaime Llosa at SINAMOS national headquarters also complained that "there do not exist mechanisms which allow the participation of the socios in the elaboration of development planning of the cooperative," *Problemas económicos fundamentales que afrontan las cooperativas azucareras*, p. 15.

37 Interview cited in footnote 34.

much more serious experiment in participation that we will evaluate in the next section.

The resulting formula involved an inclusionary approach that allowed much greater participation and the coexistence of labor unions. It thus represented a defeat for the government's attempt to combine exclusionary and inclusionary features in the new cooperatives. In terms of the variables identified in the hypotheses in Chapter 3 concerning the feasibility of exclusionary policies, the most salient for the outcome was that in hypothesis two. The organizational and ideological development of the sugar workers gave them a *reason* to resist the government's exclusionary policy, and just as importantly, it greatly increased their *capacity* to resist.

The state's sugar cooperative policy did, of course, have many inclusionary features. It combined important distributive and symbolic acts with a major attempt to incorporate the sugar workers within new institutions. Yet, given the conditions the government encountered among the sugar workers, even inclusionary policies faced serious problems, as I will demonstrate. In terms of my hypotheses concerning inclusionary policies, the high level of union and party identification among sugar workers meant that, as hypothesis two predicted, there were few uncommitted groups available to be mobilized into new state-controlled structures. The degree of prior socioeconomic welfare and structural and sectoral reform was also a relevant variable and in the direction predicted by hypothesis four. The union has previously won many institutional prerogatives such as automatic dues checkoffs, *licencia sindical,* and the right to participate in collective bargaining. Thus in this organizational area the state's inclusionary policies had little to add, and the terms of incorporation, even when their exclusionary features were removed, involved substantial institutional threats. Finally, hypothesis five, concerning the resource/demand ratio, seems relevant and at least partially borne out. The state did have great economic resources for its overall inclusionary policy. It had the power to expropriate the haciendas, give them to the workers, and to allow major wage increases in this period (1969-1972). However the state had limited symbolic resources, both because of the anti-union orientation of the cooperatives, and because of the historic animosity that existed between many of the sugar workers and the army, dating back to the massacre of Aprista militants (the rank and file of which was largely composed of sugar workers) after the Trujillo uprising of 1932. The state did have major coercive resources that it could have used to an even greater degree. However, as hypothesis five suggests, for inclusionary policies, with their aspiration to legitimacy, coercive resources are less important than economic and symbolic resources. In fact the government's sensitivity to symbolic and ideological questions made it reluctant to use this resource to the fullest, and indeed disposed the leadership to compromise in the direction of greater participation.[38]

Let us turn now to an examination of how this compromise worked out in practice, i.e. the nature of participation in inclusionary structures.

WORKER PARTICIPATION AT THE COOPERATIVE LEVEL

In April 1972 direct, secret, and general elections without restrictions were held in the sugar cooperatives in order to elect delegates to the General Assemblies and the members of the Administrative and Vigilance Councils.[39] How free were these

---

[38] This decision had ideological implications beyond the sugar cooperatives. The government was attempting to build national and international constituencies by its change-oriented policies. The conflict in the sugar cooperatives hindered this attempt. When I asked the SAF-CAP military coordinator for Paramonga (the sugar cooperative closest to Lima) why the government had removed the restrictions, he answered that "about 40 groups of outsiders, professors, Third World representatives and journalists visited and always asked how the elections worked and what was the role of government-appointed delegates. The answers were embarrassing." Interview, June 3, 1972. The point here is that it was only because the government had embarked upon a participatory inclusionary policy that it received such extensive observation and was sensitive to this criticism.

[39] For a cooperative with under 500 workers, the highest organ of self-managing government is the cooperative as a whole. For cooperatives with over 500 workers (as in all the ones I studied), the highest organ is the General Assembly of Delegates, which ranges from 90 to 150 delegates. After the 1972 election reform, the entire cooperative voted, by secret ballot, for slates of candidates to the General Assembly and the Administrative Council, which is the managing board for the cooperative. The victorious slate to the Administrative Council then selects its own officers, but they are generally known beforehand. The slate with the second most votes gets three of the nine positions on the Administrative Council. A six-person Vigilance Council, whose main task is to monitor the finances of the cooperative, is selected by the same procedure. To be eligible for membership on either council,

elections? Did they make any difference to how the cooperative operated or to the daily life of the workers?

Interviews with scores of activists involved in the elections indicate that they felt the election proceeded with a great degree of freedom. Eloquent testimony to this are those who got elected. Some of the most forceful and effective opponents of the government's policy in 1970-1972—a number of whom were in jail or banished from their cooperatives before the elections—were voted into key positions. For example, in Tumán, Natividad Ordinola came out of jail to be elected president of the cooperative.[40] In Cartavio the three trade union leaders who had been jailed for their role in the 1971 strike and banished from the cooperative for life returned to assume the vice-presidency (and later the presidency of the Administrative Council), the presidency of the Vigilance Council, and the secretary-generalship of the union.[41] By 1974 the elected presidents of all the cooperatives in the Trujillo area—Casa Grande, Laredo, and Cartavio—were men who had been heads of their unions in the 1970-1972 period of conflict.

The change was not only at the top. In terms of officership in the Administrative Councils and the Vigilance Council, the ending of restrictions, as Table 6.1 shows, meant a clear decline in the power of the technicians and the emergence of lower-level office workers, often with trade union backgrounds, into positions of leadership.[42]

---

a candidate must have completed the five grades of primary school. Candidates are selected for three years and cannot be immediately reelected. The General Assembly can—and has—voted out of office members of the Councils. The current procedures for elections are contained in *Decreto Supremo*, No. 004-72-PM March 15, 1972.

[40] Interview with Señor Ordinola at Tumán, November 14, 1972.

[41] Interview with secretary-general of the union, Cartavio, November 20, 1972.

[42] The shortage of factory workers in the top elected positions is probably less severe than the table suggests. Many of the key trade union leaders who now are "empleados" have extensive experience in the factory. In any case, factory workers often play a key role in selecting the slate of candidates via their union. The underrepresentation of campesinos, however, is severe. The requirement that council members must have completed five years of primary school must be put in the perspective of the available data on sugar workers' educational background. A study of Cayaltí and Tumán concluded that only 50% of the workers had gone beyond the first two years of primary school and less than 13% had gone beyond the fifth year. See MacDonald, *La*

TABLE 6.1

JOB STATUS OF SIX TOP ELECTED OFFICIALS IN
SELECTED SUGAR COOPERATIVES, 1970-1975

	Cooperative				
	Casa Grande		Laredo		Cartavio
	1970-71	1972-73	1970-71	1972-73	1974-75
Technician	6	1	3	1	0
Empleado	0	5	2	4	5
Obrero & Campesino	0	0	1	1	1
(Former Trade-Union Office Holder)	(0)	(2)	(0)	(4)	(4)

SOURCES: Data supplied by personnel officers double-checked by interviews with union and cooperative officers.

Where and how did this shift in formal power affect life on the cooperatives? One researcher who lived on a sugar cooperative for over a year and visited a number of other smaller cooperatives concluded:

Agrarian reform and cooperativization have profoundly affected the social structures of the estates under study. . . . Expropriation removed the patrón and brought into question the legitimacy of power exercised by hacienda employees. Laborers and employees now occupy positions in the cooperative councils which allow them to exercise power over individuals of much higher rank in the operational organization. Since all cooperative members (including high-level technicians and administrative personnel) are subject to censuring by the workers' councils, and employees no longer are assured the backing of the owners, employees have been forced to temper their exercise of power within the operational organization and in their informal contacts with hacienda residents. The most abusive and hated employees have left the coops. . . . The

---

reforma agraria en dos complejos, p. 21. Of those few who had completed five years, almost none would still do manual work in the fields as campesinos. This underrepresentation is compounded by the relative lack of influence of campesinos in the trade unions.

emphasis placed by the hacienda on coercive control of the labor force is replaced in the cooperative by an emphasis on mutual respect and self discipline.[43]

Before encountering this assessment I had come to a similar conclusion based on: (1) my observations of General Assembly meetings, (2) the somewhat diffident conduct of technicians in the cooperative offices as they presented requests to workers in charge of the Administrative or Vigilance Councils, and (3) the numerous private complaints to me by technicians that their authority had been undermined because under the cooperative they were "forced" to plant suggestions rather than impose decisions.[44]

The power of the General Assembly and the councils is greatest concerning "local government" decisions about how to allocate the disposable surplus.[45] Heated debates precede decisions by the General Assembly as to whether, and how much, money should be spent for building new schools, hiring new teachers, buying buses, employing new doctors. Questions of equity surface over decisions as to which group of members most deserves new houses and whether pay increases should be equal for all members. In both these areas the fact that the decision forum has predominately non-technician and non-government membership significantly affects outcomes.

What of worker-participation in the management of the enterprise? In theory the supreme decision-making body is the General Assembly working with the Administrative Council.

[43] Douglas E. Horton, "Haciendas and Cooperatives: A Preliminary Study of Latifundist Agriculture and Agrarian Reform in Northern Peru" (unpublished manuscript, Cornell University, 1973) to appear in a volume to be published by the Instituto de Estudios Peruanos on the sugar cooperatives, p. 72.

[44] Many of the initial reports about the agrarian reform in the cooperatives assumed that the old technicians would simply take over the power vacated by the removal of the patrons. In fact, given worker hostility toward the patrons and their former technician allies many of the old technicians left, or were driven from their place of work. To be sure, many of them simply moved to other sugar cooperatives, but they presumably had to begin internalizing the new rules of the game and were shorn of most of their claim to traditional patronal authority.

[45] However as we shall see, external state actions via a variety of mechanisms and regulations play a major role in determining "disposable" income.

Together they employ a manager *(gerente)* and work with him to formulate and approve the annual development plan of the cooperative.

The gerente obviously has a great deal of power and the question is whether he actually makes all the key decisions. Until the adjudication debt is paid off, the gerente is selected by the minister of agriculture from a list of three names drawn up by the cooperative. The fact that the minister of agriculture, not the cooperative, makes the final selection is a limitation on worker self-management. This is somewhat mitigated by the fact that the gerente can be removed simply by the Administrative Council sending the ministry of agriculture a list of three new nominees that does not include the name of the incumbent gerente. This possibility undoubtedly introduces a degree of responsiveness on the part of the gerente to the council's opinions.[46] However, in conversation with gerentes about how they designed the initial development plans, it is evident that a significant amount of their discussion is with individuals who are outside the cooperative's representational system.

In the presence of the president of the Administrative Council, I asked a gerente how the development plan of the cooperative is drawn up. He said there were four steps:

(1) The gerente talks to his technical staff and the technical staff of CECOAAP, and formulates a tentative plan.

(2) He then discusses this plan with the Administrative Council, which revises it.

(3) The revised plan is presented to the General Assembly by the president of the Administrative Council, who directs the debate. The gerente is available for questions, but the plan is voted upon by the General Assembly.

(4) The assembly-approved plan is taken to the SAF-CAP national headquarters, where the military determines whether it conforms to the general investment and financial guidelines of the agrarian adjudication law. If parts of the plan do not conform to this law the plan is returned to the Administrative Council for redrafting.

---

[46] I asked two gerentes if this procedure had been used yet and they said that its potential use had caused the early resignations of gerentes on at least two cooperatives in order to avoid being formally "fired."

This fourth step points up another significant limitation on worker self-management. The overall financial and investment guidelines for the sugar cooperative sector have been established by the state.[47] Here is a clear area of tension between self-management and the statist components of the regime's philosophy. The state's statutory right to oversee finances until the adjudication debt is paid, and its ultimate role in granting or blocking public sector loans to cooperatives that are in financial difficulty, gives it wide power. In the case of Cayaltí, which was in severe financial difficulty, further loans were clearly made dependent upon the General Assembly's formal request to be "intervened" and to come under state management. A unilaterally issued degree law in 1977 empowered the state to intervene in the management of other financially troubled cooperatives.[48]

In sum, the participation of the workers is greatest in the area of local self-government, and within the cooperative the representative structures have curtailed the prerogative of the technicians. Concerning the overall direction of the cooperative, the state still has extensive formal and informal powers to shape decisions. Nonetheless, as we shall see in a later section, the participatory structures have been skillfully used by the cooperative leaders to strengthen their veto power over a broad range of potential state policies concerning the sugar cooperatives. This is probably not what the military designers of participation

[47] Decreto Ley No. 18299, art. 3 stipulates that, after taxes, necessary production costs, and the annual payment of the adjudication debt, the cooperatives should, at a minimum, allocate 15% of their net profit to reinvestment, 10% for a reserve fund, 10% for a social welfare fund, 5% for an education fund, and 5% for a cooperative development fund. During the financial crisis of 1977 the state even assumed the right to temporarily forbid expenditures by the cooperatives for the social welfare and education funds. See "Complejos azucareros haran sólo obras indispensables," *Correo* (May 28, 1977), p. 8.

[48] Extensive extracts from the Cayaltí General Assembly debate, which culminated in a formal vote requesting state intervention, are reproduced in Perú, SAF-CAP, *Azúcar peruana: historia de un cambio* (December 1973), pp. 48-64. The closeness with which SAF-CAP followed the economic and social affairs of the cooperatives is apparent in the 217-page report prepared eight months before the Cayaltí vote; see Perú, SINAMOS, SAF-CAP, *Diagnóstico preliminar Cap "Cayaltí": documento de trabajo* (Chiclayo, April 1973). For the details of the 1977 decree see Decreto Ley No. 21815, issued on March 15.

213

had in mind, but it nonetheless is a form of occupational group participation.

COMPARATIVE PERSPECTIVES ON THE SUGAR COOPERATIVES

How one judges the Peruvian achievement in worker participation to date depends on one's perspective. If the ideal is full worker self-management, the Peruvian sugar cooperatives—even before the 1977 set-backs—had hardly begun. However if the standard of comparison is the degree of worker self-management in liberal-capitalist systems (including the nationalized sectors), then Peru, especially in the 1972-76 period, had achieved a great deal.[49]

If the standard of comparison is the role of worker self-management in a mobilizational revolutionary regime such as China, the Peruvian experiment also compares favorably. A study of the "democratic management" movement in China concluded that the three ingredients the party most wanted to stress to increase worker participation in management were:

> 1) cadres must make periodic financial statements directly to the members; 2) cadres must discuss all cooperative affairs with members, and especially with experienced peasants; 3) cadres must participate in production to gain experience and set a good example for the masses.[50]

The revolutionary vanguard of China has without doubt made more profound advances than Peru toward equality and structural change. However to date they have not curtailed the revolutionary party's capacity for control by giving significant independent scope to worker self-management. Charles Bettelheim notes that "workers' management teams focus on orientation, inspection, investigation, ideological work, and correct style of work, rather than on management as such, which is the responsibility of the revolutionary committee" and that "since these committees are mass groupings, they must follow the leader-

---

[49] For example the major experiments in worker participation in England are reviewed in Pateman, *Participation and Democratic Theory*, pp. 60-88. Her discussion indicates that neither in the private nor the nationalized sector was worker management as advanced as it was in the Peruvian sugar cooperatives from 1972-76.

[50] Townsend, *Political Participation in Communist China*, p. 177.

ship of the party, which plays a decisive role in determining their ideological orientation."[51] For better or worse, Peru attempted to reconcile strong statist direction of the change process with a degree of worker self-management. Algeria initially attempted such a combination, but a study of the experiment concludes that after five years *"autogestion* in practice [was] all but replaced by centralized state control."[52]

Despite important differences, the Peruvian experiment gains something by comparison with Yugoslavia.[53] The Yugoslav experience is particularly valuable for highlighting problems that later systems might try to avert. For example, a special problem the Yugoslavian experience points to is the difficulty in overcoming the de facto control of the experts. The position of the director in Yugoslavia is similar to the *gerente* in Peru.[54] Nu-

---

[51] Bettelheim, *Cultural Revolution and Industrial Organization in China*, p. 23. Worker mobilization and involvement *is* certainly more intense in China than in Peru; but, mobilization and involvement—while critical factors for a revolutionary regime—do not necessarily entail worker self-management.

Starting in 1970, party leaders in Cuba began a move to increase the institutionalized participation of workers in plant management. According to the self-assessment of the minister of labor, worker participation as of 1970 lacked sufficient institutionalized channels. "Theoretically, the administration represents the interest of the worker and peasant state, the interest of all the people. Theory is one thing and practice another. . . . The administration may be making one mistake after the other, and this happens everyday, everywhere. . . . The workers cannot do anything about it." Cited in Robert E. Hernández and Carmelo Mesa-Lago "Labor Organization and Wages" in *Revolutionary Change in Cuba*, ed. Carmelo Mesa-Lago (Pittsburgh: University of Pittsburgh Press, 1971), pp. 224-45. The Thirteenth Cuban Trade Union Congress held in 1973 was a significant step forward to increase the institutionalized participation of workers and unions in plant management, see *XIII Congreso de la CTC: Memorias* (La Habana: Empresa de Medios de Propaganda, 1974).

[52] Ian Clegg, *Workers' Self-Management in Algeria*, p. 8. Some observers feel this judgment may be too harsh, but it clearly shows the tension between self-management and state control.

[53] Some crucial differences are that the experiment in self-management began only after the party had created a communist regime, that the experiment was begun much earlier (1950), and, with the exception of agriculture, it is the dominant pattern for the management of enterprises in the economy. Also unlike the Peruvian sugar cooperatives where, after payment of the adjudication debt the cooperatives will be owned outright by the workers, the enterprises in Yugoslavia are publicly owned.

[54] One important difference is that the director is selected by the enterprise, and there is no state role in the selection process.

merous empirical studies of Yugoslavian self-management concur that the director is viewed by the workers as having more influence than the workers' management committees.[55] This is a sobering conclusion, and similar studies should be carried out in Peru to see if a similar perception exists and, if so, how the conditions that contribute to this situation might be altered.

From the viewpoint of the state's goals of equality, decentralized worker self-management in Yugoslavia has come under ideological attack. Some Yugoslavs argue that the state is not able to exercise sufficient control to overcome the substantial regional inequalities.[56] Others point out that the system has been relatively weak in overcoming the problems of unemployment and of great disparities of income between different enterprises. Still others caution that self-management, unless guided by socialist theory, could contribute to the reemergence of capitalist attitudes.[57]

Let us now consider how self-managing cooperatives in Peru—with all the limitations we have discussed—have helped or hindered the overall regime goals, such as organic unity, of the Peruvian society.

THE PROBLEM OF ORGANIC UNITY AND EQUITY: TENSIONS BETWEEN STATE GOALS AND SELF-MANAGEMENT COOPERATIVES

Implicit in the Peruvian government's approach to self-managing units was the assumption that self-management would contribute to greater functional unity and equity in the overall social

[55] Seven different surveys given in enterprises, which all show the Director as having the "highest perceived relative influence," are discussed in Veljko Rus, "Influence Structure in Yugoslav Enterprise," *Industrial Relations* (February 1970). For a more extensive discussion see Jiri Kolaja, *Workers' Councils: The Yugoslav Experience.*

[56] In 1947 the area with the highest per capita income (Slovenia) had a per capita income 3.3 times as high as the area with the lowest (Kosmet). In 1964 this difference had increased to 5.3. Calculated from data in K. Mihailović, "On the Yugoslav Experience in Backward Areas" in *Backward Areas in Advanced Countries*, ed. E.A.G. Robinson, p. 266.

[57] See for example, Rudi Supek, "Some Contradictions and Insufficiencies of Yugoslav Self-Managing Socialism," *Praxis* (1971), and Edvard Kardelj, "Contradictions of Social Property in Contemporary Socialist Practice," *Socialist Thought and Practice* (August-December 1972). A useful review of the debate is William N. Dunn, "Ideology and Organization in Socialist Yugoslavia: Modernization and the Obsolescence of Praxis," *Newsletter on Comparative Studies of Communism* (August 1972).

and political system. Obviously the state was accorded a central role in the creation of the self-management system, but the rhetoric implied that the state's role in constantly regulating self-management would diminish. However in Chapter 1 I advanced the argument that organic statism as an abstract model of governance encompassed, on logical grounds, two values in tension. The goal of a strong state capable of restructuring society to conform to its vision of organic order may conflict with the value of a significant degree of autonomous participation within the functional units that compose society. In the previous section I showed how the value of autonomous participation was to a significant extent curtailed in order to pursue the goal of building a strong state. This section will explore, in the concrete context of the Peruvian sugar cooperative experiment, the other component of this tension. Specifically, I am concerned with the tension between the state's goal of creating systemic solidarity (which entails a reasonable degree of equity between the different groups that make up society) and the autonomy of each functional unit to act so as to maximize its own welfare. If the conflict predicted on analytic grounds does indeed occur, how does it express itself and what mechanisms are available to the state to attempt to diminish the conflict between system solidarity and self-management? Three areas of potential conflict will be examined: (1) conflict within the cooperative, (2) conflict between different cooperatives, and (3) conflict between the sugar cooperative sector and other sectors of society.

Let us take first the question of equity and unity within each cooperative. The basic financial principle of the cooperatives is that each *socio* (member) receives an equal share of the year-end profit in accordance with hours worked. In addition, each member receives substantial benefits such as free housing, medical programs, free schooling, and some food rations. From the perspective of the members, there is a logical tendency to maximize returns *per member*. This is consistent with Jaroslav Vanek's argument that in a labor-managed and income-sharing enterprise or system "the one key operating principle . . . is that of *maximization of income per laborer*. This principle, which is quite different from maximization of profit, is the natural and rational concern of all participants in an enterprise."[58] He admits that

[58] Jaroslav Vanek, *The General Theory of Labor-Managed Market Economies*, p. 2. Emphasis in the original.

217

the logic of maximization of net income per worker means that the enterprise should only "increase its labor employment whenever the net contribution to total income by the last man employed is more than the income per laborer currently earned."[59] Because of his numerous assumptions about "full decentralization of decision-making," "full reliance on the market mechanism," and freedom of entry and exit, Vanek argues that this will not have a net harmful effect on employment in the system. However, in Peru, where the cooperatives are only one part of the economic system and where many of his other assumptions do not hold, the impact of the logical tendency to maximize income (and services) *per member* produces a variety of effects that conflict with the regime's goal of creating a solidaristic, unified society. Given the major service and profit-sharing benefits new members receive, the cooperatives will logically attempt to increase production by purchase of new equipment rather than the admission of a new member. The logic of the system also builds in incentives for the cooperative as a whole to replace retiring members with contracted workers who do not receive full membership. The logic of the cooperative principle of "maximizing income per member" thus can generate contradictions with the government's goals of reducing the already severe unemployment problem and can also create a new source of conflict and exploitation between members and the nonmembers (or "rentados" or "eventuales") they employ.

Both of these logically predictable problems have in fact materialized in the sugar sector. A careful study of employment patterns shows that, between 1968 and 1972, the number of workers whose job category qualified them as members of the cooperative *decreased* by 941 workers, while the number of nonmember "eventuales" (part-time laborers) who did not receive the benefits of the cooperatives increased by 1,278.[60] The benefits of membership are substantial. A government study of the wages and benefits of member and nonmember field workers at Tumán shows that the nonmembers received 2,074 soles per month, while for the same work a member received 3,000 soles in direct wages, and over 5,500 soles in benefits such as food rations (1,277 soles), housing (2,000 soles), and profit sharing (1,000 soles). Members

[59] Ibid., p. 3.

[60] See the excellent study, Roca "The Peruvian Sugar Cooperatives: Some Fundamental Economic Problems," pp. 17-18.

would have in fact to pay a new member four times what they have to pay contracted labor for the same amount of work.[61] Hence the increase in nonmember labor.[62]

This sharp contrast in material rewards for the same work has generated a new source of class conflict in the sugar cooperatives. For example, in November 1972, when I visited Pucalá, the nonmember sugar cane cutters had recently threatened to strike if their benefits were not improved. The members held a general assembly and decided to go to the fields themselves to break the strike. In the words of the director of labor relations for the cooperative, "we told them that if they kept up the strike we would mechanize and they would have no jobs. We gave them higher wages and some food benefits, but not membership."[63] The members with whom I talked considered this decision a moral victory for the cooperative, and indeed a flyer was issued by the Administration Council of Pucalá and posted in the cooperative and the neighboring cooperative of Pomalca praising all the members for having:

> . . . backed the organs of government of the cooperative and going spontaneously and voluntarily to cut cane in response to the inopportune work-stoppage by the contracted cane-cutters.
>
> This significant event, which marks an historic milestone in our own self-managing life [*vida autogestionaria*] deserves praise because it constitutes an objective demonstration of the cooperative spirit and the high level of responsibility of the members.[64]

Despite this optimistic announcement, when I returned two years later the conflict had greatly intensified between the members and nonmembers at Pucalá. The nonmembers had created their own union, and in July 1974 a group of nonmembers seized the president of the Administrative Council and his legal ad-

[61] SAF-CAP, *Azúcar peruana*, p. 23.

[62] Because this is now an explosive issue, current data are hard to obtain. However the books of the Department of Personnel at Laredo showed that in 1970 there were 1505 members and 70 nonmembers on the payroll. At the end of July 1974 the payroll showed 1473 members and 207 nonmembers.

[63] Interview, November 14, 1972, Pucalá. At the time, he estimated that, of the 608 cane cutters at Pucalá, 200 were members.

[64] Flyer, "A La Opinión Pública" sent out by the Administrative Council of Pucalá. Observed posted at Pomalca, November 15, 1972.

viser, and took them to their residential area, where they paraded them around and hit them with the flat sides of machetes while making their demands. Five council members who came to the defense of the president and his legal adviser were threatened with similar treatment.[65]

In the face of the glaring inequity between workers within the cooperatives and the potential for conflict it generated, state officials, especially those from SAF-CAP and the Agrarian Reform Agency, began by 1972 to pressure the cooperatives to honor the spirit of the Agrarian Reform Law, by which anyone who worked at a cooperative for six months and did not own land elsewhere would be admitted as a member of the cooperative. By 1974 this state pressure was beginning to have an effect, but tension nonetheless remains in almost all the cooperatives, and represents a continual source of friction between the state and the worker-managed cooperatives.[66]

The second equity problem arises out of unequal factor endowments between different production units within the same sector. Upon expropriation, some cooperatives inherited more profitable production units than others in terms of such factors as quality of the industrial, irrigation, and transportation systems; quantity and quality of land; and access to water. As a consequence of this great disparity in nonlabor factors of production, the members of some cooperatives might work just as hard as members of other cooperatives but have a total profit that is substantially lower per member. For example, within the eight cooperatives under study the fixed assets at the time of appropriation in 1969, not counting land, ranged from approximately $3,500 per member at Casa Grande, to $750 per member at Cayaltí.[67] The greater initial capital assets per worker has

[65] The conflict was given page one discussion in the Chiclayo newspaper *La Industria* on July 19 and 20, 1974. A large notice taken out by the Administrative Council protesting the "kidnapping" and defending the cooperatives' position vis-à-vis the "contratados" appeared in the July 21 issue of *La Industria*.

[66] The SAF-CAP booklet, *Azúcar peruana*, pp. 31-37, discusses the legal aid SAF-CAP has given to the non-members to get them admitted as members. One rationale of the cooperatives was that the nonmembers owned parcels of land in the Sierra and were thus not eligible for cooperative membership. SAF-CAP investigated and found that less than 8% could actually be disqualified on this ground.

[67] Calculated from data contained in annexes 1 and 2 of SINAMOS, *Problemas económicos fundamentales*, pp. 61-62.

meant that, by every measurable category of benefit, the workers at Casa Grande have received much more from their cooperative than workers at Cayaltí.[68]

Any country that embarks upon a self-management scheme after the expropriation of a sector of the economy will confront the same problem of different factor endowments, and thus profitability, of the production units within the sector. One solution is for the state to create some form of sector-wide profit fund that acts as a redistributive mechanism within the sector. The Peruvian government quickly recognized the problem of inequality within production units in the sugar sector. Consequently, when the government later passed the mining and fishing laws, it built sector-wide "compensation funds" into the initial income-sharing schemes. However, although the creation of such funds represents political learning on the part of the government, it does not alter the fact that it is extremely difficult to impose such a structure on a sector retroactively. In interviews, a number of top government officials concerned with the sugar sector expressed the belief that it had been a mistake not to create a similar compensation fund in the sugar sector at the time of expropriation, but that conflict between the wealthy cooperatives and state agencies would be too intense to make the creation of such a fund likely in the foreseeable future.[69]

The greatest contradiction between the state's policy of reducing inequity in the overall political and social system and its policy of encouraging participation in self-managed cooperatives becomes apparent when one considers the sugar sector in rela-

[68] For example in 1973 Casa Grande produced 49.4 tons of sugar per worker while Cayaltí produced 9.1; Central de Cooperativas Agrarias de Producción Azucarera del Perú (CECOAAP), División Técnica, *Informe de operaciones de producción de la industria azucarera peruana-1973* (February 1974), p. 16. This greater productivity per worker (largely a result of initial advantages of capital endowment) means that Casa Grande has a much greater disposable income per worker to distribute for profit sharing, new housing, and expansion of medical, educational, and other services.

[69] The absence of such a fund contributed to the bankruptcy of Cayaltí, the cooperative that inherited the poorest capital situation, and resulted in direct state intervention. Both the bankruptcy and the intervention were undesirable from the perspective of the regime's overall policy, and both might have been avoided if the state had been able to create a sector-wide compensation fund that could have been used both for investment, as well as distributive, purposes.

221

tion to the rest of the economy.[70] The structure of income in a typical developing country concentrates income in the highly capitalized modern sector. From this perspective, all the participants in the modern sector—the owners, managers, and unionized workers (bourgeoisie and proletariat alike) —are normally in the top quartile of national income. Reform that distributes income within the modern sector—while by no means insignificant— nonetheless involves redistributing income among those whose resources and relationship to the advanced production structures already places them in the top quartile of the work force. As a number of political activists within the Peruvian government and independent scholars have noted, this is exactly what happened in Peru.[71] Reform designed to redistribute income to the workers in the modern urban industrial communities, and to the highly capitalized mining and sugar sectors, in effect redistributed income to workers who, in comparison to the rest of the work force, already formed a labor aristocracy.[72]

According to Webb's data, almost all the sugar work force in 1961 would be placed in the top quartile. After redistribution of income to sugar workers in 1969-1971, their relative position moved up. Table 6.2 shows that, even after excluding many subsistence peasants, 43 percent of the economically active population (EAP) in the national sample still earned below 1,000 soles per month. *None* of the sugar workers fell into this category. While only 7 percent of the EAP earned more than 7,500 soles

[70] My thinking on this general subject owes much to the comments, lectures, and writings of Richard Webb. For references to some of his writings, see footnote 72.

[71] In Cuba however the pro-rural ethic that characterized the first decade of the revolution had extremely important distributive effects because much of the new social investment was located outside the modern sector in rural areas. For example in 1958 there was 1 rural and 33 urban hospitals in Cuba. In 1966 there were 46 rural and 50 urban hospitals. See *Cuba 1968: Supplement to the Statistical Abstract of Latin America* (Los Angeles: Latin American Center, University of California at Los Angeles, 1970), p. 109.

[72] See for example Richard Webb, "Government Policy and the Distribution of Income in Peru, 1963-1973," in *The Peruvian Experiment*, Lowenthal, pp. 79-127; and his book with the same title (Cambridge: Harvard University Press, 1977), Adolfo Figueroa, "El impacto de los reformas actuales sobre la distribución de ingresos en el Perú," *Apuntes* (1973); and the informative discussion between Richard Webb, Adolfo Figueroa and Jurgen Schuldt, "Conversatorio sobre la redistribución del ingreso en el Perú," *Apuntes*, no. 2 (1974), pp. 81-92.

TABLE 6.2

MONTHLY CASH INCOME IN SOLES: COMPARISON OF 1971 NATIONAL SAMPLE
OF ECONOMICALLY ACTIVE POPULATION (EXCLUDING MANY SUBSISTENCE
PEASANTS) WITH INCOME BREAKDOWN OF THE 26,019
WORKERS IN SUGAR SECTOR

Monthly Cash Income in Soles (National Sample)	% of EAP	Monthly Cash Income in Soles (Sugar Workers)	% of all Sugar Workers
No Cash Income	17	No Cash Income	0
1-499	14	1-499	0
500-999	12	500-999	0
1000-1999	15	1000-1999	9
2000-2999	11	2000-2999	7
3000-4999	14	3000-4500	8
5000-7499	7	4500-6500	15
7500-9999	2	6500-8000	19
10,000-24,999	4	8000-9000	11
25,000 or more	2	9000-12,000	25
Undetermined	2	12,000-16,000	5
		16,000 or more	1
Total	100%	Total	100%

SOURCES: National Sample done by minister of labor, November 1971. Sample *excluded* 657,233 campesinos. Sugar worker data calculated from Roca, "The Peruvian Sugar Cooperatives," table 2.

per month, 42 percent of the sugar work force received more than 8,000 soles.

From the government's regional planning perspective, the sugar cooperatives represent not only wealthy enclaves due to their salary structure but also inherited power that gave them privileged access to scarce resources in a desert agricultural system—most importantly water.[73] By early 1972 key SINAMOS officials such as Jaime Llosa were extremely concerned about these inequalities. Llosa believed that the cooperatives had given the sugar workers an economic base for participation but that "group egoism" on the part of the cooperatives had emerged. He felt there was a need for the state to exercise its obligation to fulfill collective goals by extracting a greater surplus from

[73] SINAMOS, "Problemas económicos fundamentales," p. 18, noted that the cooperatives have inherited from the patrons the power to use most of the scarce water for each valley. For example Casa Grande received over three times the water per hectare than the surrounding valley farms also dependent on irrigation.

the cooperatives, but without violating their integrity as labor-managed units. Llosa's proposed solution to this conflict was an Integrated Plan of Regional Development (PIAR) in which the sugar cooperatives would be integrated into valley-wide organizations in which the technical, financial, and educational resources of the cooperatives would be utilized for the entire region. The sugar cooperatives would be the central mechanisms for funneling credit and technical assistance to a regional cooperative, where representatives from all the sugar and nonsugar cooperatives would develop a regional plan in consultation with state representatives.[74]

Five years later no such plan had been implemented. What does this reveal about the political dynamics of this type of conflict between the self-managing cooperatives and the state? No reports have yet been published about the conflict, but from interviews with elected representatives of the cooperatives it appears that the cooperatives first heard in 1973 that a state plan for integration of the cooperatives with other sectors of the economy was being considered seriously. The cooperatives responded by using their power of participation against the state. A general assembly was held at each cooperative, and the workers were asked what their reaction was to the proposed plan. The workers, knowing the plan would result in a substantial loss of income and autonomy, expressed extreme hostility. Backed by this intensely emotional support the representatives of the cooperatives invited the head of SINAMOS to a meeting and informed him of the massive resistance to the plan that had been expressed in the duly elected participatory structures of the cooperatives.

The government was thus presented with a dilemma: whether to allow the great regional inequalities to persist or to impose a plan of regional integration by force. Since, as a number of government officials acknowledged, there was great reluctance to crush one of the "first children of the revolution," no decision was taken in 1973.

[74] Interview with Jaime Llosa, October 30, 1972. The argument for this plan is spelled out in the SINAMOS study he supervised, "Problemas económicos fundamentales. . . ." Also see his article, "Reforma agraria y revolución," *Participación*, no. 3 (August 1973), pp. 44-59, especially his discussion of ways to try to avoid an authoritarian statist solution to the problems of the "antagonistic pair; participation and accumulation."

In 1974 and 1975, however, the state began restructuring the political arena in the agrarian sector in such a way as to begin to create a formula for resolving the dilemma. SINAMOS field workers supervised a system of elections for local agrarian leagues; later each province held a week-long congress out of which came a provincial league with its own delegates. Finally, in October 1974 peasant delegates from all of Peru held a convention in Lima and created a National Agrarian Confederation (CNA). My interviews with elected officials of the sugar cooperatives revealed that they had not been particularly urged by SINAMOS to participate in the provincial assemblies. However once the CNA had held its constituent assembly, it received official state endorsement to speak for the entire agrarian sector. Thus, the government had helped bring into existence a participation group that could oppose the sugar workers and claim to represent the national voice of the agrarian sector. Signs of a potential political solution to the state-sugar cooperative conflict appeared at the constituent assembly, where delegates frequently voiced opposition to the privileged position of the sugar cooperatives. Some government officials privately admitted that, if the CNA, through its own participation channels, demanded the integration of the sugar cooperatives into some form of regional structure, the state would be very responsive, for this would be a non-authoritarian, participatory solution to their current dilemma of group participation and consumption versus state accumulation for collective investment.[75]

The dynamics of the process show that (1) despite the theory of functional harmony there is often significant conflict between the participation groups and the state; (2) under special conditions the organizational and legitimacy resources enjoyed by

[75] In 1975 state officials began to give serious consideration to another way to advance their "collective goals" over the "group egoism" of the cooperatives: to integrate forcibly the cooperatives into the then-emerging social property sector. While this may have solved some of the government's economic problems with the sugar sector, it would have exacerbated political resistance. A step in this direction would have been to transfer any cooperative that might go bankrupt without new state credit (like Cayaltí and possibly Pomalca) into the Social Property sector. In the last months of his rule President Velasco indicated that the government might integrate all the cooperatives into the social property sector. Significantly this met with such resistance that the new president reversed this policy decision, see *Lima Times*, October 3, 1975, p. 1.

the participation groups can be used against the state; and (3) the creation of higher-level patricipation organs, with their own claims to represent legitimately the wider interests of the sector or all the sectors, might be the only way the state can resolve clashes between its collective state goals and the narrower goals of the participating groups of a subsector.[76]

CONCLUSION

When we compare the state's organizational problem in the sugar sector with that of the state's problem in the urban squatter sector, a number of salient differences emerge.

In both areas the government had available substantial resources for attempting inclusionary policies. In the Pueblos Jóvenes it had the power to grant individual land titles, and in the sugar sector the expropriation, and subsequent state-sponsored plan of cooperative profit sharing, led to significant income increases. By economic criteria alone, state policy seemed to deliver more tangible rewards to the sugar sector than to the squatter sector.[77] However the sugar sector has proved much more resistant to the organizational component of the inclusionary policies. The explanation for this centers on differences in the organizational and ideological patterns of the target sector. Organizationally and ideologically the squatter's previous political orientation, and demand structure, had been instrumental and clientelistic—it had been ordered toward getting a good working relationship with the government of the day in order to obtain specific outputs such as land security and infrastructure. This prior pattern of organization, ideology, and demand was relatively congruent with the organic-statist policies and structures of the military regime. However the government en-

[76] However, as Decreto Ley 21815 of March 15, 1977, which enabled the state to directly intervene in the management of some cooperatives indicates, it seems highly unlikely that the Phase II leaders will opt for this more participatory solution.

[77] If anything, as we have seen, the government gave too much—from the viewpoint of its other normative and economic goals—to the sugar workers. The great income increases of the sugar workers have deprived the state of resources needed to carry out policies in other areas. The squatter sector was an "easier" policy area because it did not raise such normative or economic conflicts with other regime goals.

countered in the sugar sector a much less pliable set of conditions. The strong union and party traditions of the sugar workers were resistant to the government's policy of creating an organic-statist policy in which political parties and nongovernmental unions "wither away."

Given this situation, how much of the significant interactions between the state and the sugar workers are actually carried out within the new formal structures created by the regime? In the case of the squatters the vast majority of interactions between the state and the squatter sector were, in reality, molded to conform to a model of group representation in which there was a single vertical structure into which inputs and outputs were made. In the case of the sugar sector, however, neither the workers nor the government confine the advancement of their interests to a single vertical structure. There is "worker parallelism" and "state parallelism."

Worker parallelism refers to the unions. The government assumed that, as the workers fully participated in the cooperative's governing structure, unions would cease to have a function. However, notwithstanding the wider worker participation in the cooperative governing structure since 1972, and the continuing attempts by the state to make union dues collection and *licencia sindical* difficult, worker commitment to unions remains strong.[78]

Within the cooperative structure, the trade unions frequently draw up the winning slate of candidates. Many of the presidents of the administrative councils are trade union leaders. Outside the cooperatives, the workers have maintained their nation-wide federation of sugar workers' FTAP (Federación de Trabajadores Azucareras del Perú). Many of the top leaders of the FTAP have now become the key leaders within the cooperative movement. In 1974-1975 all three of the Trujillo area sugar cooperatives had presidents who in the past had been presidents of FTAP.

---

[78] For example individually paid union membership at Casa Grande grew from a low of 1,500 in 1972 to 2,800 by 1974. (Interview with trade union leaders, Casa Grande, August 12, 1974. Data confirmed by figures supplied by the personnel department.) Laredo union officials said their membership by 1974 was over 90%. There has been an erosion of the *licencia sindical*. Some cooperatives retain it for some officers but the norm is to petition the Administrative Council (now normally controlled by trade union activists) for time off to carry out a specific task and such petitions are normally granted.

These same men have also held the highest posts within the National Central of Sugar Cooperatives (CECOAAP). In 1973-1974 the president of the Administrative Council of CECOAAP, and the president of the Vigilance Council of CECOAAP were former secretary-generals of the Aprista-affiliated FTAP. Thus instead of the cooperative system becoming, as the government intended, the sole channel for participation of the sugar workers, the Aprista activists have retained all their old structures as well as becoming major forces within the new cooperative structures.

State parallelism refers to SAF-CAP. Instead of the state apparatus connecting only with the peak of the cooperative movement, it has, as we have seen, a permanent staff with broad monitoring powers inside each cooperative. There are thus three lines, instead of one line, of representation and control in the sugar sector.

Because of the lack of comparable union organization in the squatter sector, and its lack of economic centrality, I did not discover any significant squatter parallel organizations, and the state in that sector has nothing equivalent to SAF-CAP.

My analysis of participation and control in the sugar sector, while dealing with a challenge to the organic-statist model of government that is much more difficult and complex than that in the squatter sector, nonetheless leaves two central questions unaddressed.

The major contradictions of the organic-statist model to be resolved in the sugar sector concerned the tensions between the conflicting logic of self-managing units on the one hand, and a powerful state attempting to direct an overall process of societal development on the other hand. There was, however, relatively little conflict between state control and the imperatives of market competition, because the state expropriated a sector in which the major capital investments had already been made, and Peruvian technocrats had the capacity not only to supervise existing technology but to create new technology. However, in many other areas the state has great need for new capital investments and new technology, neither of which are readily available. In those areas, the demands of the market, and in particular the power of foreign capital, present even greater difficulties for the organic-statist model. The capacity (or incapacity) of the state to control foreign capital is the subject of the next chapter.

The second question our analysis of participation at the sectoral level has not addressed is the possibility of merging all the different sectors within the country into an authoritative national system of political participation. This is discussed in the concluding chapter of the book.

SEVEN · *The State and Foreign Capital*

IN ITS first months in office, the Peruvian military regime announced its intention to build a new political order on an economic foundation that was "neither capitalist nor communist." In fact, from the perspective of the models developed in Chapter 1, the Phase I military leader's conception of a participatory, solidaristic society, and a state-forged yet decentralized economy in which self-managing groups would play an important part, approximated at least in aspiration the organic-statist model.

In 1968, however, much of the national economy of Peru was dominated by foreign rather than national capital.[1] From the beginning, therefore, a central question facing the regime was how the state could regulate foreign capital to achieve its long-term goals.

Until now I have considered the possibilities and constraints facing a state in its attempts to restructure domestic social groups and sectors. The use of state-chartered, hierarchically structured organizations to shape the relations between the state and political and economic actors in its environment—virtually a defining characteristic of the organic-statist model—is easiest in relation to lower-class groups. For lower-class groups, their interest associations, such as unions, are by far the most important vehicles for making strong and sustained demands. If the state can restructure these organizations, it has gone a long way toward channeling their demand-making capacities. It is more difficult for the state to encapsulate effectively middle- and upper-class domestic economic groups within new state-chartered institutions, because associations are only one of a variety of organizational and demand-making vehicles available to powerful economic groups.[2] Nonetheless, the state can restructure associational

---

[1] This assertion is discussed and documented later in the chapter.

[2] This point is elaborated in Guillermo O'Donnell, "Corporatism and the Question of the State," in *Authoritarianism and Corporatism in Latin America*, ed. Malloy.

230

groups such as chambers of commerce or industrial and bar associations. This has in fact been done at various times in Brazil and Mexico.[3]

The ability of the state to encapsulate economic groups is most limited with regard to foreign economic groups. This is largely because the bulk of the assets and the most important decision centers of foreign capital lie outside the boundaries of the nation and therefore outside the organizational format of state-chartered corporatist structures. State-chartered, national, hierarchical organizations cannot, for example, encapsulate the leaders and owners of multinational corporations and can only affect a small part of the enterprises' total assets. There are, of course, other economic and political factors constraining the use of state-chartered structures in the area of foreign capital. Multinational corporations, for instance, have the power to lobby their own governments to impose sanctions against countries threatening action against foreign capital. In addition most Third World governments exercise self-restraint in their policies toward foreign capital, both to avoid state-to-state sanctions and to maintain some access to the capital, technology, and markets controlled by multinational firms.

Foreign capital, in short, by its very nature challenges the idea of an integrated, organic-statist society. This is not to say that a state elite cannot devise policies to limit the possible disintegrative effects of foreign capital on its organic-statist goals. However, precisely because of the special organizational characteristics of foreign capital, different strategies are called for in dealing with foreign capital than in dealing with the domestic groups and sectors examined thus far.

In Phase I the Peruvian government devised one of the Third World's most complex and ambitious programs of state policies for the control and management of foreign capital.[4] In some

[3] For Brazil see Philippe C. Schmitter, *Interest Conflict and Political Change in Brazil.* For Mexico see Frank R. Brandenburg, *The Making of Modern Mexico,* esp. pp. 86-95.

[4] Raymond Vernon notes the innovative international role Peru played in this period: "only one important project for the achievement of joint restrictions within a common market had [by 1970] actually materialized. This was an agreement adopted by the so-called Andean group of countries. . . . That group, spurred by the studies of an outstanding secretariat and bol-

231

areas this program has met with success. In others, major failures of design and execution have actually increased the regime's de facto dependency and contributed to the decidedly less nationalistic, more classically orthodox policies of stabilization and retrenchment that have characterized Phase II. Both because of the program's intrinsic theoretical and comparative significance for students of the state, and its critical role in the organic-statist experiment in Peru, this chapter will examine in detail the program of state policies to control foreign capital attempted in Phase I and indicate how some of its failures contributed to the emergence of Phase II.

To put this program in perspective let us assay an overview that highlights the interrelationships between a number of crucial themes. As I noted in Chapter 4, concern about the domestic consequences of foreign investment was an integral part of the threat perception that brought the military to power. Indeed, one of the major areas of the military's programmatic consensus involved the specific issue of the expropriation of the International Petroleum Company and the more general issue of control over natural resources. As I discuss later in this chapter, the Phase I government in Peru was one of the first "dependencia-oriented," as opposed to "import-substitution-oriented," governments in Latin America. In essence this meant that economic policies and political relationships that under earlier nationalist and/or inclusionary experiments had been viewed as appropriate to the development process were viewed by the state elite as a source of development problems and a threat to the integrity and autonomy of the state. More specifically, the military leaders of Phase I believed that the prior pattern of foreign investment was in part responsible for the existence of a weak state in Peru —a condition that was intolerable from the standpoint of a model of governance that approximated organic statism.

---

stered by the populist revolutionary bent of the Peruvian government, adopted a common requirement that will oblige new foreign investors to accompany their initial proposals with a plan for later divestiture." *Sovereignty at Bay. The Multinational Spread of U.S. Enterprises*, p. 246.

An excellent overview of Peru's Phase I policies is Shane Hunt, "Direct Foreign Investment in Peru: New Rules for an Old Game," in *The Peruvian Experiment*, ed. Lowenthal. In the early stages of my research for this chapter, Hunt graciously gave me advice and a draft of the above article, both of which greatly facilitated my study.

The policy response that emerged in Phase I was complex—involving in part tighter and more comprehensive investment policies by the Peruvian state apparatus toward foreign firms; in part the introduction of industrial communities that were intended both to balance foreign investment and to reduce domestic class-conflict—a crucial organic-statist goal; in part the active support of the Andean Pact, which, if carried to its logical conclusion, would have entailed giving up certain areas of sovereignty and autonomy to other South American countries as the necessary means of achieving greater sovereignty and autonomy with respect to international capitalism; and finally the development of an aggressive and integrated global foreign policy aimed at expanding Peru's degrees of freedom and lessening dependencia, a policy that was closely related to the organic-statist concern for the autonomy and integrity of the state.

The central role played by foreign capital in the Third World justifies a careful examination of this Peruvian experiment. It also allows us to focus attention on the predicaments faced by countries attempting to bring foreign capital under greater state control while concurrently using such capital to further their own economic and political goals. Such a focus thus not only addresses crucial issues of organic statism per se, but also raises crucial issues in the analysis of state power vis-à-vis foreign capital in general.[5]

FOREIGN CAPITAL AND STATE POLICIES: COMPETING CONCEPTIONS

Surprisingly, until the recent appearance of a third approach pioneered by such writers as Constantine Vaitsos, Jorge Katz, Theodore Moran, and Franklin Tugwell, the two most important bodies of literature on foreign capital devoted relatively little attention to the general question of state policies toward foreign

---

[5] This focus must not be restricted to the study of the direct foreign investment of multinational corporations. Lessening dependency also entails consideration of such factors as private and public foreign lending, access to markets and technology, and expanding internal savings capacity. This point is well developed in Louis Wolf Goodman, "The Social Organization of Decision-Making in the Multinational Corporation," in *The Multinational Corporation and Social Change*, ed. David E. Apter and Louis Wolf Goodman, pp. 63-95.

capital.[6] One of these bodies of literature examines the role of multinational corporations in international business, as seen from the perspective of industrialized nations.[7] Mainly the work of social scientists from the industrialized world, this literature is concerned primarily with how multinational corporations work, rather than with how they might be controlled. The second body of literature, although focusing on the Third World, also misses our concerns here. It examines the nature of dependency, and is mainly the work of social scientists from the Third World, notably Latin America. In this literature, national self-determination and international equity are the chief themes, and much of the literature is devoted to documenting the negative impact of foreign capital.[8] Here again, little attention is paid to possible state strategies to alter the impact of foreign capital on Third World societies.[9]

[6] See footnote 11.

[7] Many works have been associated with the Multinational Enterprise Project of the Harvard Business School directed by Raymond Vernon. Among them are John M. Stopford and Louis T. Wells, Jr., *Managing the Multinational Enterprise: Organization of the Firm and Ownership of the Subsidiaries*; Frederick T. Knickerbocker, *Oligopolistic Reaction and Multinational Enterprise*; and Vernon's own *Sovereignty at Bay*. Much of the raw data for this project are presented in tabular form in the invaluable sourcebook by James W. Vaupel and Joan P. Curhan, *The Making of Multinational Enterprise*. The book can be used to create a "prerevolutionary" baseline for Peru because Peru is one of the seven Latin American countries for which the data are presented individually, and the data go from 1900-67. Also see Jack N. Behrman, *Decision Criteria for Direct Investment in Latin America*.

[8] One of the most sophisticated formulations of the dependency argument is found in Fernando Henrique Cardoso y Enzo Faletto, *Dependencia y desarrollo en América Latina*. Also see Cardoso's *Ideologías de la burguesía industrial en sociedades dependientes (Argentina y Brasil)*. A succinct statement is Theotonio dos Santos, "The Structure of Dependence," *American Economic Review* (May 1970). For a bibliographical guide see W. C. Smith, Jr., "A Dependency Bibliography," in *Structures of Dependency*, ed. Frank Bonilla and Robert Girling.

[9] There is often an appeal in the dependency literature for a revolution to overthrow the entire capitalist structure (see, for example, the dos Santos article in the previous footnote), but almost never is there serious analysis of the strategic policies necessary to make a revolution in the specific dependent context. An additional point is that even in those cases where there is revolution (as in Cuba), it is highly likely that the revolutionary regime

In fact, these two bodies of literature taken together contributed to the widespread belief that multinational corporations had the power to grow independently of, or in spite of, state policies in Third World countries. There was frequently even the suggestion that multinational corporations contribute to the erosion of the nation-state. Both these propositions are qualified in this chapter. In the case of the growth of multinational industrial firms in Latin America since World War II, I argue that this growth did not occur independently of state policies, but instead was greatly aided by state policies of import substitution, which gave tariff, foreign exchange, and import incentives (and even subsidies) to multinational firms to locate their subsidiaries in Latin America. If this argument is sound, it follows that different policies might well have a different effect on foreign capital.

To the proposition that multinational corporations contribute to the erosion of the nation state I offer a counter-hypothesis: the growth of multinationals may well help generate in some countries normative and administrative aspirations to create mechanisms to control multinationals. The strong presence of multinationals will thus often result in an increase rather than a decrease of the state's role in the management of the economy. There is also the very real possibility that the growth of multinationals will stimulate the appearance of multistate planning and bargaining organizations such as the Andean Pact and OPEC. There is thus reason to think that the multinational corporations may well encourage the rise of countervailing bureaucracies in which the state will play a key role.[10]

Intellectually and politically, therefore, we are ready for development of the third body of literature concerning the state and foreign capital, a new literature focused on the systematic exploration of policies, strategies, and institutional mechanisms

---

will eventually want (as all Eastern European countries have done) to utilize, under highly regulated conditions, some of the resources of the multinational corporations. Thus even for Marxist regimes, the study of policies to control and utilize multinational corporations effectively is essential.

[10] The national and international strategies of the Peruvian regime in Phase I are a clear case in point, as I show later in the chapter.

available to countries attempting to expand their degrees of freedom in their relations with foreign capital and the international economic system.[11] For such countries, the locus of coun-

11 Fortunately this third body of literature is strong and growing. This chapter attempts to contribute to, and build upon, the approaches developed by this new school of policy analysts. It is significant that some of the most important books and articles of this school have been written by analysts who are fully versed in both the other schools of thought about multinationals. Their intimate knowledge of the business environment within which these corporations act, and their keen awareness of the problems identified by the dependency literature, has put them in a good position to think analytically about meaningful policies to alter the bargaining arena in directions that will increase the gains and decrease the costs for Third World states in their relations with multinational corporations. Because this literature is much more scattered and less widely known than the literature previously cited it deserves extensive citation here. Some of the most important works are: Constantine Vaitsos, *Intercountry Income Distribution and Transnational Enterprises,* his "Power, Knowledge and Development Policy: Relations Between Transnational Enterprises and Developing Countries," (The 1974 Dag Hammarskjöld Seminar on The Third World and International Economic Change, Uppsala, Sweden, August 1974) (mimeographed), and his *Comercialización de tecnología en el Pacto Andino.* From 1972 to 1976 Vaitsos headed the Department of Science and Technology Policy, Secretariat of the Andean Common Market, located in Lima. On policies toward technology, see Jorge Katz, "Patentes, corporaciones multinacionales y tecnología. Un examen crítico de la legislación internacional," *Desarrollo Económico* (April-June 1972). A general approach toward policy in the context of dependency is Osvaldo Sunkel, "National Development Policy and External Dependence in Latin America," *Journal of Development Studies* (October 1969). The Andean Pact's "Acuerdo de Cartagena" is itself a major document of this school. See especially Decision #24, "By-Laws for Common Treatment of Foreign Capital, Trademarks, Patents, Licensing Agreements and Royalties." An astute analysis of the Andean Pact is found in Miguel Wionczek, "Problems Involved in the Establishment of a Common Agreement for Foreign Investment in the Andean Common Market" (mimeo, 1974). Among the works by U.S.-based scholars are: Carlos F. Díaz-Alejandro, "North-South Relations: The Economic Component," *International Organization* (Winter 1975), Albert O. Hirschman, "How to Divest in Latin America, and Why," in his *A Bias For Hope: Essays on Development and Latin America,* Franklin Tugwell, "Petroleum Policy in Venezuela: Lessons in the Politics of Dependence Management," *Studies in Comparative International Development* (Spring 1974), Franklin Tugwell, *The Politics of Oil in Venezuela* (Stanford: Stanford University Press, 1975), and Theodore H. Moran, *Multinational Corporations and the Politics of Dependence: Copper in Chile,* esp. Chapters 7 and 8, and his "Multinational Corporations and Dependency: A Dialogue for 'Dependentistas' and 'Non-Dependentistas,'" *International Organization,* 32 (Winter 1978): 79-100.

tervailing power will be the state.[12] Any study of state-foreign capital relations should begin, therefore, with the analysis of the factors that, considered abstractly, would have a bearing on the capacity of a state in the early stages of industrialization to control the use of foreign capital in the development process. Once such factors have been examined in the abstract, we can assess the range of policies available to a country such as Peru. Peru is especially interesting for such an assessment because in Phase I it made a much more systematic effort to control foreign capital and to give labor ownership and participation in the economy than has any other inclusionary experiment in Latin America. However, these efforts have met with success in some sectors of the economy and failure in others. The study of the range of factors affecting state power in relation to foreign capital allows us to place these successes and failures in a larger analytic framework as well as to assess how the goal of controlling foreign capital reinforced or conflicted with Peru's other organic-statist goals.

VARIABLES AFFECTING THE CAPACITY OF THE STATE TO CONTROL FOREIGN CAPITAL

Because of the different issues involved in controlling foreign economic elites—as opposed to domestic lower-class groups—a

[12] This is not to deny that the state itself in dependent countries often plays an important role in inviting and protecting foreign capital.

As I stressed in Chapters 2 and 3 this has been the essence of the development strategies of the exclusionary regimes in Brazil, Argentina, and Chile. Since 1940 this process has become increasingly important in Mexico. For the often symbiotic relationship between the state and foreign capital, see in addition Guillermo O'Donnell and Delfina Linck, *Dependencia y autonomía*, pp. 199-218, and Luciano Martins, "The Politics of U.S. Multinational Corporations in Latin America," in *Latin America and the United States: The Changing Political Realities*, ed. Julio Cotler and Richard R. Fagen. Nonetheless, if policies and mechanisms to control foreign capital are to be applied at all they must come from the state apparatus. An earlier body of development theory "assigned" the task of protecting Third World societies from foreign capital to the middle classes (especially the national industrial bourgeoisie) and to urban labor. It is now much clearer that the process of dependent development itself neutralizes, quantitatively and qualitatively, these groups to a significant effect. In any case, should revolutionary forces emerge, they must first capture the state apparatus and then try to use the power of the state to control foreign capital.

237

somewhat different, though partly overlapping set of variables from those proposed in Chapter 3 will help to understand the degree of success of the state in dealing with different areas of foreign investment.

Any assessment of the factors that affect the capacity of the state to control foreign capital must begin with factors stemming from the *internal characteristics of the state itself.*

A. *State Elite's Internal Strength and Commitment to Control*

Logically, the political strength of the strategic state elite and its commitment to a policy of control is the first variable affecting the state's power to control foreign capital. The state's power to control capital is obviously increased when the state elite has reasonably great internal strength to impose a consistent strategy of control, and a reasonably high degree of ideological and programmatic unity about *why* such control has high priority and *how* a control strategy might be devised and implemented.[13]

B. *State Elite's Technical and Evaluative Capacity to Determine Preferred Role of Foreign Capital in the Overall Development Plan*

The greater the degree to which the state elite has the technical and economic sophistication to define its own long-term goals and the planning capacity and ability to identify the precise packages of foreign investment and borrowing required to complement national investment, the greater the potential to channel foreign capital into preferred areas and prevent foreign capital from entering nonpreferred areas.

C. *State Elite's Administrative and Political Capacity to Monitor Foreign Capital*

The state elite's capacity to implement its preferred investment strategy is increased to the degree that the bureaucratic apparatus of the state develops efficient administrative pro-

[13] High internal power, unity, and stability of the state elite translates into bargaining strength because it means that the environment is more "predictable" for foreign capital. This predictability enables the state to bargain for more favorable terms than if the political context were less stable. The Soviet Union and Brazil, despite different ideologies, both "offer" a predictable business context. Note that repression itself does not ensure predictability. Chile is even more repressive than Brazil but less predictable.

cedures, as well as necessary technical skills, to monitor the inflow and outflow of foreign capital, and to the degree that credible sanctions can be created to ensure non-automatic, negotiated entry for new and major reinvested foreign capital.[14] Such monitoring procedures would include the capacity to identify, specify, and negotiate effectively for the various components of an investment package, such as its sectoral and spatial location, the source of credit, the ratio of labor to capital, the import coefficient, export potential, and the rate of local integration.

A second set of factors involves the characteristics of the domestic public and private sectors.

D. *State/National Savings and Investment Capacity*

A crucial factor affecting state policy toward foreign capital is the capacity of the state and the domestic private sector to generate new investments. The greater the degree to which the state's development goals can be financed by domestically generated state savings or by capital generated by national entrepreneurs, the less dependent the state will be on borrowing abroad or on direct foreign investment to meet its investment goals. In turn, the greater will be the capacity of the state to dispense with and/or control foreign capital.

Various policies carried out by the state can affect investment capacity. The state can expand its own savings-investment capacity through increasing its tax base or by generating a surplus in state-controlled enterprises. The state can also increase incentives for savings and investment in the national private sector and disincentives for consumption in this sector. Last, the state can define investment priorities in such a way as to diminish or postpone large projects requiring great amounts of foreign exchange.[15]

E. *State/National Technological Capacity*

Technological capacity is a combination of (1) knowledge-making capacity, (2) access to machines and techniques, and

[14] Vaitsos, in "Power, Knowledge and Development Policy," shows why a policy of "non-automatic, negotiated entry" is crucial to an integrated control strategy.

[15] Later in this chapter I argue that the greatest errors of conception, prediction, and execution by Phase I policy makers concerned this variable and contributed directly to Peru's increasing vulnerability to pressures from international lenders and to the policy retrenchments of Phase II.

239

(3) the capacity of the social organizations required to put knowledge, machines, and techniques to use.[16] Viewed in this way, the greater the state's or national firms' technological capacity for carrying out the state's investment goals, the greater the state's potential to be independent of imported technology. Obviously this capacity varies greatly from sector to sector in the economy, and from project to project. State policies that can affect this variable include the creation of centers for scanning patents and technology in order to (1) increase knowledge about existing technological capabilities so that no unnecessary technology is purchased; (2) increase knowledge about the global availability and costs of technology so that only the cheapest and most appropriate technology is imported; (3) attempt to break down technological "packages" so that the state imports only those components in a package that are missing; and (4) scrutinize the patents built into incoming multinational investments in order to reduce, if possible, such provisions as those against exporting a product made with these patents, or those stipulating that all inputs for the patented process be imported from the parent firm, even though comparable inputs are available in the local market. Long-run state policies to reduce technological dependency include the selective channeling of funds for the development of those technologies most relevant for the effective exploitation of the special factor endowments of the nation, especially in those areas where the nation has a potential comparative advantage in export.[17]

F. *State/National Marketing Capacity*

The capacity of the state and of the national private sector to market exports abroad is another variable that underlies dependency and dependency-reducing policies. Once again this capacity will vary from sector to sector and project to project. The state can attempt to expand its international marketing capacity by creating its own network of world-wide marketing

[16] The phrase "technology transfer" is obviously misleading because it understates the problem of knowledge-making capacity and social organization.

[17] The politics of technology are discussed in Vaitsos, *Comercialización de tecnología en el Pacto Andino.* Also see the previously cited article by Katz. Some of the most advanced thinking on the subject is found in Andean Pact documents, particularly Acuerdo de Cartagena, "Fundamentos para una política subregional de desarrollo tecnológico" (Lima: May 16, 1974), and Decisions 84 and 85 of the Andean Pact.

agencies, and by developing relations with countries previously marginal to the established, informal networks of foreign capital. In the long run, in cases where the state produces commodities for which there are more diverse market outlets for refined than for raw materials, the state can also increase the internal value added and its range of potential buyers by developing a refining capacity.[18]

A third set of variables can be called economic background variables.

G. *Domestic Market Size*

The greater the size and growth potential of the local market, the greater the potential rewards and economies of scale for the foreign investor wishing to sell to such a market. Consequently the greater is the potential for the host state to demand a more sophisticated set of requirements as the price paid by foreign capital for continued access to the local market. This variable is relatively intractable to state policy, but it can be affected in the medium-to-long run in two ways: the state can offer a foreign investor a larger (or exclusive) share of the market by denying access to other competitors, in return for the investor's meeting an agreed-upon set of state-designated requirements; and/or the state can attempt to expand the effective market by forming common market agreements with other countries.

H. *The Value and Quantity of Export Items*

The greater the quantity and value of a nation's exportable items (normally extractive resources) and the scarcer these items are on the world market, the greater the potential bargaining power of the state vis-à-vis foreign investment and/or lending capital. Once again, this variable is relatively intractable to state policy. Potential state actions to alter its position on this variable are for the state to play an entrepreneurial role in at least attempting to establish the existence of previously unde-

[18] For example there are about 20 (closely connected) buyers of blister copper in the world, whereas there are 500-600 buyers for refined copper. Peru is thus developing its own refining capacity to attempt to decrease its vulnerability to oligopolistic marketing pressures. See Janet Ballantyne's indispensable "The Political Economy of Peruvian Gran Mineria" (Ph.D. dissertation, Cornell University, Latin American Studies Program, Dissertation Series, Number 60, 1976), pp. 234-35.

veloped export commodities, and/or for the state to play an active role in creating relevant producer cartels to raise the relative scarcity of the commodities on the world market.[19]

I. *"Sunken" Versus "Uncommitted" Foreign Capital in High State Priority vs. Low State Priority Foreign Investment Sectors*

The literature on the bargaining power of foreign capital in extractive industries points to the existence of a bargaining cycle:

> the older the concession, or the more "committed" the company, the larger is the share of total rents the government can expect to get. . . . When large new investments are being contemplated, the tables are turned on the host government. Now it must compete with all other possible areas open to foreign companies for investments and it must offer an expected profitability to the foreign company as great as that the company could get at any other site. *The moment of new investment is the moment of greatest bargaining strength for the company.*[20]

Though direct foreign investment in manufacturing is by its nature often less "sunken" than direct foreign investment in extractive industries, the insight seems of general applicability.

However, for purposes of our analysis, the bargaining cycle model may be refined by adding another variable relating to

---

[19] A strategy to increase exports might be to eliminate gradually tariffs to stimulate competition and thus increase the efficiency and quality of the production of manufactured goods. The risk is that in the "rationalization process" the existing multinational firms have the special advantage that they can draw upon the credit and marketing facilities of their parent firms, thus giving them a greater survival capacity than the national firms.

Another strategy is for the state to try to keep labor costs low and not to make any local integration requirements. The state elites in Hong Kong, Taiwan, Singapore, and South Korea have encouraged such a multinational-dominated, "export-platform" strategy for assembling labor intensive manufactured goods.

[20] Raymond F. Mikesell, "Conflict in Foreign Investor-Host Country Relations: A Preliminary Analysis" in *Foreign Investment in the Petroleum and Mineral Industries: Case Studies of Investor-Host Relations*, ed. Mikesell, p. 54 (emphasis added). Variants of this bargaining cycle approach are also found in Vernon's discussion of "The Obsolescing Bargain" in *Sovereignty at Bay*, pp. 46-59, and in Moran's discussion of a "balance of power bargaining model" in *Multinational Corporations and the Politics of Dependence*, pp. 153-224.

whether foreign investment in a given sector has a low or a high priority within the state's development plans. Whether "uncommitted" foreign capital is a source of bargaining weakness for the state (as in the standard model), or a source of state strength, depends on whether the sector is one of low or high priority for the state.

The state is in the weakest position to place controls on foreign capital in those sectors where foreign investment has a high priority in the state's development plan (because of the sector's high potential productivity and the absence of one of the state/national factors of production, such as capital, technology, or marketing capacity) *and* when there is no existing foreign investment in the sector. In these circumstances the state may be compelled to forego making exacting specifications for entry, and may in fact have to extend special subsidies to attract "uncommitted" foreign capital.

The state is in the *strongest* position to control foreign capital at a low economic and political costs if the proposed investment involves an area of the economy that is given a low priority by the state (because state/national factors of production can adequately meet planned investment targets in the sector) *and* there is no existing foreign investment in the sector. In this case the state will be most inclined to use its monitoring capacity to keep foreign capital completely out of the sector.

Between these extremes fall two other positions of potential state power. If a sector has low priority for new foreign investment (because all the state/national factors of production exist) but there is already "sunken" foreign investment, the state has a reasonable amount of leverage against this existing foreign investment. Because the investment is "sunken," it is vulnerable to the broad range of control measures the state can apply. In addition, since the "low priority" evaluation is partly a function of the state's high investment and technological capacity in the sector, the state's negotiating hand is strengthened by the credible threat that it can nationalize and effectively run the sector. Strong control measures against "sunken" investment, however, are not costless, as they are in the case of "uncommitted investment," because, if the existing investment is nationalized, it must be compensated for in some form or the state will risk formal and informal sanctions from the firms and governments of the industrialized countries.

243

The state is in a weaker position to control foreign capital if sunken investment is in a high priority sector in which the state wants a continued foreign presence because it believes that some crucial factors of production are missing on the state/national level. However, precisely because the foreign investment is sunken (it is most sunken in mining), the state can begin to use its control devices to renegotiate the original terms of entry in its favor. (Table 7.1 summarizes the above argument.)

TABLE 7.1

POWER POTENTIAL OF THE STATE IN FOUR DIFFERENT
POSITIONS IN THE BARGAINING CYCLE WITH FOREIGN CAPITAL

Previous Status of Foreign Investment		*Importance to State of Attracting Foreign Investment in the Particular Sector*	
		Low Priority	*High Priority*
	Uncommitted	1 State can bar entry of foreign capital at almost no economic or political cost	4 State has to offer incentives to attract foreign capital
	"Sunken"	2 State can control or even eliminate foreign capital but at some economic and political cost	3 State cannot eliminate foreign capital but has some capacity to impose greater controls and exact greater rents

Scale of State Potential to Control Foreign Capital
1 = Highest
4 = Lowest

What policies can the state adopt to change its position in Table 7.1 with regard to foreign capital in general and with regard to any particular area of investment? The state can attempt to obtain the missing factors of production in cell 3 and thus shift its position in that sector to cell 2. Concerning cell 4, in the long run an integrated program of lessening dependency must devote great effort to increasing the state/national technological, marketing, and especially savings and investment capacities so that the quantity of cell 4 cases it accepts declines. In the short run the only way the state can avoid a compromise of autonomy by allowing direct foreign investment on relatively easy terms is to incur the economic loss of potential new production by postponing its investment target in this sector. If the state decides against this, it must accept an initial cell 4 position. Once the investment is "sunken," it can shift to cell 3. Over time, if it can develop the missing factors of production, it can then shift to cell 2.[21] Finally, in cell 1, by combining a policy of non-automatic, negotiated entry with the creation of effective evaluative procedures, the state can assess whether new foreign investment proposals are in fact needed. In those cases where they are not, the state can bar entry and thus slow the growth of foreign investment in cell 2.

A final variable stems from the political and economic relationship of the state to the international economic system.

J. *Position of the State in the International Political System*

It is assumed that any attempt to increase control over foreign capital may generate resistance by the governments of the countries where the state's principal trade, investment, and lending "partners" in the developed world are located.[22] Factors mitigat-

[21] Much of the best work of what I termed the "third school" concerning foreign capital is dedicated largely to questions concerning the control of direct, "sunken," foreign investment and analyzes how the state can work its way up a "learning curve" so that it can exploit the potential vulnerability of sunken investment and thus shift from a cell 3 to a cell 2 position. This is the major theoretical concern of the works by Moran on copper in Chile and by Tugwell on petroleum in Venezuela. Excellent as these works are, Table 7.1 points to the need for broadening the range of policy and analysis to address cells 4 and 1. The main implications of these cells are that the state can best lessen its dependency on foreign capital, not merely by negative measures against existing foreign capital, but by a positive package of policies aimed at strengthening state/national technological, marketing, and especially domestic savings and investment capacities. If these are strengthened, there is a crucial shift from cell 4 (the position of greatest state bargaining weakness) to cell 1 (the position of greatest state bargaining strength). Insistence on the importance of the variable of state/national savings and investment capacity also allows us to address the question of foreign capital (direct foreign investment *and* loans) rather than just direct foreign investment as much of the literature does. For countries such as Peru or Brazil, *loans* rather than direct foreign investment constitute the bulk of foreign capital. Obviously if the state increased its domestic savings capacity it would be less dependent on foreign loans to increase its investment capacity.

[22] Issues of international security beyond the control of a Third World state can affect seriously how any particular developed state will respond. If the developed state values the maintenance of a security alliance with the Third World state, it might not apply economic sanctions and might even encourage its nationals to maintain economic links. However, if the

ing the effectiveness and intensity of this resistance are (1) the continuing value of the economic and political assets over which the state has control,[23] (2) the ability of the state to develop a credible range of alternative political, trade, investment, and lending partners, and (3) the diplomatic and bargaining skills of the state elite in changing the rules of the investment game while avoiding policies, such as wholesale expropriation and the refusal to negotiate about compensation, that generate almost automatic international sanctions. Thus the greater the political and economic assets the state has in the international system, the more diverse its alternative partners, and the more skillful its crisis-containing diplomacy, the greater will be its ability to increase control over foreign capital without generating effective countercontrols from the international system.

Several conclusions may be drawn from an examination of the variables presented. First, despite the fact that there is power asymmetry between a Third World state and foreign capital, the state has the potential to construct policies for almost every one of the relevant variables in order to increase its bargaining position vis-à-vis foreign capital.

Second, it is necessary to talk not of a state policy toward foreign capital but of state *policies*. This is because the state's capacity to control varies greatly from sector to sector of the economy, according to the state's specific position on each of the variables (especially variables D to I). For any given country, therefore, we can identify sectors in which the state has great potential power vis-à-vis foreign capital and sectors in which the state has relatively little. The state elite, in attempting to lessen dependence upon foreign capital, thus must formulate an ini-

---

Third World state is defined as a strategic enemy, strong sanctions might be applied to discourage nationals from doing business, even though such nationals might want to engage in business for economic reasons.

[23] Economic assets could be the "hostage value" of the remaining foreign investment, which could be subjected to greatly increased state sanctions. Other economic assets could be the right to grant or deny access to the local market and to raw materials. Political assets are less tangible but if a state occupies a strategic position politically, the threat that the Third World state has the power to shift its policy in an even more harmful direction in response to sanctions by the developed state may lessen the likelihood of the application of such sanctions.

tially appropriate policy toward foreign capital for the concrete situation in each sector and devise strategies that over time will expand its degrees of freedom in each sector.

Third, it is necessary to draw a sharp distinction between (1) preventing unwanted foreign capital, (2) controlling existing foreign investment, and (3) attracting the desired types of new investment. Different variables are relevant for predicting the success of policy measures with regard to each of these three policy tasks. To prevent unwanted foreign investment (either new or reinvested), variables A to C are the most important; the state must have a commitment to control, the capacity to evaluate and identify areas of unwanted investment, and must have a policy of non-automatic entry and effective monitoring mechanisms backed by credible sanctions. Over time the capacity to deny access selectively to the market has a significant impact on the foreign investment profile, in that it will slow the growth of unwanted investment and alter the character of new investment, since new investment will go into areas consistent with the regime's priorities.

The control of existing foreign investment brings into play all of the variables, but the state's bargaining position begins with the fact that the investment is "committed" and therefore exposed to a broad range of state policies aimed at increased control. If the state's position is very strong on all 10 variables, the state can expropriate the investment. If the state is very weak on all variables, the state can often do little in the short run. Between these two positions, it can use its power of sovereignty and coercion to carry out a range of policies from increased taxation, renegotiation of terms of continued presence, to sophisticated schemes of phase-out or increased national participation in ownership and management.

Concerning new foreign investment desired by the state, the basic process has already been spelled out in the discussion of state investment priorities and the bargaining cycle (variable I). The combination of high state foreign investment needs and "uncommitted" investment is the point in the bargaining cycle of maximum state weakness, where almost all the state's coercive powers are neutralized. The dilemma for the state is that, if it articulates the conditions for entry of foreign capital too rigidly, potential investors will stay away. The only variables that the state can manipulate are that of access to the market or the size of the market. The state can deny access to an investor's competitors, thereby giving the investor a guarantee of a significant portion of the market in return for acceptance of new strict conditions of entry, or the state can attempt to increase the size of the market (and thus increase the state's potential bargaining power) by creating a common market with other countries.

To clarify this discussion of the variables involved, we can present the "poles" of the state's potential sectoral power vis-à-vis foreign capital. Let us first make an initial simplifying assumption of holding variables A to C and J constant, i.e. we assume the state has a high commitment to control, reasonably strong evaluative and monitoring capacities and has been able to contain international opposition at a moderate subcrisis level. Even with this assumption, the state's capacity to control foreign capital in any given sector will nonetheless vary greatly along a continuum stretching from a position of minimum potential for control to maximum potential, depending on the state's position in regard to variables D to I. (See Table 7.2.) Before applying this general framework to Peru, let us first put the Phase I policies to control foreign capital into an historical and comparative perspective.

PERU'S ANTI-DEPENDENCIA PROGRAM: ORIGINS AND ORIENTATION

As we stated earlier, Peru is especially interesting because, compared to all the other inclusionary experiments in Latin America, it embarked on a much more systematic effort to control foreign capital. This is not to argue that Peru succeeded in constructing an effective evaluative and monitoring capacity, nor that it was able to resist international pressures without significant compromises. Peru did, however, develop a reasonably comprehensive policy toward foreign capital and carried out an overall policy aimed at increasing its bargaining position in the international system.

In considering Peru's policies toward foreign capital, and its attempt to combine a policy of control with its domestic organic-statist goals, it seems reasonable to assume that the internal characteristics of the state, and Peru's position in the international economic system (variables A to C and J) had an important, but roughly equivalent, impact on all sectors of the economy. My

TABLE 7.2

STATE'S POTENTIAL SECTORIAL POWER VIS-À-VIS FOREIGN CAPITAL FOR SIX VARIABLES

Variables	High Potential State Power in Sector	Low Potential State Power in Sector
D State/National Savings and Investment Capacity	State can fully finance with internal state/national resources all new planned investment in the sector.	State cannot generate internal public or private capital to carry out planned projects and thus needs to go to international capital market.
E State/National Technological Capacity	State and national entrepreneurs dominate existing technology and have knowledge making capacity to generate new technology as required.	State and national entrepreneurs do not have adequate knowledge making capacity, access to machines and techniques or the social organization to put knowledge and machines to work.
F State/National Marketing Capacity	State-national exporters have internal capital and external marketing outlets and customers.	State-national potential exporters must rely on international marketing firms to get domestic products on world markets and to locate buyers.
G Domestic Market Size	A sufficiently large, valuable and growing market that foreign capitalists do not want to lose market to competition and will be willing to submit to stringent and time consuming regulations as the price of entry.	Actual and potential effective market so small that there is little competition to enter and in fact state has to offer a package of incentives to attract foreign investment.
H Value and Quality of Export Items	State controls large quantities of valuable scarce resources.	State does not control any known large quantity of valuable scarce resources.
I "Sunken" versus "Uncommitted" Foreign Investment in High Priority and Low Priority Foreign Investment Sectors	Because of D-H, the state attaches a very low priority to attracting or retaining foreign investment in the sector. If foreign investment not already "committed" in sector, state can block any new foreign investment. If "sunken," state can extract much better terms by credibly threatening with nationalization.	Because of D-H, state can only develop sector if it attracts foreign capital. The combination of high state foreign investment priority plus uncommitted foreign investment places state in weakest of four possible bargaining positions.

working hypothesis is that the great variation found in the success of Peru's policies in controlling foreign capital in different sectors of the economy is due to the different positions the state found itself on variables D to I for each sector. Before we analyze this variance, let us first examine the origins and general characteristics of Peru's overall strategy.

Despite serious compromises that are discussed later, the Peruvian state in Phase I followed a strongly nationalistic policy toward foreign capital. The first major act of the regime was to dramatically expropriate the International Petroleum Corporation. In 1973 the Cerro de Pasco Corporation, the largest foreign company in the export sector of mining, was expropriated. All foreign holdings in the next two most important export sectors, anchovy fishing and sugar, were taken over. New foreign investments in domestic banking, insurance, and communications were forbidden. Peru also played a leading role in the Andean Pact, which links Peru, Ecuador, Bolivia, Colombia and Venezuela in a common market that could increase these states' bargaining power vis-à-vis multinational corporations, impose strong constraints on incoming capital, and will, if the legislation of the pact is enforced, eventually reduce almost all foreign manufacturing firms participating in the pact to a minority position.[24]

How does Peru's relation to foreign capital compare with other inclusionary experiments in Latin America? Almost all state elites whose orientation or philosophy places them in the "organic-statist" category have attacked the "egoism" and "individualism" of liberal capitalism. In addition, in almost all attempts to impose inclusionary corporatism, particularly the attempts led by Perón, Vargas, and Cárdenas, nationalism has figured prominently and there has been an effort to increase state control of the economy. However, the specific content of such nationalist and statist actions has varied, depending to some extent on inter-

[24] The economic rationale for the pact is discussed in Carlos F. Díaz-Alejandro, "The Andean Common Market: Gestation and Outlook" in *Analysis of Development Problems*, ed. R. S. Eckaus and P. N. Rosenstein-Rodan (Amsterdam: North-Holland Publishing Co., 1973), pp. 293-326 and David Morawetz, *The Andean Group: A Case Study in Economic Integration Among Developing Countries*. The bargaining and geopolitical dimensions of the pact, as well as the details of the "fade-out" formula, are discussed later in this chapter. Chile was an initial member of the pact but withdrew in 1976.

250

national factors such as world ideologies and the international bargaining context.

The nationalism of Vargas, for example, largely manifested itself in the formation of a state steel industry and a state oil monopoly. During the epoch of Cárdenas, nationalism centered around the nationalization of the oil industry.[25] With Perón, the content of nationalism was expanded to include the expropriation of a wider range of foreign-owned property, including railroads and some utilities. Perón also made some attempt to generate a "third path" of industrial development. However, this third path met with an extremely unsupportive world environment because, in the strategic context of World War II and later the beginnings of the Cold War, a third path was strongly opposed by the United States. Given the economic and political conditions of the immediate postwar period, neither the Soviet Union, Japan, nor Europe was in a position to provide alternative international supports. In addition, in the 1940s and early 1950s, the decolonization that eventually gave third world countries majorities in the United Nations had hardly begun.

The dominant definitions of the nature of the development problem also play a key role in shaping the context of nationalism in any particular period. During the first Perón regime (the most nationalist inclusionary experiment before Peru), the most prominent school of Latin American thought concerning development was led by Raúl Prebisch at the United Nations Economic Commission for Latin America (ECLA), with its headquarters in Chile.[26] ECLA focused on the need for governments of developing countries to formulate mechanisms and tariff policies to encourage industrialization. The fact that many of the initial beneficiaries of the generous tariff, import, and quasi-monopolistic

[25] The major Mexican legislation to control technology (1972) and to reduce foreign ownership in industry (1973) comes after, and is partly based upon, the Peruvian and Andean Pact formulas. Unlike Peruvian legislation, it has no role for worker ownership or participation in industry. See Samuel del Villar, "El sistema mexicano de regulación de la inversión extranjera: elementos y deficiencias," *Foro Internacional*, 15 (1975), pp. 331-78.

[26] The "manifesto" of this school was written by Prebisch in 1949 and published as *The Economic Development of Latin America and Its Principal Problems* (New York: United Nations, 1950), also see *Theoretical and Practical Problems of Economic Growth* (New York: United Nations, E/CN 12/221, 1951).

251

market incentives for investors were foreign had not, even by the late 1950s, been identified as a central problem by Latin American nationalists of the ECLA school. But as a United States international financier specializing in Latin America later noted, the ECLA doctrine actually accelerated the growth of foreign capital, and most notably the U.S. multinational corporation:

> The rationale of the strategy was that Latin America was caught in a vicious circle of underdevelopment because it exported primary products and imported manufactured goods under deteriorating terms of trade. The solution was import substitution through protection of infant industries behind high tariff barriers. This meant keeping out imported manufactures and granting incentives to companies producing those manufactures locally.
>
> One can see in retrospect that this amounted to an invitation to foreign firms to set up local subsidiaries.[27]

When the history of this period is fully documented, it almost surely will show that in country after country in Latin America, the multinational corporations benefited from government incentives to invest in the import substitution process. Thus, though it is true that the multinationals, through their great financial and market strength, *have* absorbed the dynamic sectors of the industrialization process in many Latin American countries, by and large this growth did not occur independently of, or despite, government attempts to control them. On the contrary, they grew in a political and ideological context in which the host states established policies that encouraged and aided direct investment in modern industry by foreign multinationals.

In terms of the variables affecting state-foreign capital relations presented earlier, therefore, most Latin American countries, including Perón's Argentina and Peru before 1968, made a positive assessment as to the usefulness of modern foreign investment in industry. On the first variable, state commitment to control foreign capital, most countries scored low. Because of this, most also had only a rudimentary capacity to evaluate individual industrial investments (variable B), and did not develop sophisticated and flexible policy mechanisms to regulate foreign

[27] Richard S. Weinert, review of *Global Reach* in *The Yale Review* (Summer 1975), p. 632.

investment (variable C). Most countries in Latin America warmly welcomed foreign investment in manufacturing, and assumed it brought new capital and industries, would eventually contribute to exports and make an overall, positive contribution to "modernization." Some investments undoubtedly did bring advantages to host countries. The critical point is that Latin American countries had not developed a state capacity to evaluate, regulate, and, depending on the assessment, deny access to proposed new investment that did not meet expectations.[28]

By the time the Peruvian regime seized power in 1968, several of the factors discussed here had changed. The international environment was very different from what it had been during early inclusionary experiments in Mexico, Brazil, and Argentina. It was now largely "decolonized" and no longer rigidly bipolar. Thus it presented greater opportunities for exploring a variety of political and economic alliances. By the early 1970s, in addition, the global economy of scarce resources had increased the bargaining power of those developing countries that had access to those resources.

The military in Peru came to power at a time when the import substitution process had already encountered serious diffi-

[28] Only now with the growth of evaluating capacity is evidence accumulating to show how problematical many of the above expectations were. For example, far from bringing in new capital, the evidence now shows that worldwide, less than 15% of the total financial needs of U.S.-based manufacturing subsidiaries abroad originated from U.S. sources; see, United States Senate, Committee on Finance, *Implications of Multinational Firms for World Trade and Investment for U.S. Trade and Labor* (Washington, D.C.: February 1973), p. 38. The growth of individual multinational firms is often not a gain for the industrial base of a country because frequently—especially in light industry and services—they grow by absorbing viable local firms. For example in Colombia between 1958 and 1967 only 27 of the 51 U.S. subsidiaries that were created were completely new enterprises; see, Miguel S. Wionczek, "Problems Involved in the Establishment of a Common Agreement for Foreign Investment in The Andean Common Market" (unpublished Working Paper for The Andean Pact Staff, July, 1970), p. 8. The export potential of the foreign industrial firms was often thwarted by clauses in the original technological agreements, which forbade the new subsidiaries to export, undoubtedly so as not to compete with the parent firm. For example, the current Peruvian regime has set up an office to evaluate contracts to import technology; of the 102 contracts studied in the first control group, 42 had restrictions against exports. For these and other restrictions, see Eduardo Anaya Franco, *Imperialismo, industrialización y transferencia de tecnología en el Perú* (Lima: Editorial Horizonte, 1975), pp. 65-69.

culties in countries such as Brazil, Chile, and Argentina. Frustrations with import substitution industrialization had led to new analyses of the problem of development. By the mid-1960s, Prebisch and ECLA were being challenged by the "dependencia" school of theorists, who argued that one of the greatest threats to Latin American autonomy lay precisely in the indiscriminate growth of foreign investment, especially the growth of the multinational firms in the modern industrial sector. "Dependencia," not industrial growth, was now a watchword for many social scientists, and the freeing of countries from economic and political dependency was considered the essence of progressive forms of nationalism.

Some key sectors of the Peruvian army were especially responsive to the new "dependencia" formulation because it reinforced, and put into global perspective, some of their specific institutional frustrations. As we saw in Chapter 4, throughout the 1960s the Peruvian army had been concerned about the effect the development process was having on internal security. They believed that, although basic changes were absolutely necessary, alliances between domestic economic elites and international economic elites made these changes extremely difficult. As early as 1963, for example, a CAEM document concluded that

> The sad and desperate truth is that in Peru, the real powers are not the Executive, the Legislative, the Judicial or the Electoral, but the latifundists, the exporters, the bankers, and the American [U.S.] investors.[29]

The guerrillas' campaign, the compromises of the Belaúnde government with IPC, and devaluation heightened "new professional" military concern that the path of development itself was generating severe national problems. Economic policies and political relationships that under earlier nationalist and/or inclusionary experiments had been viewed as appropriate to the development process were now seen as a source of development problems and a threat to the integrity and autonomy of the state.[30]

[29] Perú, Centro de Altos Estudios Militares, *El estado y la política general* (1963), p. 92.

[30] There were, in addition, some specific military reasons for sensitivity to dependency. Because of the Peruvian government's threat to expropriate IPC, the U.S. government had severely reduced aid to Peru at the same

For all these reasons the desire to reduce the internal role of foreign economic power in Peru was one of the central goals of Phase I. The first manifesto published on assuming power in 1968 called attention to

> the power of economic forces, national and foreign, which have frustrated the realization of basic structural reforms and have helped maintain an unjust social and economic order, an order which permits the utilization of our national resources for the few while the majority suffers the consequences of their marginal position.[31]

The new Peruvian regime's sensitivity to the issue of dependency also manifested itself in a speech by President Velasco before a group of Latin American industrialists:

> The most radical significance of this historical moment in Latin America rests precisely in the fact that we are more and more conscious of our situation of underdevelopment and dependency. . . . The moment has now passed when we judged the process of industrialization in the abstract as a panacea for all our problems. Now it is imperative to determine the type of industrialization. . . . We do not want an industrialization that tends to perpetuate the defects and injustices of a system that has condemned the majority of our people to ignorance, misery, and backwardness. Neither do we want an industrialization which tends to deepen the dependent condition of our countries. We want on the contrary an industrialization that helps to liberate man."[32]

By the late 1960s, thus, the very definition of development had changed, and mere industrial growth, especially via foreign capi-

---

time it was giving Chile, Peru's most feared enemy, the highest per capita aid in Latin America. During the guerrilla campaign, the U.S. reportedly denied the Peruvian military's request for some anti-guerrilla materials. The U.S. also blocked the Peruvian air force's attempt to purchase F-5s, and later applied economic sanctions when Peru purchased Mirages from France. For growing tensions, especially over the F-5 case, see Luigi Einaudi, "Peruvian Military Relations with the United States" (Santa Monica: The Rand Corporation, P-4389, June 1970).

[31] *Manifesto del Gobierno Revolucionario de la Fuerza Armada* (Lima, October 2, 1968).

[32] Speech given by President Velasco on April 6, 1970, reproduced in *Velasco: la voz de la revolución*, Vol. 1 (Lima: Editorial Peisa, 1971), pp. 207-11.

tal, had been rejected in favor of addressing internal and external structural change. In 1968, therefore, both the content and the possibilities of nationalism were broader for the Peruvian nationalists than for any other inclusionary government before them.

From the military viewpoint, internal conflicts within Peruvian society and the external dependency of the Peruvian nation could only be overcome if the military elite captured and transformed the state apparatus and used the resources of the state to restructure the internal and external components of the economy.

ASSESSING PHASE I PERU: VARIABLES CONCERNING THE INTERNAL CHARACTERISTICS OF THE STATE AND THE POSITION OF THE STATE IN THE INTERNATIONAL POLITICAL SYSTEM

In terms of the variables affecting the power of the state to control foreign capital, it is clear that the state elite in Peru scored reasonably high on its commitment to achieve control (variable A). The regime also took steps to increase its technical and evaluative capacity to determine the preferred role of foreign capital in the overall development plan (variable B) as well as to increase its administrative and political capacity to regulate foreign capital (variable C). Despite the fact that overall planning was rudimentary when the military came to power, the planning system was strengthened and the role of foreign capital received special attention in all planning efforts.[33] Peru played a major role in persuading members of the Andean Pact to subject foreign capital to stringent guidelines.[34] The agreement,

[33] A Cambridge University economist who had worked in the Peruvian Institute of National Planning recently judged that: "the national planning system in Peru appears to be the most effective in continental Latin America, and compares favourably with any in the non-socialist underdeveloped world." Despite this judgment he correctly points out numerous areas of weakness within the planning system. See E.V.K. Fitzgerald, *The State and Economic Development: Peru Since 1968*, p. 90.

Brazilian planning, while much less comprehensive, is undoubtedly more technically sophisticated. This, coupled with the great size, potential, and "predictability" of the Brazilian market, gives the government much more effective bargaining room over the details of incoming direct foreign investment than the popular or academic literature suggests.

[34] Decision 24 of the Cartagena Agreement Commission, "By-Laws for Common Treatment of Foreign Capital, Trademarks, Patents, Licensing Agreements and Royalties" (December 1970).

which was enacted into Peruvian law, stipulated that no new foreign investment could be made without submitting an application to national agencies created to regulate foreign capital.[35] The application required a detailed breakdown of the major technological, capital, and balance-of-payments effects of the investment, a breakdown needed by national planning bodies to determine whether such investment was consistent with national development plans and met some major shortages in the state-national capacity to carry out the plan.[36] The new procedure applied both to incoming investment and to any reinvestment of profits by foreign firms that exceeded 5 percent of their authorized capital.[37]

That this new system, despite numerous weaknesses, was perceived to have teeth was obvious from a report by a consultant to the American Chamber of Commerce in Lima:

> Along with the shift in emphasis to development planning and controlled development has come the notion that foreign inputs must be *selected* according to the needs of the overall scheme, and that they be *controlled* to assure that they fulfill a beneficial role within it. Hence, the days when foreign companies came to these countries seeking markets and were permitted relatively free entry are now past. . . . The new criterion is clearly and absolutely that foreign inputs must have a positive developmental effect in terms of capital inputs, import substitution products, increased foreign exchange, new technologies, etc.[38]

[35] Article 2 of Decision 24.

[36] Appendix 1 of Decision 24 suggests approximately 50 information categories that must be answered before an application to invest is formally considered.

[37] See the investment guide prepared by one of the major U.S. accounting firms used by multinationals in Peru, Price Waterhouse and Co. *Information Guide for Doing Business in Peru* (Lima: 1973), p. 71. From 1971 to 1976, foreign firms could only repatriate up to 14% net profits on their officially registered capital base. Thus if they reinvested without official authorization, they did not increase their registered capital base. In addition, unauthorized reinvestments could well be "unrepatriatable" if the company were liquidated or the foreign investor sold his shares. In 1976 the authorized level of profit remission was raised from 14% to 20% of net profits and the reinvestment limit was raised from 5% to 7%. For details, see footnote 96 in this chapter.

[38] Dr. John R. Pate, "Foreign Investment in The Andean Pact" in Coun-

257

Strict legal rules were also established to prevent foreign firms from buying out viable national firms or from using local capital to finance new investment projects. Sensitive areas, such as domestic banking and insurance, where Peruvian nationals had reasonably strong financial and technological capacity to carry out necessary functions, were closed to all new foreign investment by law. While there was no law against new investment in commerce, an investment specialist noted in early 1975 that "no new foreign investment in commerce is being authorized and existing commercial companies report that they cannot obtain authorization to reinvest profits over the statutory 5 percent."[39] In addition, all basic industries (steel, nonferrous metallurgy, basic chemicals, fertilizers, cement and paper) were declared the investment prerogative of the state, and were being placed under state ownership. While new foreign capital would be permitted in this sector, it would be as a minority partner of the state.[40]

Apart from altering the internal characteristics of the state (variables A to C) in directions that increased its capacity to control foreign capital, the Phase I government attempted to limit or neutralize countermeasures from the governments of the international political system (variable J).[41] Peru was aggressive in seeking out alternative partners for trade, aid, borrowing, and new political allies, thereby lessening to some extent its heavy

---

cil of the Americas, *Andean Pact: Definition, Design and Analysis* (New York: 1973), p. 43 (emphasis in original).

[39] See Stanley F. Rose, "The Andean Pact and its Foreign Investment Code —Need for Clarity?" *Tax Management International Journal* (January 1975), p. 15. This is a systematic comparative analysis of the actual enforcement of the Andean Pact's Investment Code in the countries of the pact. The study was based upon the author's interviews (supplemented with a questionnaire) with foreign investment consultants and lawyers in all the pact countries. This information built upon Rose's prior experience as an investment consultant and lawyer at Price Waterhouse and Co., Lima. Also see his meticulously documented "Peru: An Introduction to Peruvian Law for Lawyers and Businessmen," *Tax Management International Journal* (February 1975), pp. 3-43.

[40] Perú, Decreto Ley No. 18350, *Ley General de Industrias* (July 30, 1970), articles 4-20.

[41] I have already mentioned some long range trends in the international economic and political system that had, by 1968, increased Peru's potential bargaining power. Here I concentrate on specific international policies of the regime.

reliance on the United States.[42] It established close relations with almost all the communist countries. China (along with India) became one of the first major buyers for the state's copper marketing efforts, and Rumania was the first country to enter a joint venture with the Peruvian state to develop copper.[43] The government used its known mining and potential oil resources to secure major loans from Japan, in return for granting Japan a first-option buyer status for these resources. The Peruvian authorities also attempted to increase their bargaining power to get new, but highly regulated, investment by playing a major role in the creation and framing of the Andean Pact's Decision 24 on the "Common Treatment of Foreign Capital."[44]

Peru in Phase I also played a reasonably skillful and firm bargaining game with the United States.[45] Many U.S.-owned enterprises were nationalized, and from 1968 to early 1974 the U.S. government informally closed many credit lines to Peru. However, while continuing to nationalize a range of U.S. firms, and diversify its non-U.S. international partners, Peru kept negotiations open with the United States by insisting that, in principle, appropriate legal compensation for each company was under consideration and that new U.S. private investment was welcome if it directly complemented the state's development plan and adhered to the new investment codes and procedures.[46] Finally,

[42] See for example Robert H. Swansbrough, "Peru's Diplomatic Offensive: Solidarity for Latin American Independence," in *Latin America: The Search for a New International Role,* ed. Ronald G. Hellman and H. Jon Rosenbaum (New York: John Wiley & Sons, Halsted Press Division, 1975), pp. 115-130.

Fitzgerald cites figures that show U.S. banks, USAID and the U.S. government's Export-Import Bank provided 41% of Peru's external finance in 1966 and only 10% in 1974. In the same period, Europe went from 29% to 42%, IBRD and IDB went from 18% to 21%, and "other" sources of finance went from 12% to 27%. See Fitzgerald, *The State and Economic Development,* p. 71. However during the financial crisis of 1976-1978 U.S. sources of external financing once again assumed a much more significant role.

[43] For details on these projects, see Ballantyne "The Political Economy of Peruvian Gran Mineria."

[44] This is discussed at length later in the chapter.

[45] Before and during the Allende government, the U.S. for strategic reasons wanted to follow a policy that would avoid a complete break with Peru out of fear of creating a strong regional anti-U.S. bloc.

[46] The Peruvian government statements (and actions) helped build a constituency against heavy sanctions by the U.S. government among many

after long and difficult negotiations, the Peruvian and U.S. governments arrived at a formula in February 1974 by which the U.S. government agreed that, in return for $74 million of blocked funds and a payment of the lump sum of $76 million to the U.S. government (which in turn would reimburse U.S. firms), the United States would consider all previous claims by expropriated U.S.-owned firms settled.[47] This agreement paved the way for unfreezing loans from the U.S. government-controlled Export-Import Bank.[48] It also caused a rapid turnabout on the part of the United States from a near veto in the Inter-American Development Bank and the World Bank to cautious approval of loans to Peru.[49] The agreement also apparently had a substantial impact on Peru's credit rating with some private sector European bankers, who had indicated they would enter the huge financial consortium to develop the copper mine, Cuajone, only if the

---

of the U.S. investors who were still "hostages" in Peru, and among those investors in petroleum and mining who were considering new investments that they wanted to go forward. These in turn (coupled with the U.S. strategic fears of completely alienating Peru) helped prevent the application of the Hickenlooper amendment and other formal sanctions by the U.S. government.

[47] The Peruvian government has released a 137-page booklet containing the official correspondence concerning the agreement. See Perú, Oficina del Primer Ministro, *Información oficial sobre el convenio entre los gobiernos del Perú y de los Estados Unidos de América, suscrito el 19 de febrero de 1974* (Lima: 1974). While the agreement did not list IPC as a beneficiary (it explicitly listed all the other nationalized U.S. firms), the allocation of the lump sum was done by the U.S. government. Former President Fernando Belaúnde caused a stir by circulating a photostat of a check for over $23 million that IPC received.

[48] For this sequence of events, see Hunt, "Direct Foreign Investment in Peru," pp. 326-31. The chief U.S. negotiator was James R. Greene, a New York banker, and the complex agreement is often referred to as the Greene agreement.

[49] The Peruvian delegate to the Inter-American Development Bank wrote a special report in which he noted that the United States for most of 1972 had over 42% of the votes in the bank and lamented that Peru did not receive any new development loans in 1972. See Armando Prugue, Director Ejecutivo Alterno por Colombia y el Perú, *El Perú en el Banco Inter-americano de Desarrollo (panorama y perspectivas institucionales)* (Washington, D.C.: Banco Interamericano de Desarrollo, June 24, 1974), p. 59. In interviews with three different high executives of the bank concerned with Peru all stressed that after Peru had settled its expropriation conflict with the U.S. government the bank was given the "Greene light" to explore major new loans to Peru.

investment was "protected" by the presence of the Export-Import Bank. After more than four years of delays, the key part of the Cuajone financing was put together rapidly, following the U.S.-Peruvian agreement.

In sum, there is considerable evidence that in terms of the internal characteristics of the state (variables A to C), and the regime's position in the international economic and political system (variable J), the Phase I state elite developed a comprehensive and consistent control policy and executed an overall foreign policy aimed at increasing its international bargaining capacity. Despite this, a great deal of variation existed in the success the Phase I military rulers had in controlling foreign capital in different sectors of the economy. We may assume, therefore, that this variation was due to the different positions the state found itself on variables D to I. This proposition is now examined by comparing the government's success in controlling foreign capital in a number of different sectors.

Sugar: High Capacity for Control

In the sugar sector the Peruvian state was in a strong position in regard to variables D to I. This sector was amenable to strong state action to diminish foreign investment (through expropriation of all foreign holdings) and amenable as well to the relatively successful pursuit of the state's other goals of worker participation and economic growth.

The Peruvian state/national savings and investment capabilities (variable D), were sufficient to meet foreseeable investment needs. Almost all the land and water available for sugar production in Peru were being utilized in 1968, so that further investments would not be massive and could be financed largely out of the industry's own profits. No major foreign loans were contemplated.

Technologically (variable E) Peru already had a fully installed production system, and Peruvian sugar specialists were in abundance because they ran the majority of the sugar estates in Peru. Peruvian sugar technologists were, in fact, among the best trained in the world. Peru therefore had the capability to manage existing sugar technologies and to make any further refinements necessary.[50]

[50] A self-assessment to this effect is found in Central de Cooperativas Agrarias de Producción Azucarera del Perú, División Técnica, "Situación

261

In regard to variable I, the Peruvian government was in the second strongest bargaining position indicated in Table 7.1, i.e., there was "committed" foreign investment in a low priority sector (because of the state/national strength on variables D and E).[51] Thus the committed foreign investment was vulnerable to a wide range of state policies to exact greater control, including the policy of maximum control, namely the expropriation of all foreign holdings.[52]

The only area of potential weakness was Peru's access to world markets (variable F). Peruvians had long experience in international sugar markets and were not dependent upon foreign marketing skills or contacts. However, over 90 percent of Peru's sugar was normally sold to the U.S. market via the sugar quota at a price that was often over the world price.[53] The Grace Company lobbied forcefully in Washington to have Peru's sugar quota cut.[54] However, since the Greene Agreement specifically included Grace as a beneficiary of the lump-sum agreement between Peru and the United States, the legal basis for retaliatory action on the part of the United States was removed.[55] In any case, the threat

---

actual y futura del potencial técnico de la industria azucarera" (Lima: September 1974), pp. 2-3. The report, however, stressed that the initially strong position in regard to technical personnel might be eroded unless the government took strong measures to retain old, and train new professionals in sugar technology.

[51] Precisely because of Peru's strong position on variables D and E the state did not need to attract any new foreign investment to the sector, so variable G (Domestic Market Size), which is primarily relevant in the case of new investment, is not important for our analysis.

[52] Of the twelve major sugar haciendas in Peru, only two were fully foreign owned. Paramonga and Cartavio were both owned by the W. R. Grace Company of New York City and accounted for approximately 20% of the total production of sugar. See Charles T. Goodsell, *American Corporations and Peruvian Politics*, pp. 72-75. Casa Grande, the largest hacienda, was headed by the Gildemeister family, who, though considered Peruvian oligarchs, registered much of their holdings in a corporation located outside of Peru.

[53] Central de Cooperativas Agrarias de Producción Azucarera del Perú, División Técnica, *Informe de operaciones de producción de la industria azucarera peruana—1973* (Lima: February 1974), p. 30.

[54] Grace's efforts (which were opposed by the American Chamber of Commerce in Lima, which feared it would hurt all the rest of the U.S. companies in Peru) are described by Goodsell, *American Corporations and Peruvian Politics*, pp. 134-38.

[55] See Perú, *Información oficial sobre el convenio entre los gobiernos del*

from the United States of a possible cut in the sugar quota was made less credible by a worldwide shortage of sugar that increased the value (variable H) of Peru's sugar and generated alternative buyers at a price higher than that specified in the U.S. sugar quota.

In the circumstances, all the factors were thus favorable to Peru, and the Peruvian state successfully removed all foreign investment in the sector through expropriation. The state was also able to carry out policies consistent with its social and political goals of worker self-management and participation by yielding ownership of the sugar sector to worker cooperatives, as described in Chapter 6. The same favorable conditions meant that the state was able to maintain its objective of economic growth under conditions of lessened dependency upon foreign capital. The sugar industry, which had never produced more than 840 thousand tons in any one year before 1968, produced over 900 thousand tons for all years between 1971-1976. The strong world market for sugar increased the foreign exchange earnings from $60 million in 1970 to a record of nearly $265 million in the sugar boom year of 1975.[56]

Oil: Low Capacity to Control

Between 1969 and 1971, the new Peruvian government attempted to devise an overall policy for the exploration of oil. However, with the important exception of access to world markets, the conditions in the oil sector for the relevant variables were at the opposite pole from those in the sugar sector, and the state elite was in a weak position to control foreign capital. In contrast to the sugar sector, state planners believed that the oil

---

Perú y de los Estados Unidos de América; pp. 17-18, 43-52. The agreement included compensation for Grace's chemical and paper industrial holdings which were expropriated.

[56] The foreign exchange figures are from Peru, Central Reserve Bank, *Aide Memoire on the Economic Situation in Peru* (Lima: 1976), Table 8.

While the Peruvian government was able to carry out its expropriation policy in the sugar sector successfully, increasing production costs, declining volume of the profitable export sector due to increasing domestic consumption, and erratic world sugar prices threatens the sugar sector with financial difficulties in the future that will necessitate continued policy innovation and attention. For an assessment of some of these problems and governmental policy response see "Agriculture: Bitter Pill for Sugar Cooperatives," *The Andean Report* 3 (April 1977), pp. 68-69.

sector required massive new investments. The discovery of large amounts of commercial oil in neighboring Ecuador in 1967, in a geological province that extended into the jungle area of Peru, raised hopes that similar finds could be made in Peru.[57] The prospect that such finds could increase Peru's foreign exchange for its development projects, and provide the government with additional funds for its ambitious social reforms, was enticing.[58]

However, the government faced important constraints in its technological capabilities (variable E). The state oil company, PETROPERU, had been created in 1969 following the expropriation of IPC.[59] IPC provided a valuable core for PETROPERU, but not one foreign geological or petroleum engineer stayed with the national company. In addition, since IPC had been engaged in a bitter conflict with the Peruvian government throughout the 1960s, it had not expanded the training of high-level Peruvian oil exploration and managerial professionals. Peru's national educational system was not capable of filling the gap by training oil engineers at home. In 1969 there were no Ph.D. or M.A. programs in the country specializing in oil technology. In fact, while the country graduated 600 B.S.'s annually in mechanical engineering, there were only 10-15 graduating in petroleum

57 By mid-1974, 245,000 barrels a day were being piped through Ecuador's Trans-Andean pipeline, and Ecuador had already joined Venezuela as Latin America's only members of OPEC. See *The Petroleum Economist* (August 1974), p. 292.

58 In informal conversations, various military officers stressed geopolitical reasons for wanting to invest heavily in the Amazon region: it was a nearly uninhabited area of Peru with borders with Ecuador, from whom Peru had won territory in 1941 and with Brazil, who they feared harbored expansionist intentions. Development of oil would bring people, roads, and, because of the rough terrain, extensive use of helicopters. Since the state could give the Peruvian air force a virtual monopoly of helicopter transportation this would subsidize the expansion of Peru's helicopter force. Peru's air force helicopter squadrons in the Amazon increased from one to five from 1971 to 1974, and a Bell helicopter representative estimated that the Peruvian air force (even before a planned $50 million of scheduled investment) was already the "world's fourth or fifth largest commercial helicopter operator"; see "Air Support Soars in Jungle Oil Push," in the *Peruvian Times* Special Issue. *Peru Petroleum Survey—1974* (September 20, 1974), pp. 42-43.

59 A small state company had existed before, Empresa Petrolera Fiscal, but it was an undynamic enterprise with little independent exploration capacity.

engineering.[60] PETROPERU carried out an aggressive program of exploration, but its managerial and technical personnel were already severely strained and it could not greatly expand its program into other regions of the country that preliminary studies indicated were ripe for intense exploration.[61]

However, state/national investment capacity (variable D) was the most important constraint in the oil sector. It was estimated that it would cost over $500 million (with a high foreign exchange component) just to explore intensively Peru's potential oil areas—not to mention the task of developing any commercial finds. Even should the technological problems be overcome by subcontracting (which would have been somewhat difficult because major oil companies had first call on many of the subcontractors), the cost would have severely strained Peru's budget and balance of payments. The prospects of borrowing this sum in 1969 were extremely low because, as a major study of petroleum and mineral development noted,

> International loan sources are usually not available for these purposes, partly because of the risk involved and partly because international financial institutions, such as the World Bank, have taken the position that since capital for the extractive industries is available from private sources, the international institutions should employ their own limited loan funds for transportation, power, and other industries for which private capital is not ordinarily available.[62]

It should be remembered that the policy-making period under consideration, 1969-1971, was well before the Libyan expropriation in August 1973 and the large OPEC price rises of fall 1973 that so changed the world oil supply situation. In fact Raymond Mikesell, writing shortly before the new Peruvian government began to evaluate how to explore and develop oil prospects, devoted attention to the "tremendous increase of oil reserves," asked whether "crude oil prices will continue to fall," and was skeptical about OPEC arriving at any strong policies concerning

[60] Interview with Dr. Froilan Miranda, Manager of the Personnel Training Program of PETROPERU, Lima, October 2, 1974.

[61] Interviews with General Marco Fernández Baca, Executive President, PETROPERU, September 19 and 24, 1974, Lima.

[62] *Foreign Investment in the Petroleum and Mineral Industries*, ed. Mikesell, p. 26.

production and marketing.[63] The state's bargaining position was further weakened by the fact that in regard to the value and quantity of export items (variable G), no major commercial discoveries of oil in the Peruvian Amazon had been made.

Thus when the Peruvian government decided to begin informal exploratory talks with foreign oil companies in mid-1969, it found itself in the weakest of the four possible bargaining positions under variable I: oil was a high priority area in which there was no committed investment.

Given Peru's weak position on all the relevant variables, it is not surprising that when it entered into agreement with foreign capital in order to pursue the state's goals for economic development, it had to compromise its goal of autonomy at least in the short run. After approximately a year and a half of negotiations, Occidental Petroleum Corporation signed an oil exploration contract in 1971 with the government of Peru. Before the government curtailed further contracts in August 1973, seventeen similar contracts had been signed with other foreign oil companies or consortiums. In these contracts, the foreign company generally received a "block" of a million hectares and agreed to bear all the expenses of exploration and development of the wells. In exchange for these services, PETROPERU, on behalf of the state, agreed to compensate the contractor with a remuneration varying from 44 to 50 percent of the product obtained.[64]

The compromise with autonomy consisted in the fact that foreign firms were allowed to explore and produce, a privilege the exclusionary regime in Brazil only granted after eleven years despite the fact that Brazil imported over 75 percent of its oil.[65]

[63] See his "Conflict in Foreign Investor-Host Country Relations: A Preliminary Analysis" in ibid., p. 46.

[64] See a speech describing the contract by General Marco Fernández Baca, Executive President, PETROPERU, *El contrato de operaciones Modelo Perú* (Lima: Departamento de Relaciones Públicas de Petróleos del Perú, 1973), p. 4. All the contracts were printed in the official newspaper *El Peruano*. In Occidental's contract they would receive 50% (*El Peruano*, June 23, 1971, pp. 4-8), whereas in some of the later contracts such as Signal's the amount was reduced to 44% or 45% depending on the amount of oil produced (*El Peruano*, July 4, 1973), pp. 10-15.

[65] For a discussion of the nationalist movement that led to the creation of the state entity PETROBRAS, which from 1953 to 1975 had monopoly rights to explore and produce, see John D. Wirth, *The Politics of Brazilian*

While we recognize this compromise, two questions still need to be raised about any agreement between the state elite and a multinational corporation in a country trying to lessen dependency. First is the question of how the state elite ensures that the foreign companies deliver fully the services for which the state has agreed to come to a compromise over such things as state autonomy. Second is the question of how the state elite can act to overcome the initial weaknesses in its bargaining position and expand its degree of freedom in subsequent stages. On both points the Phase I rulers pursued policies that shed light on this often neglected area of state-multinational bargaining.

The major areas of failure to deliver services in extractive contracts are the foreign company's slow development of the site to which it has rights or the low rent paid by the multinationals in order to keep the site as an undeveloped strategic reserve as part of their worldwide sourcing strategy. The Peruvian government virtually precluded both of these possibilities by building into the contracts a detailed time schedule for a "guaranteed program of exploration," and by ensuring that companies sign a bank guarantee for the cost of the guaranteed program, which goes to the state in cases of noncompliance. Typically, the contracts specify the exact amount of kilometers of seismic studies to be carried out and the minimum amount of money to be spent executing the studies, the quantity and quality of aeroradar and aeromagnetic surveys to be made of the block, and the number of holes in new structures that must be drilled in the first seven years of the contract.[66] A rough estimate is that companies signed bank guarantees to carry out at least $350 million worth of exploration in the first seven years.[67]

Development, 1930-1954 (Stanford: Stanford University Press, 1970), pp. 173-216.

Venezuela's apparently more nationalistic policy toward oil companies compared to Peru should be put in the perspective of the overall argument advanced in this section. Venezuela had vast sunken foreign investment, in proven fields, producing great revenues, whereas Peru began with unsunken investment, no proven reserves, and no revenues from production.

[66] Based on my study of the contracts and conversations with exploration managers of the private companies and with Eng. Arturo Tresierra, Gerente, Departamento Contratos de Operaciones, PETROPERU, September 3, 1974.

[67] Actual expenditures are undoubtedly much higher. The exploration manager of one of the most active firms estimated that his company alone, by June 1975, had spent approximately $90 million.

Having started from a weak position, did the Peruvian state take steps to lessen its degree of dependency in the oil sector at a later stage? The existence of a state company actively engaged in parallel production, research, and marketing may be the essential element in any strategy to expand the state's degree of freedom during later interactions with foreign companies. In the case of foreign oil companies in Peru, it is PETROPERU that extracts and uses the knowledge and data generated by the presence of these companies. PETROPERU receives complete copies of all seismic data and other studies carried out by the foreign oil companies. It also receives computer print-outs of all drilling reports. PETROPERU has a supervisory committee for each block, which carries out on-site visits, and student trainees are sent to each block as part of a summer training program. PETROPERU's access to the information, especially drilling reports, should strengthen further its capacity to select future drilling sites for its own exploration program.[68]

The state company also played an active role in developing the capacity of Peru's educational system to produce technicians in the oil sector. In addition to an active in-house training program, PETROPERU helped establish Peru's first graduate programs in oil technology, and it linked these to employment.[69] The state company therefore was attempting to create a scientific-technological subsystem that conbined education, employment,

[68] Interview with PETROPERU's chief executive concerned with monitoring the operations contracts of the foreign companies, Eng. Tresierra, previously cited and corroborated by interviews with exploration managers of the companies.

[69] For example, PETROPERU assumed approximately two-thirds of the cost of starting an M.A. program in Petroleum Engineering at the National University of Engineering and was in the process of creating other graduate programs in Exploration Geology and Operations Research. In these programs PETROPERU will help in problem definition and help supply research materials, adjunct professors, field research opportunities, and subsequent employment opportunities. It was also planned to increase Peru's annual output of 10-15 B.A. graduates in Petroleum Engineering to at least 50 students and then finance B.A. theses research in Petroleum for 50 students a year. Of the 50 with thesis support PETROPERU hoped to hire 25 and to give them a "Petroleum Adaptation Course" of from 6-12 months depending on their specialty. Interviews with Doctor Miranda of PETROPERU previously cited and Eng. José Robles, Gerente, Área de Investigación y Desarrollo, October 7, 1974.

and basic and applied research of the sort that is usually absent in dependent countries.[70]

A public sector company whose technological and managerial capabilities are growing is also a direct asset to the state in its relations with foreign companies because it increases monitoring and bargaining capacities. As the public sector company develops a parallel capacity in all the areas in which foreign firms are engaged, the credibility of the state in further bargaining goes up, because it may have by then the capacity to take over and run the developed operations that foreign capital has created.

This latter point leads to a final comment. If the initial extractive investment is successful and oil is discovered and pipelines completely built, then the bargaining position of the state vis-à-vis foreign companies is automatically increased because foreign capital has already been committed, its investment "sunk," and foreign firms are therefore open to a broad range of controls not available to the state at the earlier stage when investment was merely contemplated.

Unfortunately for Peru, however, by the end of 1976 the country still found itself in a very weak position in the oil sector. Of the 19 new exploration units, only Occidental and PETRO-PERU had found commercial oil. Thus, concerning the value and quantity of oil (variable H), Peru remained very weak because there were still no large quantities of proven export reserves. Because no foreign companies had completed the development process, there were still no "sunken investments." Worse still, the minister of mines and energy acknowledged that Peru, in the midst of the worst balance of payments crisis in its history, was spending $600,000 a day on oil imports. He said the country needed massive new investments in oil exploration and that the state did not have sufficient investment capacity. In terms of Table 7.1, the Peruvian state was still in the weakest bargaining position, cell 4; i.e., there existed a very "high priority" need for extremely large "uncommitted" investments. In this situation the minister announced in November 1976 that Peru, which

[70] Concerning the absence of such integrated science systems in dependent countries and policy proposals for their creation, see the last chapter in Nancy Stepan, *Beginnings of Brazilian Science: Oswaldo Cruz, Medical Research and Policy, 1890-1920*, pp. 157-81.

269

had refused to issue any new oil exploration contracts to foreign capital since August 1973, had re-opened its doors to foreign oil exploration and that, to encourage such investment, the government would modify the existing model of oil contracts to make it conform with the reality of Peru's oil requirements.[71]

Manufacturing: Moderate Control

The Peruvian military encountered a diverse set of conditions in manufacturing. In some areas (e.g., petrochemicals, automobiles) Peru scored very low on most of the variables, and in others (e.g., furniture, textiles), reasonably high. In much of the manufacturing sector the new government found itself roughly mid-way between the positions it encountered in sugar and oil. Analytically, manufacturing is best treated in our framework not as a coherent "sector," such as sugar or petroleum, but rather as a group of "subsectors." Politically, however, the Peruvian regime attempted in Phase I to formulate a strategy that, while taking into account its only moderately good position to control foreign capital, would nonetheless enable it to simultaneously promote and reconcile its goals of increased worker participation in management, increased overall investment rates, and increased control over foreign capital. My analysis concentrates on the goal of increased control over foreign capital and shows how it did or did not further the two other goals.

Recognizing the diverse conditions it had to cope with in the industrial sector, the government formulated not a policy, but a package of policies to address three distinct problems in regard to foreign capital in industry: (1) how to prevent unwanted, "low priority" new foreign investment, (2) how to increase control over existing foreign investment, and (3) how to attract new foreign investment into "high priority" development projects. Let us analyze each problem in turn.

The problem of regulating and, wherever Peru's position on the relevant variables was favorable, stemming the inflow of new foreign capital was identified as an important policy area relatively early in Phase I. One of the first tasks of the Ministry of Industry and Commerce was to carry out an inventory of all foreign holdings in the manufacturing sector and to identify the

[71] For his speech, see *El Comercio* (November 21, 1976), p. 1. Also see the press conference given by President Morales Bermúdez, *El Comercio* (November 10, 1976), p. 4.

year of entry. The results showed that 242 firms in which foreign capital played a significant role were responsible for 44 percent of all industrial production.[72] Foreign firms had a particularly strong production position in such modern sectors as automobiles (94.5%), basic industries for nonferrous metals (97.9%), heavy rubber (87.5%), and industrial chemicals (73.4%). The trend was alarming because, out of 231 firms for which data were available, 164 (71%) had come to Peru since 1960.[73]

The institutional procedures discussed above, by which the government allowed new foreign capital a highly regulated entry only after a full evaluation process had been completed, gave the Phase I rulers a strong capacity to block the entry of any unwanted foreign capital.[74]

But what about existing foreign investment? As already argued, existing foreign investment is vulnerable to the coercive powers of the state. In Phase I the Peruvian government devised a number of strategies to increase state and national control over existing foreign investment.

As a member of the Andean Pact, the Peruvian government played a major role in getting the pact members to construct a tough, innovative, and comprehensive law (Decision 24) in 1971 that required all existing foreign-controlled manufacturing firms wanting to participate in the tariff reduction program of the pact to gradually 'divest' their equity. The new law required that, fifteen years after the law went into effect, national shareholders must own 51 percent of the shares of the company.[75]

---

[72] In 128 of these firms foreign capital controlled over 75% of the firm's shares, 46 controlled between 50% to 75% of the shares, and in the remaining 68 firms foreign capital controlled between 25 to 49.9% of the shares. The results of this census are contained in Perú, Ministerio de Industria y Comercio, Oficina Sectorial de Planificación, *Estadística Industrial Manufacturera: Resultados de 1968-1969-1970* (Preliminares) (Lima: 1970). The results are available in a more assembled form in Franco, *Imperialismo, industrialización y transferencia de tecnología en el Perú*, cuadros 13A-C.

[73] Ibid.

[74] In Phase II the state elite has been more preoccupied with increasing investment so changes are being made in these institutional procedures created in Phase I.

[75] For this decision, see the careful discussion in Stanley F. Rose, *Business Operations in Peru* (Washington, D.C.: Bureau of National Affairs, Tax Management Foreign Income, No. 329, 1975), pp. A26-27. Venezuela did not join the pact until 1973 and did not ratify Decision 24 until 1974. Due to pressures on the pact to act slowly and to have a uniform policy, the pact

Stanley Rose, a lawyer who served as foreign investment adviser to Price Waterhouse, Peat and Company's Lima office (which acted as an accounting firm for many foreign as well as national manufacturing firms), notes that the Peruvian national law, and actual practice, went further than in other pact countries in enforcing the divestment required of foreign industrial firms. "The requirement to have 15 percent national shareholders by July 1, 1974, 45 percent by July 1, 1981, and 51 percent by July 1, 1986, was made obligatory for foreign industrial companies in Peru *regardless* of a company's desires to use the Andean Zone. . . . Almost *all* (foreign) industrial companies had signed transformation contracts by the end of June, 1974."[76]

A more direct and quick method for the state to gain control over existing foreign investment in "basic" industries was built into the General Law of Industries. In this law all industries were grouped according to their strategic relation to Peru's overall industrial plan. Highest priority was given to the basic industrial sector (such as steel, nonferrous metallurgy, heavy chemicals, fertilizers, cement, and paper).[77] The General Law decreed that all such basic industries be reserved for the state.[78] As a consequence, the state used its scarce economic and political resources to nationalize progressively the basic industry sector.[79] By 1974 the state had expropriated, and begun to compensate, over thirty foreign and domestic firms, including all the foreign firms in the basic sector area of cement and paper and all foreign

---

members agreed in November 1976 that the 15-year period for completing the transition would date from January 1, 1974.

[76] Rose, *Business Operations in Peru*, pp. 26-27 (emphasis added). In October 1976, in the aftermath of Chile's withdrawal from the Andean Pact, a number of revisions of Decision 24 were made. See *The Andean Report* (November 1976), pp. 208-11.

[77] *Ley General de Industrias*, Decreto Ley No. 18350, July 30, 1970. Article 4.

[78] Article 4. However, Article 8 lists the special conditions in which the state may temporarily waive this requirement.

[79] See Franco, *Imperialismo, industrialización y tranferencia de tecnología en el Perú*, pp. 70-75, for a complete list of all the firms purchased between 1969-1974. Another policy that has reduced the number of foreign industrial firms is a rationalization policy by which the state holds competitive bidding for monopoly rights to produce a product with greater economies of scale. After General Motors, Ford, Fiat and other firms lost the bidding for automobiles, they closed their plants.

firms engaged in catching and processing anchovy, one of Peru's leading exports.[80]

The Industrial Community Law represented a somewhat more complex, innovative (though by late 1976 watered-down) mechanism to pursue the organic-statist goal of increased control over existing foreign capital in industry while at the same time increasing worker participation. This law covered both national and foreign firms and, if it had been applied, would have reduced the role of foreign ownership. The key legal stipulations of this law were that every industrial firm employing at least six workers or having a gross annual income over approximately $25,000 had to give 15 percent of annual net profits before taxes to an association of all the workers of the firm called "The Industrial Community." These funds were to be reinvested by the Industrial Community in the firm itself, in exchange for share ownership, or to be used to purchase shares of existing shareholders until the Industrial Community owned 50 percent of the firm. The workers were also supposed to assume positions on the Board of Directors proportional to their ownership. In addition, 10 percent of the pre-tax profit was to be distributed each year directly to the workers.[81] As a policy the measure thus had strong inclusionary features.

[80] In Phase II the utilization of this mechanism of expanding state control over foreign investment has slowed greatly. Indeed, by March 1976 the government began to consider selling some of the far-flung state-controlled firms to national private capital. As of January 1977 only one of the 180 state companies had been divested and that was only partially divested. In July 1976 PESCAPERU, the state anchovy fishing and processing corporation announced it would sell the fishing fleet of over 500 boats to small national private firms, none of which could purchase more than 4 boats. For a description of the pressures on the state to divest and for a nearly complete listing of the 180 state companies, see *The Andean Report* (September 1976), pp. 164-66, 177-80. For details of the divestment of PESCA-PERU, see *The Andean Report* (August 1976), pp. 146-47.

[81] Decreto Ley No. 18384 del 1º de Septiembre 1970, *Ley de Comunidad Industrial.* A succinct discussion of the law is contained in Peter Knight, "New Forms of Economic Organization in Peru: Toward Workers' Self-Management" in *The Peruvian Experiment*, ed. Lowenthal, pp. 367-71. In late February 1976 in an effort to encourage investment among small and medium industries, the government exempted firms whose gross annual income was less than $500,000 from the industrial community legislation. See "Peru: Reconciliation," *Latin America* (March 5, 1976), p. 79. In late 1976 even greater changes were introduced. See footnote 87, this chapter.

273

The state elite's response to what it perceived was a situation of deep conflict between different groups in society was "organic-statist" in that it attempted to use the power of the state to restructure the organization of society to forge greater functional harmony. In Velasco's words,

The Industrial Community is fundamentally an institution of participation, an institution which makes possible the direct intervention of the workers in the total life of the enterprise, in property, in decisions. . . . The basis of the revolutionary plan [of the government] consists in affirming that the apparently irreducible contradiction "capital versus labor" should be and can be overcome.

He went on to say that, by the time the industrial community had arrived at 50 percent ownership, "there will have conceivably emerged a new form of relations between the factors of production. Managers as well as labor will have been reeducated in the daily exercise of a new form of social solidarity."[82]

How did this scheme to reduce Peruvian and foreign industrialists to 50 percent ownership of their firms actually work? In 1974, according to government figures, there were 3,352 recognized industrial communities, with 195,532 workers who had acquired an average of 9 percent of the shares of their firms.[83]

[82] *Velasco: la voz de la revolución*, 2 vols. (Lima: Ediciones Participación, 1972), 1:22-25. Carlos Delgado, one of major ideologues of Phase I went further, arguing that once the workers had reached 50% ownership; "the irreducible opposition between the traditional 'bourgeoisie' and 'proletariat' will not exist, not because the interests of both social classes will have been conciliated but because there will have ceased to exist the polarity between total ownership on one hand and total propertylessness on the other. In synthesis, both the 'proletariat' and the 'bourgeoisie' will have ceased to exist as social classes." Quoted in a chapter that reviews the government's ideological statements about the Industrial Community, Diego García-Sayán, "La Comunidad Industrial y los concepciones doctrinarias del gobierno" in *Dinámica de la Comunidad Industrial*, Luis Pásara et al. (Lima: DESCO, 1974), p. 54.

[83] Perú, Ministerio de Industria y Turismo, Oficina de Comunidades Laborales, *Estadística de Comunidades Industriales* (Lima: 1974). Share ownership rose from roughly 3% in 1971 to 6% in 1972. In addition the average profit distributed directly to the workers went from 4,720 soles in 1972 to 7,201 soles in 1973. The latter figure represented approximately $163 at 1973 prices. The monthly minimum wage in Lima in 1973 was 3,000 soles. For the above figures and a useful review see Jorge Santistevan, "Industrial Communities: Achievements and (or?) Problems," (paper pre-

Numerous studies have documented the legal loopholes and quasilegal tactics that would have allowed firms to hold off until the distant future (or in some cases possibly forever) the acquisition by the workers of 50 percent control.[84] However, most analysts failed to note the combination of laws that made the position of the foreign firms quite different from that of the national firms in Peru, or from foreign firms in other Andean Pact countries. In addition to the Industrial Community Law, Peru, as we have seen, had enacted the stiffest version within the Andean Pact of the "fade-out" formula. Foreign industrial firms already in existence in Peru on July 1, 1971, were required to sell a portion of their shares to national investors and reach a 49 percent foreign-ownership level by June 30, 1986. Thus, unlike national firms in Peru, the foreign firms were faced with a fixed date. And, unlike foreign industrialists in other Andean Pact countries who had the option of getting down to 49 percent by selling to numerous national buyers and thus still being in a good position to control the firm, in Peru (except in those cases where the foreign firms' partner was the state) the Industrial Community was eventually to own 50 percent.[85] Had these laws been fully implemented, the Industrial Communities would

---

sented before the Second International Conference on Self-Management, Cornell University, June 6-8, 1975), pp. 6-8. He notes however that since, as in the sugar sector, there was not yet a compensation fund to assure a more equal distribution, the workers in the most profitable firms had received over 30,000 soles ($680) while some workers in less profitable firms received less than 3,000 soles.

[84] For legal loopholes see Pedro de las Casas Grieve et al., *Análises de la participación de la Comunidad Industrial en el capital social de la empresa* (Lima: Universidad del Pacífico, 1970). Abuses of the law were denounced by the labor representative at the "Primer Seminario de Comunidades Industriales Para Directivos de Empresas" I attended as an observer in October 1972. These charges were formally elaborated later at the First National Congress of the Industrial Communities. See Primer Congreso Nacional de Comunidades Industriales, *Resoluciones* (Lima: Confederación Nacional de Comunidades Industriales, March 1973, mimeo), pp. 10-13. In 1975 the Phase I government issued a draft law which proposed to correct many of these loopholes. See "El gobierno revolucionario de la Fuerza Armada entrego para debate, el anteproyecto de Ley de Comunidades Industriales," *El Peruano* (May 31, 1975), pp. 6-7. However, this draft law was shelved early in Phase II.

[85] For the distinctiveness of Peru's position, compare Peru's Decree No. 19262, article 11, issued January 6, 1972 with the Andean Pact's Decision 24, articles 18 and 30.

have grown faster in the foreign-owned than in the domestically-owned industrial sector. Also the loss of de facto control by 1986 was much more likely for foreign-owned industrial forms in Peru than it was for similar firms in the rest of the Andean Pact countries.

By late 1976 the Phase II leaders, faced with what they perceived as growing conflict in the industrial sector and, most importantly, a major investment shortage, announced basic revisions in the Industrial Community Law.[86] The key changes were that worker shares in industrial firms would be limited to 33 percent (rather than 50 percent) of total shares, and that these shares would be distributed to workers as *individuals* rather than to the industrial community as a bloc. While workers would still have some participation on the Board of Directors, control was nonetheless ensured for the owner-managers. President Morales Bermúdez in a speech before the Annual Executives Conference (CADE) explained the reasons for the change. "Distortions within the productive system and social conflicts oblige a revision of the rules of the game between entrepreneurs and workers concerning labor community participation. For management to function well it is necessary to preserve the power of decision of those share-holders who have assumed the entrepreneurial initiative, have supplied the capital, and assumed the risks."[87]

In May 1977 the Phase II leaders also revised the law compelling *all* foreign industrial firms to fade out by making such transformation provisions compulsory *only* for those firms who wished to participate in the Andean Pact or which had entered Peru after January 1, 1974.[88] The changes in the Industrial Com-

[86] The workers in the industrial sector displayed neither a tendency toward increased "harmony" with owners that the government hoped for nor the erosion of class militancy that some of the left feared. Strikes in the manufacturing sector in 1973-75 were significantly higher than in any other three-year period in Peru's history for which there are data. Also the government's attempt to guide the first Congress of the Confederation of Industrial Communities and its subsequent organizations had at best been only moderately successful. For the latter point see Santistevan, "Industrial Communities: Achievements and (or?) Problems."

[87] More than probably any other early Phase II pronouncement, this speech displayed the distinctive ideological and policy approach that differentiated this phase from Phase I. The complete text is printed in *El Comercio* (November 22, 1976), p. 2.

[88] See Decreto Ley No. 21849 of May 10, 1977 published in *El Peruano* the following day.

munity Law also meant that those foreign industrial firms com-pelled to fade out were given the *option* of whether to sell to the Industrial Community or not.[89] Thus the attempt to increase national control over foreign industry by fade out has been sig-nificantly watered down by Phase II leaders, and the organic participatory feature of the fade-out formula implied in the original Industrial Community Law, which was one of the most ambitious and original features of the initial plan to control foreign industry, was in essence abandoned.[90]

Let us now turn to the final, most difficult, aspect of the con-trol of foreign capital in the manufacturing sector. How has the Peruvian regime attempted to handle the problem of attracting new foreign capital into its "high priority" areas of manufactur-ing? From the perspective of the variables presented, Peru faced almost insoluble problems in regard to attracting new foreign in-vestment on the favorable terms it demanded, and in fact it has to date attracted little new industrial investment. Its policies of forced divestment and selective nationalization have made foreign investors extremely cautious. Though Peru's policy of eventual compensation has prevented a crisis in the terms of variable J, in that the U.S. government has not applied major sanctions, it has not allayed the suspicions of most potential new investors in industry. In addition, the size and the value of the Peruvian mar-ket for industrial products (variable G) is small, and this is one of the most salient variables affecting new industrial investment. Under these conditions, any attempt by the Peruvian state to tighten the regulations concerning incoming foreign capital cre-ates an almost insoluble dilemma, namely that such controls might greatly diminish the capacity of the state to attract foreign capital into those areas where the state planners have determined that the need is high.

A recognition of this dilemma is crucial to an understanding of the Peruvian military's decision to play a leading role in bolster-ing the Andean Pact and to seek to strengthen Third World political and economic collaboration. Just as an understanding of the military's policies toward the Industrial Community was essential for grasping their overall strategy toward the control

[89] See, "Dictan normas complementarias para la adecuación de Ley de Comunidad Industrial," *El Peruano* (May 27, 1977), pp. 2-3.

[90] More analysis of the political and financial pressures that led to these changes is supplied later in the book.

of existing investment, we cannot understand the Phase I strategy
to *simultaneously attract and control new investment* without
putting this strategy in the context of the military's overall perception of geopolitical power relationships and the need to follow
an aggressive Third World foreign policy.

This perception, which, with variants, was repeatedly presented to me when I visited or lectured at CAEM or interviewed
such key army officers as the former foreign minister (and later
minister of war and prime minister), General Mercado Jarrín,
can be paraphrased in the following way:[91]

> The Peruvian military has a basic security interest in achiev-
> ing integral development. We recognize, however, that Peru is
> a small country, with little power to advance these security
> interests by itself, given present geo-political realities. The
> most important security struggle is no longer between East
> and West, but between North and South. To be able to nego-
> tiate effectively with the industrialized powers of the North,
> Peru has no alternative but to seek to expand its factors of
> power by uniting with other Third World countries. Only
> then can Peru hope to alter the existing power asymmetry
> which is the basis of imperialism. A crucial factor of negotiat-
> ing power with multinationals is the size of the market. If
> Peru can help mold the Andean Pact countries into an effective
> economic and planning market of over 75 million people, this
> becomes an attractive market. Then, and only then, can Peru
> have the power to greatly tighten the restrictions for entry.
>
> In a global context, international trade patterns, patent
> systems, and commodity flows were all initially structured to
> serve the interests of the dominant industrial powers. This
> situation can only be restructured so that it is less detrimental
> to the basic interests of the industrializing countries if the
> entire Third World pools its power to deny resources the
> industrialized countries need. Brazil may delude itself that
> because of its greater size it can negotiate alone. The Peruvian
> military, however, bases its position on a realistic military
> assessment about the Peruvian state's fundamental geopolitical

[91] Note: This is not a direct quotation but a summary paraphrase of a
position widely espoused among the leaders of Phase I. I have taken the
license of using the first-person plural format to capture the emotive quality
that I think is essential to understanding their adherence to this position.

weakness unless we are able to join forces with other Third World countries.[92]

Given this general position, how was the Andean Pact supposed to aid Peru in attracting, on its own stiffer terms, the specific types of new foreign investment wanted? Here the key policy is the Andean Pact's Sectoral Program of Investment. Under this program, an entire potential investment growth area —such as petrochemicals, the automotive industry, fertilizers or metal processing machinery—will be subject to regional planning by the Junta of the Andean Pact, and specific products within each area will be allocated on a monopoly or near-monopoly basis to a particular country.[93] For Peru this would mean that, when Peru is assigned the exclusive right to develop a particular product, the other Andean countries should erect a common external tariff against imports of the product from countries outside the Andean Pact. They should also agree not to authorize any investment in their own territories for projects to manufacture products assigned to Peru. Furthermore, under the sectoral program of investment, not only will Peru receive an initial monopoly for some products but, once monopoly is granted, the foreign investor will either have to invest in Peru or stay completely outside the entire Andean Common Market.[94]

[92] The core of this position was presented to me in an interview with Prime Minister Mercado Jarrín in Lima, October 10, 1974. Much of this argument is contained in his "El poderío de los pobres," talk given before the Plenary Session of the Reunion of the Chiefs of State of the Non-Allied Countries held in Algeria in September, 1973 and reproduced in *Proceso*, no. 2 (September 1973), pp. 22-31. See also two of his articles in the same journal on the Andean Pact "Perspectivas del Acuerdo de Cartagena," no. 1 (June 1973), pp. 7-22, and "Hacia un sistema andino," no. 3 (December 1973), pp. 6-14.

[93] To date the only sectoral programs to have been fully approved are for the light metal-working and petrochemical industries, and negotiations for investment are still in the early stage. Under the terms of the initial light metal agreement, 25 products were assigned to Peru, 16 on an exclusive basis. See Acuerdo de Cartagena, *Grupo Andino: primer programa sectorial de desarrollo industrial de sector metal-mecánico* (Lima: Junta del Acuerdo de Cartagena, March 1973), pp. 78-79. For aspects of the petrochemical negotiations, see "Petrochemicals Agreement Signed by Andean Pact," *Latin American Economic Report* (September 5, 1975), p. 1. For details of an automotive agreement that was signed in September 1977 see, *The Andean Report* (September 1977), pp. 170-72.

[94] The idea is to give a start-up capability and not an indefinite monopoly.

279

During Phase I, but even in Phase II, the sectoral programs have played and will continue to play a more critical role in Peru's capacity to attract high priority new investment than in the other pact countries, with the possible exception of Allende's Chile. Even with the modifications we have noted, the Peruvian Industrial Community Law still requires firms to distribute 25 percent of pre-tax profits to the workers in cash or some kind of dividend-earning securities. This, coupled with the generally tough policy toward foreign investment, would make it extremely difficult for Peru to attract investment into high priority sectors without the special market advantages provided by the Andean Pact's sectoral program.

Although the sectoral program is still in its early stages, the potential for increasing the state's power vis-à-vis foreign capital was made clear in the negotiations for Peru's automotive industry. Initial talks in the Andean Pact had indicated that Peru stood a good chance of being granted nearly exclusive rights to develop tractors and diesel engines for trucks and buses. With this strong possibility strengthening its hand, Peru held competitive biddings for exclusive Peruvian rights to manufacture each line. Peru built in stiff regulations in order that its major industrial goals should be met. These goals included: (1) state control (the state would own over 50 percent of the shares, and there were provisions for progressive selling to Peruvian buyers); (2) an improvement in the balance of payments (for every dollar of inputs imported a dollar's-worth of goods must be exported); (3) the establishment of linkages to other Peruvian industries (once production has reached scheduled capacity, over 60 percent of all inputs must be purchased from local enterprises); (4) decentralization (the bidders had to agree to build their plants in the new industrial park created by the government in the northern city of Trujillo); and even (5) worker participation in management (via the original Industrial Community Law). Despite these exacting specifications, the Peruvian government received seven tenders for each exclusive contract. The first contracts to be signed were awarded to Massey-Ferguson (an English-Canadi-

---

Thus Peru's monopoly rights in the metal-making industry would terminate the last day of 1982. For these aspects of the metal-making industries' agreement, see Decision 57, articles 10, 16, and 25 in *Grupo Andino: primer programa sectorial de desarrollo industrial de sector metal-mecánico*, pp. 64-68.

an Company) to build a $2.5-million tractor plant, and to Volvo and a Massey subsidiary to build an $8.2-million diesel engine plant.[95]

The Andean Pact's sectoral program thus offered Peru some chance of attaining an acceptable balance between its often conflicting goals of increased state control, programmed foreign investment in key industrial areas, and at least some worker participation. The program, however, was not without its perils. Peru's strategy of using the Andean Pact's sectoral program to attract investment under stiff terms depended on the unified action of six countries with very different perceived needs for foreign capital. Chile and Colombia expressed considerable ambivalence about the wisdom of the strict application of Decision 24, and in 1976 Chile caused a crisis by threatening to leave, and eventually leaving the Andean Pact. The Chilean crisis brought about a collective effort to save the pact by softening a number of the foreign investment guidelines while retaining the essential component of sectoral programs.[96] Nonetheless, the sectoral programs themselves continue to be difficult to forge and to implement. While arriving at an acceptable allocation of each program is difficult in itself, it is also hard to assure that countries not allocated a specific product but with existing capacities to produce it, nonetheless adhere to the pact's guidelines and do not give

[95] The details of these contracts are discussed in "Peruvian Car Assembly and Manufacture," *Latin American Economic Report* (April 12, 1974), pp. 57-58, and "Andean Vehicle Production," *Latin American Economic Report* (May 10, 1974), pp. 69-70. For an insightful analysis see Hunt, "Direct Foreign Investment in Peru: New Rules for an Old Game," pp. 320-25, 337-39. Also see John R. Pate, Jr. "New Joint Venture Approaches and a Review of Competitive Forces Within Ancom," in *Andean Pact: Definition, Design and Analysis*, pp. 12-20.

[96] Some of the major changes were an increase in the automatic reinvestment allowance from 5% of capital per year to 7%, an increase in the profit remittance from 14% of capital a year to 20% (with some provisions for individual countries to fix higher remittance levels of their own), the prohibition on foreign firms having access to local long-term credit (defined as any credit over three years) was retained, but access to short and medium term local credit was authorized, and foreign companies were allowed to meet the fade-out requirement by bringing in local shareholders via increases in capital, in addition to having the option to sell off existing shares. For an excellent summary of these changes and the continuing efforts by the remaining members to keep the pact viable see, "Andean Pact: The Five Trying Hard to Pick Up The Pieces," *The Andean Report* (November 1976), pp. 208-11.

their existing enterprises special privileges.[97] Despite these and other difficulties, the potential advantages of the pact are such that Peru will press to maintain this important Third World institution.

International Borrowing Versus Internal Saving

Until now I have focused on direct foreign investment in specific sectors of the Peruvian economy. I now wish to give special attention to the public sector's and the national private sector's capacity to invest, and examine how this affects the Peruvian state's ability to lessen dependency by lessening reliance on foreign capital. Such an examination allows us to explore a different aspect of dependency, namely the relationship between the state and the international financial community. Since the state/ domestic investment and savings capacity (variable D) is a crucial factor that underlies all sectors, improvement or deterioration concerning this variable has a direct impact on the degree of autonomy or dependence the state has in relation to the international financial community and, indeed, in the very formation of its development strategy.

At the aggregate level, there are standard national accounts indicators that allow us to present some crucial relationships in very clear terms. Specifically, gross national investment equals gross savings, and gross savings equals domestic savings plus foreign savings. Thus if the state wants to increase investment (one of its goals), while decreasing external financial dependency (another of its goals), it must increase domestic savings. How has the Peruvian state dealt with these very basic relationships?

Table 7.3 presents the relationship between gross national product and gross investment in Peru. This table shows that, although the yearly figures are somewhat erratic, gross investment as a percentage of GNP had increased from 14.3 during the 1970-1973 period, to an estimated 16.0 during 1974-1976. However, when we examine the relationship between internal national savings and GNP, we see that the former had fallen sharply

[97] The major new sectoral programs that had been presented to the Andean Pact Commission but that were still being negotiated in early 1977 were autos, fertilizers, electronics, and steel. Still in the pre-presentation stage were plans for sectoral programs in chemicals and pharmochemicals, pulp and paper, glass, and shipbuilding. Ibid., p. 211.

TABLE 7.3

RELATIONSHIP BETWEEN PERU'S GNP AND GROSS INVESTMENT, 1970-1976
(In billions of current soles)

Year	GNP	Gross Investment	Gross Investment as % of GNP
1970	235.0	31.0	13.2
1971	259.7	39.6	15.2
1972	290.0	41.8	14.4
1973	350.6	50.7	14.5
1974	428.5	70.0	16.3
1975 (est.)	549.0	91.4	16.6
1976 (est.)	700.7	105.9	15.1

SOURCES: Three of the basic sources for Peru's recent national accounts are Banco Central de Reserva del Perú, *Cuentas Nacionales del Perú, 1960-1973* (Lima: 1974), Banco Central de Reserva del Perú, *El Desarrollo Económico y Financiero del Perú; 1968-1973* (Lima: 1974) and the monthly bulletin of the Banco Central de Reserva del Perú. Much data for 1973-74 is contained in the 81 page, Exposición al país del Ministro de Economía y Finanzas, General de Brig. E. P. Amílcar Vargas Gavilano, efectivado el 13 de Febrero de 1975, *Evaluación económica 1973-1974 y perspectivas para 1975-1976* (Lima: Ministerio de Economía y Finanzas, Oficina de Relaciones Públicas, 1975). Projections for 1975 and 1976 come from unpublished figures supplied to me in June 1975 by the Dirección General Estudios Economicos, Ministerio de Economía y Finanzas. Since this source updates some estimates for earlier years tables 7.3, 7.4, and 7.5 are based on this last source to maintain internal consistency. Two other valuable sources that present less complete and slightly different but basically congruent data are Banco Central de Reserva del Perú, *Aide Memoire on the Economic Situation of Peru* (Lima: 1976) and the Wells Fargo Bank's, *Economic Report on Peru* (October 1976).

in the period (Table 7.4).[98] Since national savings capacity has declined as a percentage of the GNP, any increase in gross investment could have only been accomplished by an increase in foreign loans plus direct foreign investment (which over the

[98] One U.S. bank with substantial loans to Peru cites figures that indicate a somewhat worse deterioration in the investment/savings ratio than presented in Tables 7.3 and 7.4. They state that "investment as a share of GNP rose from less than 13% in 1970 to approximately 19% in 1975, largely as a result of the rapid build-up of public capital outlays. The favorable trends in investment have not been matched by an improvement in domestic savings performance. Domestic savings as a share of GNP fell from over 16% in 1970 to an estimated 7.5% in 1975." See, *Economic Report on Peru* (Wells Fargo Bank N.A., October 1976), p. 1.

TABLE 7.4

RELATIONSHIP OF GNP TO INTERNAL NATIONAL SAVINGS IN PERU, 1970-1976
(In billions of current soles)

Year	GNP	Internal National Savings	Internal Savings as % of GNP
1970	235.0	38.3	16.3
1971	259.7	38.8	14.9
1972	290.0	40.9	14.1
1973	350.6	45.4	12.9
1974	428.5	38.8	9.1
1975 (est.)	549.0	42.3	7.7
1976 (est.)	700.7	53.5	7.6

SOURCES: See Table 7.3.

long run make up the vast bulk of the national accounts entries labeled "foreign savings").

The importance of the position of the state in the international system (variable J) is nowhere more obvious for Peru than when we consider Peru's borrowing capacity. International investors and buyers, as well as the U.S. government, were interested in Peru's resources such as copper, fishmeal, and oil. But before they would extend significant credit lines to Peru, they wanted the country to give minimal recognition to the right of foreign firms to be compensated if they were expropriated. In this context, Peru's capacity to borrow from U.S.-government-associated organizations was limited until it settled its conflict with the United States over the expropriation of U.S. firms.

As we saw, in February 1974 Peru and the United States finally arrived at the complicated formula of the Greene Agreement, by which the United States considered all outstanding claims by U.S. firms against the Peruvian government settled. As a result of the agreement, the United States government facilitated official credit to Peru, and Peru's standing in the international financial community improved immediately. The dramatic increase in Peru's external borrowing is shown in Table 7.5.

The counterpart to the foreign "savings" was rapid accumulation of debt based on favorable assessments (by the Peruvian government and foreign lenders) of Peru's prospects for petroleum and of reasonably good prices for Peru's export commodi-

284

TABLE 7.5

FOREIGN "SAVINGS"[a] AS A PERCENTAGE OF GROSS INVESTMENT IN PERU
1970-1976

(In billions of current soles)

Year	Gross Investment	Total Foreign "Savings"	Foreign "Savings" as Percentage of Gross Investment
1970	31.0	−7.3	—
1971	39.6	0.8	2.0
1972	41.8	0.9	2.1
1973	50.7	5.3	10.5
1974	70.0	31.2	44.6
1975 (est.)	91.4	49.1	53.7
1976 (est.)	105.9	52.4	49.5

SOURCES: See Table 7.3.

[a] Two caveats: first, as noted earlier, the vast bulk of the national account entry "foreign savings" came from external loans and direct private investment; second, "foreign savings" were especially low in 1970-72 because of large debt repayments which canceled out some new loans that did in fact come in.

ties. Copper in particular looked like a good source of new foreign exchange earning because the huge new copper mine Cuajone would be in full production by 1976. Table 7.6 shows the great growth of Peru's foreign debt in the mid-1970s.

Thus, after over eight years of struggle to reduce dependency, Peru continued to have a low state/national investment capacity (variable D). Because the state had not been able to extract a sufficient investment surplus from the national economy by measures such as increased taxes, and because it still wanted to push forward on its goal of rapid economic growth, it was forced to compromise on its goal of autonomy by greatly increasing external borrowing. The revised 1975-1976 investment plan showed that approximately 50 percent of all the country's proposed new investment projects were dependent on foreign financing. The state proposed to use these loans to pay for service contracts for ongoing state enterprises that still lacked technological and managerial capacity, for major state infrastructure investments such as the oil pipeline and irrigation projects, and for turn-key projects in which foreign firms would build factories for the state in such technologically sophisticated areas as refining, chemical

285

TABLE 7.6

PERU'S FOREIGN DEBT, 1960-1976
(In millions of U.S. dollars)

	1960	1965	1969	1971	1973	1974	1975	1976
Public Debt	265	688	1,116	1,195	1,495	2,050	2,670	3,070
Non-publicly guaranteed debt	—a	—	—	—	—	1,080	1,250	1,450
Total Debt	—	—	—	—	—	3,130	3,920	4,520

SOURCES: Data for 1960, 1965, 1969, 1971 from Inter-American Development Bank, *Economic and Social Progress in Latin America: Annual Report, 1972* (Washington, 1973), p. 407. Data for 1973 from Ministro de Economía y Finanzas, "Evaluación económica 1973-74 y perspectivas para 1975-1976," p. 36. Data for 1974, 1975, and 1976 are from Carlos Massad and Roberto Zahler, *Dos estudios sobre endeudamiento externo* (Santiago de Chile: Cuadernos de la CEPAL, Naciones Unidas, 1977), p. 19. The Wells Fargo Bank projected a foreign debt of $5,404 million for Peru by 1980, see their *Economic Report on Peru* (October 1976), pp. 27-30.
a Dash indicates no data available.

fertilizers, and massive fish processing. The state's leaders argued that such external finance capital was much less threatening to national autonomy than direct foreign investment.

The Peruvian government delayed hard choices about how and where it could increase internal savings or decrease new investments, partly because of the widespread expectations within the government as late as early 1975 that there would be important petroleum earnings beginning in 1977. Unfortunately for the Peruvian planners, big oil finds never materialized. Moreover, the prolonged recession in the industrialized countries depressed the price of Peru's commodity exports. To compound the external difficulties, the anchovy catch never fully recovered from a disastrous decline caused in part by changes in ocean currents in 1972. When Peru's revised export forecast is measured against its projected debt service, the full dimensions of the country's foreign exchange crisis is crushingly apparent (Table 7.7).

Whatever the combination of causes, the reality was that by the middle of 1975 Peru was increasingly dependent on the international financial community for credit to fund its development program. It became devastatingly clear that the development priorities of international financial institutions were not necessarily those of a state whose announced goal was to "revolutionize its internal and external structures of domination."

TABLE 7.7

PERU'S PROJECTED PUBLIC DEBT SERVICE AS A PERCENTAGE OF EXPORT VALUE
1977-1980

	Service			Service as Percentage of FOB Export Value
	Amortization	*Interest (In U.S. $ millions)*	*Total*	*Based on a 10% growth rate in export value*
1977	440	314	754	39
1978	707	351	1,058	49
1979	959	408	1,367	58
1980	1,171	423	1,594	62

SOURCES: International Monetary Fund reproduced in *The Andean Report* (September 1977), p. 180. Some projections are even more pessimistic. Ronald Muller of American University estimates that even if there were no new financing after 1976 the total debt service would approach 100% of forecast export earning in the 1980-1984 period; see *Latin American Economic Report* (July 29, 1977), p. 115.

In April 1976 Peru had virtually exhausted its foreign reserves and initiated a major loan request. While other factors were also at work, it is impressive that in the thirty days before the vital loan was finally approved by a consortium of U.S. bankers, the Phase II government (1) imposed a stabilization package involving a wage freeze, devaluation, and public sector budget cuts, a package that led one radical minister to apologize for the "capitalist cut" of the measures; (2) announced a state of emergency by which the unions' right to strike was canceled; (3) changed the cabinet, in which the most prominent remaining military radicals from Phase I (Generals Maldonado, Gallegos, and de la Flor) were removed, while the civilian head of social property resigned; (4) ended the ban on new oil contracts with foreign firms; (5) announced the first sale of a state company to the private sector; and (6) reached agreement in principle to pay compensation for the expropriation of Marcona Mining.[99]

When the loan was finally announced, many of the financial journals suggested that the price of the loan had been high in terms of the policy autonomy that had been given up. One jour-

[99] For a calendar showing this close relationship between the economic crisis and political change, see "Politics: The Year of the Neo-Revolution," *The Andean Report* (August 1976), pp. 142-43.

287

nal asserted that "the New York bankers are to make payment of each instalment of the loan contingent on the rigorous application by Peru of the economic policies prescribed by the banks. This will mean permanent monitoring of the government's performance by the consortium."[100]

After coming to power in 1968, the leaders of Phase I, despite problems, setbacks, and some compromises, pioneered a variety of new formulas for handling the direct investment component of dependency. However, the major weakness of their strategy was their inability to devise and implement a policy to strengthen state/national savings and investment capacity. Weakness in this area meant that the state elite was able to pursue its economic development goals only by increasing financial dependency. By 1976 this dependency in turn had undermined much of the motivation as well as the mechanisms necessary for the control of foreign direct investment.

Conclusion

In the first chapter I argued that there was a built-in political tension in organic-statism between the "self-managing" and the "centralizing" components of the model. Much of the conflict in the Peruvian sugar sector stemmed from this tension. The analysis of the state and foreign capital in this chapter suggests that there are also economic tensions in organic-statism that can exacerbate the question of external dependency. The strongly statist direction of the economy in Peru frightened private national capitalists, who cut down their contribution to national investment capacity. However, since the organic component of the regime's ideology put limits on the legitimacy of complete

---

[100] See "U.S. Banks to Vet Peruvian Economy as Price of Loan," *Latin American Economic Report* (July 30, 1976), p. 117. See also "Peru: The Economy, The Revolution Sobers Down and Takes Advice from the New York Bankers," *The Andean Report* (August 1976), pp. 141-44. Because of the markedly political overtones of private monitoring, the banks in 1977 let the IMF make the hard demands, and made their bank loans conditional upon Peru's satisfactorily responding to the IMF's suggested policy changes. For details of these negotiations see "Peru's Central Bank Protests at Draconian IMF Program," *Latin American Economic Report* (April 22, 1977) the lead articles in *The Andean Report* of April, May, and December 1977, and the candid, "Why the Banks Bailed Out Peru," *Business Week* (March 21, 1977), pp. 117-18.

state ownership of the means of production, the government often did not go into the more profitable economic areas, and gave special financial incentives, such as major tax write-offs, to encourage private sector reinvestment. This frequently eroded the state's investment planning capacity because the tax deductions reduced the state's tax base, and part of the tax deductions found their way into private consumption. Furthermore, the private sector reinvestment often went into producing consumer goods that did not have a high priority in the state's investment plan.

The Peruvian regime frequently asserted that its economic formula was "neither communist nor capitalist." This is not a theoretically impossible position to maintain, but by early 1976 the organic-participatory aspects of the Peruvian regime meant that Peru did not have the advantages of a communist regime, with a high capacity to reduce consumption and extract an investment surplus, while the statist policies had led to a decline in domestic capitalist private sector savings. Since neither the state nor the national private sector was generating an investment surplus, the regime increasingly intensified its reliance on foreign borrowing to finance the organic-statist revolution. Clearly, if the regime was to endure as a major experiment, it had to find ways to resolve this contradiction or, by a series of policy shifts, it would continue to be drawn back toward the position of financial, economic, and political dependency on the foreign capital that the experiment was originally devised to transcend.

EIGHT · *The Institutionalization of Organic-Statist Regimes*

THIS book has analyzed the characteristics of the organic-statist model, as well as the conditions under which regimes are likely to be installed successfully by the use of inclusionary and/or exclusionary corporatist policies. Among the variables found to be particularly useful for predicting the installation of regimes by such policies were the organizational strength and ideological unity of the state elite; the degree of prior development of autonomous political parties and interest groups; the degree of societal polarization; the extent of prior social welfare and other structural reforms; and the ratio of the state elite's coercive, economic, and symbolic resource capacity to the effective demands made on them by civil society. For each variable a hypothesis was formulated as to the conditions that were supportive or resistant to the installation of a regime by the use of inclusionary and/or exclusionary policies.

This explanatory framework yielded a series of insights in the cross-national analysis of the patterns of installation of a number of Latin American regimes. The success or failure of installation attempts in Argentina, Brazil, Chile, Mexico, and Peru was in all cases in the hypothesized direction, given the net assigned value they received for the variables listed above. The framework, modified somewhat for the case of foreign capital, also provided important insights for the within-nation comparison of the degree of successful or unsuccessful installation across three policy sectors in Phase I of the Peruvian regime.

It has not been the purpose of this analysis to provide a definitive empirical test of these explanations of regime installation, nor to construct a model that may be applied uncritically to other empirical settings. Instead the analysis has had two goals —to provide insights into the actual cases considered, involving comparisons both across nations and across policy sectors within Peru, and to demonstrate the viability of a type of analysis that stands between the single-country case study and highly statistical

290

cross-national comparisons involving large numbers of cases. In case studies, the orientation of the study is often too idiosyncratic to be useful to the researcher interested in systematic comparative analysis, while highly statistical cross-national studies often sacrifice an adequate command of substantive, conceptual, and theoretical issues for the sake of technical sophistication. I hope that my efforts in this book may stimulate other scholars to explore further the promising but relatively neglected middle ground of substantively based, conceptually oriented, hypothesis-testing comparative analysis utilizing an intermediate number of cases. Given the current state of the art in comparative politics, the greatest potential for theory building and cumulative research would seem to be in this direction.[1]

The Failure to Institutionalize

Though the present study has been concerned largely with the problems of *installation* by inclusionary or exclusionary policies, neither the theoretical discussion of organic-statism nor the substantive discussion of Peru would be complete without considering briefly the problem of the *institutionalization* of such a regime. This final chapter explores, in a necessarily tentative and speculative manner, two questions regarding institutionalization. Specifically, why has the Peruvian military not been able to institutionalize the regime? And, more generally, does the organic-statist model itself present generic predicaments for the task of institutionalization?

By focusing in this final chapter on the inability of the Peruvian regime to become institutionalized, it is not my intention to suggest that the regime was a complete failure. Quite the contrary. The 1968-1975 government in Peru stands along with the Cárdenas government in Mexico, the first Peronist government in Argentina, and perhaps one or two other governments as one of the more important reformist, incorporating periods in modern Latin American history. After decades of "postponed revolution"

---

[1] For a similar argument see the conclusion of David Collier and Ruth Berins Collier, "Who Does What, To Whom, and How: Toward a Comparative Analysis of Latin American Corporatism." Ruth Collier demonstrates the feasibility and the value of such an approach in her "Parties, Coups, and Authoritarian Rule: Patterns of Political Change in Tropical Africa," *Comparative Political Studies*, 11 (April 1978): 62-93.

291

in Peru, the Peruvian military regime initiated profound reform and structural change in the country. Indeed, in comparison with the majority of reform governments in Latin America, the length of the initial phase of vigorous reform in Peru is exceptional.[2] From this perspective, what is striking is not so much that by 1975 there had emerged a clear failure of institutionalization, but rather that the intense reform period of the regime in fact lasted as long as it did.

Nonetheless, it was evident by the mid-1970s that as an organic-statist experiment the Peruvian regime had failed. The regime, which had been successfully installed, had not succeeded in institutionalizing itself. Institutionalization is a distinct process from that of installation and is not just a matter of longevity. Institutionalization implies that a regime has consolidated the new political patterns of succession, control, and participation; has managed to establish a viable pattern of economic accumulation; has forged extensive constituencies for its rule; and has created a significant degree of Gramscian "hegemonic acceptance" in civil society. It also implies that the majority of the weighty political actors in the polity are pursuing strategies to further their positions within the new institutional framework, rather than directing their energies to resisting, eroding or terminating that framework.

By virtually all the criteria, it was evident by 1977 that the Peruvian regime was not institutionalized. Indeed the prospects for institutionalization were substantially poorer than they had been five years earlier.

Despite the absence of open conflict, the military-enforced succession from President Velasco, the regime's first president, to President Morales Bermúdez in August 1975 was accomplished only by initial pronouncements by key army commanders, followed by three separate declarations by the navy, air force, and

---

[2] Phase I of the Peruvian regime lasted almost seven years, at least five of which could be characterized as years in which vigorous structural change was pursued. In Chile, the period of structural change under Allende lasted less than three years; the populist reform under Goulart in Brazil endured less than three years and accomplished little; Perón carried out nearly all of his policy innovations in the first four years of his regime; while the change-oriented governments of Torres in Bolivia in 1970-71, Grau San Martín in Cuba in 1933, and the populist military in the Dominican Republic in 1965, as well as many others in modern Latin American history lasted less than twelve months.

police in support of the pronouncements.[3] The succession thus had the reasonably coherent backing of the different uniformed services, but in no sense involved an institutionalized formula of succession. The period 1975-1977 saw the emergence of the sharpest conflict within the military since the inauguration of the regime.[4]

Equally important, despite the many changes introduced by the state elite during Phase I, the military rulers did not manage to generate either stable constituencies or hegemonic acceptance in civil society. SINAMOS, the most important organization for the coordination of participation, control and mobilization yet created by the regime has not been institutionalized. It was completely reorganized and deemphasized following intense criticisms both within and outside the state apparatus, and is due to be phased out by September 1978.

Economically, from the viewpoint of both trade unionists and private investors, the rules of the game were still undergoing fundamental alteration in 1976-1977, with major changes occurring in such basic institutions as the Industrial Community. Finally, the economic and political difficulties that the state faced were of such magnitude that many key civilian and even some military figures were devoting more energy to developing strategies of military extrication and regime termination than to completing the effort to institutionalize the organic-statist experiment in governance embarked upon in Phase I. Indeed in February 1977 the government announced its intention to hold general elections in 1980.[5] The first concrete steps toward the transfer of power were

[3] The pronouncements and adherences are reproduced in *La Prensa* (August 30, 1975), pp. 1-2.

[4] This period saw the purge from high office of almost all the Phase I military radicals such as Generals Maldonado, de la Flor, and Gallegos. In addition, Generals Rodriguez, Dellapiane, and Valdez Palacios were deported for associating themselves with a new opposition political party. Possibly to preclude a succession crisis, the heads of the three military services on April 22, 1977, announced that President Bermúdez would not leave the presidency upon his retirement from active duty in February 1978, but would remain in office until the end of the 1977-1980 Development Plan. See "Peru: Old Soldiers Never Die," *Latin American Political Report* (April 29, 1977), pp. 124-25.

[5] The draft of the 1977-1980 development plan specifically stated that general elections would be held in the plan period. See Perú, Comisión de la Fuerza Armada y Fuerzas Policiales, "Proyecto: Plan de Gobierno 'Tupac Amaru' (Periodo 1977-1980)." *La Prensa,* suplemento especial (February 6,

to be elections for a constituent assembly in June 1978. The decision to hold elections, however, did not mean that the military had abandoned all hope of institutionalizing some of the economic reforms and political structures initiated since 1968. The law announcing the elections for the constituent assembly stated explicitly that the duties of the assembly would be restricted to constitution-making and that a major task would be to formulate legal measures that "would institutionalize the structural reforms carried out by the Revolutionary Government of the Armed Forces."[6] The president, General Morales Bermúdez, caused great

---

1977), p. 3. No details were given about the rules of the game for the elections. The announcement that general elections would be held by 1980 inaugurated a sharp debate about the nature of the future political system. The National Agrarian Confederation (CNA) opposed a return to traditional elections and proposed a political system which would "make possible the real transfer of political and economic power to workers' organizations," see "Peru: Forlorn Hopes," *Latin American Political Report* (April 22, 1977), p. 119. The Peruvian Communist party called for a constitutional assembly before elections and wanted workers organizations such as the CNA to play a key role, see "Sobre entrevista con Morales Bermúdez dio informe el PCP," *El Comercio* (May 17, 1977), p. 4. However, many of the pre-1968 political party leaders immediately began to maneuver for rapid elections and a return to the old electoral system. For this political atmosphere, which is quite different in tone from that of Phase I, see "Peru: A Great Debate," *Latin American Political Report* (February 25, 1977), p. 60; "Peru: Dialogues," *Latin American Political Report* (June 3, 1977), p. 166, and the Popular Christian party's official communiqué calling for congressional elections in June 1978 in *El Comercio* (May 11, 1977), p. 6, 8. My point is not that the military will definitely yield power by 1980. There are obviously many factors that could preclude military extrication. However the fact that many key political actors strove to bring about a return to traditional party politics showed how little progress had been made toward legitimizing and institutionalizing national political formulae consistent with the organic-statist design.

6 Article 2 of Decreto Ley No. 21949, October 4, 1977. Exactly what the Phase II military considered were the structural reforms that should be institutionalized was left unclear. The reforms will certainly not be as great as the early Phase I program implied. For example, when the detailed electoral law governing the constituent assembly was released, the base organizations such as the industrial communities and the official peasant organization (CNA) were not allocated seats. Furthermore, the electoral jury eventually denied CNA the right accorded to all political parties to nominate slates for the 100-person, nation-at-large, proportional representation elections, on condition they could raise at least 40,000 voters' signatures and show evidence that they had functioning committees in at least 12 of the country's 23 departments. In addition, Peru's estimated two and a half million illiterates of voting age were not given the vote. The government defended its decisions

concern among the political parties by asserting at his year-end press conference that the military government would annul the proceedings of the constituent assembly should the assembly not reaffirm the structural reforms. He stated pointedly that the armed forces "will maintain their vigilance over what happens. In reality it is a transference of government and not of power."[7] The point to stress, however, is that the political and economic changes begun by the regime were not institutionalized during Phase I, were partly reversed in Phase II, and their future status was the subject of much debate as the major political actors began to maneuver for a possible transfer of power by 1980. This is not to say that none of the reforms will endure. It is merely to underscore that by 1977 it was clear that the prospects for institutionalizing anything but a small part of the ambitious organic-statist program of Phase I were extremely slight. This last chapter will explore the reasons for this inability to institutionalize.

A significant part of the failure to institutionalize can be explained by a series of *conjunctural* factors that eroded drastically the resources and, increasingly, the will of the state elite to push forward their initial policies and organic-statist designs. This is important to stress, because even had the model of governance remained the same, we can readily conceive of a plausible alternative series of circumstances that would have been much less damaging to the process of institutionalization than those that actually occurred. Thus, before we can assess how much weight to give to generic predicaments as the explanation for the failure to institutionalize, we have to evaluate the degree to which non-

concerning the base organizations and the illiterate population with the argument that these were fundamental issues that should be decided by the constituent assembly. Other reasons for the non-allocation of seats to base organizations were no doubt the sharp opposition of the traditional parties and the fact that the retrenchments of Phase II had brought the military into conflict with the largest of the base organizations, the CNA. With the prohibition against base organizations in national political elections and the phasing-out of SINAMOS the experiment with functional participation initiated in Phase I was virtually ended. Concerning electoral registration, see *The Andean Report* of December 1977 and February 1978.

[7] See "Nadie ni nada podrá detener el advance de la Revolución dijo el Presidente de la Republica," *El Comercio* (December 31, 1977), p. 6. For separate protests signed by the leaderships of APRA, Acción Popular, Movimiento Democrático Peruano, and the Partido Popular Cristiano, see editions of *OJO* and *Correo* for January 3, 1978.

inevitable, conjunctural factors weakened or strengthened the institutionalization effort. If, as I contend, we determine that conjunctural factors had a major weakening effect on institutionalization, and that by counterfactual analysis we could construct a plausible series of events (which though they did not actually occur might reasonably have occurred) that would have strengthened the institutionalization effort (also my contention), then we have made a convincing case that the analysis of conjunctural events is a legitimate, even a necessary, part of the overall analysis of the failure to institutionalize.

Notwithstanding the above argument, it is also true that, when we explore more deeply certain characteristics of the organic-statist model, we can also see that the model itself contains *generic predicaments* or contradictions for institutionalization, predicaments that no amount of "counterfactual" analysis can eliminate. In Chapter One I discussed at length the predicaments of organic-statism considered purely as an abstract model of governance.[8] These generic predicaments become especially critical when the question is not merely the installation of a regime but its institutionalization. While many of the factors aiding installation may also aid institutionalization, the converse may also be true. This general statement seems particularly germane when we consider the problem of institutionalizing organic statism.

Some of the specific elements of the organic-statist model (such as the relative autonomy of the state, the subsidiarity principle, and the role of the state elite with the power to impose an architectonic design on society) take on new theoretical and political significance when the analysis turns to the question of institutionalization. For example, the organic-statist model posits the relative autonomy of the state. Such autonomy may be consistent with the tasks of installation, but is it compatible with the broad constituency that is needed for institutionalization? The model posits that the state restructure all sectors of civil society so that they become harmoniously interrelated units. Such restructuring would seem to require immense penetration and mobilization. Yet the model's requirement of subsidiarity precludes the existence of a monist political party as an aid to institutionalization. Furthermore, the model posits a state elite

[8] See pp. 40-45.

with the power to restructure the component parts of civil society into an organic, self-managing polity. Yet the organizational
imperatives of maintaining the unity of the state elite (a requirement of the model) may conflict with the political imperatives of devolving meaningful power to the participating, self-
managing units of the polity (another element of the model).

If we take the arguments of the last few pages into account,
then, both for the specific purpose of explaining the failure
to institutionalize inclusionary policies in Peru, and for the theoretical purpose of exploring certain fundamental dilemmas of
organic-statist institutionalization, we need to analyze both *conjunctural* and *generic factors*.

Conjunctural Pressures

Between 1972 and 1976 a number of events came together in
Peru that had the effect of hindering the institutionalization of
the regime along the lines originally indicated by the strategic
elite in Phase I.

In the preceding chapter I discussed the economic crises that
by 1976 had brought a series of policy reversals. I suggested that
these crises derived in part from generic predicaments of the
economic model followed by the government. However, the
analysis of Peru would not be complete without some attention
to conjunctural factors that intensified the economic crisis. By
the standards of the Third World, Peru in 1971 had a reasonably
diversified export economy of fishmeal, sugar, copper, and
other ores as well as prospects for oil. Despite this diversified
range of actual and potential exports, none fared well. In the
1960s anchovy catches had increased, and Peru had embarked
upon an expensive effort to develop a fishmeal industry to meet
the growing world market for fertilizer. However, primarily because of ecological changes beyond the control of the government (specifically a change in ocean currents), the anchovy
catches dropped drastically toward the end of Phase I. The
three-year average yield of export fishmeal in 1970-1973 had been
1,715,000 tons, and represented Peru's largest foreign exchange
earning export. For the next three years (1973-1976) the average
yield was only 575,000 tons.[9] The drop caused a lowering of

[9] Peru, Central Reserve Bank, *Aide Memoire on the Economic Situation of*

dollar earnings, hurt Peru's credit rating as a future source of fishmeal, and caused politically costly mass layoffs in the fishmeal industry in 1976.

In the case of oil exploration begun in the Peruvian jungle in 1971, both PETROPERU and the U.S. oil-firm, Occidental Petroleum, made a rapid string of early finds. Indeed, between October 1972 and August 1974 Occidental made "ten straight discoveries."[10] The finds themselves were not large, but since the oil wells were in the same geological province as rich finds in Ecuador, expectations rose, Peru's capacity to borrow increased greatly, and the military elite felt less pressured to finance their ambitious investment and social welfare plans by stringent policies of internal savings such as a major taxation reform. However, after the widely heralded early discoveries, almost no major wells were discovered. Had oil actually been found—not an implausible *counterfactual*—the external financing crisis that led to the termination of many of the policies of Phase I would have been much less severe. Note that it was not only the absence of oil that was the major problem; it was the combination of the enticing early finds and the later paucity of finds that contributed to the deleterious national accounts pattern of declining internal savings, increasing investments, and soaring foreign borrowing. It was this pattern that made Peru so vulnerable to the foreign financial pressure described in the preceding chapter.

There was no major setback to Peru's copper and iron exports, but the worldwide recession of 1974-1975 lowered the industrial world's demand and world prices have remained sluggish. Sugar prices were extremely good in 1974, but just at the height of the foreign exchange crisis in 1976, the average price for Peru's sugar exports fell disastrously.[11]

I do not want to overstress the conjunctural aspect of the failure to institutionalize. I want merely to point out that factors

---

Peru (Lima: 1976), Table 8. Overfishing also compounded the anchovy shortage.

[10] See the special issue "Peru Petroleum Survey—1974" of the *Peruvian Times* (September 20, 1974), p. 40.

[11] Peru, *Aide Memoire on the Economic Situation of Peru*, Table 8. The *Andean Report* asserts that international prices for Peruvian sugar which rose "to a record of 65 cents a pound and over in 1974, plummeted last year and have at times been below 10 cents a pound this year" (April 1977), p. 68.

extrinsic to the basic model of governance can play a major role in helping or hindering the institutionalization of any regime. In this particular case, consolidation of the new institutions to be built on the basis of inclusionary policies required economic resources, resources that many professional observers in 1972-1973 felt Peru could reasonably expect through the discovery of oil and continuing fish meal and ore revenues. But Peru did not discover oil, and this model of governance experienced crisis. Had oil been discovered, the identical model of governance, with all the generic predicaments that I analyze later in the chapter, might have been strengthened significantly.

Let me now turn to a set of external foreign policy events that also had a major impact on the military's commitment to push forward the attempt to institutionalize the experiment begun in 1968. The military's willingness to go along with the Phase I state elite's inclusionary organic-statist experiment had a clear connection with their assessment of Peru's security needs. As I have shown elsewhere, part of the military's programmatic consensus when they assumed power derived from their belief that structural changes were necessary to achieve national security. The lack of internal change was seen as contributing to domestic revolutionary pressures. The lack of national integration of the marginal classes was seen as contributing to a weakening of Peru's security in the eventuality of any external conflict. It was this perception—that structural changes were essential for national security—that changed between 1973 and 1977.

In the early period of Phase I, the external border situation was not threatening to Peru. Chile was first under the Chrisian Democrat reform government of Eduardo Frei, and later under the Marxist coalition of Salvador Allende. For a time Bolivia was under the rule of a populist military coalition led by General Torres and modeled on Peru. Ecuador, whose long-standing border claims had been effectively silenced by the Peruvian army in 1941, was financially weak in 1968, while Brazil, in the pre-boom period before 1968, was not viewed as threatening.

Toward the end of Phase I, however, many of the military officers in Peru saw their geopolitical and military situation in very different terms. Chile, Argentina, Uruguay, and Bolivia had all shifted to the right and constituted an informal coalition with Brazil, a coalition with which Peru was jarringly out of step. Ecuador's oil gave it revenue with which to increase its air force.

By 1975 the Peruvian military was worried about the possibility of conflict with Chile as the 100th anniversary of the War of the Pacific approached. Chile and Brazil were seen as sympathetic to Bolivia's desire to have an exit to the Pacific. Peru's military strategists pondered the fact that its borders blocked what they saw as Brazil's desire to be a continental power stretching to the Pacific.

Given this radically different set of conditions and perceptions, the aggressive nationalistic, antidependency foreign policies and internal structural reform programs that had been a fundamental part of the military's national security strategy between 1968 and 1972 were increasingly seen by military officers as exacerbating rather than ameliorating the threat to Peru's national security. The national security rationale that had been such an important factor in forging the programmatic consensus for internal change was thus severely eroded by external changes. For many officers the new security situation seemed to be a compelling reason for policy retrenchment and indeed even for extrication from the tasks of governance, tasks they came to see as alienating the military from society and diverting the military from the newly threatening external security situation. Once again, it is easy to imagine a different set of events, presenting far fewer obstacles to the institutionalization of the policies of Phase I.

It is also interesting to speculate about what would have happened had President Velasco not been stricken seriously ill in March 1973. By many accounts Velasco's illness severely altered the political dynamics of Peru. His energy and power as head of the experiment in Peru gave strength to the core of radical officers discussed in Chapter Four. Had he been able to stay in power until 1980, these radical officers would have headed the seniority list and one of them might have become the next president.[12] As it was, after Velasco's near death he was often only able to devote three days a week to his presidential and military functions. In addition, rumors were widespread that, due to his poor

[12] The list of all active-duty line generals with their seniority and retirement dates was published in the Lima weekly *Caretas* (February 5, 1975), p. 8. According to this schedule, by 1978 Morales Bermúdez was to retire, and by 1980 the "radical colonels" of 1968 such as Leonidas Rodríguez Figueroa, Enrique Gallegos Venero, and Miguel Angel de la Flor were to have been the most senior officers. Almost none of the radical officers of Phase I was on active duty by the end of one year of Phase II.

health, his behavior was at times erratic, and this further weakened his position within a military worried about external threats to Peru. The power that adhered to Velasco as the founder of the regime, who had the ability to monitor closely career patterns of officers, increasingly slipped away.[13] Structural factors are always extremely important in any regime, but the deep changes in Spain and China after the deaths of Franco and Mao show how important a critical leader can be to the maintenance of cohesion within a delicate balance of forces.

The conjuncture of so many negative economic events, so many threatening geopolitical changes, and the sharp decline in the coordinating and leading capacity of the president, must be weighed seriously when historians come to analyze the loss of forward movement in Phase I and the failure to institutionalize the regime in Peru.[14]

However, for our understanding of Peru and, even more, for our broader theoretical analysis of the problems of institutionalizing organic-statist systems, we must not let attention to conjunctural events obscure the fundamental dilemmas to institutionalization that are presented by certain characteristics of the organic-statist model.

GENERIC PREDICAMENTS: AUTONOMY AND PENETRATION VS. CONSTITUENCY

One of the chief characteristics of the organic-statist model is that the state is a relatively autonomous actor in the political system. The phrase "relative autonomy of the state" implies that the state elite is not *constrained* by class fractions and has a

[13] At this stage of documentation, my analysis of these events is necessarily tentative. However the above description is based on conversations with a number of participants in high level governmental meetings, including one military officer cabinet member. When Velasco died in December 1977, an emotional and unruly crowd of approximately 200,000 people accompanied his funeral procession in what was widely interpreted as a massive demonstration against the retrenchments of Phase II. See "Peru: Last Farewell," *Latin American Political Report* (January 6, 1978), pp. 6-7.

[14] This discussion of negative conjunctural factors is of course not exhaustive. My brief analysis benefited from the more extensive discussion of the factors contributing to the erosion of Phase I policies contained in the last chapter of Peter S. Cleaves and Martin J. Scurrah, *Agriculture, Bureaucracy and Society: Reform in Peru Under Military Rule* (New Haven: draft manuscript, March 1977).

significant degree of freedom to impose its design on society. "Autonomy" is therefore often interpreted to mean strength. However, while autonomy may be a source of strength in the installation phase, in the institutionalization phase relative autonomy may be a source of weakness because a state elite is not *sustained* by constituencies in civil society and therefore is almost exclusively dependent upon its own internal unity and coercive powers. The other side of the coin of autonomy is thus isolation and fragility.

The problem of isolation is overcome in many corporatist systems because the state, while enjoying considerable autonomy, nonetheless frequently utilizes existing social structures and attempts to establish complex patron-client relationships throughout the political system. In this way the state elite builds constituencies because specific brokers benefit from the new state-chartered structures and therefore aid the state elite in its institutionalization efforts. Vargas in Brazil, for example, incorporated labor into new state structures, but in doing so created, as did Cárdenas in Mexico, an aristocracy of trade union leaders who helped control and deliver their labor constituency to the government. This demonstrated ability to control the laboring classes in turn increased the regime's support by the owner classes.

In the organic-statist model, however, the relation between the autonomy and the constituency of the state is more complex. On the one hand the model posits a society composed of decentralized self-managing and harmoniously interrelated units. On the other hand, because such units rarely arise spontaneously, it is assumed that the power of the state will be used to *restratify* almost all groups in civil society and to create new functional groups. Thus the organic-statist model does not assume that an initial constituency for the organic-statist regime exists. It is posited, however, that such a constituency could come into being once the new functional groups have been created, owing to the social equity, justice, and participation these groups provide.

In any concrete situation, of course, such restratification of society profoundly threatens existing organizations and leaders because, if the state elite is successful in its organic-statist designs, it will transform the economic and political base of such organizations and leaders. The difference between the organic-statist model as it was approximated in Peru and the command-socialist model as followed in China is that in China the revolutionary elite openly acknowledged that restratification required conflict and a monist party, whereas in Peru the Phase I strategic elite placed a high value on the "bloodless" nature of the changes involved in restratification, as well as the principles of subsidiarity and self-management, and rejected the idea of a revolutionary one-party state as inconsistent with these principles.

The particular mix of grand aspirations for social engineering and self-imposed limitations on state power to control social groups that is found in the organic-statist model presents greater predicaments for the institutionalization of patterns of participation and control than those presented by the command-socialist model. The organic-statist model also presents more predicaments for participation and control than less ambitious corporatist systems, such as those in Mexico under Cárdenas and in Brazil under Vargas. In these latter systems few attempts were made to restratify social groups, and the elites were not inhibited about imposing complex controls on labor.

The predicaments organic statism presents for the institutionalization of the regime are clearly seen in Peru. Many observers commented on the relative autonomy of the state in Peru vis-à-vis domestic groups during the installation phase of the regime.[15] This autonomy meant that the state elite, free of parliamentary, electoral and most judicial constraints, was able to carry out sweeping agrarian reform, to construct new organizations for the urban poor, and to begin to restructure patterns of ownership and participation in industry.

Since, however, no legitimate role is assigned in organic statism to a mobilizing, deeply penetrating, single revolutionary party, as in command-socialism, such transformations can be carried out only by the state bureaucracy. The attempt of the state elite in Phase I to impose an architectonic design on society meant that virtually every group in society, including rightist *and* leftist political parties, industrialists *and* trade unionists, landlords *and* traditional Indian peasants, were (or felt they might be) subjected to restratification by the state.[16] The threat of penetration by the state, in the context of a model that allowed limited

15 As noted in Chapter 7, this autonomy was far more limited in relation to foreign groups.
16 Abraham F. Lowenthal skillfully develops this theme in his excellent introduction to the book he edited; *The Peruvian Experiment: Continuity and Change Under Military Rule*, see esp. pp. 9-11.

pluralism, contributed to the result that, despite the existence of reforms that were more extensive than in any other regime in Latin American history (with the exception of Cuba), no group —even the presumed beneficiaries of governmental policy—felt entirely safe from the hand of the state bureaucracy. As a consequence no group provided the Phase I state elite with a stable constituency. Indeed, I would go so far as to say that the exclusionary corporatist policies in Brazil produced a larger constituency than did the inclusionary policies of the Peruvian state elite in Phase I. This is not as paradoxical an assertion as it seems. Major sectors of the national and international bourgeoisie in Brazil perceived the Brazilian state elite as carrying out policies they desired and required. The more obvious class basis of the Brazilian state thus gave it a greater constituency than the Peruvian state, which, in its efforts to restratify all classes in order to build an organic-statist society, did not clearly identify itself with any major existing social formations.

The contrast with Mexico also helps place the Peruvian case in clearer perspective since Mexico is the only contemporary regime that made the transition to institutionalization by the use of inclusionary policies. Mexico's more orthodox inclusionary corporatist policies toward two key support groups, peasant communities and urban labor, simultaneously engendered broader constituencies and firmer control than did the more organic-statist formulae used to incorporate similar groups in Peru.[17]

[17] My attention to these points is meant to add to, not supplant, other explanatory factors already advanced concerning institutionalization outcomes in Peru and Mexico. In contrast to Peru after Phase I, the Mexican regime in the period after Cárdenas was fully institutionalized. I have indicated some of the reasons for the differences between Mexico and Peru in this respect. The mystique of popular revolution gave the political elite in Mexico at the time of Cárdenas great symbolic resources which the Peruvian military with their historic image as the "watchdogs of the oligarchy" and the "oppressors of people" were never able to approximate. The revolutionary mystique in Mexico, combined with the virtual absence of any significant prior experience with political parties, gave the Mexican strategic elite much greater organizational space than the Peruvian elite, who instead encountered institutionalized Aprista party identifications. These identifications, moreover, had a strong antimilitary bias. In Mexico, by comparison, trade union ties to parties were much weaker than those between the Communist and Aprista trade unions to their respective parties in Peru. Despite this, the military in Peru encountered great reform space and used their power to carry out sweeping reforms. This explains why, in the installation phase,

In the case of agrarian reform, Peru attempted far greater restratification than occurred in Mexico under Cárdenas. Under Cárdenas, in essence the *ejido* reform was a return to the status quo ante. The Mexican land reform was to a large extent congruent with preexisting structures of peasant society, and the state did not attempt to carry out major restructuring within the corporate structure of the *ejidos*. Often the state political apparatus accepted existing land-tenure inequalities within the *ejidos*, and the state was linked to the leaders of the *ejidos* in a patron-client relationship. As one field study noted, the state authorities by:

> permitting certain members of the *ejido* communities to enjoy special privileges ensured their strong support for the political machine. As long as local *presidentes* of the *comisariados ejidales* received a personal gain from the unequal land distribution, they supported the higher authorities who allowed the system to continue.[18]

As a consequence, agrarian reform has provided the Mexican regime with an important "constituency."

By contrast, the Peruvian government's commitment to forging an organic-statist society in rural communities was deeper than Mexico's and consequently a more difficult task of state engineering. Government policy toward traditional indigenous communities allowed a minimal "family agricultural unit" to be worked individually. The rest had to be worked communally. The government believed it was applying traditional, communal, socioeconomic principles, which they saw as congruent with their overall organic-statist philosophy. In fact, however, the individual tenant system had long since superseded communal ownership

---

the Apristas assumed no worse than a passive stance toward the military government, while the Communists actually gave their active support. In the long run, of course, given the organic-statist designs the Phase I state elite had for the future of Peru, the Aprista and Communist party structures, by their very existence, represented obstacles to the full institutionalization of the regime.

[18] Glen Fisher, "Directed Cultural Change in Nayarit, Mexico," in *Synoptic Studies of Mexican Culture*, edited by Robert Wauchope (New Orleans: Tulane University, Middle American Research Institute, 1957), p. 153, cited in Roger Hansen, *The Politics of Mexican Development*, p. 128. Also see Hansen's supporting data, pp. 31-32.

as the dominant property form.[19] The government's agrarian reform law therefore implied considerable state-imposed redistribution *within* the indigenous communities. Thus while in Mexico the state aligned itself with the dominant groups in the *ejidos*, in Peru, as one of the top advisers to the Ministry of Agriculture acknowledged, the state found itself aligned with the politically and economically weakest sectors of the community.[20] The traditional leaders were suspicious of state policy, and this suspicion was reinforced by the fact that, again unlike Mexico, the peasants played no part in initiating the agrarian reform. As a consequence the leaders of the Indian communities were often able to turn the community against the agrarian reform. In fact, many communities were frightened by the agrarian reform law because they believed it attacked the firmly established principle of family ownership.[21]

The idea of production cooperatives also met resistance in those former haciendas where much of the land was sharecropped and the peasants were the de facto owners of the land. A scholar who observed the first two years of agrarian reform at two such cooperatives concluded:

> By law, all productive assets of a production cooperative must be utilized collectively; no individual or "peasant" production can be carried out. . . . Officials from the Ministry of Agriculture have insisted that production cooperatives be established in these estates, but the residents resist. In Udima, a workable

[19] For example, the 1961 National Agrarian Census figures on indigenous communities show that only 38% of the leaders of 1,568 recognized communities "considered that the lands of the community were predominantly communal." See David Scott Palmer, "Revolution from Above: Military Government and Popular Participation in Peru, 1968-1972" (Ph.D. dissertation, Cornell University, Latin American Studies Program, Dissertation Series, Number 47, 1973). This dissertation is particularly strong on the question of peasant communities, see esp. pp. 143-53, 216-28.

[20] Interview, August 5, 1974, Lima. In the Chinese model this contradiction would be significantly lessened because the monist party would use its power to remove, or control, the members of the community who had the most privileged economic positions in the pre-revolutionary social structure.

[21] One of the communities studied by Palmer "sent a commission of authorities to Lima to request their dissolution as a recognized community. They interpret the law as implying the end of private holdings and inheritance in the community, and they vehemently oppose it," see "Revolution from Above: . . . ," pp. 218-19.

solution has been found whereby the residents continue to cultivate and graze individually, and operate the lands of the ex-hacienda collectively. (This is clearly an extra-legal solution.) In Espinal, the situation is very critical since Ministry officials insist upon de facto collectivization of production while the residents refuse to give up their lands . . .[22]

He concluded that, in these two cases, "the agrarian reform beneficiaries . . . see the formation of production cooperatives as a more serious threat than any posed by their ex-landlord. Never was [he] able to force them off the land. Collectivization to them connotes primarily the collection of surplus by the state and its agents."[23]

Few systematic surveys have yet been published about attitudes toward agrarian reform in Peru. One of the first to be released indicates that, even in the two former coastal haciendas that the government expropriated and adjudicated to the workers as cooperatives, support for the regime *declined* in the five years after agrarian reform began (see Table 8.1) .

To increase organized support for the regime, the government attempted to institutionalize a pyramidal system of representation that began with election to local "agrarian leagues" and culminated in the creation in 1974 of a National Agrarian Confederation (CNA). However there was still much peasant skepticism about the new institution. Indeed, McClintock's 1974 study of agrarian attitudes showed that only "a scant 6% in all sites was positive about the Agrarian League System."[24]

To turn to organized labor, here again we find that, in keeping with its organic-statist goals, the Peruvian regime reorganized both labor and management into new institutions such as the industrial communities. This was done in the belief that the new structures were not only consistent with the regime's normative values but would yield substantial dividends by creating a

[22] Douglas Horton, "Haciendas and Cooperatives: A Preliminary Study of Latifundist Agriculture and Agrarian Reform in Northern Peru" (University of Wisconsin, Land Tenure Center. Unpublished manuscript, September 1973), p. 79.

[23] Ibid., p. 67.

[24] Cynthia McClintock, "Socioeconomic Status and Political Participation in Peru: The Impact of the Agrarian Cooperatives, 1969-1975" (paper prepared for delivery at the 1975 Annual Meeting of the American Political Science Association, San Francisco, September 2-5, 1975), p. 51.

TABLE 8.1

Attitudes Toward the Government in Two Land Reform Cooperatives,
1969 and 1974

Question: "Do you think that in general what the government does
helps to improve the country?"

	Government helps	Government helps more or less	Government does not help	No answer	Don't know (other)	N
Cooperatives:						
Marla 1969	50	11	22	3	14	40
Marla 1974	7	40	36	3	15	62
Estrella 1969	33	25	27	0	15	79
Estrella 1974	13	32	25	3	27	88

SOURCES: The 1969 survey was administered by the Instituto de Estudios Peruanos shortly after the agrarian reform began. The 1974 data come from a follow-up survey administered to the same cooperatives by Cynthia McClintock. See her "Self-Management and Political Participation in Peru, 1969-1975: The Corporatist Illusion" (paper prepared for delivery at the 1976 Annual Meeting of the American Political Science Association, Chicago, September 2-5, 1976), Table 9.

labor constituency and reducing labor conflict, thereby aiding the policies of rapid industrialization. However, precisely because the state elite's design was more organic-statist than corporatist, the complex control mechanisms of the kind that made strikes so difficult under Cárdenas or Vargas were not built into the industrial communities in Phase I.[25] The state elite instead stressed repeatedly that new behavior by labor would flow from the incentive system provided by industrial communities themselves.

If we use strikes as a key indicator, however, a very different pattern of labor behavior emerged in Phase I in Peru than emerged under Cárdenas in Mexico. Under Cárdenas, in the period in which he was mobilizing labor against his enemies and into new corporatist structures, the number of workers involved

[25] For a documented comparison of the Brazilian and Mexican union legislation with the less restrictive union legislation of Peru during Phase I see the section on "Legal Controls" in Evelyne Huber Stephens, "The Politics of Workers' Participation: The Peruvian Approach in Comparative Perspective" (Ph.D. dissertation, Yale University, 1977), Chapter 5.

in strikes rose sharply to an average of about 130,000 workers in 1935 and 1936. By 1938 and 1939, however, Cárdenas had already institutionalized a complex "carrot and stick" control system and strikes in the two-year period involved, on the average, less than 14,000 workers.[26]

In Peru, despite the charges of corporatism, the Phase I leaders did not attempt to construct complex mechanisms to reduce labor's capacity to strike. Instead the government relied on the incorporation of labor and management into the industrial communities, which were supposed to bring about a new solidarity between labor and management. The available data indicate that the expected pattern of self-adjusting, institutionalized harmony between labor and management did not emerge. Instead, if strikes are an accurate indicator of labor-management conflict, in the last three years for which data are available, strikes reached an all-time high since modern records began to be compiled in 1957 (see Table 8.2). Since the current Peruvian regime has attempted to pursuade labor not to strike, the data clearly indicate that the industrial communities did not contribute to the new pattern of labor relations that the state had aspired to institutionalize. Using 1965 as the base year, the number of industrial strikes declined to a low of 71.2 percent in 1970, but had risen to 224.1 percent in 1975 (see Table 8.2). Some authors have made a strong case that the 1970 Industrial Communities Law played an important role in the escalation of conflict between workers and managers.[27] Certainly this inference seems to have been drawn by the Phase II leaders and was one of the reasons why the most innovative organic-statist features of the Industrial Community Law were revised in the drastic legal restructuring of the industrial communities in 1977.[28] Indeed, government preoccupation with rising strike levels led to the 1976 decrees virtually forbidding strikes, decrees that were more explicitly control-oriented than the existing Mexican legislation. The explicitness of these decrees in turn further exacerbated the problem of trying to create an urban labor constituency for the regime. Labor unrest reached a new peak during the General Strike of July 19, 1977, which has

---

[26] The strike pattern under Cárdenas was discussed in Chapter 3.

[27] See in particular the excellent study by Stephens cited in footnote 25.

[28] Perú, Decreto Ley 21789, of 1 February, 1977. For a detailed comparison of the 1970 and the 1977 industrial community laws see, *The Andean Report*, (February 1977), pp. 21-25.

TABLE 8.2

STRIKE DATA FOR PERU, 1957-1976

Year	Total Number of Strikes	% of Economically Active Population Involved in Strikes	Total Number of Strikes in Industrial-Manu-facturing	Index of Variation for Industrial-Manufacturing Strikes
1957	161		71	
1958	213		63	
1959	233		82	
1960	285		109	
1961	341		183	
1962	380		167	
1963	422		210	
1964	398		168	
1965	397	3.70	191	100
1966	394	3.21	191	100
1967	414	3.66	207	108.4
1968	364	2.68	198	103.7
1969	372	2.21	143	74.9
1970	345	2.60	136	71.2
1971	377	3.65	184	96.3
1972	409	2.86	259	135.6
1973	788	8.80	423	221.5
1974	562	7.10	315	163.9
1975	779	N/A	428	224.1
1976	Decrees issued virtually making all strikes illegal			

SOURCES: Perú, Ministerio de Trabajo, Dirección General de Empleo, *Las huelgas en el Perú: 1957-1972* (Lima: August, 1973), Cuadros Nº 2.2 and Nº 3.2. Data for 1973-1974 are from Perú, Instituto Nacional de Planificación, *Informe socio económico: 1974* (Lima: March, 1975), pp. 11, 70. The index of variation and the 1975 data are from Stephens, "The Politics of Workers' Participation," Chapter 5. Data on strikes are regularly contained in a private sector publication, *Industria Peruana*, see esp. Nº 502 (September 1974) for a detailed sectorial analysis of industrial strikes.

Despite the decrees against strikes the Ministry of Labor's data indicates there were 35 strikes involving 34,475 work hours lost in the first trimester of 1977. This contrasted with 181 strikes and 3,907,302 work hours lost in the first trimester of 1976. For the decrees and strike data see *La Crónica* (April 26, 1977), p. 8. The same source indicates that sabotage and deliberate inefficiency are growing problems.

been described by one observer as "the most important united action by labor in Peru since the general strike of 1919."[29]

GENERIC PREDICAMENTS: INTERNAL ORGANIZATIONAL NORMS OF THE STATE ELITE VS. INSTITUTIONALIZED SOCIETAL PARTICIPATION

The organic-statist model posits state-structured functional units in which participation and self-management occur. In any organic-statist attempt, however, there is the danger that, in the process of forging new structures in society, the state elite will retain so much power for itself that the organs of representation never achieve the authoritative decision-making capacity posited. This problem would be present no matter what the power base of the strategic state elite, but it will be compounded when, as in Peru, the state elite's power base is the military which has a series of special internal norms about the organization and distribution of power.

The character of the strategic elite makes a crucial difference, and the general problem that assets in the installation phase may become liabilities in the institutionalization phase again arises. In Peru the core of the state elite in Phase I derived much of their initial power to impose their architectonic design on society from their ability to maintain the continued support of the new professional army. However, the very qualities of relative autonomy, institutional cohesion, and monopoly of force that gave the Peruvian strategic elite strength in the installation phase presented special obstacles for the institutionalization phase.

These obstacles to institutionalization were present in Peru at all levels of the national political system. At the apex, the presidency had by 1977 been filled by only two people, both from the very top of the army hierarchy. Given the fact that the army provided the critical base of support for the regime, the recruitment to the highest political office in the country had to satisfy first the requirements of internal cohesion, hierarchy, and in-

---

[29] See "For the Record: The Peruvian General Strike," *Latin American Political Report* (August 19, 1977), p. 251. The strike was particularly ominous for the government because it marked the first open confrontation between the Communist party and the government since the military assumed power in 1968. A further sign of growing labor autonomy and militance was that a key organizing role in the strike was played by the Lima branch of the Central de Trabajadores de la Revolución Peruana (CTRP), which originally had been created in Phase I as a pro-government trade union organization.

stitutional acceptance within the army as a corporate unit, and only secondarily satisfy the requirements of the new national political system the state elite was attempting to forge. This recruitment structure reduced the potential for a political leader with charisma to emerge, and there was a built-in tension between the bureaucratic and hierarchical requirements necessary for maintaining military cohesion and the requirements of responding to rapidly changing pressures or opportunities in the political system. Such a recruitment structure also exists in Brazil, but in Brazil the presidential term is fixed and thus succession is institutionalized, and military and to some degree even nonmilitary discontent finds an outlet in the process of selection of the next president. In Peru, where the term of the president is not fixed, a logical focus for internal military and external civilian discontent involves a more explosive process of presidential change. The presidential selection process in Peru thus remains too narrow in its recruitment base to fit the organic-statist model and completely lacks an institutionalized succession procedure.

At the next level, the leadership of the strategic elite is found in the cabinet, in the President's Advisory Council, and in the administrative controllers of the territorial units. The new professional army again presented problems for the institutionalization of the regime because, in its desire to maintain unity and secrecy about decision making, the military in Phase I retained a virtual monopoly of all key positions in the state apparatus. David E. Apter, in his discussion of the modernization process, identifies three functions of modernizing elites: achieving "goal specification," "institutional coherence," and "central control." He suggests that these functions are normally performed in different political systems by individuals from a variety of career roles, such as the civil servant, manager, political entrepreneur and broker.[30]

What was unusual about the Peruvian regime before the succession of President Morales was that the military attempted to maximize their unity by monopolizing all three elite functions and closely supervising career roles. In the installation phase, such a pattern does not necessarily present system-level conflicts among elites because pro-government elites may believe such

[30] Apter, *The Politics of Modernization*, pp. 164-67.

monopoly a short-run necessity. Over the long run, however, the requirements of information, coordination and support necessary to institutionalize the system entails some sharing of elite functions. Once again it is crucially important whether the state elite is a military bureaucracy or a political party. A revolutionary party may monopolize all elite functions yet be able to recruit into its top echelons members from all important career roles. In the case of Peru, regardless of the loyalty, brilliance, or technical skill of civilians, they cannot be recruited into the strategic state elite as long as that elite is a military bureaucracy, because the military carry with them their own institutional recruitment patterns. In Peru for example, recruitment to the military career occurs before 20 years of age; during the entire period of Phase I no nonuniformed military or police officer held a cabinet position or was even a member of the President's Advisory Council.[31] The core state elite of Velasco probably felt that this exclusively military recruitment pattern was necessary to ensure that they did not lose the support of the rank and file military officers as their Phase I policies went beyond the programmatic consensus developed before the military assumed power.

The dilemma for the Phase I strategic elite was that, precisely because their architectonic design was so ambitious, they could not afford to alienate their only safe power base. However this power base itself had relatively traditional institutional concerns that were not fully consistent with many of the policies needed to institutionalize the organic-statist design.

The exclusion of civilians imposed three kinds of costs during Phase I. First, military bureaucrats at times had to fill roles that,

[31] The hermetic "uniformed services only" quality about the Peruvian strategic elite is in sharp contrast to most other important military regimes. For example, in Egypt, an analysis of 131 individuals who held cabinet or higher positions from 1952-1969, showed that 66.4% were civilians and that "ministries with uninterrupted civilian leadership were Justice, Public Works, Housing and Utilities, Irrigation, Commerce, Agriculture, Treasury and Higher Education." See R. H. Dekmejian, *Egypt Under Nasser: A Study in Political Dynamics*, pp. 171-72. In Brazil since 1964, the key ministries of Planning and Finance have been held exclusively by professional civilian economists and, at the symbolic level, Brazilian Presidents, though all military men, never wear a uniform. In contrast, all military members of the cabinet in Peru always wear uniforms and the government is still officially—and repeatedly—referred to as the "Revolutionary Government of the Armed Forces."

despite their "new professionalism," they were not technically qualified to perform. Second, because governance, even military rule, has an indispensable political component, key governmental positions were occasionally filled in violation of strict seniority patterns in order to meet political requirements. This in turn weakened the institutional unity that was the regime's most secure base. Third, important civilians with technical, managerial, and political skills became alienated from the regime, which appeared hermetically sealed off from their influence.[32] The succession from Velasco to Morales was partly intended to respond to these problems, and Morales recruited some civilians to cabinet level posts. The predicament faced by the military elite as of 1977 concerned whether they could retain the cohesion and monopoly of force necessary to impose their design while still finding ways to attract civilians to play the key technical and political roles required for the successful institutionalization of the ambitious organic-statist design or even for a well-orchestrated extrication from direct military rule.

At the next level in the national political system, where the government is supposedly linked to a mass base, there were also constraints to institution building. The major linkage organization the regime created was SINAMOS. As a bureaucratic "sponsored organization," dependent upon the government and therefore upon the army, SINAMOS had inherent limitations. On the one hand it could not make any key tactical or strategic political decisions because it was not a political party with operational or ideological autonomy.[33] On the other hand, it was given the extremely difficult task of penetrating, and linking, many sectors of society to the state. To do this, it needed permanent activists in each locality. Given the military nature of the elite designing organic statism in Peru, SINAMOS could not function as a monist party capable of recruiting permanent cadres close to the

[32] My sample is far too small to draw anything more than a tentative conclusion, but those pro-regime elite civilians whom I observed over a four-year period did seem increasingly frustrated as it became clear that, despite their loyalty or achievement, entry into the strategic state elite was barred. In a party system many of these activisits would have risen, or had clear hopes of rising, to critical leadership positions.

[33] For the concept of "sponsored organizations" and a discussion of their problems in the context of catholic politics in Italy see G. Poggi, *Catholic Action in Italy: The Sociology of a Sponsored Organization*, esp. pp. 45-59, 228-29.

base (as in a system such as China), nor could it work out flexible patron-client relationships with strategically placed brokers throughout the political system (as in Mexico). Again, because it was a sponsored bureaucratic organization and not a political party, SINAMOS's mobilization efforts were constantly supervised and were constrained and frequently checked or altered by the national military government and/or by regional military commanders. These contradictions in SINAMOS were so severe that by 1975 it was widely accepted even by the military that it was a failure. When it became clear in 1975 that SINAMOS was to be completely reorganized in an attempt to deal with these problems, I asked one of the original deputy director-generals of SINAMOS why this apparently massive and powerful organization had failed so dramatically after only three years. He answered: "SINAMOS is being changed because it exhausted its political capital very rapidly. It was feared by groups we were trying to organize. Also sectors within the bureaucracy felt we were assuming their functions and politicizing their technical workers. We had a bad situation in that we were not a political organization that could respond quickly and tactically to problems. We were a representative of the state."[34]

Finally let us consider the question of the relationship of the new professional army base to the presumed structure of an organic-statist national political system of authority. During the last half of Phase I, the government devoted much of its efforts to creating units of functional participation at the base level and to gradually constructing these into pyramid-shaped national organizations for each sector. Two such peak organizations were created, the Confederation of Industrial Communities (CONACAI) and the National Agrarian Confederation (CNA). But to date most of Peruvian society is still not incorporated into any group.

Even if all the economic and social groups were eventually organized at the national level—an extremely unlikely possibility —several difficulties would still remain for the institutionalization of an organic-statist regime by a military elite. A national organization of functional groups with a system of elected officials from the base up is an organ of representation and consultation, but not yet one of authoritative participation in national decision making. Furthermore, the power to rule and make binding decisions entails resolving conflicts between sectors and im-

[34] Interview, June 1975, Lima.

posing priorities. The system of vertical representation within peak organizations does not address these questions of horizontal integration between sectors, just as it does not in itself resolve the question of turning *representation into participation, voice into command.* To go beyond consultation toward the power to make binding decisions and the capacity to work out priorities between sectors entails devolution of power from the strategic state elite to the new organs of participation. This is not a logical impossibility in the model. However, to date, no regime that has forged such a system of consultation has yet devolved sufficient power to the consultative organs to make them an authoritative part of national decision-making. In my book on the military in Brazil, I concluded by drawing attention to the distinction that must be made between the *military as government* and the *military as institution.* The same distinction is crucial to Peru. Undoubtedly some members of the military as government in Phase I might have wanted to devolve power to the emerging functional representation groups. However the central fact was that the military as institution never made such a commitment, and no significant devolution occurred.

Although the difficulties confronting institutionalization of the regime in Peru appear insurmountable, the military government has several achievements. Agrarian reform in Peru has ameliorated one of the most unequal land tenure systems in the world. The educational system has become more open and more focused on Peru's culture. Despite Phase II retrenchments, the experiments with social property, the industrial community, participation, and the Andean Pact have both broadened the scope, and added to the content, of the worldwide debate about alternative forms of state-society relations, and alternative approaches to the problems between rich and poor nations.

The period 1968 through 1975 in Peru will ultimately be remembered as a controversial military interlude in Peru's history rather than as the formative phase of an enduring regime. A major reason for this is the inability of the military to find solutions to the generic problems of organic-statist institutionalization. Rather than institutionalization via the military's scheme, the future holds more transformations of the scheme.

Selected Bibliography

1. Books and Monographs

Agulla, Juan Carlos. *Diagnóstico social de una crisis: Córdoba, mayo de 1969*. Córdoba: Editel, 1969.

Alexander, Robert J. *Labor Relations in Argentina, Brazil and Chile*. New York: McGraw-Hill Book Company, Inc., 1962.

Almond, Gabriel, and Coleman, James S. *The Politics of the Developing Areas*. Princeton: Princeton University Press, 1960.

Almond, Gabriel, and Verba, Sidney. *The Civic Culture: Political Attitudes and Democracy in Five Nations*. Princeton: Princeton University Press, 1963.

Althusser, Louis. *Lenin and Philosophy and Other Essays*. New York and London: Monthly Review Press, 1971.

Amaral, Azevedo. *O estado autoritário*. Rio de Janeiro: José Olympio, 1939.

Anaya Franco, Eduardo. *Imperialismo, industrialización y transferencia de tecnologia en el Perú*. Lima: Editorial Horizonte, 1975.

Anderson, Charles W. *The Political Economy of Modern Spain: Policy-Making in an Authoritarian System*. Madison: University of Wisconsin Press, 1970.

Apter, David E. *The Politics of Modernization*. Chicago: University of Chicago Press, 1965.

———. *Choice and the Politics of Allocation: A Developmental Theory*. New Haven and London: Yale University Press, 1971.

———. *Political Change: Collected Essays*. London: Frank Cass and Company Limited, 1973.

Apter, David E., and Goodman, Louis Wolf, eds. *The Multinational Corporation and Social Change*. New York: Praeger Publishers, 1976.

Aquarone, Alberto. *L'organizzazione dello Stato totalitario*. Turin: Giulio Einaudi editore, 1965.

Aristotle. *The Politics*. Translated by E. Barker. New York: Oxford University Press, 1962.

Ashby, Joe C. *Organized Labor and the Mexican Revolution Under Lázaro Cárdenas*. Chapel Hill: University of North Carolina Press, 1967.

Astiz, Carlos A. *Pressure Groups and Power Elites in Peruvian Politics*. Ithaca: Cornell University Press, 1969.

317

Avineri, Shlomo. *The Social and Politicial Thought of Karl Marx.* Cambridge: Cambridge University Press, 1968.

Baella Tuesta, Alfonso. *El poder invisible.* Lima: Editorial Andina, 1977.

Balvé, Beba; Marín, Juan Carlos; and Murmis, Miguel, eds. *Lucha de calles, lucha de clases.* Buenos Aires: La Rosa Blindada, 1973.

Beer, Samuel H. *British Politics in the Collectivist Age.* New York: Alfred A. Knopf, 1965.

Behrman, Jack N. *Decision Criteria for Direct Investment in Latin America.* New York: Council of the Americas, 1974.

Béjar, Héctor. *Peru 1965: Notes on a Guerrilla Experience.* New York: Monthly Review Press, 1969.

———. *La revolución en la trampa.* Lima: Ediciones Socialismo y Participación, 1976.

Bentley, Arthur. *The Process of Government: A Study of Social Pressures.* Chicago: University of Chicago Press, 1908.

Bettelheim, Charles. *Cultural Revolution and Industrial Organization in China: Changes in Management and the Division of Labor.* Translated by Alfred Ehrenfeld. New York: Monthly Review Press, 1974.

———. *Class Struggles in the USSR: First Period; 1917-1923.* Translated by Brian Pearce. New York: Monthly Review Press, 1977.

Bourricaud, François. *Power and Society in Contemporary Peru.* Translated by Paul Stevenson. New York: Praeger Publishers, 1970.

Brandenburg, Frank R. *The Making of Modern Mexico.* Englewood Cliffs, New Jersey: Prentice-Hall, Inc., 1964.

Briones, Guillermo, and Mejía Valera, José. *El obrero industrial.* Lima: Universidad de San Marcos, Instituto de Investigaciones Sociológicos, 1964.

Buckland, W. W. *Roman Law and Common Law: A Comparison in Outline.* Cambridge: Cambridge University Press, 1936.

Bullock, Alan, and Shock, Maurice, eds. *The Liberal Tradition: From Fox to Keynes.* Oxford: Oxford University Press, 1967.

Cardoso, Fernando Henrique, and Faletto, Enzo. *Dependencia y desarrollo en América Latina.* México: Siglo Veintiuno Editores, 1969.

Cardoso, Fernando Henrique. *Ideologías de la burguesia industrial en sociedades dependientes (Argentina y Brasil).* México: Siglo Veintiuno Editores, 1971.

———. *Estado y sociedad en América Latina.* Buenos Aires: Ediciones Nueva Visión, 1972.

———. *Autoritarismo e democratização.* Rio de Janeiro: Editôra Paz E Terra, 1975.

Clegg, Ian. *Workers' Self-Management in Algeria.* London: Allen Lane, The Penguin Press, 1971.

Collier, David. *Squatters and Oligarchs: Authoritarian Rule and Policy*

Change in Peru. Baltimore: The Johns Hopkins University Press, 1976.

Connolly, William E., ed. *The Bias of Pluralism.* New York: Atherton Press, 1967.

Cotler, Julio. *Clases, estado y nación en el Perú.* Lima: Instituto de Estudios Peruanos ediciones, 1978.

Dahl, Robert A. *Polyarchy: Participation and Opposition.* New Haven: Yale University Press, 1971.

Dekmejian, R. H. *Egypt Under Nasser: A Study in Political Dynamics.* Albany: State University of New York Press, 1971.

Delgado, Carlos. *El proceso revolucionario peruano: testimonio de lucha.* México: Siglo Veintiuno Editores, 1972.

———. *Revolución y participación.* Lima: Ediciones del Centro, 1974.

Delich, Francisco. *Crisis y protesta social: Córdoba, mayo de 1969.* Buenos Aires: Ediciones Signos, 1970.

Durkheim, Emile. *The Division of Labor in Society.* Translated by G. Simpson. New York: The Free Press, 1964.

Einaudi, Luigi; Maullin, Richard; Stepan, Alfred; and Fleet, Michael. *Latin American Institutional Development: The Changing Catholic Church.* Santa Monica: The Rand Corporation, October 1969.

Einaudi, Luigi, and Stepan, Alfred. *Latin American Institutional Development: Changing Military Perspectives in Peru and Brazil.* Santa Monica: The Rand Corporation, 1971.

Engels, Frederick. *The Origin of the Family, Private Property, and the State.* New York: International Publishers, 1942.

Espinoza Uriarte, H., and Osorio Torres, J. *El poder económico en la industria.* Lima: Universidad Nacional Federico Villarreal, 1972.

Ezcurdia, Mario. *Análisis teórico del Partido Revolucionario Institucional.* México: B. Costa-Amic, Editor, 1968.

Fitzgerald, E.V.K. *The State and Economic Development: Peru Since 1968.* Cambridge, England: Cambridge University Press, University of Cambridge, Department of Applied Economics, Occasional Paper 49, 1976.

Franco, Carlos. *La revolución participatoria.* Lima: Mosca Azul Editores, 1975.

Galbraith, J. K. *American Capitalism: The Concept of Countervailing Power.* Revised edition. London: Hamish Hamilton, 1957.

Garcés, Joan. *El estado y los problemas tácticos en el gobierno de Allende.* Buenos Aires: Siglo Veintiuno Editores, 1973.

García, Pío, ed. *Las fuerzas armadas y el golpe de estado en Chile.* México: Siglo Veintiuno Editores, 1974.

Gerschenkron, Alexander. *Economic Backwardness in Historical Perspective: A Book of Essays.* Cambridge: Harvard University Press, 1966.

Gianella, Jaime. *Marginalidad en Lima Metropolitana: una investigación exploratoria*. Lima: Centro de Estudios y Promoción del Desarrollo. Cuadernos DESCO, Series A, no. 8. 1970.

Goodsell, Charles T. *American Corporations and Peruvian Politics*. Cambridge: Harvard University Press, 1974.

Gramsci, Antonio. *The Modern Prince and Other Writings*. Translated by Louis Marks. New York: International Publishers, 1970.

————. *Selections from the Prison Notebooks*. Translated by Quintin Hoare and Geoffrey Nowell Smith. New York: International Publishers, 1971.

Hamilton, Bernice. *Political Thought in Sixteenth-Century Spain: A Study of the Political Ideas of Vitoria, de Soto, Suárez, and Molina*. Oxford: Oxford University Press, 1963.

Handelman, Howard. *Struggle in the Andes: Peasant Political Mobilization in Peru*. Austin: University of Texas Press, 1975.

Hansen, Roger D. *The Politics of Mexican Development*. Baltimore: The Johns Hopkins University Press, 1971.

Haya de la Torre, Víctor Raúl, *El antimperialismo y el Apra*. 4th ed. Lima: Editoria Imprenta Amauta, 1972.

Heclo, Hugh. *Modern Social Politics in Britain and Sweden: From Relief to Income Maintenance*. New Haven: Yale University Press, 1974.

Herbold, Carl, Jr. and Stein, Steve. *Guía bibliográfica para la historia social y política del Perú en el siglo XX (1895-1960)*. Lima: Instituto de Estudios Peruanos ediciones y Campodónicoediciones, 1971.

Hirschman, Albert O. *A Bias for Hope: Essays on Development and Latin America*. New Haven: Yale University Press, 1971.

Huntington, Samuel P. *Political Order in Changing Societies*. New Haven: Yale University Press, 1968.

————. *The Soldier and the State: The Theory and Politics of Civil-Military Relations*. New York: Vintage Books, 1964.

Ilchman, Warren F., and Uphoff, Norman Thomas. *The Political Economy of Change*. Berkeley: University of California Press, 1969.

Jaguaribe, Hélio. *Desenvolvimento econômico e desenvolvimento político*. Rio de Janeiro: Editôra Fundo de Cultura, 1962.

Kaplán, Marcos. *La formación del estado nacional en América Latina*. Santiago: Editorial Universitaria, 1969.

Kaufman, Robert F. *Transitions to Stable Authoritarian Corporate Regimes: The Chilean Case?* Beverly Hills: Sage Comparative Politics Series, Series 01-060, Vol. 5, 1976.

Kirkpatrick, Jeane. *Leader and Vanguard in Mass Society: A Study of Peronist Argentina*. Cambridge: The M.I.T. Press, 1971.

Klarén, Peter F. *Modernization, Dislocation, and Aprismo: Origins of the Peruvian Aprista Party, 1870-1932*. Austin: University of Texas Press, 1973.

320

Klinghoffer, Hans, ed. *La pensée politique du Président Getúlio Vargas: sélection, classement systématique et traduction française.* Rio de Janeiro: Imprensa Nacional, 1942.

Knickerbocker, Frederick T. *Oligopolistic Reaction and Multinational Enterprise.* Boston: Harvard University, Graduate School of Business Administration, Division of Research, 1973.

Kolaja, Jiri. *Workers' Councils: The Yugoslav Experience.* New York: Praeger, 1966.

Kuczynski, Pedro-Pablo. *Peruvian Democracy under Economic Stress: An Account of the Belaúnde Administration, 1963-1968.* Princeton: Princeton University Press, 1977.

LaPalombara, Joseph. *Interest Groups in Italian Politics.* Princeton: Princeton University Press, 1964.

Larson, Magali Sarfatti, and Bergman, Arlene Eisen. *Social Stratification in Peru.* Berkeley: Institute of International Studies, University of California, 1969.

Lenin, V. I. *Selected Works.* 3 vols. Moscow: Progress Publishers, 1970.

———. *The State and Revolution.* New York: International Publishers, 1971.

Linz, Juan J., and Stepan, Alfred, eds. *Breakdowns of Democratic Regimes: The European and Latin American Experience.* Baltimore: The Johns Hopkins University Press, forthcoming: tentative title.

Lowenthal, Abraham F., ed. *The Peruvian Experiment: Continuity and Change Under a Military Regime.* Princeton: Princeton University Press, 1975.

Lowi, Theodore J. *The End of Liberalism: Ideology, Policy, and the Crisis of Public Authority.* New York: W. W. Norton and Company, 1969.

MacDonald, Alphonse L. *La reforma agraria en dos complejos agro-industriales, Cayaltí y Tumán: informe preliminar.* Lima: Pontificia Universidad Católica del Perú, 1970.

Malloy, James M. *Bolivia: The Uncompleted Revolution.* Pittsburgh: University of Pittsburgh Press, 1970.

———, ed. *Authoritarianism and Corporatism in Latin America.* Pittsburgh: Pittsburgh University Press, 1977.

Malpica, Carlos. *Los dueños del Perú.* 6th ed., revised. Lima: Ediciones Peisa, 1974.

Mariátegui, José Carlos. *Seven Interpretive Essays on Peruvian Reality.* Austin and London: University of Texas Press, 1971.

Marx, Karl, and Engels, Frederick. *Selected Correspondence.* London: Lawrence and Wishart Ltd., 1956.

———. *Selected Works.* 2 vols. Moscow: Foreign Languages Publishing House, 1958.

Marx, Karl. *The 18th Brumaire of Louis Bonaparte.* New York: International Publishers, 1963.

321

Maser, Werner. *Hitler's Mein Kampf: An Analysis*. Translated by R. H. Barry. London: Faber and Faber, 1970.

Matos Mar, José. *Urbanización y barriadas en América Latina*. Lima: Instituto de Estudios Peruanos, 1968.

Matos Mar, José, and Ravines, Rogger. *Bibliografía peruana de ciencias sociales (1957-1969)*. Lima: Instituto de Estudios Peruanos ediciones y Campodónicoediciones, 1971.

Mercado Jarrín, Edgardo. *Ensayos por Edgardo Mercado Jarrín: Primer Ministro, Ministro de Guerra y Comandante General del Ejército*. Lima: Biblioteca Militar del Oficial, 1974.

Mikesell, Raymond, ed. *Foreign Investment in the Petroleum and Mineral Industries: Case Studies of Investor-Host Relations*. Baltimore: The Johns Hopkins Press, 1971.

Miliband, Ralph. *The State in Capitalist Society*. New York: Basic Books, 1969.

Moncloa, Francisco. *Perú: ¿Qué pasó? (1968-1976)*. Lima: Editorial Horizonte, 1977.

Moran, Theodore H. *Multinational Corporations and the Politics of Dependence: Copper in Chile*. Princeton: Princeton University Press, 1974.

Morawetz, David. *The Andean Group: A Case Study in Economic Integration Among Developing Countries*. Cambridge: The MIT Press, 1974.

Mussolini, Benito. *The Political and Social Doctrine of Fascism*. London: The Hogarth Press, Day to Day Pamphlet No. 18, 1933.

Nolte, Ernst. *Three Faces of Fascism: Action Française, Italian Fascism, National Socialism*. Translated by Leila Vennewitz. New York, Chicago, San Francisco: Holt, Rinehart and Winston, 1966.

Nordlinger, Eric A. *Conflict Regulation in Divided Societies*. Cambridge: Center For International Affairs, Harvard University Press, 1972.

North, Liisa. *Civil-Military Relations in Argentina, Chile and Peru*. Berkeley: Institute of International Studies, University of California, 1966.

O'Donnell, Guillermo A. *Modernization and Bureaucratic Authoritarianism: Studies in South American Politics*. Berkeley: Institute of International Studies, University of California, 1973.

O'Donnell, Guillermo, and Linck, Delfina. *Dependencia y autonomía*. Buenos Aires: Amorrortu Editores, 1973.

Pareto, Vilfredo. *The Mind and Society: A Treatise in General Sociology*. New York: Dover Publications, Inc., 1935.

Pásara, Luis; Santistevan, Jorge; Bustamante, Alberto; and García-Sayán, Diego. *Dinámica de la comunidad industrial*. Lima: Centro de Estudios y Promoción del Desarrollo, DESCO, 1974.

Pateman, Carole. *Participation and Democratic Theory.* London: Cambridge University Press, 1970.

Pease García, Henry and Verme Insúa, Olga. *Perú 1968-1973: cronología política.* 2 vols. Lima: Centro de Estudios y Promoción del Desarrollo, DESCO, 1974.

Perón, Juan. *Expone su doctrina.* Buenos Aires: n.p., 1952.

————. *Mensajes de Perón.* Buenos Aires: Ediciones Mundo Peronista, 1952.

Pike, Fredrick B. *The Modern History of Peru.* New York: Frederick A. Praeger, 1967.

Pike, Fredrick B., and Stritch, Thomas, eds. *The New Corporatism: Social-Political Structures in the Iberian World.* Notre Dame and London: University of Notre Dame Press, 1974.

Poggi, G. *Catholic Action in Italy: The Sociology of a Sponsored Organization.* Stanford: Stanford University Press, 1967.

Poulantzas, Nicos. *Political Power and Social Classes.* Translated by Timothy O'Hagan. London: New Left Books and Sheed and Ward, 1973.

Prugue, Armando. *El Perú en el Banco Interamericano de Desarrollo: panorama y perspectivas institucionales.* Washington, D.C.: Banco Interamericano de Desarrollo, 1974.

Purcell, Susan Kaufman. *The Mexican Profit-Sharing Decision: Politics in an Authoritarian Regime.* Berkeley and Los Angeles: University of California Press, 1975.

Quijano, Aníbal. *Nationalism and Capitalism in Peru: A Study in Neo-Imperialism.* New York: Monthly Review Press, 1971.

Reyna, José Luis, and Weinert, Richard S., eds. *Authoritarianism in Mexico.* Philadelphia: ISHI Publications, 1977.

Reynolds, Clark W. *The Mexican Economy: Twentieth Century Structure and Growth.* New Haven: Yale University Press, 1970.

Rommen, Heinrich A. *The State in Catholic Social Thought: A Treatise in Political Philosophy.* St. Louis and London: B. Herder Book Company, 1945.

Ronfeldt, David. *Atencingo: The Politics of Agrarian Struggle in a Mexican Ejido.* Stanford: Stanford University Press, 1973.

Rose, Stanley F. *Business Operations in Peru.* Washington, D.C.: Bureau of National Affairs, Tax Management Foreign Income, No. 329, 1975.

Russett, Bruce M., and Stepan, Alfred, eds. *Military Force and American Society.* New York: Harper Torchbooks, 1973.

Salazar Bondy, Augusto. *Historia de las ideas en el Perú contemporáneo.* 2 vols. 2nd ed. Lima: Francisco Moncloa, 1967.

Sarti, Roland. *Fascism and the Industrial Leadership in Italy, 1919-1940: A Study in the Expansion of Private Power Under Fascism.* Berkeley: University of California Press, 1971.

323

Schmitter, Philippe. *Interest Conflict and Political Change in Brazil.* Stanford: Stanford University Press, 1971.

Schumpeter, Joseph A. *Capitalism, Socialism and Democracy.* New York: Harper Torchbooks, 1962.

Schurmann, Franz. *Ideology and Organization in Communist China.* 2nd ed., revised. Berkeley: University of California Press, 1968.

Scott, Robert. *Mexican Government in Transition.* Revised edition. Urbana: University of Illinois Press, 1964.

Senén González, Santiago. *El sindicalismo después de Perón.* Buenos Aires: Editorial Galerna, 1971.

Seoane, Edgardo. *Ni tiranos ni caudillos: cartas y hechos del proceso político.* Lima: Editora Italperu, n.d.

Simão, Azis. *Sindicato e estado.* São Paulo: Dominus Editôra, 1966.

Skilling, H. Gordon, and Griffiths, Franklin, eds. *Interest Groups in Soviet Politics.* Princeton: Princeton University Press, 1970.

Smith, Adam. *The Wealth of Nations.* 2 vols. London: J. M. Dent and Sons, Everyman's Library Edition, 1910.

Sohm, Rudolph. *The Institutes: A Textbook of the History and System of Roman Law.* Translated by J. C. Ledlie. 2nd ed., revised. Oxford: Clarendon Press, 1901.

Stepan, Alfred. *The Military in Politics: Changing Patterns in Brazil.* Princeton: Princeton University Press, 1971.

———, ed. *Authoritarian Brazil: Origins, Policies, and Future.* New Haven and London: Yale University Press, 1973.

Stepan, Nancy. *Beginnings of Brazilian Science: Oswaldo Cruz, Medical Research and Policy, 1890-1920.* New York: Science History Publications, 1975.

Stojanović, Svetozar. *Between Ideals and Reality: A Critique of Socialism and Its Future.* Translated by Gerson S. Sher. New York: Oxford University Press, 1973.

Stopford, John M., and Wells, Louis T., Jr. *Managing the Multinational Enterprise: Organization of the Firm and Ownership of the Subsidiaries.* New York: Basic Books, Inc., 1972.

Tilley, Charles, ed. *The Formation of National States in Western Europe.* Princeton: Princeton University Press, 1975.

Townsend, James R. *Political Participation in Communist China.* Berkeley: University of California Press, 1969.

Truman, David B. *The Governmental Process: Political Interests and Public Opinion.* New York: Alfred A. Knopf, 1951.

Tucker, Robert C. *The Marxian Revolutionary Idea.* New York: W. W. Norton and Company, 1969.

Tugwell, Franklin. *The Politics of Oil in Venezuela.* Stanford: Stanford University Press, 1975.

Ugalde, Antonio. *Power and Conflict in a Mexican Community: A*

Study of Political Integration. Albuquerque: University of New Mexico Press, 1970.

Unsain, Alejandro. *Ordenamiento de las leyes obreras argentinas.* 4th ed. Buenos Aires: El Ateneo, 1952.

Vaitsos, Constantine V. *Comercialización de tecnología en el Pacto Andino.* Lima: Instituto de Estudios Peruanos, 1973.

————. *Intercountry Income Distribution and Transnational Enterprises.* Oxford: Oxford University Press, 1974.

Vanek, Jaroslav. *The General Theory of Labor-Managed Market Economies.* Ithaca: Cornell University Press, 1970.

Vaupel, James W., and Curhan, Joan P. *The Making of Multinational Enterprise.* Boston: Harvard University, Graduate School of Business Administration, Division of Research, 1969.

Velasco Alvarado, General Juan. *Velasco: la voz de la revolución.* 2 vols. Lima: Ediciones Participación, 1972.

Vernon, Raymond. *Sovereignty at Bay: The Multinational Spread of U.S. Enterprises.* New York: Basic Books, Inc., 1971.

————, ed. *Big Business and the State: Changing Relations in Western Europe.* Cambridge: Harvard University Press, 1974.

Villanueva, Víctor. *¿Nueva mentalidad militar en el Perú?* Lima: Librería-Editorial Juan Mejía Baca, 1969.

————. *El CAEM y la revolución de la Fuerza Armada.* Lima: IEP ediciones y Campodónico ediciones, 1972.

————. *Ejército Peruano: del caudillaje anárquico al militarismo reformista.* Lima: Librería-Editorial Juan Mejía Baca, 1973.

Webb, Richard. *Government Policy and the Distribution of Income in Peru, 1963-1973.* Cambridge: Harvard University Press, 1977.

Weber, Eugen. *Varieties of Fascism: Doctrines of Revolution in the Twentieth Century.* New York: Van Nostrand Reinhold Company, 1964.

Weber, Max. *The Theory of Social and Economic Organization.* Translated by A. M. Henderson and Talcott Parsons. New York: The Free Press of Glencoe, 1964.

Welsh, Eileen. *Bibliografía sobre el crecimiento dinámico de Lima, referente al proceso de urbanización en el Perú.* Lima: Centro de Estudios y Promoción de Desarrollo. Cuadernos DESCO, Series A, no. 3, 1970.

Wilkie, James W., and Monzón de Wilkie, Edna, eds. *México visto en el siglo XX: entrevistas de historia oral.* México: Instituto Mexicano de Investigaciones Económicas, 1969.

Wolin, Sheldon. *Politics and Vision: Continuity and Innovation in Western Political Thought.* Boston: Little, Brown and Company, 1960.

Yugoslavia's Way: The Program of the League of Communists of Yugo-

slavia. Translated by Stoyan Pribechevich. New York: All Nations Press, 1958.

Zimmerman Zavala, Augusto. *El Plan Inca, objectivo: revolución peruana*. Lima: Empresa Editora del Diario Oficial "El Peruano," 1974.

2. ARTICLES

Ai Camp, Roderic. "The Cabinet and the Técnico in Mexico and the United States." *Journal of Comparative Administration* 3 (May 1971): 188-214.

Anderson, Bo, and Cockcroft, James D. "Control and Cooptation in Mexican Politics." *International Journal of Comparative Sociology* 7 (March 1966): 11-28.

Andrews, Frank M., and Phillips, George W. "The Squatters of Lima: Who They Are and What They Want." *The Journal of Developing Areas* 4 (January 1970): 211-24.

Apter, David. "Radicalization and Embourgeoisement: Some Hypotheses for a Comparative Study of History" *The Journal of Interdisciplinary History* 1 (Winter 1971): 265-303.

Bachrach, Peter, and Baratz, Morton S. "Two Faces of Power." *American Political Science Review* 56 (December 1962): 947-52.

Baer, Werner; Kerstenetzsky, Isaac; and Vittella, Aníbal V. "The Changing Role of the State in the Brazilian Economy." *World Development* 1 (November 1973): 23-34.

Baer, Werner; Newfarmer, Richard; and Trebart, Thomas. "On State Capitalism in Brazil: Some New Issues and Questions." *Inter-American Economic Affairs* 30 (Winter 1976): 63-93.

Basurto, Jorge. "Populismo y movilización de masas en México durante el régimen cardenista." *Revista Mexicana de Sociología* 31 (October-December 1969): 853-92.

Béjar, Héctor. "El neocapitalismo del Señor Quijano." *Participación*, no. 1 (December 1972): 17-22.

Bendix, Reinhard. "Social Stratification and the Political Community." *European Journal of Sociology* 1 (1960): 181-210.

Bezold, Willy; Cabrera, Jorge; and Jaworski, Hélan. "La planificación participante y la planificación de base en el Perú." *Revista Interamericana de Planificación* 9 (June 1975): 5-15.

Bobbio Centurión, Lt. Coronel Carlos. ¿Qué ejército necesita el Perú?: *Revista Militar del Perú*, no. 675 (March-April 1963): 132-36.

Bourricaud, François. "Los militares: ¿por qué y para qué?" In Mercier Vega, Luis; Cuéllar, Oscar; Bourricaud, François; Valdez Pallete, Luis; Alberto Lozoya, Jorge; Bañales G., Carlos; Camacho Peña, Alfonso; and Rouquié, Alain. *Fuerzas armadas, poder y cambio*. Caracas: Editorial Tiempo Nuevo, 1971, pp. 101-71.

Cardoso, Fernando Henrique. "The Industrial Elite." In *Elites in Latin America*. Edited by Seymour Martin Lipset and Aldo Solari. New York: Oxford University Press, 1967, pp. 94-114.

Carrión, Jorge. "La represión también es militante." In Carmona, Fernando; Montaño, Guillermo; Carrión, Jorge; and Aguilar M., Alonso. *El milagro mexicano*. México: Editorial Nuestro Tiempo, S.A., 1970, pp. 210-20.

Collier, David, and Collier, Ruth Berins. "Who Does What, To Whom, and How: Toward a Comparative Analysis of Latin American Corporatism." In *Authoritarianism and Corporatism in Latin America*. Edited by James M. Malloy. Pittsburgh: University of Pittsburgh Press, 1977, pp. 489-512.

Collier, Ruth. "Parties, Coups, and Authoritarian Rule: Patterns of Political Change in Tropical Africa," *Comparative Political Studies* 11 (April 1978): 62-93.

Cornelius, Wayne, Jr. "Urbanization as an Agent in Latin American Political Instability: The Case of Mexico." *American Political Science Review* 63 (September 1969): 833-57.

————. "Nation Building, Participation, and Distribution: The Politics of Social Reform Under Cárdenas." In *Crisis, Choice, and Change: Historical Studies of Political Development*. Edited by Gabriel A. Almond, Scott C. Flanagan, and Robert J. Mundt. Boston: Little, Brown and Company, 1973, pp. 392-498.

Cotler, Julio. "Political Crisis and Military Populism in Peru." *Studies in Comparative International Development* 6 (1970-71): 95-113.

————. "Crisis política y populismo militar." In Matos Mar, José; Fuenzalida Vollmar, Fernando; Cotler, Julio; Escobar, Alberto; Salazar Bondy, Augusto; and Bravo Bresani, Jorge. *Perú: hoy*. México: Siglo Veintiuno Editores, 1971, pp. 86-104.

————. "Bases del corporativismo en el Perú." *Sociedad y Política* 1 (October 1972): 3-12.

————. "Peru: A Structural-Historical Approach to the Breakdown of Democratic Institutions." In *Breakdowns of Democratic Regimes: The European and Latin American Experience*. Edited by Juan J. Linz and Alfred Stepan. Baltimore: The Johns Hopkins University Press, 1978.

Daalder, Hans. "The Consociational Democracy Theme." *World Politics* 26 (July 1974): 604-21.

Dados, no. 7 (1970). Special issue devoted to "Sociedad e Estado" in Brazil.

Dealy, Glen Caudill. "The Tradition of Monistic Democracy in Latin America." *Journal of the History of Ideas* 35 (October-December 1974): 625-46.

de la Flor Valle, Lt. Col. Miguel. "La guerra en Argelia." *Revista de la Escuela Superior de Guerra* 4 (October-December 1962): 19-44.

del Prado, Jorge. "Is there a Revolution in Peru?" *World Marxist Review.* (January 1971), pp. 17-27.

de Navarrete, Ifigenia M. "La distribución del ingreso en México: tendencias y perspectivas." In *El perfil de México en 1980.* Instituto de Investigaciones Sociales, Universidad Nacional Autónoma de México. México: Siglo Veintiuno Editores, 1970, vol. 1, pp. 15-71.

Deutsch, Karl. "Social Mobilization and Political Development." *American Political Science Review* 55 (September 1961): 493-514.

Díaz-Alejandro, Carlos F. "The Andean Common Market: Gestation and Outlook." In *Analysis of Development Problems.* Edited by R. S. Eckaus and P.N. Rosenstein-Rodan. Amsterdam: North-Holland Publishing Co., 1973, pp. 293-326.

―――. "North-South Relations: The Economic Component." *International Organization* 29 (Winter 1975): 214-41.

Dietz, Henry. "Urban Squatter Settlements in Peru: A Case History and Analysis." *Journal of Inter-American Development* 11 (July 1969): 353-70.

di Tella, Torcuato. "Populism and Reform in Latin America." In *Obstacles to Change in Latin America.* Edited by Claudio Veliz. London: Oxford University Press, 1965, pp. 47-74.

dos Santos, Theotonio. "The Structure of Dependence." *American Economic Review* 60 (May 1970): 231-36.

Dowse, Robert A. "A Functionalist's Logic." *World Politics* 18 (June 1966): 607-22.

Dunn, William N. "Ideology and Organization in Socialist Yugoslavia: Modernization and the Obsolescence of Praxis." *Newsletter on Comparative Studies of Communism* 5 (August 1972): 21-56.

Einaudi, Luigi R. "Peruvian Military Relations With the United States." Santa Monica: The Rand Corporation, P-4389, 1970.

Escudero, Lt. Colonel Víctor M. "El movimiento cooperativista." *Revista Militar del Perú,* no. 684 (September-October 1964): 1-49.

Fagen, Richard R., and Tuohy, William S. "Aspects of the Mexican Political System." *Studies in Comparative International Development* 7 (Fall 1973): 208-20.

Femia, Joseph. "Hegemony and Consciousness in the Thought of Antonio Gramsci." *Political Studies* 23 (March 1975): 29-48.

Figueroa, Adolfo. "El impacto de las reformas actuales sobre la distribución de ingresos en el Perú." *Apuntes* (Lima) 1 (1973): 67-82.

Gallegos Venero, Lt. Colonel Enrique. "¿Debe preocuparnos la guerra subversiva?" *Revista de la Escuela Superior de Guerra* 7 (January-March 1960): 18-20.

Gallegos Venero, Enrique. "Un combate victorioso en guerra contrarevolucionaria." *Revista de la Escuela Superior de Guerra* 10 (July-September 1963): 7-26.

328

————. "Inteligencia y guerra no convencional." *Revista de la Escuela Superior de Guerra* 13 (July-September 1966): 7-18.

Gilpin, Robert. "The Politics of Transnational Economic Relations." In *Transnational Relations and World Politics*. Edited by Robert O. Keohane and Joseph S. Nye, Jr. Cambridge: Harvard University Press, 1972, pp. 48-69.

Girardin, Jean-Claude. "Sur la théorie marxiste de l'Etat." *Les Temps Modernes*, no. 314-315 (Sept.-Oct. 1972): 634-83.

Guignabaudet, Philipe. "Concepción de una economía racional." *Revista de la Escuela Superior de Guerra* 10 (October-December 1963): 51-72.

Hobsbawm, Eric. "Peru: The Peculiar 'Revolution.' " *New York Review of Books*, December 16, 1971, pp. 29-36.

Huntington, Samuel P. "Civilian Control of the Military: A Theoretical Statement." In *Political Behavior: A Reader in Theory and Research*. Edited by H. Eulau, S. Eldersveld, and M. Janowitz. New York: Free Press, 1956, pp. 380-85.

Información Política Mensual. Useful 30 to 40-page documentation of major political events in Peru, published monthly since late 1972 by DESCO in Lima.

Janos, Andrew C. "Group Politics in Communist Society: A Second Look at the Pluralist Model." In *Authoritarian Politics in Modern Society: The Dynamics of Established One-Party Systems*. Edited by Samuel P. Huntington and Clement H. Moore. New York: Basic Books, 1970, pp. 437-50.

John XXIII, Pope. "Mater et Magistra." In *The Social Teachings of the Church*. Edited by Anne Freemantle. New York: The New American Library, 1963, pp. 223-76.

Kardelj, Edvard. "The Principal Dilemma: Self-Management or Statism." *Socialist Thought and Practice* (Belgrade), no. 24 (October-December 1966): 3-29.

————. "Contradictions of Social Property in Contemporary Socialist Practice." *Socialist Thought and Practice* (Belgrade), no. 49 (August-December 1972): 25-53.

Katz, Jorge. "Patentes, corporaciones multinacionales y tecnología: un examen crítico de la legislación internacional." *Desarrollo Económico* (Buenos Aires) 12 (April-June 1972) : 105-49.

LaPalombara, Joseph. "The Utility and Limitations of Interest Group Theory in Non-American Field Situations." *The Journal of Politics* 22 (February 1960): 29-49.

————. "Political Power and Political Development." *Yale Law Journal* 78 (June 1969): 1253-75.

Latin American Perspectives, issue 14 (Summer 1977). Special issue entitled "Peru: Bourgeois Revolution and Class Struggle."

329

Linz, Juan J. "An Authoritarian Regime: Spain." In *Mass Politics: Studies in Political Sociology*. Edited by Erik Allardt and Stein Rokkan. New York: Free Press, 1970, pp. 251-83, 374-81.

————. "Totalitarian and Authoritarian Regimes." In *Handbook of Political Science*. Edited by Fred Greenstein and Nelson Polsby. Reading, Massachusetts: Addison-Wesley Publishing Co., 1975, Vol. 3, pp. 175-411.

————. "Some Notes Toward a Comparative Study of Fascism in Sociological Historical Perspective." In *Fascism: A Reader's Guide; Analyses, Interpretations, Bibliography*. Edited by Walter Laqueur. Berkeley: University of California Press, 1976, pp. 3-121.

Lijphart, Arend. "Consociational Democracy." *World Politics* 21 (January 1969): 207-25.

Llosa, Jaime. "Reforma agraria y revolución." *Participación*, no. 3 (August 1973): 44-59.

Lowenthal, Abraham F. "United States Policy Toward Latin America: 'Liberal,' 'Radical,' and 'Bureaucratic' Perspectives." *Latin American Research Review* 8 (Fall 1973): 3-25.

————. "Peru's 'Revolutionary Government of the Armed Forces': Background and Context." In *Political-Military Systems: Comparative Perspectives*. Edited by Catherine McArdle Kelleher. Beverly Hills, Calif.: Sage Publications, 1974, pp. 147-59.

Manaster, Kenneth A. "The Problem of Urban Settlement in Developing Countries: Peru." *Wisconsin Law Review* 1 (1968): 23-61.

Mangin, William. "Latin American Squatter Settlements: A Problem and A Solution." *Latin American Research Review* 11 (Summer 1967): 28-64.

Martins, Luciano. "The Politics of U.S. Multinational Corporations in Latin America." In *Latin America and the United States: Changing Political Realities*. Edited by Julio Cotler and Richard R. Fagen. Stanford: Stanford University Press, 1974, pp. 368-402.

Meijer, Hans. "Bureaucracy and Policy Formulation in Sweden." *Scandinavian Political Studies* 4 (1969): 103-16.

Mejía Zagastizábal, Capitan Lizandro. "Acción cívica en el campo laboral." *Revista Militar del Perú*, no. 680 (January-February 1964): 100-15.

Mercado Jarrín, Edgardo. "El ejército de hoy y su proyección en nuestra sociedad en período de transición." *Revista Militar del Perú*, no. 685 (November-December 1964): 1-20.

————. "La política y la estrategia militar en la guerra contrasubversiva en la América Latina." *Revista Militar del Perú*, no. 701 (November-December 1967): 4-33.

————. "La seguridad integral en el proceso revolucionario peruano." *Participación* 1 (December 1972): 7-12.

Michl, Sara. "Urban Squatter Organization as a National Government Tool: The Case of Lima" in Rabinovitz, Francine F. and Trueblood, Felicity M., eds. *Latin American Urban Research*, vol. 3. Beverly Hills, Calif.: Sage Publications, 1973, pp. 155-80.

Mikhailović, K. "On the Yugoslav Experience in Backward Areas." In *Backward Areas in Advanced Countries.* Edited by E.A.G. Robinson. London: St. Martins Press, 1969, pp. 256-75.

Morse, Richard M. "The Heritage of Latin America." In *The Founding of New Societies.* Edited by Louis Hartz. New York: Harcourt, Brace and World, Inc., 1964, pp. 123-77.

Neira, Hugo. "El poder de informar." *Participación* 2 (February 1973): 50-73.

Nettl, J. P. "The State as a Conceptual Variable." *World Politics* 20 (July 1968): 559-92.

Newton, Ronald C. "On 'Functional Groups,' 'Fragmentation,' and 'Pluralism,' in Spanish American Political Society." *Hispanic American Historical Review* 50 (February 1970): 1-29.

O'Donnell, Guillermo A. "Reflexiones sobre las tendencias generales de cambio en el Estado burocrático-autoritario." Centro de Estudios de Estado y Sociedad, Documento CEDES/G.E. CLACSO/Nº 1, Buenos Aires, August 1975.

———. "Estado y alianzas en Argentina, 1956-1976." Centro de Estudios de Estado y Sociedad, Buenos Aires, October 1976.

———. "Corporatism and the Question of the State." In *Authoritarianism and Corporatism in Latin America.* Edited by James M. Malloy. Pittsburgh: University of Pittsburgh Press, 1977, pp. 47-87.

Parenti, Michael. "Power and Pluralism: A View from the Bottom." *Journal of Politics* 32 (August 1970): 501-30.

Pašić, Najdan. "Dictatorship by the Proletariat or over the Proletariat." *Socialist Thought and Practice* (Belgrade), no. 32 (October-December 1968): 104-14.

Pius XI, Pope. "Quadragesimo Anno." In *The Papal Encyclicals in Their Historical Context.* Edited by Anne Freemantle. New York: New American Library, 1963, pp. 228-35.

Pius XII, Pope. "Summi Pontificatus." In *The Papal Encyclicals in Their Historical Context.* Edited by Anne Freemantle. New York: New American Library, 1963, pp. 263-69.

Poulantzas, Nicos. "The Problem of the Capitalist State." *New Left Review*, no. 34 (November-December 1969): 67-78.

Powell, John Duncan. "Peasant Politics and Clientelist Politics." *American Political Science Review* 64 (June 1970): 411-25.

Purcell, John F. H., and Purcell, Susan Kaufman. "Machine Politics and Socioeconomic Change in Mexico." In *Contemporary Mexico: Papers of the 4th International Congress of Mexican History.* Edited by James W. Wilkie, Michael C. Meyer, and Edna Monzón de Wilkie. Berkeley: University of California Press, 1975, pp. 348-66.

Reyna, José Luis. "Movilización y participación políticas: discusión de algunas hipótesis para el caso mexicano." In *El perfil de México en 1980.* Instituto de Investigaciones Sociales, Universidad Nacional Autónoma de México. México: Siglo Veintiuno Editores, S. A., 1972, vol. 3, pp. 503-35.

————. "Control político, estabilidad y desarrollo en México." México: Centro de Estudios Sociológicos, El Colegio de México, 1974.

Rivas Gazo, Colonel Alejandro. "Primer foro nacional de la energía." *Revista Militar del Perú,* no. 690 (January-July 1966): 53-54.

Rokkan, Stein. "Norway: Numerical Democracy and Corporate Pluralism." In *Political Oppositions in Western Democracies.* Edited by Robert A. Dahl. New Haven: Yale University Press, 1968, pp. 70-115.

Rose, Stanley F. "The Andean Pact and Its Foreign Investment Code— Need for Clarity?" *Tax Management International Journal* (January 1975): 1-16.

————. "Peru: An Introduction to Peruvian Law for Lawyers and Businessmen." *Tax Management International Journal* (February 1975): 3-43.

Rus, Veljko. "Influence Structure in Yugoslav Enterprise." *Industrial Relations* 9 (February 1960): 148-60.

Sanderson, John. "Marx and Engels on the State." *Western Political Quarterly* 16 (December 1963): 946-55.

Sarti, Roland. "Fascist Modernization in Italy: Traditional or Revolutionary?" *American Historical Review* 75 (April 1970): 1020-45.

Schmitter, Philippe C. "Still the Century of Corporatism?" In *The New Corporatism: Social-Political Structures in the Iberian World.* Edited by Fredrick B. Pike and Thomas Stritch. Notre Dame and London: University of Notre Dame Press, 1974, pp. 85-131.

Smith, Brian H., and Rodríguez, José Luis. "Comparative Working Class Behavior: Chile, France, and Italy." *American Behavioral Scientist* 18 (September 1974): 59-96.

Stavenhagen, Rodolfo. "Un modelo para el estudio de las organizaciones políticas en México." *Revista Mexicana de Sociología* 29 (April-June 1967): 329-36.

————. "Marginalidad y participación en la reforma agraria mexicana." In Stavenhagen, Rodolfo, *Sociología y subdesarrollo.* México: Editorial Nuestro Tiempo, S.A.: 1972, pp. 145-81.

Stepan, Alfred. "Political Development Theory: The Latin American Experience." *Journal of International Affairs* 20 (1966): 223-34.

————. "The Continuing Problem of Brazilian Integration—The Monarchical and Republican Periods." In *Latin American History:*

Select Problems: Identity, Integration, and Nationhood. Edited by Fredrick B. Pike. New York: Harcourt, Brace and World, Inc., 1969, pp. 259-96.

Sunkel, Osvaldo. "National Development Policy and External Dependence in Latin America." *Journal of Development Studies* 6 (October 1969): 23-48.

Supek, Rudi. "Some Contradictions and Insufficiencies of Yugoslav Self-Managing Socialism." *Praxis* (Belgrade), no. 3/4 (1971): 375-97.

Trubek, David. "Law, Planning and the Development of the Brazilian Capital Market." *The Bulletin*, New York University Graduate School of Business Administration, nos. 72-73 (April 1971).

Tugwell, Franklin. "Petroleum Policy in Venezuela: Lessons in the Politics of Dependence Management." *Studies in Comparative International Development* 9 (Spring 1974): 84-120.

Turner, John F. "Lima's Barriadas and Corralones: Suburbs vs. Slums." *Ekistics* (Greece) 19 (1965): 152-56.

Wiarda, Howard. "Toward a Framework for the Study of Political Change in the Iberic-Latin Tradition: The Corporative Model." *World Politics* 25 (January 1973): 206-35.

Williams, Gwyn A. "The Concept of 'Egemonia' in the Thought of Antonio Gramsci: Some Notes on Interpretation." *Journal of the History of Ideas* 21 (October-December 1960): 586-99.

Zeña, Major Agustín León. "La infantería en la guerra revolucionaria." *Revista Militar del Perú*, no. 675 (March-April 1963): 3-7.

3. Dissertations and Unpublished Manuscripts

Ballantyne, Janet C. "The Political Economy of Peruvian Gran Mineria." Ph.D. dissertation, Cornell University, 1976. Latin American Studies Program Dissertation Series, Number 60.

Brown, Lyle C. "General Lázaro Cárdenas and Mexican Presidential Politics, 1933-1940: A Study in the Acquisition and Manipulation of Political Power." Ph.D. dissertation, University of Texas, 1964.

Cinta, Ricardo. "La burguesía y el estado en México." Paper prepared for delivery at the Seminar on the State and the Economy in Contemporary Mexico, Center for Inter-American Relations, New York, Spring 1975.

Cleaves, Peter S., and Scurrah, Martin J. *Agriculture, Bureaucracy and Society: Reform in Peru Under Military Rule.* New Haven: draft manuscript, March 1977.

Collier, David; Spencer, Leslie; Waters, Cherri. "Varieties of Latin American 'Corporatism.'" Paper presented at the Annual Meeting of the American Political Science Association, Sept. 2-5, 1975, San Francisco.

Collier, David, ed. "The New Authoritarianism in Latin America." Bloomington: draft manuscript, January 1978.

Córdova, Arnaldo. "La transformación del PNR en PRM: el triunfo del corporativismo en México." Paper presented at the 4th International Congress of Mexican Studies, Santa Monica, California, October 1973.

Erickson, Kenneth Paul. "Labor in the Political Process in Brazil: Corporatism in a Modernizing Nation." Ph.D. dissertation, Columbia University, 1970.

————. "Corporative Control of Labor in Brazil." Paper presented at the 1971 Annual Meeting of the American Political Science Association, Chicago.

Erickson, Kenneth Paul, and Peppe, Patrick V. "The Dynamics of Dependency: Industrial Modernization and Tightening Controls Over the Working Class in Brazil and Chile." Paper prepared for Latin American Studies Association, San Francisco, November 1974.

Everett, Michael David. "The Role of the Mexican Trade Unions, 1950-1963." Ph.D. dissertation, Washington University, Missouri, 1967.

Glade, William P. "The State and Economic Development in Mediterranean Politics." Paper prepared for delivery at the 1973 Annual Meeting of the American Political Science Association, New Orleans, Louisiana, September 4-8, 1973.

Horton, Douglas E. "Haciendas and Cooperatives: A Preliminary Study of Latifundist Agriculture and Agrarian Reform in Northern Peru." Manuscript, Cornell University, 1973.

Kaufman, Robert R. "Industrial Change and Authoritarian Rule in South America: A Concrete Review of the Bureaucratic-Authoritarian Model." Prepared for the Working Group on the State and Public Policy of the Joint Committee on Latin American Studies, June, 1977.

Lamounier, Bolivar. "Ideology and Authoritarian Regimes: Theoretical Perspectives and a Study of the Brazilian Case." Ph.D. dissertation, University of California, Los Angeles, 1974.

McClintock, Cynthia. "Socioeconomic Status and Political Participation in Peru: The Impact of the Agrarian Cooperatives, 1969-1975." Paper prepared for delivery at the 1975 Annual Meeting of the American Political Science Association, San Francisco, September 2-5, 1975.

Mericle, Kenneth S. "Conflict Regulation in the Brazilian Industrial Relations System." Ph.D. dissertation, University of Wisconsin, 1974.

Miller, Richard Ulric. "The Role of Labor Organizations in a Developing Country: The Case of Mexico." Ph.D. dissertation, Cornell University, 1966.

Palmer, David Scott. "Revolution from Above: Military Government and Popular Participation in Peru, 1968-1972." Ph.D. dissertation, Cornell University, 1973. Latin American Studies Program Dissertation Series, Number 47.

Richmond, Patricia McIntire. "Mexico: A Case Study of One-Party Politics." Ph.D. dissertation, University of California, Berkeley, 1965.

Roca, Santiago. "The Peruvian Sugar Cooperatives: Some Fundamental Economic Problems, 1968-1972." In Knight, Peter T.; Roca, Santiago; Vanek, Jaroslav; and Collazo, F. "Self-Management in Peru," pp. 1-47. Manuscript no. 10, Program on Participation and Labor-Managed Systems, Cornell University, June 1975.

Santistevan, Jorge. "Industrial Communities: Achievements and (or?) Problems." Paper presented at the 2nd Inter-national Conference on Self-Management, Cornell University, 6-8 June 1975.

Sarti, Roland. "Italian Workers Under Fascism." Paper prepared for delivery at the Annual Meeting of the American Historical Association, San Francisco, 1973.

Schmitter, Philippe C. "Corporatist Interest Representation and Public Policy-Making in Portugal." Paper presented at the Conference Group on Modern Portugal, Durham, N. H., October 10-14, 1973.

Stephens, Evelyn Huber. "The Politics of Workers' Participation: The Peruvian Approach in Comparative Perspective." Ph.D. dissertation, Yale University, 1977.

Vaitsos, Constantine V. "The Changing Policies of Latin American Governments Toward Economic Development and Direct Foreign Investments." Manuscript, Junta del Acuerdo de Cartagena, Lima, March 1973.

———. "Power, Knowledge, and Development Policy: Relations Between Transnational Enterprises and Developing Countries." Paper presented at the 1974 Dag Hammarskjöld Seminar on the Third World and International Economic Change, Uppsala, Sweden, August 1974. (Mimeographed.)

Wionczek, Miguel. "Problems Involved in the Establishment of a Common Agreement for Foreign Investment in the Andean Common Market." Working paper prepared for the Andean Pact Staff, July 1970. (Mimeographed.)

Witte, John F., "Theories of American Pluralism: The Writings of Arthur F. Bentley, David Truman, and Robert A. Dahl." Manuscript, Yale University, 17 May 1973.

335

4. PUBLICATIONS OF GOVERNMENTS AND PUBLIC AND PRIVATE ORGANIZATIONS

Acuerdo de Cartagena. Decision 24, "By-Laws for Common Treatment of Foreign Capital, Trademarks, Patents, Licensing Agreements and Royalties." Lima: Junta del Acuerdo de Cartagena, December 1970.

Acuerdo de Cartagena. *Grupo Andino: primer programa sectorial de desarrollo industrial del sector metalmecánico.* Lima: Junta del Acuerdo de Cartagena, March 1973.

Argentina. Ministerio de Trabajo y Seguridad Social. *Análisis económico financiero de las cajas nacionales de seguridad social.* Buenos Aires: 1963.

Central de Cooperativas Agrarias de Producción Azucarera del Perú. *Caña de azúcar: plan de cultivo en base al incremento de la demanda interna.* Lima: 1974.

Central de Cooperativas Agrarias de Producción Azucarera del Perú. División Técnica. *Informe de operaciones de producción de la industria azucarera peruana–1973.* Lima: February 1974.

Central de Cooperativas Agrarias de Producción Azucarera del Perú. División Técnica. *Situación actual y futura del potencial técnico de la industria azucarera.* Lima: 1974.

Comité Interamericano de Desarrollo Agrícola. *Tenencia de la tierra y desarrollo socio-económico del sector agrícola*: Perú. Washington, D.C.: Pan American Union, 1966.

Confederación Nacional de Comunidades Industriales. Primer Congreso. *Resoluciones.* Lima: March 1973. (Mimeographed.)

Council of the Americas. *Andean Pact: Definition, Design and Analysis.* New York: Council of the Americas, 1973.

Inter-American Development Bank. *Economic and Social Progress in Latin America: Annual Report: 1973.* Washington, D.C.

International Monetary Fund. *International Financial Statistics.* (Various issues.)

Perú. Banco Central de Reserva del Perú. *Cuentas Nacionales del Perú, 1960-1973.* Lima: 1974.

Perú. Banco Central de Reserva del Perú. *El desarrollo económico y financiero del Perú: 1968-1973.* Lima: 1974.

Perú. Central Reserve Bank. *Aide Memoire on the Economic Situation in Peru.* Lima, 1976.

Perú. Centro Nacional de Capacitación e Investigación para la Reforma Agraria. *Participación, organización y poder en Casa-Grande.* April 1972.

Perú. Comité de Asesoramiento de la Presidencia de la República. *Filosofía de la revolución peruana: la comunidad laboral, la comunidad pesquera.* General José Graham Hurtado. Lima: Oficina Nacional de Información, 1971.

336

Perú. Comité de Asesoramiento de la Presidencia de la República. *La Revolución Nacional Peruana: "Manifiesto," "Estatuto," "Plan," del Gobierno Revolucionario de la Fuerza Armada.* Lima: 1974.

Perú. *Estatuto de Prensa.* Decreto Ley No. 20680, 26 July 1974.

Perú. Instituto Nacional de Planificación. *Informe socio-económico: 1974.* Lima: March 1975.

Perú. *Ley de Comunidad Industrial.* Decreto Ley No. 18384, 1 September 1970.

Perú. *Ley General de Industrias.* Decreto Ley No. 18350, 30 July 1970.

Perú. *Ley Orgánica del Sistema Nacional de Apoyo a la Movilización Social.* Decreto Ley No. 19352, 4 April 1972.

Perú. Ministerio de Economía y Finanzas. Oficina de Relaciones Públicas. *Evaluación económica 1973-74 y perspectivas para 1975-76.* General Amílcar Vargas Gavilano. Lima: 1975.

Perú. Ministerio de Guerra. *Las guerrillas en el Perú y su represión.* Lima: 1966.

Perú. Ministerio de Industria y Comercio. Oficina Sectorial de Planificación. *Estadística industrial manufacturera: resultados de 1968-1969-1970* (Preliminares). Lima: 1970.

Perú. Ministerio de Trabajo. Dirección General de Empleo. *Las huelgas en el Perú: 1957-1972.* Lima: August 1973.

Perú. Oficina Central de Información, *Bases ideológicas de la Revolución Peruana.* Lima: February 25, 1975.

Perú. Oficina del Primer Ministro. *Información oficial sobre el convenio entre los gobiernos del Perú y de los Estados Unidos de América, suscrito el 19 de febrero de 1974.* Lima: 1974.

Perú. PETROPERU. *El contrato de operaciones Modelo Perú.* Lima: Departamento de Relaciones Públicas de Petróleos del Perú, 1973.

Perú. Presidencia de la República. Instituto Nacional de Planificación. *Plan Nacional de Desarrollo para 1971-1975.* 5 vols. Lima: 1971.

Perú. Presidencia de la República. SINAMOS. *Problemas económicas fundamentales que afrontan las cooperativas azucareras.* (Lima: 1972).

Perú. Presidencia de la República. SINAMOS. Oficina Nacional de Desarrollo Cooperativa. *Apreciación sobre la situación económica, financiera, organizativa, sindical y social de las cooperativas agrarias de producción azucarera del Departamento de la Libertad.* Lima: January 1972.

Perú. Presidencia de la República. SINAMOS. Dirección General de Pueblos Jóvenes y Areas de Subdesarrollo Urbano Interno. *Diagnóstico nacional de la problematica de los pueblos jóvenes: documento de trabajo.* Lima: 1973.

Perú. Presidencia de la República. SINAMOS. Oficina Nacional de Desarrollo de Pueblos Jóvenes. *Censo de población y vivienda de pueblos jóvenes: cifras preliminares.* 1971.

Perú. Presidencia de la República. SINAMOS. Oficina Nacional de Desarrollo de Pueblos Jóvenes. *Organización vecinal.* Lima: n.d.

Perú. Presidencia de la República. SINAMOS. Oficina Nacional de Desarrollo de Pueblos Jóvenes. *Guía para la organización de los pueblos jóvenes.* Lima: n.d.

Perú. Presidencia de la República. SINAMOS. SAF-CAP. *Diagnóstico preliminar Cap "Cayaltí": documento de trabajo.* Chiclayo, April 1973.

Perú. Presidencia de la República. SINAMOS. SAF-CAP. *Azúcar peruana: historia de un cambio.* December 1973.

Perú. *Se Crea El Sistema Nacional de Apoyo a la Movilización Social.* Decreto Ley No. 18896. 22 June 1971.

Price Waterhouse and Co. *Information Guide for Doing Business in Peru.* February 1973.

Price Waterhouse and Co. *Information Guide for Doing Business in the Andean Common Market.* March 1974.

United Nations. Economic Commission for Latin America. *Theoretical and Practical Problems of Economic Growth.* New York: United Nations, 1951. (E/CN 12/221.)

United Nations. Department of Economic and Social Affairs. *The Impact of Multinational Corporations on Development and on International Relations.* New York: United Nations, 1974. (E.5500/Rev. 1 ST/ ESA/6.)

United Nations. Department of Economic and Social Affairs. *Summary of the Hearings Before the Group of Eminent Persons to Study the Impact of Multinational Corporations on Development and on International Relations.* New York: United Nations, 1974. (ST/ESA/ 15.)

U.S. Congress. Senate. Committee on Finance. *Implications of Multinational Firms for World Trade and Investment and for U.S. Trade and Labor.* Washington, D.C.: Government Printing Office, 1973.

U.S. Department of Commerce. *Survey of Current Business.* Volumes 42-54 (1962-1974).

Wells Fargo Bank N.A. *Economic Report on Peru.* San Francisco, October 1976.

Index

Library of Congress Cataloging in Publication Data

Stepan, Alfred C.
  The state and society.

  Bibliography: p.
  1. Peru—Politics and government—1968-
  2. Peru—Social policy.   3. Peru—Economic policy.
  4. State, The.   5. Corporate state.   I. Title.
JL3431.S73   321.9   77-85567
ISBN 0-691-07591-3
ISBN 0-691-02179-1 pbk.